I0890561

Perspectives on Blockchain Technology and Responsible Investing

Sonal Trivedi
Chitkara Business School, Chitkara University, India

Rashmi Aggarwal
Chitkara Business School, Chitkara University, India

Gurmeet Singh
The University of the South Pacific, Fiji

A volume in the Advances in Finance, Accounting, and Economics (AFAE) Book Series

IGI Global
PUBLISHER of TIMELY KNOWLEDGE

Published in the United States of America by
IGI Global
Business Science Reference (an imprint of IGI Global)
701 E. Chocolate Avenue
Hershey PA, USA 17033
Tel: 717-533-8845
Fax: 717-533-8661
E-mail: cust@igi-global.com
Web site: http://www.igi-global.com

Library of Congress Cataloging-in-Publication Data

Names: Trivedi, Sonal, 1986- editor. | Aggarwal, Rashmi, 1974- editor. | Singh, Gurmeet, 1967- editor.
Title: Perspectives on blockchain technology and responsible investing / edited by Sonal Trivedi, Rashmi Aggarwal, Gurmeet Singh.
Description: Hershey, PA : Engineering Science Reference, [2023] | Includes bibliographical references and index. | Summary: "The transformation of green investment and climate finance by blockchain analyzes and establishes the relationship between global effort for climate adaptation and this innovative technology. The benefit of blockchain in financial sector is realized as it has brought various operational changes such as smart contracts, changes in regulation and governance, changes in transaction etc. Each chapter of this edited book will cover blockchain, innovation, climate adaptation, ESG investing, Responsible investing. This book will provide insight to entrepreneurs, practitioners, professionals, leaders, academicians, research scholars, regulators, policy makers and more. This book is significant for readers as it understands the concept of Blockchain, sustainability and finance together"-- Provided by publisher.
Identifiers: LCCN 2023005807 (print) | LCCN 2023005808 (ebook) | ISBN 9781668483619 (hardcover) | ISBN 9781668483626 (paperback) | ISBN 9781668483633 (ebook)
Subjects: LCSH: Sustainable development. | Social responsibility of business. | Blockchains (Databases)--Social aspects. | Investments--Social aspects.
Classification: LCC HC79.E5 P45618 2023 (print) | LCC HC79.E5 (ebook) | DDC 338.9/27--dc23/eng/20230221
LC record available at https://lccn.loc.gov/2023005807
LC ebook record available at https://lccn.loc.gov/2023005808

This book is published in the IGI Global book series Advances in Finance, Accounting, and Economics (AFAE) (ISSN: 2327-5677; eISSN: 2327-5685)

British Cataloguing in Publication Data
A Cataloguing in Publication record for this book is available from the British Library.

For electronic access to this publication, please contact: eresources@igi-global.com.

Advances in Finance, Accounting, and Economics (AFAE) Book Series

Ahmed Driouchi
Al Akhawayn University, Morocco

ISSN:2327-5677
EISSN:2327-5685

MISSION

In our changing economic and business environment, it is important to consider the financial changes occurring internationally as well as within individual organizations and business environments. Understanding these changes as well as the factors that influence them is crucial in preparing for our financial future and ensuring economic sustainability and growth.

The **Advances in Finance, Accounting, and Economics (AFAE)** book series aims to publish comprehensive and informative titles in all areas of economics and economic theory, finance, and accounting to assist in advancing the available knowledge and providing for further research development in these dynamic fields.

COVERAGE

- Managerial Accounting
- Finance and Accounting in SMEs
- Finance
- Evidence-Based Studies
- Interest Rates and Annuities
- Economic Policy
- Theoretical Issues in Economics, Finance, and Accounting
- E-Finance
- Economics of Natural and Environmental Resources
- Economics Geography

IGI Global is currently accepting manuscripts for publication within this series. To submit a proposal for a volume in this series, please contact our Acquisition Editors at Acquisitions@igi-global.com or visit: http://www.igi-global.com/publish/.

The Advances in Finance, Accounting, and Economics (AFAE) Book Series (ISSN 2327-5677) is published by IGI Global, 701 E. Chocolate Avenue, Hershey, PA 17033-1240, USA, www.igi-global.com. This series is composed of titles available for purchase individually; each title is edited to be contextually exclusive from any other title within the series. For pricing and ordering information please visit http://www.igi-global.com/book-series/advances-finance-accounting-economics/73685. Postmaster: Send all address changes to above address.

Titles in this Series

For a list of additional titles in this series, please visit: http://www.igi-global.com/book-series/

Handbook of Research on Designing Sustainable Supply Chains to Achieve a Circular Economy
Yanamandra Ramakrishna (Skyline University College, UAE) and Siti Norida Wahab (Universiti Teknologi MARA, Malaysia)
Business Science Reference • © 2023 • 697pp • H/C (ISBN: 9781668476642) • US $295.00

Emerging Insights on the Relationship Between Cryptocurrencies and Decentralized Economic Models
Dhanapal Kesavan (SRM Institute of Science and Technology, India) and N. Mari Anand (Department of Business Studies, University of Technology and Applied Sciences, Salalah, Oman)
Business Science Reference • © 2023 • 256pp • H/C (ISBN: 9781668456910) • US $250.00

Exploring Business Ecosystems and Innovation Capacity Building in Global Economics
Mihir Joshi (Banasthali Vidyapith University, India) Mohsen Brahmi (University of Sfax, Tunisia) Luigi Aldieri (University of Salerno, Italy) and Concetto Paolo Vinci (University of Salerno, Italy)
Business Science Reference • © 2023 • 393pp • H/C (ISBN: 9781668467664) • US $250.00

Accounting and Financial Reporting Challenges for Government, Non-Profits, and the Private Sector
Fábio Albuquerque (Instituto Politécnico de Lisboa, Portugal) and Paula Gomes dos Santos (Instituto Politécnico de Lisboa, Portugal)
Business Science Reference • © 2023 • 320pp • H/C (ISBN: 9781668472934) • US $240.00

Handbook of Research on Changing World Economic Order in the Post-Pandemic Period
Sushanta Kumar Mahapatra (IBS Hyderabad, The ICFAI Foundation for Higher Education, India) and Vishal Sarin (Lovely Professional University, India)
Business Science Reference • © 2023 • 470pp • H/C (ISBN: 9781799868965) • US $325.00

Concepts, Cases, and Regulations in Financial Fraud and Corruption
Abdul Rafay (University of Management and Technology, Pakistan)
Business Science Reference • © 2023 • 419pp • H/C (ISBN: 9781668450079) • US $250.00

IGI Global
PUBLISHER of TIMELY KNOWLEDGE

701 East Chocolate Avenue, Hershey, PA 17033, USA
Tel: 717-533-8845 x100 • Fax: 717-533-8661
E-Mail: cust@igi-global.com • www.igi-global.com

Table of Contents

Detailed Table of Contents

The use of blockchain in the banking sector has drawn more attention globally. There are a lot of advantages and drawbacks to implementing blockchain in the financial sector, according to academics. These papers will be examined in this scoping review in order to determine the knowledge gaps in the subject area. To find pertinent publications for the study, a thorough manual search was done in the electronic Science Direct database. Articles were manually evaluated and vetted for eligibility by reading the abstract. Data were taken from the appropriate studies in order to synthesize, collect, rate the quality, and create a narrative summary of the results. A total of 100 articles (both review articles and research articles) were included in our final analysis. The results of the current study point to areas that need further investigation, such as the general public's ignorance about blockchain technology and its potential outside of the banking sector.

Blockchain technology is gaining popularity in the financial sector and specifically in banking. Its implementation will result into increased transparency and reduced cost. Distributed ledger technology (DLT) is primarily a payment system that is well adopted by the financial sector and will have significant impact on future of

low-emission technological developments in the 4IR and 5IR by using the practical-sense mechanism. Reading this chapter will therefore increase the knowledge of blockchain technology (BT), artificial intelligence (AI), and climate finance in the low carbon economic sustainability. Furthermore, the proposed green development themes (i.e., hybrid green city and industrial layout, hybrid low emission agriculture farm) affirms the sustainable low carbon economic developments in the forthcoming Industry 5.0. Finally, the strategic recommendations will assist in developing the low carbon economy with the perfection of BT, AI, and global climate finance in the world.

The main purpose of the research is to provide a solution that can resolve the well-known issues in the current smart contract concept and fully change the architecture used in smart contracts and blockchain. For this purpose, the author lists the issues, analyzes them, and provides the solution explaining how it will change the situation and what kind of positive impact it will have not only on the performance of smart contracts and their extensibility but also the impact on pollution and saving of energy.

Young investors, fuelled by the hype and ads, are rushing to cryptocurrency exchanges with the hopes of generating rapid riches, and investors of the millennial generation especially believe cryptocurrency can make them billionaires. Crypto Research and Intelligence Business found that over 15 million Indians had accepted cryptocurrencies and invested close to $10 billion in crypto assets. Because of the ongoing changes over the last few years, changing from paper to virtual currency, a new type of currency, namely cryptocurrency, has emerged. Shorter transaction times and lower transfer fees are two of the advantages that cryptocurrencies offer to their potential users. The concept of cryptocurrency is underpinned by decentralised technology, which has captivated the interest of a variety of stakeholders. This research examines millennial cryptocurrency adoption behaviour in India.

The disastrous impacts of catastrophic events, droughts, and severe weather on people throughout the globe forced everyone to think about global warming and its implications and do all they can to fix it. Global warming prevention and sustainability include governments, corporations, and people. The topic of environmentally responsible banking has been widely covered in the media since the turn of the century. As a result, there is an urgent need to understand and categorise the growing body of sustainable banking research. The present study is intended to conduct a bibliometric analysis of green banking literature for the duration of 2001-2022. The findings offer a view on the development of the academic literature relating to sustainable banking all through the course of time as well as throughout academic disciplines and publications.

Blockchain technology is a multidisciplinary approach that is growing fast in the economy. The attributes possessed by blockchain are evident in many sectors in the economy such as banking, financial services, innovation, creativity, etc. Blockchain has brought out a revolutionary change in the economy as it provides transparency, cost efficiency, accuracy. Application of blockchain technologies in finance will help in attaining sustainability. The chapter provides comprehensive review of past studies on the role of blockchain technologies in financial services and in enhancing financial performances. The study will provide better insights to the managers of the financial institutions regarding the pros and cons of blockchain technology.

Sustainable development is a worldwide priority and the main objective of all countries. The sustainability concept focuses on economic, social, and ecological pillars. Every nation tries to bring sustainability to the economy, and financial development plays a major role. The financial sector actively promotes technological advancements in power production to lower emissions, significantly reducing energy pollution. The prior studies have shown mixed results on the interconnection between financial development and carbon dioxide emissions. The results also differ in developed and developing nations. The study shows that seventeen sustainability goals developed by the United Nations to achieve in the year 2030 have been affected due to COVID-19 and the Ukraine War. Hence, it has become imperative for nations to emphasize sustainable development.

A distributed ledger, called blockchain, keeps track of every detail about a digital asset. Using this technology, users can utilize the benefits of digital currency. Digital currency has a massive effect on the banking sector. It would be wise to be informed of the technologies that might seriously disrupt the Indian banking sector's operations because it plays a crucial part in the economy and contributes considerably to the nation's gross domestic product. The introduction of this technology in the banking industry significantly reduces fraud resulting from mistakes and identity theft. The specifics of blockchain technology and how it affects the Indian banking industry are discussed in this chapter. It also provides details about various types of digital currency, highlighting their advantages and disadvantages. Much emphasis will be on the importance of blockchain technologies in the future of digital currency. The research's conclusions were strengthened and condensed using SWOT analysis.

Green finance is an important source for raising necessary funds for preserving/ conserving the environment through developments of green projects. It is a loan raised especially for environmentally friendly activities such as biodiversity financing, optimum use of natural resources, etc. Prudent use of green finance attracts the use of digitized technologies which will facilitate prosperous accomplishment of environmental projects. One of the primary and significant digitized technology is blockchain. Further, it ensures effective monitoring of environmental projects, enhances transparency and accountability, and minimizes greenwashing risk. The bank for international settlement (BIS) has stressed blockchain for bringing transparency in usage of green finance thereby improving efficiency. Thus, the present study is an attempt to have insights on the use of blockchain for streamlining green finance. The study proposes the use of digitalized technologies for supporting and promoting green finance.

The word 'blockchain' was introduced years ago, but the meaning has changed over time. Initially it was developed only as the tool for bitcoin cryptocurrency transactions. Developed countries like US and China show the positive relationship between blockchain and financial market innovation. In the present era of initialization where people are more concerned about the safety and security of transaction, blockchain is seen as a solution in the financial market sustainability. The Indian government in association with RBI has planned to launch virtual currency for the development of the Indian financial market and economy. This study reveals the relationship between blockchain and financial market innovation in the Indian context and the factors that impact the significance and relationship. The purpose of the study is to estimate the conceptual framework of blockchain in the field of financial market innovation and sustainability. Thus, this study tries to reveal the key factors of blockchain technology that impact the innovation in the field of financial markets.

Large-scale and small-scale industries as well as entrepreneurs are struggling to find various ways to reduce pollution and move towards a more ecofriendly environment. One of the most forthcoming technologies is blockchain, which has entered the market but is not yet that prominent amongst people. Food suppliers in many countries have started using this technology, and various other companies have also taken interest in using this system to reduce their paperwork and to become faster and more reliable in their work. Blockchain technology is not a popular term for small entrepreneurs or small business, so to justify the above problem, this chapter gives brief idea about how blockchain can be helpful for sustainable growth with green innovation. It sheds light on the importance of blockchain technology in various innovations, which are ecofriendly. The study will add in the broader idea about green innovation and its link with blockchain technology.

Preface

The transformation of green investment and climate finance by blockchain analyzes and establishes the relationship between global effort for climate adaptation and this innovative technology. The benefit of blockchain in financial sector is realized as it has brought various operational changes such as smart contracts, changes in regulation and governance, changes in transaction etc. Each chapter of this edited book will cover blockchain, innovation, climate adaptation, ESG investing, Responsible investing. This book will provide insight to entrepreneurs, practitioners, professionals, leaders, academicians, research scholars, regulators, policy makers and more. This book is significant for readers as it understands the concept of Blockchain, sustainability and finance together.

Of the 21 chapters submitted for possible inclusion in this book, 14 chapters met the requirements of a rigorous double-blind review process. These chapters were organized into five sections covering introduction, responsible investing, sustainability, technology, and innovation.

SECTION 1: INTRODUCTION

Section 1 explores the introduction to application of blockchain in financial sector. This section features two chapters exploring the literature review related to application of blockchain in financial sector. In the first chapter of this section, Vinita Choudhary and Neha Kamboj from K R Mangalam University, Gurugram, India with Sonal Trivedi, Chitkara University, Punjab, India has focused on potential of blockchain technology in financial sector. The chapter title "Scoping Review of Literature on Application of Blockchain in Finance" coined the concept that the use of blockchain in the financial sector has drawn more attention globally. There are a lot of advantages and drawbacks to implementing blockchain in the financial sector, according to academics. These papers will be examined in this scoping review in order to determine the knowledge gaps in the subject area. To find pertinent publications for the study, a thorough manual search was done in the electronic

Science Direct database. Articles were manually evaluated and vetted for eligibility by reading the abstract. Data were taken from the appropriate studies in order to synthesize, collect, rate the quality, and create a narrative summary of the results. A total of 100 articles (both review articles and research articles) were included in our final analysis. The results of the current study point to areas that need further investigation, such as the general public's ignorance about blockchain technology and its potential outside of the banking sector.

The second chapter titled "An Umbrella Review of the Literature on Blockchain and Distributed Ledger Technology and Their Role in Future Banking" authored by Ms. Ankita and Sonal Trivedi from Chitkara University, Punjab, India has focused on potential usage of blockchain technology in the field of banking. Blockchain technology is gaining popularity in financial sector, specifically, in banking. Its implementation will result into increased transparency and reduced cost. Though, Distributed Ledger Technology (DLT) is primarily a payment system very the well adopted by financial sector and will have significant impact on future of banking. The purpose of the study is to identify that whether this novel technology is good enough to replace and compete with traditional financial system. The current study followed the umbrella review limiting the studies based on blockchain, DLT and Banking beyond 2015 till today published in Scopus indexed journals. The study concludes that there is evidence of adoption of blockchain technology in banking sector around the globe but there is still need to explore the application of blockchain in banking and there is need to overcome the challenges faced in implementation of blockchain in banking sector.

SECTION 2: RESPONSIBLE INVESTING

Section two explores the concept of responsible investing and sustainable finance. This section comprises of four chapters and authors from four different countries: Zimbabwe, Japan, Rome, and India.

The first chapter in this section (Chapter 3) focuses green financing strategies and SDG. The chapter is titled "Green Financing Strategies Adopted in Zimbabwe Towards Attainment of Sustainable Development Goals" and is authored by Mufaro Dzingirai, Kudakwashe Zvitambo, and Herbert Masukume from Business Management, Midlands State University, Zimbabwe. The issue of green financing has increasingly become more relevant in the 21st century intending to create a green economy. Accordingly, scholars, researchers, and policymakers are now much interested in how green finance can accelerate the attainment of Sustainable Development Goals (SDGs) across the world. Surprisingly, there is scanty evidence in the development mainstream literature that addresses the issues of green financing strategies, particularly in African countries. This chapter established eight green financing strategies that have been employed in Zimbabwe towards attaining SDGs, namely, the national climate change fund strategy, IDBZ climate finance facility strategy, domestic public finance strategy, domestic private finance, public-private partnerships (PPPs) financing strategy, foreign investment strategy, and development finance strategy. These results can help the Zimbabwean government, NGOs, financial institutions, and society at larger as well as educators and researchers.

The second chapter of this section is authored by Amitab Bhattacharjee, Graduate School of Management, Sophia University, Tokyo and Vikram Bansal, Atal Bihari Vajpayee School of Management and Entrepreneurship, Jawaharlal Nehru University, Delhi, India. It is titled "Sustainable Approaches of Blockchain Tech, Artificial Intelligence, and Climate Finance in the 4&5IR: Low Emission Technologies amd Economy" and is Chapter 4 of this book. Save the green and live in the green should be the motto of the modern high-tech world. Industry 4.0 introduces the most advanced automated technologies, but many of them cause high CO2 emission around the globe that needs strong compelling force because any catastrophic changes in the climate causes dreadful vandalization in the economy, and society. This chapter (Chapter 4) discusses the climate friendly economic and low emission technological developments in the 4IR & 5IR by using the practical-sense mechanism. Reading this chapter will therefore increase the knowledge of blockchain technology (BT), artificial intelligence (AI), and climate finance in the low carbon economic sustainability. Furthermore, the proposed green development themes (i.e., hybrid green city and industrial layout, hybrid low emission agriculture farm) affirms the sustainable low carbon economic developments in the forthcoming industry 5.0. Finally, the strategic recommendations will assist to develop the low carbon economy with the perfection of BT, AI, and global climate finance in the world.

The third chapter of this section (Chapter 5) is authored by Rinat Galiautdinov, Independent Researcher, Principal Software Developer and Software Architect, Rome. It is titled "The New Architecture of Smart Contracts and Its Impact on Performance, Vulnerability, Pollution, and Energy Saving." This chapter provides a solution which can resolve the well-known issues in the current smart contract concept and fully change the architecture used in smart contracts and blockchain. For this purpose, the author list such the issues, analyzes them and provides the solution explaining how it will change the situation and what kind of positive impact it will have not only on the performance of smart contracts and their extensibility but also the impact on pollution and saving of energy.

The fourth chapter of this section and title of Chapter 6 of this book is "Cryptocurrency Adoption Behavior of Millennials Investors in India," which is authored by Renuka Sharma, Kiran Mehta, and Ritik Rana from Chitkara Business School, Chitkara University, Punjab, India. Young investors, fueled by the hype and ads, are rushing to cryptocurrency exchanges with the hopes of generating rapid riches, and investors of the millennial generation especially believe cryptocurrency can make them billionaires. Crypto Research and Intelligence Business found that over 15 million Indians had accepted cryptocurrencies and invested close to $10 billion in crypto assets. Because of the ongoing changes over the last few years, changing from paper to virtual currency, a new type of currency, namely cryptocurrency, has emerged. Shorter transaction times and lower transfer fees are two of the few advantages that cryptocurrencies offer to their potential users. The concept of cryptocurrency is underpinned by decentralised technology, which has captivated the interest of a variety of stakeholders. This chapter examines millennial cryptocurrency adoption behaviour in India.

SECTION 3: SUSTAINABILITY

Section 3 explores the prospects of blockchain in bringing sustainable finance. This section comprises of three chapters.

The first chapter of this section titled "A Bibliometrics Analysis of Green Banking: Present State and Future Directions" is Chapter 7 of this book and is authored by Kiran Mehta, Renuka Sharma, and S. Jalotra from Chitkara Business School, Chitkara University, Punjab, India. This chapter is intended to conduct a bibliometric analysis of green banking literature for the duration of 2001-2022. The findings offer a view on the development of the academic literature relating to sustainable banking all through the course of time as well as throughout academic disciplines and publications.

In the context of blockchain technology as a multidisciplinary approach which is growing fast in the economy, the second chapter of this section explores the attributes possessed by blockchain is evident in many sectors in the economy such as banking, financial services, innovation, creativity etc. The second chapter of this section titled "Prospects of Blockchain Technology in Finance Sustainability" is Chapter 8 of this book and is authored by Gurpreet Kaur, Mehak Gupta and Taranpreet Kaur from Chitkara Business School, Chitkara University, Punjab, India. Application of blockchain technologies in finance will help in attaining sustainability. This chapter provides comprehensive review of past studies on role of blockchain technologies in financial services and in enhancing financial performances. The study will provide better insights to the managers of the financial institutions regarding the pros and cons of blockchain technology.

The third chapter of this section is titled "Sustainability as a Catalyst of Financial Development" which is Chapter 9 of this book. This chapter is authored by Ms. Soumya Singhal, Management, Trinity Institute of Professional Studies, GGSIPU,

New Delhi, India; Ms. Khushboo Gulati, School of Management and Commerce, Manav Rachna University, Faridabad, Haryana, India; and Isha Chhabra, K R Mangalam University, Gurugram, India. The financial sector actively promotes technological advancements in the power production in order to lower emissions, which contributes significantly to the reduction of energy pollution. The prior studies have shown the mixed results of interconnection between financial development and carbon dioxide emissions. This chapter shows the seventeen sustainability goals developed by united nations to achieve in the year 2030 has been affected due to Covid-19 and Ukraine War.

SECTION 4: TECHNOLOGY

This section features two chapters. The first chapter of this section and the title of the 10th chapter of this book is "Digital Currency and Blockchain Technology in the Financial World," which is authored By Jyoti Verma and Monica Gupta from Chitkara Business School, Chitkara University, Punjab, India with Jyotsna Sharma, School of Management Studies and Commerce, RIMT University, Mandi Gobindgarh, Punjab, India. A distributed ledger, called blockchain, keeps track of every detail about a digital asset. Using this technology, users can utilize the benefits of digital currency. Digital currency has a massive effect on the banking sector. It would be wise to be informed of the technologies that might seriously disrupt the Indian banking sector's operations because it plays a crucial part in the economy and contributes considerably to the nation's gross domestic product. The introduction of this technology in the banking industry significantly reduces fraud resulting from mistakes and identity theft. The specifics of blockchain technology and how it affects the Indian banking industry are discussed in this chapter. It also provides details about various types of digital currency, highlighting their advantages and disadvantages. Much emphasis will be on the importance of Blockchain technologies in the future of Digital Currency. The research's conclusions were strengthened and condensed using SWOT analysis.

The second chapter of this section and title of Chapter 11 is "Application of Blockchain for Sustaining Green Finance," which is authored by Gurpreet Kaur & Aadheesh from Chitkara Business School, Chitkara University, Punjab, India. Green finance is an important source for raising necessary funds for preserving/conserving the environment through developments of green projects. It is loan raised especially for environment friendly activities such as biodiversity financing, optimum use of natural resources etc. Prudent use of green finance attracts the use of digitized technologies which will facilitate prosperous accomplishment of environmental projects. One of the primary and significant digitized technology is Block chain. Further it ensures effective monitoring of environmental projects, enhances transparency& accountability, minimizes greenwashing risk. The bank for International Settlement (BIS) has stressed on the blockchain for bringing transparency in usage of green finance thereby improving efficiency. Thus, this chapter is an attempt to have an insight on the use of block chain for streamlining the green finance. The study proposes the use of digitalized technologies for supporting, promoting green finance.

SECTION 5: INNOVATION

This section features three chapters. The first chapter of this section (Chapter 12) is titled as "Financial Market Innovation, Blockchain, and Sustainability" and is authored by Manavati Panwar, Rajasthan College of Engineering for Women, Jaipur, India. The word ' Blockchain' was introduced years ago, but the meaning has changed over time. Initially it was developed only as the tool for bitcoin cryptocurrency transactions. In developed countries like US and China shows the positive relationship between block chain and financial market innovation. In the present era of initialization where people are more concerned about the safety and security of transaction, block chain seen as a solution in the financial market sustainability. Indian government in association with RBI has planned to launch virtual currency for the development of the Indian financial market and economy. This chapter reveals the relationship between block chain and financial market innovation in Indian context and the factors that impact the significance & relationship. The purpose of the study is to estimate the conceptual framework of block chain in the field of financial market innovation and sustainability. Thus, this study tries to reveal the key factors of block chain technology that impact the innovation in the field of financial markets.

The second chapter of this section (Chapter 13) is titled "Importance of Blockchain Technology in Green Innovation" and authored by Tushti Bakrania and Chirag Vipulbhai Erda from Atmiya University, Rajkot, Gujarat, India. Large-scale, small-scale industries as well as entrepreneurs are struggling to find various ways to reduce pollution and move towards more ecofriendly environment and their products. One of the most forthcoming technologies is of blockchain which has entered the market but not yet that prominent amongst people. Food suppliers in many countries have started using this technology as well as various other companies have also taken interest in using this system to reduce their paperwork and to become faster and more reliable in their work. The blockchain technology is not much popular term for small entrepreneurs or small business, so to justify the above problem this chapter gives brief idea about how block chain can be helpful for sustainable growth with green innovation. It gives light on the importance of block chain technology in various innovations which are ecofriendly. This chapter will add in the broader idea about green innovation and its link with blockchain technology.

The third chapter of this section is "Blockchain Technology Usage to Streamline Climate Investment," which is Chapter 14 of this book. It is authored by Surabhi Sugathan, Om Sterling Global University, Haryana, India. The main objective of this chapter is to contour the climate investing by implementing block chain technology which will lead a transparency within the network. Climate investing aids the companies which are involved in reducing carbon emission subsidising the usage of fossil fuels and manufacturing alternate options. This investment will be directly propositional to the "Green Revolution" which our Indian government is making efforts for. Block chain technology will help towards this investment by creating a transparent and secured network which is impossible to get hacked. The database management will be designed using the latest programming techniques which may also include artificial intelligence. Climate finance includes the financial resources which is been used to support the sustainability and climate change.

Sonal Trivedi
Chitkara Business School, Chitkara University, India

Rashmi Aggarwal
Chitkara Business School, Chitkara University, India

Gurmeet Singh
The University of the South Pacific, Fiji

Chapter 1
Scoping Review of Literature on the Application of Blockchain in Finance

Vinita Choudhary
https://orcid.org/0000-0002-6705-0956
School of Management and Commerce, K.R. Mangalam University, Gurugram, India

Neha Kamboj
https://orcid.org/Orcid
K.R. Mangalam University, Gurgaon, India

Sonal Trivedi
https://orcid.org/0000-0001-8711-2977
Chitkara Business School, Chitkara University, India

ABSTRACT

The use of blockchain in the banking sector has drawn more attention globally. There are a lot of advantages and drawbacks to implementing blockchain in the financial sector, according to academics. These papers will be examined in this scoping review in order to determine the knowledge gaps in the subject area. To find pertinent publications for the study, a thorough manual search was done in the electronic Science Direct database. Articles were manually evaluated and vetted for eligibility by reading the abstract. Data were taken from the appropriate studies in order to synthesize, collect, rate the quality, and create a narrative summary of the results. A total of 100 articles (both review articles and research articles) were included in our final analysis. The results of the current study point to areas that need further investigation, such as the general public's ignorance about blockchain technology and its potential outside of the banking sector.

DOI: 10.4018/978-1-6684-8361-9.ch001

1. BACKGROUND

Scoping reviews are a perfect technique for determining the scope or depth of a specific body of literature. They provide an explicit indication of the volume of literature and research that are currently accessible as well as a synopsis (broad or thorough) of their key ideas. Scoping studies might be beneficial for analyzing new information if it is unclear. The more specific issues can be presented and productively answered by a more detailed systematic review.

Recent years have seen a rise in the use of scoping reviews, which have been documented in a variety of academic fields and specialties (Davis & Gould, 2009). Few articles about the scope, makeup, and application of finished scoping reviews have been published yet.

The scoping methodology is the one that best fits the goals of this study among the several information creation procedures (Parkhill et al., 2022; Eling & Lehmann, 2018). The scoping review is also known as a scoping study. It is a type of information creation that discourses an empirical research query with the goal of mapping key ideas, forms of evidence, and research gaps pertaining to a specific area or field. It does this by methodically searching for, evaluating, and creating existing information (Chang et al. 2020). Its versatility and extremely methodical approach are its strong points. Despite this fact that the scoping methodology was first used in clinical research to draw knowledge about therapies. It has also been applied to record other occurrences of interest viz study designs, structures, hypotheses, or categorizations (Leong & Chen, 2020).

An arranged process is used for the scoping review, including the registering of a protocol, the establishment of exclusion and inclusion measures, an orderly database search and the selection of records by unprejudiced assessors (Arksey & O'Malley, 2005). These were specifically applied in the current study (Abramova & Bohme, 2016; Janssen et al., 2020). The protocol for this paper was developed by the authors in the year 2015, and it was registered on December 7th (Nakhuva & Champaneria, 2015).

The purpose of this study is to present a summary of the literature that has been published thus far on the usage of blockchain in the financial sector covering the banking, insurance, and financial markets.

CHAPTER FLOW

Before proceeding further, the clear view of organization of paper is mentioned to understand the proper flow of paper in Figure 1.

Figure 1. Proper flow of a paper

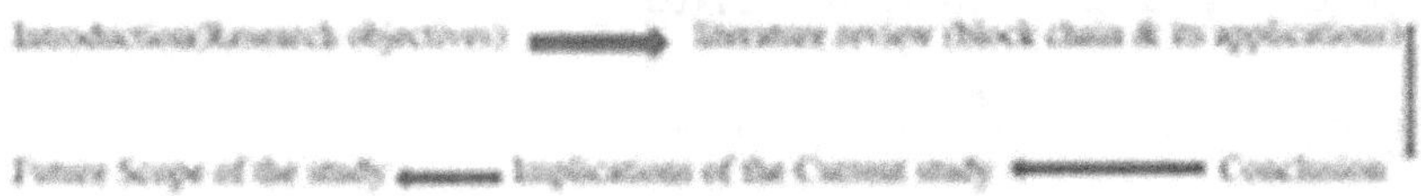

1.1. Research Objective

A scoping review is carried out in the recent study to identify the methods used in the research and the state of the knack in the field of blockchain applications in finance. The goal of this paper is to present an outline or overview of the available information.

The objectives for a scoping review in this paper are as follows:

- To determine the many forms of evidence that can be used to support the use of blockchain in finance.
- To examine how research is conducted on blockchain's application in finance.
- To determine important aspects or components of blockchain in finance.

1.2. Study Question

RQ 1: What sources of evidence are pertinent to the study related to application of blockchain in finance?

RQ 2: Look over and explain any definitions that are utilized in application of blockchain in finance.

1.3. Method of Research

The scoping review methodology approach was developed by Arksey and O'Malley in 2005 and further improved by the many researchers like Munn, Z and others for the current study.

The study's main objective is to identify specific traits or ideas in papers or research and to map, describe, or explain these traits or ideas. In these situations, a scoping review is preferable than a systematic study. When a researcher has a doubt about the viability, suitability, significance, or efficacy of a particular procedure, an orderly review is probably the utmost reliable course of action.

1.4. Inclusion and Exclusion Criteria

The following sorts of papers were included in the current study:

1. All reviews published since 2018 that describe the literature;
2. Papers outlining the creation, usage, or appraisal of scoping review methodologies with other information fusion techniques; and
3. Studies evaluating the use of blockchain in finance.

The inclusion norms for the present study were centered on capturing review-based papers published since 2018 that fell within the category of "Blockchain Applications in Finance," encompassing financial markets, insurance, and banking. Other than papers based on reviews, the study also covered research papers published since 2018. Publications that did not fit our purpose were omitted from the study. Table 1 shows the process of sorting.

Table 1. The process of sorting

Search Topology	Basis: Science Direct	Papers Count
Keywords	Financial Market, Blockchain, Banking, Insurance	595 Articles
Year of Publication	2018 to 2022 (5 years)	532 Articles 2022 (190) 2021 (124) 2020 (101) 2019 (58) 2018 (59)
Articles type	Review articles Research articles	56 337
Subject range	Business, Management and Accounting	156
After using exclusion/inclusion criteria	The papers which matched our research objective Initial screening of papers reading abstract	80
Searched reference list of pertinent articles	Manual searching of selected articles	20
Number of Articles for Scoping review		100

1.5. Look Up, Pick Out, and Retrieve Evidence

Science direct, an electronic database, served as the study's primary source. The search approach was constrained by the type of study (review-based publications, mostly, but a few research papers as well), the language (English), the year (since 2018), and the subject categories (business and management).

The following steps are included in "Look Up, Pick Out and Retrieve Evidence":

1. Clarify and link the aim and research problems;
2. Identify studies that are pertinent; weigh practicality, extensiveness, and extensiveness.
3. Select studies using an iterative collaborative method for data extraction;
4. Table all the papers found by integrating quantitative details and qualitative theme analysis;
5. Compile, summarize, and present the findings, together with any implications for research, practice, or policy.

1.6. Data Extraction

Each study's data was extracted, which then entered it into an Excel spreadsheet. Author, year, title, keywords, nation or location, purpose, method, findings, and study recommendations were among the data retrieved.

2. LITERATURE REVIEW

The structure (presentation of) of scoping review of review-based papers in the field of Blockchain, Insurance, Banking, financial market since 2018 is shown in Table 2.

Table 2. The structure of scoping review

2.1	Introduction: Blockchain	2.1.1 Blockchain technology: Meaning 2.1.2 Evolution of Blockchain technology
2.2	Application of blockchain in Finance	2.2.1 Solicitation of blockchain in financial markets 2.2.2 Solicitation of blockchain in Insurance 2.2.3 Solicitation of blockchain in Banking

2.1. Introduction: Blockchain

Blockchain technology- is a type of distributed ledger technology (DLT) that is decentralized. It is a "chain of blocks," with each block holding a hash and timestamped digital data that serves as an identification. The solicitation of blockchain in financial markets has been seen as the chief case for the technology since its evolution. When it was used in 2009 to describe the cryptocurrency Bitcoin, it attracted a lot of attention. The incredible capabilities of blockchain have the potential to greatly help the financial sector (Trivedi & Malik, 2022).

2.1.1. Blockchain Technology: Meaning

A pseudonym whose name is Satoshi Nakamoto, invented and developed the first blockchain. (The Economist, 2015). Furthermore, blockchain is network-based peer-to-peer (P2P) distributed database. It is made up of a sequence of blocks that include transactions that are recorded and validated by the network community. After being added to the blockchain, a blockchain constituent cannot be reformed. It also preserves an everlasting record of previous acts (Zachariadis, et al, 2019).

Additionally, Blockchain is believed to ignite the business and profitable organizational revolutions. This also boosted worldwide economic reform. For commencing Blockchain, it is requiring to generate a digital security code via encryption. Operators can ratify the transaction without providing any personal information. Because the Blockchain record is immutable, the transaction will be completed and distributed automatically (Chang et al., 2020). Furthermore, Blockchain is referred to be the "next-generation Internet," "a new basic technology," and "a new foundational technology" due to its power to reconstruct financial transactions, alter how individuals interact in the nation and bring about economic change (Zachariadis et al., 2019). Furthermore, Blockchain appears to be a secured database and a decentralized node-based transaction mechanism (Ertz & Boily, 2019).

A ground-breaking breakthrough is blockchain that has piqued the interest of organizations and administrations around the globe. Principally, "distributed ledger technology" refers to a pool of dealings and facts that are outlined and logged sequentially over distributed account book (Rashideh, W.2020). Moreover, Blockchain is designed for the underlying technology of cryptocurrencies, which may be thought of as a register that accepts appends only (Zhang et al, 2020). The decentralized nodes of the blockchain system verify its correctness and have access to all its data to the general public.

Blockchain is however defined as a constantly growing record list, denoted as blocks, that is linked through cryptography (Eling & Lehmann 2018). Blockchains are employed in cryptocurrency systems like Bitcoin and Ethereum as transaction ledger accounts to record both the current state and prior transactions. Blockchain may alternatively be characterized as a set of blocks containing data in hash functions, a link to the previous block, and a timestamp (Janssen et al., 2020). This distributed database primarily allows for the insertion of new data to old data(Peters et al., 2015). It is made up of blocks that form a chain, with each block containing a list of transactions and a hash pointer to the block before it. For this reason, the sole option is to attach a block to the chain's destination. By using a consensus procedure, the content of a new block that will be connected is decided.

Established on the Preceding Definitions

One can say that a blockchain could be understood by means of a distributed database model that is based on a peer-to-peer network. It is taking into account a sequence of blocks inclosing time-stamped transactions that are authenticated by the network community could not be amended once included, and is safeguarded by public-key infrastructure (PKI).

The next section explains how blockchain was developed.

2.1.2. Evolution of the Blockchain Technology

Three stages, namely Blockchain 1.0, 2.0, and 3.0, can be used to explain the evolution of blockchain (Chang, et al.,2020; Kar & Navin 2021). Based on the publications, this section explains the three phases or generations of the evolution of blockchain technology.

Through three technological generations, blockchain technology has advanced: such as Bitcoin, is used by Generation 1. Apart from bitcoin, the most well-known cryptocurrency, there are about 600 others that have been formed and are used in bitcoin-based apps as exchange tokens. Other widely used ones include Ethereum, Monero, and Ripple (Kar & Navin 2021).

In addition to financial transactions, Generation 2 also includes Loans, bonds, Futures, smart contracts, and mortgages. The most important aspect of this level is the combination of blockchain technology and smart contracts. Smart contracts are hidden portions of encryption that respond in a particular way when certain conditions are satisfied (Kar & Navin 2021). A variety of uses for smart contracts are possible.

Generation 3 is used as a universal platform or instrument in the fields of government, research, medicine, the arts, literacy and culture. The blockchain is incorporated by the government to encourage inhabitant pellucidity in its processes (Kar & Navin 2021). They can save the polls on a blockchain system and surge public prominence of them.

As a result, decentralized networks and encryption were the first applications of blockchain. Later, in 2013, the Ethereum project was created by crafting a blockchain framework in all of Turing's language, allowing developers to build contracts that can perform any role and systematize business operations (Beck et al., 2017).

A significant turning point in the decentralization trend in the global securities market was reached in 2015 with the introduction of the block trading platform LINQ. Distributed Ledger Technology promoted the use of blockchain in UK government and financial issues in 2016. Besides, the Publics' Bank of China organized a conference on digital currency to explore the notion of using blockchain to introduce digital currency and enhance the efficiency, competence, and convenience of financial transactions. Blockchain technology is having ability to end financial exclusion by tackling issues including financial illiteracy, high costs, geographic access, and a lack of banking services (Schuetz & Venkatesh 2020).

As a result, this section offers an outline of the development of blockchain in several fields.

2.2. Application of Blockchain in Finance

2.2.1. Solicitation of Blockchain in Financial Markets

Machine learning, a branch of artificial intelligence, is being used by financial markets more and more to develop precise, quick models. Financial specialists can use these forecasts to better understand trends, spot dangers, manage resources, and assure better data for future planning (Mohanta et al., 2020).

To handle enormous amounts of unstructured data and spot patterns in the financial markets in real time, Kavout use machine learning and quantitative analysis. The Kai Score, an AI-powered stock ranker, is one of Kavout's offerings. The Kai Score distils enormous amounts of data—including price trends and SEC filings—after extensive analysis into a stock ranking. Alpha Sense is a financial search engine with artificial intelligence (AI) that caters to clients including banks, investment businesses, and Fortune 500 organizations (Pestovska, 2021).

In order to identify changes and trends in the financial markets, the platform analyses keyword searches inside filings, transcripts, research, and news using natural language processing.

Industry impact: A range of financial experts, organizations, and businesses find Alpha Sense useful. In particular, brokers find the platform to be of great use. Brokers and traders can access SEC and international filings, transcripts of earnings calls, news announcements, and data on both private and public firms through the search engine (Stratopoulos et al., 2020).

a. What Advantages Does Blockchain Have in the Capital Markets?

Blockchain-based solutions offer definite advantages for the following four types of market players in the financial markets:

a.1. For issuers.

Blockchain offers considerable advantages to issuers by facilitating quicker, less expensive, and easier access to capital. It happens through programmable virtual securities and assets. New securities may be formed and issued quickly. As conforming rights and obligations are automatically encoded. As a result, the velocity of funding events can be increased by issuers and facilitators of new offerings.

More flexibility and customization are possible than ever due to block chain in the case of the issuing of securities. Using a single interface, blockchain technology can streamline KYC/AML processes and provide investors with real-time updates and analytics. It results in increasing efficiency and transparency (Wu & Duan, 2019).

The capacity to fractionalize each asset is the utmost benefit of virtual assets. In some markets, the capability to divide up virtual assets into more accessible and transferable pieces allows for increased liquidity and investor variety. Additionally, the costs associated with issuing a security or assets have greatly decreased. It leads to open doors for smaller investors. It provides current issuers with access to new marketplaces or sorts of securities. Last but not least, an asset's whole lifecycle, including investor servicing and dividend event processing, has the potential to be automated (Wu et al., 2013).

a.2. For fund managers.

Profoundly, blockchain makes it possible to trade any asset peer-to-peer on a verified ledger. Funds benefit from quicker and clearer settlement and clearing because it reduces systemic risk or default risk in less open market. Faster processing allows managers and funds to use and allocate their existing money more effectively because there is less capital that is locked up. The funds will save money. Also helps in improved operational efficiency, keeping points like simplifying fund servicing, bookkeeping, apportionments, and administration. Third parties paid fees for activities like fund management and accounting, transfer agency, and custody could be reduced or even disregarded with the use of automated fund services (Fadaeddini et al., 2020)

A variety of new financial products and instruments will undoubtedly be developed, leading to the creation of innovative asset classes for capital allocation by using blockchain technology. The construction of new financial goods or instruments will be made simpler since, despite the expansion of financial services. The majority of these assets will adhere to a set of predetermined programming standards. A larger investor base will be made possible by the capacity to issue virtual assets and segregate current assets, predominantly as new-fangled investors are more at ease by owning a portfolio of virtual assets (Hodson, 2019).

a.3. Pertaining to financial investors.

Blockchain has enticingly decreased the barrier for introduction of new financial products/assets. By enhancing the capacity to match investor demand more precisely for return, time horizon, and willingness for risk, custom digital instruments may have a substantial influence on the relationship between investor and issuer. This is probably going to bring money prospective buyers and capital seekers closer together (Mazzucato et al., 2020).

An investor's objective is to minimise risk while maximising potential benefits. One of the biggest reasons for concern is a lack of money. The flexibility of electronic assets and monetary instruments addresses this concern. It allows for more complete risk management, less expensive transaction costs, and enhanced potential liquidity of an asset. Investors will notice better liquidity and better rate of return when combined with the improved connectivity and efficacies across capital markets. Additionally, the decentralized blockchain ledger will make it possible to gain stronger insights into asset quality, which could improve the due diligence procedure (Fusco et al., 2020)

a.4. Pertaining to Regulators.

Regulators are regularly condemned for intervening excessively in capital markets or for failing to act swiftly enough, as was the case during in the 2008 financial crisis. Governmental and regulatory entities benefit from the distributed ledger of a blockchain since it is always transparent and verifiable. Due to blockchain's absoluteness, which prohibits transaction data from being altered Hence, regulations may be automated (Pranto et al., 2021).

Regulators will get plenty time to focus on exploration and risk forecasting as a result of the fact that several organizations will be using the alike blockchain system to track their possessions and asset lifecycle occurrences. This would free up their time from having to familiarise themselves with the quirks of every organization's environment and unique code encryptions. The enhanced data and transparency capabilities of the blockchain's book will save administrative outlays and maybe avert some types of systemic risk (Avgouleas & Kiayias 2019).

b. What Applications of Blockchain are there in the Capital Markets?

b.1. Collateral management.

Due to physical delivery of financial instruments, which gives them little flexibility to adjust to market conditions, current security management approaches are sluggish and ineffective. It is also challenging to get a comprehensive picture of cross-entity collateral deposits due to the information being so compartmentalized. The ability of a company to enhance net balances across entities or across collateral deposits and locations is further constrained by this walled structure (Avgouleas & Kiayias 2019).

Blockchain allows for more effective collateral management by digitising collateral holdings and consolidating them into a single, streamlined registry. The introduction and digitalization of collateral tokens or assets opens up new markets and prospects (Drummer & Neumann 2020).

For instance, to eliminate delays between valuation and call, real-time redeployment and settlement of technologically represented collateral securities on the blockchain can be used.

b.2. Sales and trading.

One of the primary roles of investment banking is sales and trading. The transactions in securities and economic instruments is referred to sales and trading. Through a number of processes, such as bilateral agreements, matching algorithms, centralised exchanges, decentralised exchanges and auctions, blockchain enables the seamless go-to-market of digital securities (Drummer & Neumann 2020).

Blockchain unlocks numerous new choices, comprising the formation of novel and customised electronic instruments to fulfill the stockholder's expectations. The adaptable feature of digital security issuance has intended to smoothly carry out many corporate operations, has made these new assets conceivable (Trivedi & Malik 2022).

b.3. Issuance.

Issuance is termed as process of making securities or holdings available to savers in order to elevate money. Both totally new digital assets and digital representations of already existing traditional securities can be created using blockchain and sold on the market as tokens. Improvements in issuance can be made throughout an asset's lifecycle, containing when equity is digitized at initial stage or for the numerous changes done at later stages. Traditional collateral-backed assets can be digitally transformed to produce proofs that reflect specific securities with the inclusion of programmable functionality (Babel et al., 2021)

Decentralized crowdfunding which is a new commercial model that generates more effectively capital and improves the governance rights and distribution of equity, is made possible by blockchain technology (Beck et al., 2017).

b.4. Clearing and settlement.

Management of the handover of money and securities, as well as account updates, are all part of the clearing process. Settlement refers to the concrete exchange financial instruments. Smart contracts may be developed to connect payments to handovers utilising stablecoins, digital assets and off-chain cash payments. They can select a settlement model from a variety that takes into account the market's liquidity needs and risk forbearance, containing deferred net settlement, deferred settlement and atomic settlement.

b.5. Exchanges.

Market services viz. Derivatives, Fixed income and Trading and Management of equity etcetera. commercial services viz. OTC upgrades, IPO and savers relations, and licensing are just a few of the many responsibilities that exchanges frequently handle.

Blockchain technology has the ability to enhance a variety of exchanges' business processes. The ability to lower overhead costs and improve current procedures is offered by decreased exchange fees combined with quicker clearance and dissipating. A blockchain network-enabled shared, distributed ledger can improve KYC and AML compliance and offer trade confirmation. The clear ledger of the blockchain can help exchanges with facts validation, access control, and, in the finest scenario, by offering more effective warning systems for trading activity. With better asset servicing capabilities, new financial products and derivatives instruments are made possible by the digitization of assets (Trivedi & Malik 2022).

Additionally, the custom of blockchain in combination with new digital assets and securities creates the possibility of new prime or subordinate markets, which would increase the liquidity of particular assets.

b.6. After-trade services and structure.

After-trade services are utilised following the conclusion of a trade. Although transactions are immediate today, there are risks associated with post-trade settlement procedures because of shifting markets and pricing. The annual costs of global post-trade processing, which include corporate activities, trade expenditure management, reconciliations, and regulatory reporting, range from $17 billion to $24 billion.

Blockchain streamlines and automates these procedures, boosting their efficiency and security while cutting expenses and clearance times (Zachariadis et al., 2019)

b.7. Stablecoins.

Blockchain technology makes it possible for any company to create digital money secured by any kind of asset. Stablecoins are electronic money that is intended to maintain a fixed entity value, for example one dollar. Many organisations, including Facebook and JP Morgan have already begun to create their own electronic money. Internal resource management and reconciliation across many LEIs within a single parent business can be accomplished using stablecoins. The benefits of developing their personal private e-currency or joining a community that utilises the matching stablecoin are just now becoming clear to institutions (Wu et al., 2013).

b.8. Mutual fund administration.

Transaction management, reporting, entity registration and fund management are just a few of the procedures that make up mutual fund administration.

Currently, managing funds involves performing error-prone administrative activities and manually processing fund data. By computerizing and safeguarding fund locus information and sharing it in close to immediate time with important stakeholders, blockchain improves the fund management process. As a result, fund information and supplementary reference information are much more transparent and secure (Trivedi & Malik 2022).

Individual registration can be affluent and necessitates rigorous AML/KYC compliance measures. By design, a blockchain gives an organisation a single shared ledger where data may be automatically recorded, validated, preserved, and disseminated. Additional fund operation procedures, like the registry of fund unit owners, the recording of investor, balances of cash funds, cash distribution, and others, can be made more efficient (Zhang et al., 2020).

Funds have this opportunity for broadening up the products which have the range to create new goods and electronic financial instruments in new markets made feasible by digital securities and assets. Whenever necessary, regulators or other network members may be given access to information on a fund's compliance.

b.9. Asset servicing.

Asset management, on the other hand, is the management of currency and securities by commercial banks and other pecuniary organisations. This denotes to situations where wealth management entails certain services. With the help of blockchain technology, digital security lifespan occasions like coupons, maturity, dividends, right exercises, and price may be automated, easing administration and servicing procedures (Whittemore et al., 2014).

b.10. Replacing the transfer agent.

Transfer Agents should maintain the ownership record of the registered shareholders of an Issuer, including their addresses and telephone numbers. Transfer agents oversee the handovers, issuance, and cancellation of an issuing organization's shares and frequently support listed bondholders.

This would make it possible to pay investors, obtain investor approval, and examine papers without the need for unneeded agent duties. A digital transfer agent could have more logic, like the ability to track investor-initiated liquidations and redemptions as well as net subscriptions. Smart contracts are also used by a digital agent to ascertain the spontaneously distribute earnings i.e. dividends. Blockchain technology enables a wide number of additional functions to be fixed into a digital transfer agent, improving investors, and other key bondholders (Ukpong & Acha 2019 ; Sultana et al., 2020)

b.11. Custody.

Custody describes the holding of assets for safety or guardianship for lessening loss/theft risk. The very sophisticated security features of this technology is mentioned below

- Decentralized architecture
- Cryptographically secure code

Above mentioned features ensure that assets are handled with the highest level of protection.

2.2.2. Solicitation of blockchain in Insurance

a. Blockchain use in the insurance sector.

The insurance sector has a stigma for being slow to embrace innovative methods and technology in its field. However, this industry has also begun to investigate about adding technologies and methods into its system (Davis et al., 2009). Based on the "Gartner hype cycle", in such type of industry, this technology has yet to be completely explored and is currently in innovation trigger phase (Trivedi & Malik 2022).

Now Insurance firms are also interested in the real-world applications of blockchain and smart contracts so they have begun to inquire about it, also which type of architecture of blocks will be suitable to meet industry's demands and whether this technology is established to that level to be implemented in the this industry (Trivedi & Malik 2022).

The insurance industry' core concern for using this technology is to prevent false claims. The primary goal to implement block chain is to rationalize the processes of payments and claims settlements, so that number of fraud claims can be lower in this sector (Rajasekaran et al., 2022)

Block chain technology not only boosts-up & elevates present-day functional procedures in the insurance business, but it also has the aptitude to crack current goods into collective economic products like P-2-P insurance (Trivedi & Malik 2022).

a.1. Prevention of fraud and assessment of risk.

Many mediators like people from medical field, insurers, police force, could be involved for computation of risk profile of individuals and their to be paid premium (Gatteschi et al., 2018) As a result, all those mediators will become part of blockchain network to prevent fraud and assessment of risk (Min, 2019). From architectural standpoint consortium blockchain can be employed. A consortium blockchain is a blockchain which comprises of small number of group/nodes which represents all the players affianced in the operation (Dib et al., 2018).

The privacy & security of this network could be amended by encompassing small number of players. Moreover, as users, who are small in numbers will be directing this network, gaining agreement from handlers in event of reestablishing the present ailment of blockchain will be simple if any specious entries are added in grid (Khan et al., 2019).

a.2. Reduction of claim processing time and cost.

Blockchain can also be used for reduction of claim processing time which ultimately result into reduction of operational cost (Gatteschi et al., 2018). This goal can be met by using smart contracts to process claims without the involvement of humans, such as in the case of accident insurance, travel insurance, and so on. Furthermore, IoT can be used for specific types of insurance, such as crop insurance (Sultana et al., 2020; Rashideh, W. 2020). Furthermore, smart contracts will help in reduction of human resource need in any organization.

a.3. Use of smart contracts & IoT.

Block chain is very helpful in development of new insurance products for insurance industry. Similarly smart contracts are helping industry to attract customers as well as in development of new products. This way smart contract will lessen the operational cost which results in reduction of paid premium of consumers (Chen et al., 2021).

Furthermore, use of IoT tools like, tracking devices for theft insurance and travel insurance could also develop the working of insurance industry (Leong & Chen, 2020).

Smart contracts could be used in (P-2-P) peer-2-peer insurance which is also in its embryonic growth stage. contracts will definitely be helpful in enhancement the transparency and confidence in insurance.

a.4. Underwriting of policies.

Few companies like Standard Chatered, IBM &AIG have connected to craft a blockchain-based system. This will help them, for distribution of international insurance coverage. Introduction of blockchain in this industry has prepared the insurance processes cheaper, more customized and faster (Brophy, 2019). Presently, 3 companies have applied this concept to craft a multinational policy which uses smart contracts. They have found it efficient.

a.5. Micro-insurance.

In past Micro-insurance were not proven to be successful because of higher operational cost but use of smart contracts in micro-insurance can be helpful in making the operations and management faster and economical (Ukpong & Acha, 2019). IoT applications have made possible Pay-per-use insurance (Nakhuva & Champaneria, (2015).

a.6. Big data.

On a daily basis, more connected devices are being operated, which results in surge of amount of data which insurance firms should manage. Large amount of data (big data) might be competently achieved, pooled, & monetized by using block chain technology (Khatoon, 2020).

The big data technology has given advantage of being able to retain static record or data without demanding central coordination, & the information could be easily accessible by all parties (Wu et al., 2013)

Transparency and security are ensured when data is stored on the blockchain by creating a digital fingerprint with a time stamp and date (Khatoon, 2020). With streamlined data, risk assessment may also be done more quickly and accurately.

a.7. Reinsurance.

Based on current reinsurance contracts, block chain can provide correct reserve estimations. This makes it easier for property and casualty (P&C) insurers to calculate how much cash will be available as claims are settled. They can employ block chain to use rebalancing their exposures to certain risks (Eling & Lehmann 2018). Insurance companies can now run their operations with confidence.

a.8. Insurance for casualties and property.

Blockchain technology has full potential for making claims processing 3x faster and 5x cheaper. The claims processes and payment processes could be mechanized by leveraging pooled ledgers and smart contracts for issuing policies, which results in amplified efficiency and accurateness (Min, 2019). Smart contracts can convert paper contracts into programmable code, allowing claims processing to be automated.

a.9. Subrogation in claim.

While conventional subrogation is primarily manual, insurers may utilize smart contracts to automate loss investigation, claim notification, and payment from several other insurance companies and policy holders. This curtails the amount of communications amongst several parties, predominantly call centers. These call centers spend most of the time in answering the questions from other insurance companies, legal institutions, third parties, and claims intake (Grima et al., 2020).

a.10. Few more examples of blockchain usage in insurance sector.

Marine insurance companies, such as Danish Shipping Giant, are also using blockchain technology to monitor its supply chains and databases (Pedersen et al., 2019).

Furthermore, one Travel insurance company AXA which is a French based organization had developed one product through application of blockchain technology and named it 'fizzy' (Radanović & Likić 2018). Smart contracts were utilized in this product to compensate travellers for aircraft delays. Moreover, AON and ANZ companies has also implemented blockchain in their insurance products (Daudt et al., 2013).

2.2.3. Solicitation of Blockchain in Banking

a. Blockchain for banking.

All nations and countries rely on banks to maintain their financial stability. Currently, the system does not meet the customer's needs as it has become outdated, according to Shenzhen Research Institute (2016; Yong, 2019). The current banking system can be considered modern for a number of reasons but the current scams of Deutsche Bank and Goldman Sachs shows a different story (Mao & Motohashi 2016).

Therefore, most of the giant players in market are rigorously adopting the innovative and new technologies like blockchain to compete in the market, can provide better customer service and elevated services. As of now, Bank of America has filed 35 patents related to the use of blockchain in banks (Ertz & Boily, 2019).

The R3 CEV consortium, which consists of Citigroup, UBS, Barclays Bank, and Goldman Sachs, is examining how blockchain technology can be applied to banking. This is in order to minimize operational costs. Visa-backed startup Chain and the NASDAQ exchange have launched blockchain-based LINQ. Traditional banking has been transformed by blockchain (Cucari et al., 2019).

Here are few points which inspired local as well as international financial institutions and banks to use blockchain are as follows:

One is to diminish costs and transfer value. Investing in the central database is a major cost component for commercial banks since the terminal is expensive to purchase & maintain (Kar & Navin, 2021). In contrast, excessive bookkeeping and billing work increases operational risks and labor costs. With Blockchain technology, low-cost, transparent, and cost-free models can be developed because DLT and automated blockchain can be used (Parkhil et al., 2022; Peters et al., 2015).

The second point is about efficiently controlling risks. Banks focuses on tracking of loans & monitoring usage, but real operations are not reliable and also ineffective (Levac et al., 2010). Furthermore, global money flow control may exacerbate the problem. The blockchain's multi-center feature portrays individual user as a node in the blockchain, allowing direct point-to-point lending without the need for banks to act as middlemen and guarantee loans (Levac et al., 2010; Janssen et al., 2020). The efficacy of fund management improves, but the extent of credit risk due to information asymmetry gradually decreased. After all, it looks for creative ways to create revenue. A rising number of significant corporations, which includes banks and investment firms, are collaborating with financial entrepreneurs or funding in blockchain-based enterprises.

Banks demand a lucrative and creative business plan in this competitive market. It is clear from all angles that the application of blockchain has resulted in a positive change and innovation of commercial banks' traditional operations.

Blockchain technology has the potential to manage the complete business chain of banks in a methodical manner. Second, the use of blockchain in banks will actually boost efficiency and revolutionize the whole business paradigm. Smart contracts could save banks money on work audits and billing. Countless manuals as well as knowledge-based works are mechanized, and geniuses should maximize their cognitive abilities. Furthermore, blockchain would address inefficiencies, excessive costs, operational hazards, and fraud in a variety of financial sector activities. As a result, public sovereignty, cross blockchain, and quasi features have fundamentally impacted the bank's back-end and architecture, user experience, the centralized banking system, increased service efficiency, and offered banks with transformation chances. Banks provide traditional financial services as well as Internet financial services (Grant & Booth 2009).

b. Blockchain, distributed ledger technology, and the future of banking.

The advent of corporate blockchains has resulted in large investments in multiple emerging protocols that fulfil payment system privacy and authorization standards (Chang et al., 2020) The study focuses specifically on the most probable outcome use cases beyond the cross-border payments in this part, as well as challenges to overcome and potential legislative changes with in long term. Almost all of the institutions polled plan to concentrate payment solutions during the next 12 months. According to them, DLT functionality best complements the operations required in running a payment system. This use case may deliver the best long-term return on investment (Mohanta et al., 2020).

More individuals will embrace stable coins in the coming years, and these stable coins will mostly be relied on fiat currencies. This is being driven by initiatives like Facebook's Libra and Finality, as well as JPMorgan Chase's stable coins. The People's Bank of China will become the first issuer of the national bank's digital currency later this year. The interoperability of blockchain platforms has increased. The differences between the various blockchain protocols remain significant, but there is an ongoing discussion about collaboration and study into how assets might survive in multiple chains (Radanović & Likić 2018).

The year before, a multi-cloud blockchain really was installed, which could result in a successful cross-blockchain pilot in the coming months. Regulators will become more creative in managing fintech innovation by new microenterprises and established financial institutions. They can, in a way, create their own "consortium." GFIN is one of the early initiatives to develop standard rules for cross-border unification of financial innovation (Pranto et al. 2021).

c. Trade finance opportunities.

The majority of the banks polled felt that the sector had practically unlimited possibilities. Those banks predict that blockchain will make substantial headway in trade finance during the next five years. DLT has demonstrated considerable benefits in terms of speed, transparency, and capital release. Some noteworthy use cases for such banking consortium's development of capabilities in this subject. In 2017, nine banks like KBC, Santander UniCredit, HSBC, and Societe Generale, Deutsche Bank, and Nordea, Rabobank, Natixis, launched a blockchain-based platform to facilitate cross-border trading. Batavia, a comparable platform, was built in 2016 which was based on a solid evidence begun by IBM and UBS, with additional partners including Commerzbank, Caixa Bank, and Bank of Montreal. Batavia and Trade, both are constructed on the Hyperledger Fabric platform, and their trade finance blockchain platforms were integrated in 2018. Marco Polo and Voltron, which employ the R3 Corda architecture, and Komgo, which is based on quorum, are two more blockchain trade finance ideas (Sorgente & Lanz, 2017).

However, trade finance apps continue to have issues. The problem is that even if they did develop a system, "it will only operate if the paper is on both sides of international trade and customers agreed to use it, and this is not always successful." There is also the possibility of centralised and significant multinational commerce difficulties that can prevent the involvement of "smaller third parties." Trade financing is a less apparent use than cross-border payments, but it is one that banks are trying hard to develop (Mohanta et al., 2020; Joanna Briggs Institute 2011).

d. Primary securities issuance.

Blockchain technology has the potential to make it easier to issue primary assets such as corporate bonds. Currently, cash flow tracking and execution are mostly done manually. Certain bond life cycle operations can be automated by utilizing certain smart contracts & immutability of blockchain transactions (Mazzucato, et al., 2020). Bond proceeds, for example, might be issued on a parametric basis and instantly triggered upon the fulfilment of defined trigger conditions. The World Bank released Bondi, the first public bond generated and managed using DLT, in 2018. This two-year blockchain bond sponsored by the Common Wealth Bank of Australia garnered $80 million in its inaugural issuance. Similar problems are expected to arise in the future (Fusco et al., 2020).

Tokenization of Asset has expanded steadily (Pestovska, 2021). Technology has enabled an environment in which authorized natural or legal persons. This person could provide as well as exchange regulated digital stocks. The tokenization of securities will significantly reduce the cost of international transactions for banks. In the tokenized economy, there is the prospect of a more efficient system that eliminates the friction of creating, purchasing, and selling tokens. Tokenization "might help in making the financial industry more accessible, cheaper, faster, and easier, as well as release trillions of euros of current illiquid assets and considerably boost transaction volume," according to one bank. It is capable of supplying storage tokens (Munn et al., 2019). When decentralized alternatives are insufficient, the platform may serve as a trusted intermediary to suit the demands of the token economy. In the medium term, effective oversight and cross-border cooperation are required. Record speed, security, transparency, and immutability have all grown in 2019 as a result of substantial technological developments in the securities tokenization industry. This study is still a long way from accomplishing that aim.

Using DLT, clearing and settlement will improve. Banks regard clearing and settlement as additional critical applications (Fadaeddini, et al., 2020). A shared ledger helps speed up asset clearing and settlement when big and complicated multi-party transactions occur on a regular basis (Davis et al., 2009; Hodson, 2019). Exchanges and other financial organizations that trade substantial volumes of securities and derivatives on a regular basis have already experimented using blockchain platforms in the settlement process. Goldman Sachs received a patent in 2017 for the blockchain-based transaction processing system SETL coin. In 2015, the Nasdaq exchange created the first blockchain-based securities trading platform, LINQ. According to the article, industry groupings are striving toward "24-hour continuous settlement," or establishing a real "global settlement day." The existing real-time total billing system has a finite lifespan. Continuous Linked Settlement refers to a platform that serves as a worldwide multi-currency settlement system.

CONCLUSION

The current study includes a scoping evaluation of 100 review-based publications published between 2018 and 2019, utilizing Science Direct as a source. The review-based publications included in this study focused on the usage of blockchain in the financial sector, insurance, or banking. As a result, this paper discusses the use of blockchain in the sector of finance. The current study sought to identify, present, and define significant terminology used in review-based publications explaining the implementation of blockchain technology in the financial market, insurance, or banking. The important concepts are specified in the study's literature review section. The identification of important phrases and their definitions in these 100 review-based articles was done using an excel sheet, and afterwards thematic analysis of terminology was performed by coloring comparable themes with the same color.

The same subject is then utilized as broad headings in the literature review section. The current study assists researchers in identifying research gaps.

IMPLICATIONS OF CURRENT STUDY

This research Paper proposed few implications in order to promote the acceptance and usage of blockchain-based financial solutions. It is vital for financial firms to work through the blockchain consortium for blockchain technology to be adopted and used throughout the financial industry (wu et al., 2021). Regarding the decentralization of the present financial system, it is extremely possible that the blockchain would take long to be embraced and used throughout the banking sector since changes in financial systems and transformation of financial organizations' systems must typically be supplied in simultaneously (Trivedi & Malik, 2022). In interbank payments cases, the transition to the closed distributed ledger that bypasses the central bank is intensifying. The closed distributed ledger service, which includes banks and clients for transactions in international finances, is emerging in the international payment service.

Blockchain technology is already growing as a novel flow of money, founded on the beginnings of the distributed ledger provided by Bitcoin.

As distributed ledgers focusing on financial institutions become more prevalent, closed distributed ledger technology is expected to be a pioneer in future financial innovation in terms of dependability, stability, and efficiency (Davis et al., 2009). Consumer and associated environment demands alter as technology advances. During the same period, there is an additional layer for consumers to be compromised by information, such as hacking, and there is a great demand for blockchain technology as a result of businesses' attempts to protect against hacking (Trivedi & Malik, 2022). To encourage market movements, the government and relevant institutions should recognize and enable the strength of blockchain in individual and company transactions, public services, and so on, through the creation of new technologies and the dissemination of best - practice information.

FUTURE SCOPE OF STUDY

Here are few scopes to explore blockchain for new researches:

- From the standpoints of financial technology and systems, the features, and drawbacks of implementing the blockchain system. This includes its application in payment system. This may be backed up by research on the level to which blockchain systems have the ability to offer traditional bank funding to those who have previously been denied credit by financial institutions.

- Blockchain applications, particularly in the financial industry, are still in their early stages. There is a request for researchers to examine and construct additional prototypes in order to have a better understanding of the technology's use in the financial industry. There are several frameworks, concepts, and models that must be evaluated and applied in order to assess their strengths and limitations.
- There is a need of copyleft licenses to ensure interoperability among various blockchain solutions. To yet, the primary goal has been to concentrate on the functioning of blockchain prototypes for proof-of-concept purposes. However, copyleft licenses for interoperability must be created before blockchain can be adopted and used in the financial industry. At this point in the technology's life cycle, researchers must begin investigating interoperability difficulties and the standardization process.

Based on our results, there are several routes for academics to pursue, notably technology-related study focused on scalability and interoperability, as well as sociotechnical research focused on the development and consequences of blockchain for individuals, organizations, and society. While most of the present study focuses on technological advancements, models, architectures, and use cases, the ramifications of technology on society and the changes anticipated to be brought about by the various suggested cases of current businesses must also be investigated.

REFERENCES

Abramova, S., & Böhme, R. (2016). *Perceived benefit and risk as multidimensional determinants of bitcoin use: A quantitative exploratory study*. Academic Press.

Arksey, H., & O'Malley, L. (2005). Scoping studies: Towards a methodological framework. *International Journal of Social Research Methodology*, *8*(1), 19–32. doi:10.1080/1364557032000119616

Avgouleas, E., & Kiayias, A. (2019). The promise of blockchain technology for global securities and derivatives markets: The new financial ecosystem and the 'holy grail' of systemic risk containment. *European Business Organization Law Review*, *20*(1), 81–110. doi:10.100740804-019-00133-3

Babel, K., Daian, P., Kelkar, M., & Juels, A. (2021). *Clockwork finance: Automated analysis of economic security in smart contracts*. arXiv preprint arXiv:2109.04347

Beck, R., Avital, M., Rossi, M., & Thatcher, J. B. (2017). Blockchain technology in business and information systems research. *Business & Information Systems Engineering*, *59*(6), 381–384. doi:10.100712599-017-0505-1

Brophy, R. (2019). Blockchain and insurance: a review for operations and regulation. *Journal of Financial Regulation and Compliance, 28*(2), 215-234.

Chang, V., Baudier, P., Zhang, H., Xu, Q., Zhang, J., & Arami, M. (2020). How Blockchain can impact financial services–The overview, challenges and recommendations from expert interviewees. *Technological Forecasting and Social Change*, *158*, 120166. doi:10.1016/j.techfore.2020.120166 PMID:32834134

Chen, C. L., Deng, Y. Y., Tsaur, W. J., Li, C. T., Lee, C. C., & Wu, C. M. (2021). A traceable online insurance claims system based on blockchain and smart contract technology. *Sustainability*, *13*(16), 9386. doi:10.3390u13169386

Colquhoun, H. L., Levac, D., O'Brien, K. K., Straus, S., Tricco, A. C., Perrier, L., & Moher, D. (2014). Scoping reviews: Time for clarity in definition, methods, and reporting. *Journal of Clinical Epidemiology*, *67*(12), 1291–1294. doi:10.1016/j.jclinepi.2014.03.013 PMID:25034198

Cucari, N., Wankowicz, E., & De Falco, S. E. (2019). Rural tourism and Albergo Diffuso: A case study for sustainable land-use planning. *Land Use Policy*, *82*, 105–119. doi:10.1016/j.landusepol.2018.11.050

Daudt, H. M., van Mossel, C., & Scott, S. J. (2013). Enhancing the scoping study methodology: A large, inter-professional team's experience with Arksey and O'Malley's framework. *BMC Medical Research Methodology*, *13*(1), 1–9. doi:10.1186/1471-2288-13-48 PMID:23522333

Davis, K., Drey, N., & Gould, D. (2009). What are scoping studies? A review of the nursing literature. *International Journal of Nursing Studies*, *46*(10), 1386–1400. doi:10.1016/j.ijnurstu.2009.02.010 PMID:19328488

Dib, O., Brousmiche, K. L., Durand, A., Thea, E., & Hamida, E. B. (2018). Consortium blockchains: Overview, applications and challenges. *International Journal On Advances in Telecommunications*, *11*(1&2), 51–64.

Drummer, D., & Neumann, D. (2020). Is code law? Current legal and technical adoption issues and remedies for blockchain-enabled smart contracts. *Journal of Information Technology*, *35*(4), 337–360. doi:10.1177/0268396220924669

Eling, M., & Lehmann, M. (2018). The impact of digitalization on the insurance value chain and the insurability of risks. *The Geneva Papers on Risk and Insurance. Issues and Practice*, *43*(3), 359–396. doi:10.105741288-017-0073-0

Ertz, M., & Boily, É. (2019). The rise of the digital economy: Thoughts on blockchain technology and cryptocurrencies for the collaborative economy. *International Journal of Innovation Studies*, *3*(4), 84–93. doi:10.1016/j.ijis.2019.12.002

Fadaeddini, A., Majidi, B., & Eshghi, M. (2020). Secure decentralized peer-to-peer training of deep neural networks based on distributed ledger technology. *The Journal of Supercomputing*, *76*(12), 10354–10368. doi:10.100711227-020-03251-9

Fusco, A., Dicuonzo, G., Dell'Atti, V., & Tatullo, M. (2020). Blockchain in healthcare: Insights on COVID-19. *International Journal of Environmental Research and Public Health*, *17*(19), 7167. doi:10.3390/ijerph17197167 PMID:33007951

Gatteschi, V., Lamberti, F., Demartini, C., Pranteda, C., & Santamaría, V. (2018). Blockchain and smart contracts for insurance: Is the technology mature enough?. *Future Internet*, *10*(2), 20.

Grant, M. J., & Booth, A. (2009). A typology of reviews: An analysis of 14 review types and associated methodologies. *Health Information and Libraries Journal*, *26*(2), 91–108. doi:10.1111/j.1471-1842.2009.00848.x PMID:19490148

Grima, S., Spiteri, J., & Romānova, I. (2020). A STEEP framework analysis of the key factors impacting the use of blockchain technology in the insurance industry. *The Geneva Papers on Risk and Insurance. Issues and Practice*, *45*(3), 398–425. doi:10.105741288-020-00162-x

Hodson, C. J. (2019). *Cyber risk management: Prioritize threats, identify vulnerabilities and apply controls*. Kogan Page Publishers.

Janssen, M., Weerakkody, V., Ismagilova, E., Sivarajah, U., & Irani, Z. (2020). A framework for analysing blockchain technology adoption: Integrating institutional, market and technical factors. *International Journal of Information Management*, *50*, 302–309. doi:10.1016/j.ijinfomgt.2019.08.012

Joanna Briggs Institute. (2011). The Joanna Briggs Institute best practice information sheet: Music as an intervention in hospitals. *Nursing & Health Sciences*, *13*(1), 99–102. doi:10.1111/j.1442-2018.2011.00583.x PMID:21426462

Kar, A. K., & Navin, L. (2021). Diffusion of blockchain in insurance industry: An analysis through the review of academic and trade literature. *Telematics and Informatics*, *58*, 101532. doi:10.1016/j.tele.2020.101532

Khan, R., Kumar, P., Jayakody, D. N. K., & Liyanage, M. (2019). A survey on security and privacy of 5G technologies: Potential solutions, recent advancements, and future directions. *IEEE Communications Surveys and Tutorials*, *22*(1), 196–248. doi:10.1109/COMST.2019.2933899

Khatoon, A. (2020). A blockchain-based smart contract system for healthcare management. *Electronics (Basel)*, *9*(1), 94. doi:10.3390/electronics9010094

Leong, Y. Y., & Chen, Y. C. (2020). Cyber risk cost and management in IoT devices-linked health insurance. *The Geneva Papers on Risk and Insurance. Issues and Practice*, *45*(4), 737–759. doi:10.105741288-020-00169-4

Levac, D., Colquhoun, H., & O'Brien, K. K. (2010). Scoping studies: Advancing the methodology. *Implementation Science; IS*, *5*(1), 1–9. doi:10.1186/1748-5908-5-69 PMID:20854677

Mao, H., & Motohashi, K. (2016). A Comparative Study on Tenant Firms in Beijing Tsinghua University Science Park and Shenzhen Research Institute of Tsinghua University. *Asian Journal of Innovation and Policy*, *5*(3), 225–250. doi:10.7545/ajip.2016.5.3.225

Mazzucato, M., Kattel, R., & Ryan-Collins, J. (2020). Challenge-driven innovation policy: Towards a new policy toolkit. *Journal of Industry, Competition and Trade*, *20*(2), 421–437. doi:10.100710842-019-00329-w

Min, H. (2019). Blockchain technology for enhancing supply chain resilience. *Business Horizons*, *62*(1), 35–45. doi:10.1016/j.bushor.2018.08.012

Mohanta, B. K., Jena, D., Satapathy, U., & Patnaik, S. (2020). Survey on IoT security: Challenges and solution using machine learning, artificial intelligence and blockchain technology. *Internet of Things*, *11*, 100227. doi:10.1016/j.iot.2020.100227

Munn, Z., Aromataris, E., Tufanaru, C., Stern, C., Porritt, K., Farrow, J., ... Jordan, Z. (2019). The development of software to support multiple systematic review types: The Joanna Briggs Institute System for the Unified Management, Assessment and Review of Information (JBI SUMARI). *JBI Evidence Implementation*, *17*(1), 36–43. PMID:30239357

Nakhuva, B., & Champaneria, T. (2015). Study of various internet of things platforms. *International Journal of Computer Science & Engineering Survey*, *6*(6), 61–74. doi:10.5121/ijcses.2015.6605

Parkhill, A. J., Nixon, M., & McEwan, T. E. (2022). A critical analysis of stalking theory and implications for research and practice. *Behavioral Sciences & the Law, 40*(5), 562–583. doi:10.1002/bsl.2598 PMID:36134723

Pedersen, A. B., Risius, M., & Beck, R. (2019). A ten-step decision path to determine when to use blockchain technologies. *MIS Quarterly Executive, 18*(2), 99–115. doi:10.17705/2msqe.00010

Pestovska, Z. (2021). Changes in the financial services market under the influence of AI. *Artificial Intelligence as a Basis for the Development of the Digital Economy*, 85.

Peters, M. D., Godfrey, C. M., Khalil, H., McInerney, P., Parker, D., & Soares, C. B. (2015). Guidance for conducting systematic scoping reviews. *JBI Evidence Implementation, 13*(3), 141–146. PMID:26134548

Pranto, T. H., Noman, A. A., Mahmud, A., & Haque, A. B. (2021). Blockchain and smart contract for IoT enabled smart agriculture. *PeerJ. Computer Science, 7*, e407. doi:10.7717/peerj-cs.407 PMID:33834098

Radanović, I., & Likić, R. (2018). Opportunities for use of blockchain technology in medicine. *Applied Health Economics and Health Policy, 16*(5), 583–590. doi:10.100740258-018-0412-8 PMID:30022440

Rajasekaran, A. S., Azees, M., & Al-Turjman, F. (2022). A comprehensive survey on blockchain technology. *Sustainable Energy Technologies and Assessments, 52*, 102039. doi:10.1016/j.seta.2022.102039

Rashideh, W. (2020). Blockchain technology framework: Current and future perspectives for the tourism industry. *Tourism Management, 80*, 104125. doi:10.1016/j.tourman.2020.104125

Schuetz, S., & Venkatesh, V. (2020). Blockchain, adoption, and financial inclusion in India: Research opportunities. *International Journal of Information Management, 52*, 101936. doi:10.1016/j.ijinfomgt.2019.04.009

Sorgente, A., & Lanz, M. (2017). Emerging adults' financial well-being: A scoping review. *Adolescent Research Review, 2*(4), 255–292. doi:10.100740894-016-0052-x

Stratopoulos, T. C., Wang, V. X., & Ye, J. (2020). Blockchain technology adoption. *Accounting Horizons, 36*(1), 197-220.

Sultana, T., Almogren, A., Akbar, M., Zuair, M., Ullah, I., & Javaid, N. (2020). Data sharing system integrating access control mechanism using blockchain-based smart contracts for IoT devices. *Applied Sciences (Basel, Switzerland), 10*(2), 488. doi:10.3390/app10020488

Trivedi, S., & Malik, R. (2022). Blockchain Technology as an Emerging Technology in the Insurance Market. In *Big Data: A Game Changer for Insurance Industry* (pp. 81–100). Emerald Publishing Limited. doi:10.1108/978-1-80262-605-620221006

Ukpong, M. S., & Acha, I. A. (2019). A Critique of Micro-Insurance Models for Microfinance Banks to Boost SMEs in Nigeria. *Noble International Journal of Economics and Financial Research, 4*(1), 1-9.

Whittemore, R., Chao, A., Jang, M., Minges, K. E., & Park, C. (2014). Methods for knowledge synthesis: An overview. *Heart & Lung*, *43*(5), 453–461. doi:10.1016/j.hrtlng.2014.05.014 PMID:25012634

Wu, B., & Duan, T. (2019, March). The application of blockchain technology in financial markets. *Journal of Physics: Conference Series*, *1176*(4), 042094. doi:10.1088/1742-6596/1176/4/042094

Wu, X., Zhu, X., Wu, G. Q., & Ding, W. (2013). Data mining with big data. *IEEE Transactions on Knowledge and Data Engineering*, *26*(1), 97–107.

Yong, W. (2019). Report on the Development of Qianhai, Shenzhen. In *Annual Report on the Development of China's Special Economic Zones (2018)* (pp. 41–57). Springer. doi:10.1007/978-981-13-9837-7_4

Zachariadis, M., Hileman, G., & Scott, S. V. (2019). Governance and control in distributed ledgers: Understanding the challenges facing blockchain technology in financial services. *Information and Organization*, *29*(2), 105–117. doi:10.1016/j.infoandorg.2019.03.001

Zhang, A., Zhong, R. Y., Farooque, M., Kang, K., & Venkatesh, V. G. (2020). Blockchain-based life cycle assessment: An implementation framework and system architecture. *Resources, Conservation and Recycling*, *152*, 104512. doi:10.1016/j.resconrec.2019.104512

Chapter 2
An Umbrella Review of the Literature on Blockchain and Distributed Ledger Technology and Their Roles in Future Banking

Ankita
Chitkara Business School, Chitkara University, India

Sonal Trivedi
https://orcid.org/0000-0001-8711-2977
Chitkara Business School, Chitkara University, India

ABSTRACT

Blockchain technology is gaining popularity in the financial sector and specifically in banking. Its implementation will result into increased transparency and reduced cost. Distributed ledger technology (DLT) is primarily a payment system that is well adopted by the financial sector and will have significant impact on future of banking. The purpose of the study is to identify whether this novel technology is good enough to replace and compete with the traditional financial system. The current study followed the umbrella review limiting the studies based on blockchain, DLT, and banking from 2015 until today published in Scopus-indexed journals. The study concludes that there is evidence of adoption of blockchain technology in banking sectors around the globe, but there is still need to explore the application of blockchain in banking, and there is a need to overcome the challenges faced in implementation of blockchain in the banking sector.

DOI: 10.4018/978-1-6684-8361-9.ch002

INTRODUCTION

Blockchain technology is also known as the "next-generation Internet" (Shermin, 2017) and a "foundational technology" (Lele, 2019) having the ability to transform transactions, impact in what way individuals interrelate in the economy, and even transform society. It is expected to revolutionise a wide range of operations, from government, healthcare, manufacturing to finance and beyond, according to analysts.

It is frequently referred to as a disruptive, "game-changing" breakthrough, with some arguing that its lasting impact may be even greater than that of the "World Wide Web or Internet media" (Gleim & Stevens, 2021). Despite the widespread interest and acceptance of blockchain technology, numerous applications have raised concerns. Many digital currencies such as Bitcoin have been described as "solutions in search of a problem," whether they are distributed autonomous organisations which exists on upper position of blockchain structure or ICO (Initial Coin Offerings) which use current digital tokens to attract fund (Matzutt et al. 2018).

Some critics have warned that embracing such a technology transition could attract criminal behaviour, if not opening the door for disorder, then at the very slightest fueling the growth of authoritarianism.

Contrary to the existing basic technologies (such as the Internet), the existing basic technologies used by established international organizations and alliances (such as 7 Internet Society, 6 ICANN, 5 W3C, 4 Internet Governance Forum, IETF etc.) are disordered at finest. There is no structure for reaching consensus, resolving differences and coordinating actions. Reasonably, it may affect the future of adoption and application of blockchain which in increasing presently. Additionally, it brings substantial risk for users and arouses increasing concerns from regulators, especially in the financial sector. In the service sector, the stability and confidence of financial services are threatened. The environment of taxation concerns is the most important.

Blockchain for Responsible Investor

Responsible investment includes considerations of ESG issues (Environment, Social, Governance) while making investment decisions. Responsible investors are those which not only look at financial returns but also impact on planet and people. This has influenced financial institutions to come up with financial products with sustainable attributes.

Blockchain increased usage in finance is brought by objective to cut cost and to increase profits of businesses. There is an increased usage of blockchain for responsible investing also taking into consideration the good impact of blockchain on environment. Such initiative includes 'blockchain for impact coalition' which is an initiative by UN agencies for engaging with vendors providing blockchain technology services. Another initiative is a project with social impact run by 'ConsesSys' (Developer of Ethereum application). Also, in year 2017, UNFCCC have suggested another usage of blockchain to report and track reduction in emission of greenhouse gases and thus avoid the issue of double counting. To achieve this in practical UNFCC has partnered with 'HackForClimate' group for bringing such solutions. There are technologies to track and report the attributes of sustainability in a commodity such as presence of carbon footprint but all such projects are at nascent stage. Thus, it is not only blockchain technology alone which is a solution to track and report the attributes of sustainability in a commodity.

With respect to checking sustainability attributes in financial products, various financial institutions have now started offering financial products with sustainability attributes such as ETFs and other funds such as cryptocurrency funds, crypto venture capital funds. Also, Bitcoin Investment Trust is launched by Greyscale. Furthermore, Ethereum and Bitcoin Trackers is launched by 'XBT Provider AB Sweden' in 2017. Also, Leonteq and Vontobel, the providers of Swiss structured products have released certificates for Bitcoin tracker counting 'Bitcoin shorting products'. This is a beginning of development of structured products in financial sector with the launch of Bitcoin futures by 'CME Group'.

In the present study, the paper clarified the characteristics of distributed ledger technologies inspired by blockchain and checked their effectiveness as part of the financial service infrastructure. Our approach is based on completed academic research and reference points recommended by comprehensive practitioners to generate core insights into current governance issues. The paper has adopted a transformation process to guide us in solving current and future related issues related to financial services governance practices. As a guideline for our thinking, the paper relies on the literature on IT platform governance and use this as a perspective to study important governance characteristics, such as for making decision, incentive structures and mechanism for controlling in digital infrastructure. As the discussion about blockchain continues to evolve and surpass, policy makers and practitioners of Bitcoin have begun to consider not only the basic characteristics of blockchain technology, but also the complexity of the socio-economic, legal and institutional requirements of the atmosphere being developed. The paper illustrated our discussions with the help of critical situations in which the existing blockchain was questioned and experienced a crisis of testing its governance model. The paper use these "important moments" to assess efficiency, risk and trust issues that are at the core of a robust and effective financial system. This allows us to briefly discuss the skills and conditions of governance and provide insights on missionary or overcoming challenges.

The structure of current paper is (as shown in Figure 1): The paper first uses existing literature on Blockchain, DLT and banking to prove our ideas. Then, before reviewing their promise as fundamental technologies for financial services, the paper provides description of blockchain and DLT. The paper also presents examples of DLT and how DLT & blockchain relate and differ from each other. This allows us to determine the boundaries of existing practices in distributed ledger systems, blockchain and banking. Based on the illustrations and literature the paper discussed, the paper re-examines the review-based papers on 5 criteria. Our conclusions summarize the impact of our discussion on the future development of review-based paper in the field of blockchain, DLT and banking. Also, the paper identifies key fields for future research in blockchain as well as umbrella review.

Figure 1. Structure of current study

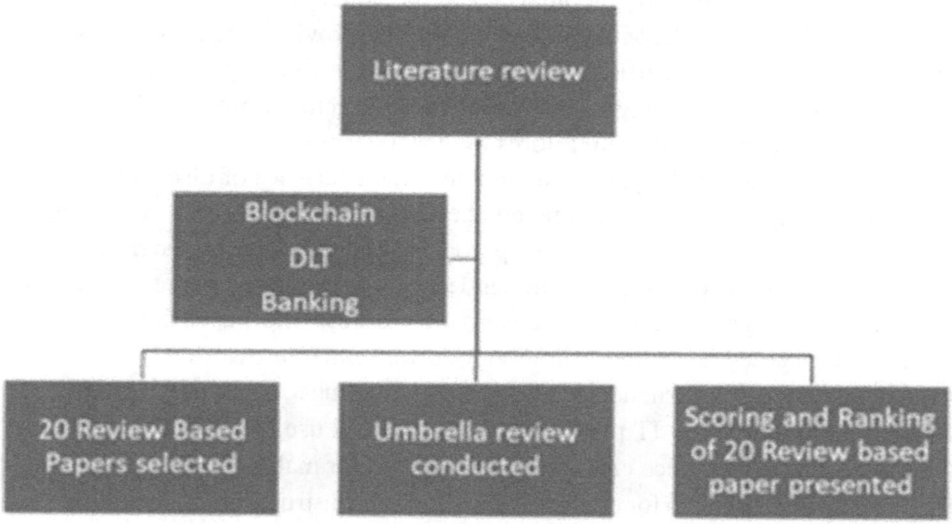

Research Method

Table 1 shows that the complete drive of present umbrella review is to provide a valuation that requires a conceptual framework. Thus, the section below introduces a literature review on blockchain, distributed ledger technology (DLT), and the banking industry.

Table 1. Research methodology used in the present paper

Scope	Research problem	The review-based papers are not given similar attention as given to exploratory studies. The present study gives emphasis on methodical reviews as there are very limited studies based of umbrella review in the field of management, particularly in blockchain and banking.
	Research question	Whether the review-based papers clearly define their research methodology used for reviewing the paper as empirical studies presents their methodology used for research.
	Research Objective	To review review-based papers in the field of Blockchain, DLT and banking
Data selection	Source	Science Direct
	Search term	Blockchain, DLT and Banking
	Process of screening	The abstract of selected papers was considered to eliminate the ineligible papers
	Inclusion of studies	The review papers with focus on blockchain in banking the paperre considered for inclusion of umbrella review
	Exclusion of studies	Grey papers the paperre excluded such as books, editorials, conference papers, etc.
Data processing	Criteria for appraisal of study	Five criteria the paperre used to appraise the review paper i.e. whether the review papers have clearly defined their research methodology i.e. research problem, research objective, research question, source of data based and tool of analysis.
	Method of data extraction	Data was manually updated on spreadsheet by author, no software or the paperb application was used for data extraction
	Method of data analysis	Checklist
	Method of synthesizing result	Scoring from 0 to 5
Data reporting	Findings	In a scoring from 0 to 5, none of the review paper got a score of 4 and 5. Thus, there is need that review-based papers clearly define their methodology used for reviewing the paper.
	Limitation	The number of review paper was merely 20 and only one database was used as a source.
	Conclusion	The current study concludes that reviethe paperd papers in the field of 'Blockchain, DLT and banking' require to be more clearly defined to identify the research gap in the field.
	Implication for future research	Based on the limitations and challenges faced in implementing blockchain in banking, the future research can provide suggestions and recommendations to improve the applicability of blockchain in banking.

LITERATURE REVIEW

Blockchain

Blockchain-a shared ledger technology that allows anyone in the corporate network to view the system of record-will change many industries in the future, including financial services. Blockchain is still in its infancy, but some ongoing initiatives are already driving the development of industrial solutions, which will bring several important benefits when transferring assets within corporate networks (Efanov & Roschin, 2018).

Today, all participants in the corporate network keep their own traditional ledger to record their transactions in the ecosystem. Despite investing in integration and B2B technology to reduce complexity and increase the network of these systems, corporate network participants often still exchange data files between them (Niranjanamurthy, Nithya & Jagannatha, 2019) As a result, the processes used to support asset ownership and transfer assets across corporate networks are often inefficient, costly, and fragile.

Blockchain has the potential to allow all participants in the company's network to share the system of record (Beck et al. 2017). When moving assets across corporate networks, this replicated shared ledger provides consensus, lineage, immutability, and finality-reducing cost, complexity, and time, supporting sharing, trusted processes, enabling trusted records, and improving discoverability (Lemieux, 2016).

The current study focuses on the current state of blockchain in financial services as shown in Figure 2, studies the challenges and opportunities of implementing the technology in banks and capital markets, and studies many use cases, many of which are already undergoing feasibility studies. Financial services will not be the only industry affected by blockchain, but it is currently at the forefront of experimenting and implementing the technology.

Distributed Ledger Technology

DLT specifically denotes to technical protocols and infrastructure that can simultaneously access, verify, and update data sets that characterize distributed ledgers (Sunyaev, 2020). It is suitable for computer networks distributed in multiple units or locations.

DLT uses encryption technology to firmly cryptographic signatures, store data, and keys so that only authorized users can access them (Maull et al., 2017).

The technology also develops database which is immutable, which means that once information is saved, it cannot be removed, and permanent records of all updates are kept for future generations to use (Liu, Farahani, & Firouzi, 2020).

Figure 2. Potential of blockchain
Source: Developed by author.

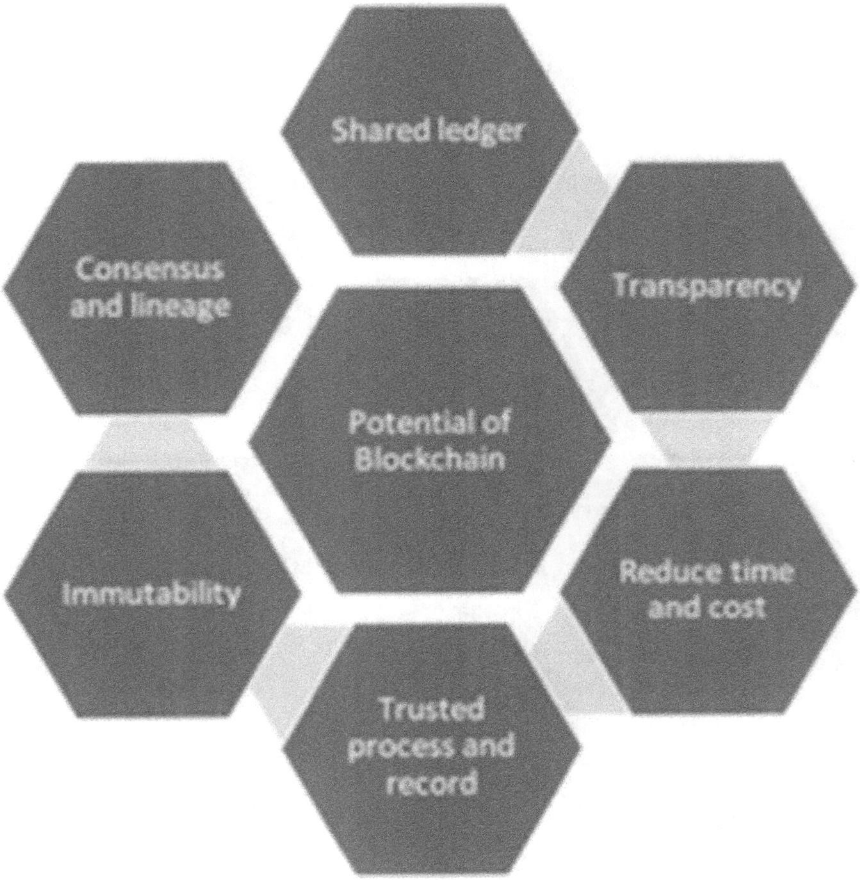

By transferring records to a decentralized system from a single authoritative location where all related parties can see and change the ledger, this architecture represents a major change in the way information is collected and communicated. This allows all other parties to view who is using and changing the ledger. Thus, DLT has transparency, and it ensures increased trust among participating entities and virtually removes the possibility of frauds in the ledger.

Therefore, DLT eliminates requirement for parties to depend on a central authority which can be trusted and which controls the ledger or external third parties to accomplish this role and act as tamper protection.

Figure 3. Features of DLT
Source: Developed by author.

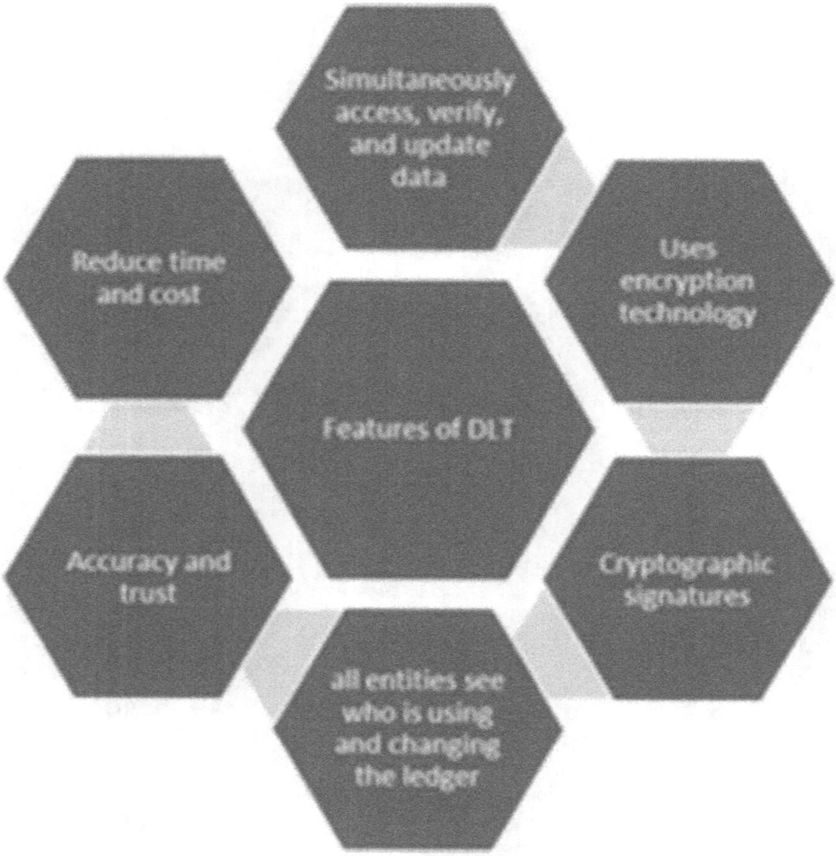

In the ten years since the introduction of Bitcoin in 2009, people's interest in distributed ledger technology has grown significantly. Bitcoin is a cryptocurrency based on blockchain technology. It is the first to prove that the technology is not only effective, but also scalable and Safety.

Since then, companies in all industries have done experiments with DLT to find its application in business processes. Healthcare, financial services, supply chain management and pharmaceuticals were early leaders in applying DLT.

It is significant to observe that DLT is a novel concept. For a long time, companies collected and saved data in various locations, whether on paper or in isolated software, and the data was only regularly merged into a central database. For example, each business unit of a company may have different data bits, and the business unit enters these data into the centralized general ledger only when needed. Similarly, several cooperative organizations usually hold their own data and only record it in a central ledger controlled by authorized parties upon request or need. The huge advancement of DLT is that it can eliminate or minimize the usually error-prone and time-consuming process required to match various involvement of ledger which provide surety that everybody has access leading to trust and accuracy (refer Figure 3).

Examples of Distributed Ledger Technology

Various kinds of distributed ledger technologies are presently in use. The blockchain is the most popular type of DLT, which bundles transactions into linked blocks and then sends them to nodes on the network. It was Bitcoin & some additional cryptocurrencies.

For the IoT ecosystem, another kind of DLT is Tangle. The IOTA Foundation and the Eclipse Foundation have launched the Tangle EE Working Group, that Tangle defines as "a permissionless, contactless, and scalable distributed ledger designed to support trustworthy data and Value transmission". Other popular DLT include Hyperledger Fabric, Ethereum and Corda.

Blockchain and DLT: How They Relate and Differ

The terms blockchain & DLT are often used interchangeably and sometimes together. In other words, blockchain is a type of DLT, but not all DLT use blockchain technology (Ølnes, Ubacht, & Janssen, 2017).

Figure 4. Blockchain vs. DLT
Source: Developed by author.

The doubt between the use of terms DLT and blockchain is obvious as these terms become popular after the popularity of Bitcoin despite the fact that the technology is novel (refer Figure 4). No one is expert in the field and people are still exploring its use. Both are used to create remote ledgers using cryptography. Both create immutable records containing timestamps. Both are considered almost impossible to crack (Moyano & Ross, 2017). Both can be public so that everyone can access it, just like Bitcoin, or approve it (private) and therefore limited to authorized users who agree to certain usage standards (refer Figure 5).

Figure 5. Similarity between blockchain and DLT
Source: Developed by author.

Similarity	Both use cryptocurrency
	Both create immutable records
	Almost impossible to crack
	Everyone can access

This is the biggest difference: Blockchain uses data blocks linked together to develop distributed ledgers, as the name suggests (refer Figure 6). DLT also involves technologies which use different principles of design to develop distributed ledgers. In order to meet the requirements of DLT, the technology does not have to construct its data in units of blocks.

Figure 6. Difference between blockchain and DLT
Source: Developed by author.

The Future of Distributed Ledger Technology

Whether distributed ledger technologies like blockchain will completely change the way industries and government work is an open environment.

Experts in this field promote DLT as a significant technology who can not only greatly progress existing procedures, but also initiate novel and innovative applications.

In addition, they view DLT as component of the "Internet of Value", for conducting transactions in real time on a global network. In fact, DLT exists only as the Internet which supports it is ubiquitous (Arslan et al. 2020).

The view of experts is that DLT will also have same technology curve as any other technology i.e. initially few leading companies will adopt DLT resulting into more competitive position, then fast followers will also adopt this technology and lastly, laggers. Like any other technology adoption, companies will face challenges in adopting, operating & expanding the usage of DLT.

For this reason, visionaries, entrepreneurs and corporate executives are now facing the challenge of building a corporate network. These companies can use DLT together to fundamentally change the way they share and manage data, and innovate DLT brand new Process and business model.

Blockchain and DLT for Banking

Banks are considered as the backbone of any country's/nation's financial system. According to the Shenzhen Research Institute (2016), the current system of bank is outdated and it no longer satisfies the need of customer. There are arguments in favor of current banking system as modern but the recent scams like Deutsche Bank and Goldman Sachs presents a different story. This is why, large organizations are adopting novel technologies such as blockchain for competitive advantage, better customer service and upgraded services. For Now, 35 patents related to use of blockchain in banks have been filed by Bank of America. Citigroup, UBS, Barclays Bank and Goldman Sachs has recognized the R3 CEV consortium to further discover possible usage of blockchain in banking to minimize the operational cost. Visabacked startup Chain and NASDAQ exchange have launched blockchain technology based Linq. Thus, blockchain has changed the face of traditional banking system (Cucari et al., 2021).

The points which motivated both local and international financial institutions and banks to use blockchain are as under: *One* is to reduce costs & transfer value. Major element of cost for Commercial banks is the fund invested with the central database, because the purchase costs & maintenance of the terminal are high (Kewell, Adams, & Parry, 2017). On the other hand, a large amount of bookkeeping and billing work increases operation risks & labor cost. The solution to such problems is Blockchain technology, because the use of DLT and automated blockchain can develop a low-cost, transparent, & cost-free model (Nguyen, 2016). The *second* is efficiently controlling risks. Banks highlight tracking loan & monitoring usage, but real operations are unreliable and ineffective (Kołodziej, 2021). In addition, global regulation of capital flows may complicate the challenge. 'The multi-center function of blockchain technology treats each user as a node in the blockchain, realizing direct point-to-point transactions and lenders without the need for banks to provide loan guarantees as intermediaries' (Kołodziej, 2021). The credit risk caused by asymmetry in information is significantly condensed, and the efficiency of fund management is improved. After all, it is looking for innovative ways to make money. In the field of finance, increasing number of large organizations are investing in start-up based on blockchain technology or cooperating with startups, including investment institutions & banks (Hassani, Huang, & Silva, 2018). In this environment of high competition, banks require a business model which is profitable and innovative. The transformation and innovation of the commercial bank's traditional business by the blockchain is reflected in all aspects.

Figure 7. Usage of blockchain in banking
Source: Developed by author.

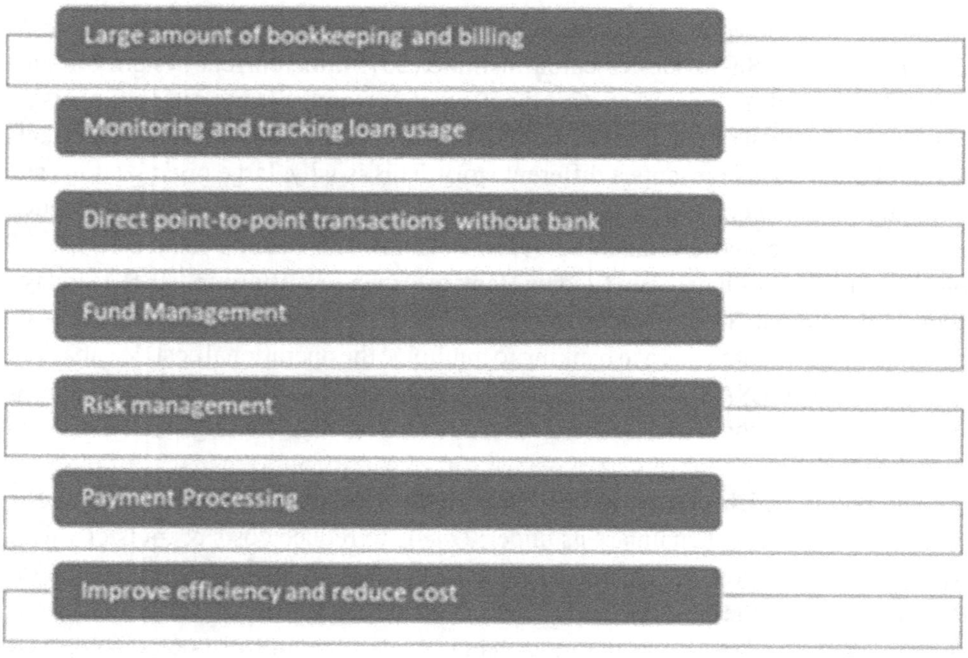

From the banking industry to transaction participants, counting those tangled in optimizing countless processes in the financial services sector (Adams, Kewell, & Parry, 2018). Blockchain technology can answer the entire business chain for banks systematically. Figure 7 shows different business areas of banks where blockchain technology is being applied, from payment processing to invoices to supply chain financing. The goal is understanding customers and possible areas of money laundering risk management. Secondly, the usage of blockchain technology in banks will improve efficiency of business and change the entire business model. For banks, the use of smart contracts can bar work auditing and billing costs. Many manuals and knowledge-based tasks are automated, and talents should make full use of their cognitive skills. In addition, blockchain can solve the inefficiency, high cost, operational risks & fraud of numerous processes in financial services. Therefore, public autonomy, the multi-center blockchain, and non-manipulable attributes have essentially altered the business model of enhanced the bank's back-end and infrastructure, user experience, the centralized banking system, improved service efficiency and provided banks with transformation opportunities. Banks range from traditional financial services to Internet financial services.

Blockchain, DLT, and the Future of Banking

The emergence of enterprise blockchains has led to significant investments in various evolving protocols that meet the privacy and permission thresholds of payment systems (Arslanian & Fischer, 2019). In this section, the paper focus on the most likely future use cases outside of cross-border payments, obstacles to overcome, and potential regulatory changes in the long run. Almost all banks surveyed will prioritize payment solutions in the next 12 months. They say that the functionality of DLT best complements the processes involved in running a payment system. In the long run, this use case may provide the highest return on investment. In the near future, stablecoins will be accepted by more people, and these stablecoins are mainly based on fiat currencies. This is driven by projects such as Facebook's Libra and Fnality and JPMorgan Chase's stablecoins. The central bank's digital currency is becoming a reality, and the People's Bank of China will become the first issuer later this year. Interoperability between blockchain platforms has been improved. The differences between the major blockchain protocols are still large, but there is an open dialogue about cooperation and research on how assets can coexist in different chains (Venegas, 2020). The multi-cloud blockchain was deployed last year, which may be a successful cross-blockchain pilot in the next few months. Regulators will be more innovative in the way they manage fintech innovation from new small businesses and existing financial institutions. In a sense, they can start forming their own "consortium." There are some early efforts to establish common principles for cross-border integration of financial innovation, including GFIN.

Trade Finance Opportunities

Most of the banks surveyed stated that almost all options are open to the industry. In particular, they believe that trade finance is an area where they hope blockchain will make significant progress within five years. As mentioned on page 6, DLT has significant advantages in terms of speed, transparency, and capital release. Some notable use cases for the banking consortium to develop skills in this field. A blockchain-based platform composed of nine banks (KBC, UniCredit, HSBC, Societe Generale, Deutsche Bank, Nordea, Rabobank, Natixis and Santander) in 2017 to simplify cross-border trade. A similar platform Batavia was developed in 2016 based on a proof-of-concept initiated by IBM and UBS, with the addition of Commerzbank, CaixaBank and Bank of Montreal as additional partners. Both Batavia and Trade are built on the Hyperledger Fabric platform and merged their trade finance blockchain platforms in 2018. Other blockchain trade financing plans include Marco Polo and Voltron, which use the R3 Corda framework, and Komgo, which is based on a quorum.

However, there are still problems with trade finance applications. The point of concern is that if they did build a system, "it will only work if [the paper] are on both sides of the international trade and both customers agree to use it, it's not always effective." There is also the prospect of centralized and large-scale international trade issues that can avoid "smaller third parties." Trade finance is not as obvious as cross-border payments, but rather an application that banks are working hard on.

Primary Securities Issuance

The blockchain system can facilitate the issuance of primary securities, such as corporate bonds. Currently, the issuance & payment of cash flow are mostly tracked & executed manually. The immutableness of blockchain transactions can assist automate certain procedures in the bond life cycle using predefined smart contracts (Le Gear, 2020). For example, bond proceeds can be issued on a parameter basis, and will be activated immediately once certain trigger conditions are met. In 2018, the World Bank issued Bondi, the first public bond created and managed through DLT. This two-year blockchain bond managed by the Common wealth Bank of Australia raised $80 million at the time of its initial issuance. Similar problems are likely to occur in the future.

Asset tokenization has steadily increased (Tian et al. 2020). Thanks to technology, there is now an ecosystem where authorized natural or legal persons can issue and trade regulated digital stocks of all assets of each asset class on the open market. This tokenization of securities will help banks significantly reduce global transaction costs. The tokenized economy provides the potential for a more efficient system that eliminates the friction of creating, buying, and selling tokens. A bank pointed out that "tokenization can make the financial industry more accessible, cheaper, faster, and easier, and may release trillions of euros of current illiquid assets and substantially increase transaction volume." It can be used to provide storage tokens (Narayan & Tidström, 2020). The platform may act as a trusted intermediary to meet the needs of the token economy when decentralized solutions are not enough. In the short term, proper supervision and cross-border coordination are needed. In 2019, major technological advancements in the securities tokenization industry have improved the speed, security, transparency, and immutability of records. The transfer of tokens between chains. But this paper is still a long way from that goal.

DLT will improve clearing and settlement. Banks treat clearing and settlement as another important application. When large and complex multi-party transactions occur on a regular basis, a common ledger can speed up asset clearing and settlement (Lipton, 2018). Exchanges and other financial institutions that frequently trade large amounts of securities and derivatives have already tried blockchain platforms in the settlement process. In 2017, Goldman Sachs obtained a patent for the blockchain-based transaction processing system SETLcoin. The Nasdaq exchange successfully completed the first blockchain-based securities trading platform through Linq in 2015. One interviethe papere said that industry groups are moving towards "24-hour continuous settlement", that is, setting up a true "global settlement day." The current real-time total billing system has a limited operating time. Continuous Linked Settlement, a platform as an international multi-currency settlement system

UMBRELLA REVIEW: REVIEW OF REVIEW

Our review type is mainly comprehensive review, because our main purpose is to review 36 existing reviews (Aromataris et al., 2015). Secondly, the paper speed up the process by applying two focused search strategies, thereby using the fast review method (Tricco et al., 2017). (a) Source strategy: The paper use one databases (science direct) to identify journals and articles. (b) Restriction strategy: The paper focused our search on review articles in peer-reviethe paperd journals that appeared in English-language journals focusing on Blockchain, DLT and Banking betthe paperen 2014 and 2021. Third, the paper analyzed the verification method used.

Therefore, the review used in present paper is a methodological review (Krezmien et al., 2017).

The paper does not examine the authors' expertise in this umbrella review. Instead, it concentrates on the 'increasing emphasis on methodical reviews,' as stated in our study question. Thus, in the present umbrella review, the focus was given on methodology of review, type of review and type of analysis used in the literature review.

Table 2 presents the Umbrella review of reviewed papers.

Explanation:

Type of review and terms used in title:

The terms which are used in a review-papers are - Synthesis review, Overview, Descriptive review, Literature review, Systematic review, Analytical review and State-of-the-art review. In the present umbrella review, it was found that out of 20 review-based paper, 5 papers did not used any term in their title; 5 used the term 'systematic literature review'; 4 used the term survey and 2 used the term review. There were only 1 paper each using the term 'state-of-the-art' and comprehensive review.

Type of finding:

According to Toye et al., the key difference between "comprehensive methods (a) methods that aim to describe or "aggregate" results and (b) methods that aim interpreting these results and developing conceptual understanding or "theory".' (2014, p. 4). Thus, the types of findings are generally distinguished as aggregate or development of a new theory. In the present umbrella review of 20 review-based paper, it was found that none of the review-paper resulted into development of a new theory.

After, identification of body of present umbrella review of 20 review-based paper, the next section presents the analysis of these 20 review-based papers.

Table 2. The list of 20 review-based papers which are reviewed in the current study

S.no	Paper Title	Author	Year	Research Methodology	Selected Sources/ Databases	Type of Review	Term Used for Review Paper	Method of Data Analysis	Type of Finding
1	Sustainability of bitcoin and blockchains	Harald Vranken	2017	not defined	not defined	proof-of-work	No term used in the title	not defined	Aggregate findings
2	Systematic Review of the Literature, Research on Blockchain Technology as Support to the Trust Model Proposed Applied to Smart Places	António Brandão, Henrique São Mamede, and Ramiro Gonçalves	2018	clearly defined	IEEE Xplore, Springer Link, ScienceDirect, YMCA, Google Scholar	Systematic literature review	Systematic literature review	Search Analysis	Aggregate findings
3	Blockchain for smart communities: Applications, challenges and opportunities	Shubhani Aggarwal, Rajat Chaudhary, Gagangeet Singh Aujla, Neeraj Kumar, Kim-Kwang Raymond Choo, Albert Y. Zomaya	2019	not defined	not defined	Descriptive review	No term used in the title	Comparative analysis	Aggregate findings
4	A systematic literature review of blockchain-based applications: Current status, classification and open issues	Fran Casino, Thomas K. Dasaklis, Constantinos Patsakis	2019	clearly defined	Scopus	Systematic literature review	Systematic literature review	Thematic content analysis.	Aggregate findings
5	The blockchain: State-of-the-art and research challenges	Lu Yang	2019	not defined	not defined	Descriptive review	State-of-the-art	not defined	Aggregate findings

continues on following page

Table 2. Continued

S.no	Paper Title	Author	Year	Research Methodology	Selected Sources/ Databases	Type of Review	Term Used for Review Paper	Method of Data Analysis	Type of Finding
6	Blockchain technology: A survey on applications and security privacy Challenges	Bhabendu Kumar Mohanta, Debasish Jena, Soumyashree S. Panda, Srichandan Sobhanayak	2019	clearly defined	IEEE Xplore, ScienceDirect, ACM Digital Library, Web of Science, Inderscience	Descriptive review	Survey	not defined	Aggregate findings
7	Understanding digital transformation: A review and a research agenda	Gregory Vial	2019	clearly defined	AIS Library, Business Source Complete, ScienceDirect	rigorously reviewing literature	Review	Bibliographic analysis	Aggregate findings
8	A systematic literature review of blockchain cyber security	Paul J. Taylor, Tooska Dargahi, Ali Dehghantanha, Reza M. Parizi, Kim-Kwang Raymond Choo	2019	clearly defined	IEEE Xplore, Digital Library, ScienceDirect, SpringerLink, ACM Digital Library, Google Scholar	Systematic literature review	Systematic literature review	Meta analysis	Aggregate findings
9	A bibliometric analysis of bitcoin scientific production	Ignasi Merediz-Solà, Aurelio F. Bariviera	2019	partly defined	Web of Science	Bibliometric Analysis	Bibliometric Analysis	Bibliometric Analysis	Aggregate findings
10	Blockchain as a disruptive technology for business: A systematic review	Julie Frizzo-Barkera, Peter A. Chow-White, Philippa R. Adams, Jennifer Mentanko, Dung Ha, Sandy Green	2019	clearly defined	Business Source Complete, SpringerLink, and Web of Science	Systematic literature review	Systematic literature review	Meta analysis	Aggregate findings
11	The state of play of blockchain technology in the financial services sector: A systematic literature review	Omar Alia, Mustafa Ally, Clutterbuck, Yogesh Dwivedi	2020	clearly defined	The digitalibraries of: Science Direct, Emerald, Scopus, ACM Digital, IEEE, and AIS e-library.	Systematic literature review	A systematic literature review	Empirical evaluations of different use cases and applications.	Aggregate findings

continues on following page

Table 2. Continued

S.no	Paper Title	Author	Year	Research Methodology	Selected Sources/ Databases	Type of Review	Term Used for Review Paper	Method of Data Analysis	Type of Finding
12	Smart Contracts on the Blockchain – A Bibliometric Analysis and Review	Lennart Ante	2020	clearly defined	Web of Science	Systematic literature review	Review	Bibliometric Analysis	Aggregate findings
13	Survey on Blockchain based Smart Contracts: Applications, Opportunities and Challenges	Tharaka Hewa, Mika Ylianttila, Madhusanka Liyanage	2020	not defined	not defined	Descriptive review	Survey	not defined	Aggregate findings
14	The decade-long cryptocurrencies and the blockchain rollercoaster: Mapping the intellectual structure and charting future directions	Anton Klarin	2020	clearly defined	Web of Science (WoS) and Scopus	Descriptive review	No term used in the title	Bibliometric co-citation analysis	Aggregate findings
15	Deep learning for financial applications: A survey	Ahmet Murat Ozbayoglu, Mehmet Ugur Gudelek, Omer Berat Sezer	2020	Partly defined	ScienceDirect, ACM Digital Library, Google Scholar, arXiv.org, ResearchGate	state-of-the-art	Survey	Histogram	Aggregate findings
16	Interpol review of digital evidence 2016 - 2019	Paul Reedy	2020	not defined	not defined	Descriptive review	interpol review	not defined	Aggregate findings
17	Financial fraud detection applying data mining techniques: A comprehensive review from 2009 to 2019	Khaled Gubran Al-Hashedi, Pritheega Magalingam	2021	clearly defined	The digital libraries that were selected in this review include IEEE, ACM, Emerald, and Elsevier.	Descriptive review	Comprehensive review	Comprehensive analysis	Aggregate findings

continues on following page

Table 2. Continued

S.no	Paper Title	Author	Year	Research Methodology	Selected Sources/ Databases	Type of Review	Term Used for Review Paper	Method of Data Analysis	Type of Finding
18	Challenges and opportunities to scale up sustainable finance after the COVID-19 crisis: Lessons and promising innovations from science and practice	Simone Quatrini	2021	partly defined	not defined	Descriptive review	No term used in the title	Comparative analysis	Aggregate findings
19	A survey of breakthrough in blockchain technology: Adoptions, applications, challenges and future research	Abdurrashid Ibrahim Sanka, Muhammad Irfan, Ian Huang, Ray C.C. Cheung	2021	not defined	not defined	state-of-the-art	Survey	statistical analysis	Aggregate findings
20	Blockchain based solutions to secure IoT: Background, integration trends and a way forward	Shivam Saxena, Bharat Bhushan b, Mohd Abdul Ahad	2021	not defined	not defined	comprehensive survey	No term used in the title	not defined	Aggregate findings

ANALYSIS

This section presents the appraisal, analysis and synthesis of present umbrella review of 20 review-based papers.

Appraisal

The tool which is used to appraise the umbrella review is by development of a checklist. The criteria used for assessing the review paper are mentioned in the table below. The papers are identified by their serial number mentioned in Table 2. The checklist explains whether the review paper clearly defines the criteria or not. Thus, the codes are given as follows – N for not clearly defined and Y for yes clearly defined.

Table 3. Checklist for umbrella review

S.No/ Criteria	Research Problem	Research Objective	Research Question	Source	Method of Analysis
1	N	N	N	N	N
2	N	Y	Y	N	Y
3	N	N	N	N	Y
4	N	Y	N	N	Y
5	N	N	N	N	N
6	N	N	N	Y	N
7	N	N	Y	Y	Y
8	N	N	Y	Y	Y
9	N	N	N	Y	Y
10	N	N	N	Y	Y
11	N	N	N	Y	Y
12	N	N	N	N	Y
13	N	N	N	N	N
14	N	N	N	Y	Y
15	N	N	Y	Y	Y
16	N	N	N	N	N
17	N	Y	N	Y	Y
18	N	N	N	N	Y
19	N	N	N	N	Y
20	N	N	N	N	N

Table 3 shows that none of the review paper defined research problem and research objective was defined by only 3 review paper. Furthermore, it is observed that research questions the paperre defined in 4 review papers but source of database was clearly defined in 9 review papers. The most important thing is that 14 review papers out of 20 described the method of analyzing the findings.

Synthesis

The result is summarized by rating the coding as N = 0 and Y = 1. Thus, in given five criteria maximum score for a review paper will be 5 and minimum score will be zero resulting into a scale of 0 to 5.

Table 4. Scoring of review-based papers

S.No	Criteria 1	Criteria 2	Criteria 3	Criteria 4	Criteria 5	Total Score	Category Given to Paper After Reviewing
1	0	0	0	0	0	0	F
2	0	1	1	0	1	3	C
3	0	0	0	0	1	1	E
4	0	1	0	0	1	2	D
5	0	0	0	0	0	0	F
6	0	0	0	1	0	1	E
7	0	0	1	1	1	3	C
8	0	0	1	1	1	3	C
9	0	0	0	1	1	2	D
10	0	0	0	1	1	2	D
11	0	0	0	1	1	2	D
12	0	0	0	0	1	1	E
13	0	0	0	0	0	0	F
14	0	0	0	1	1	2	D
15	0	0	1	1	1	3	C
16	0	0	0	0	0	0	F
17	0	1	0	1	1	3	C
18	0	0	0	0	1	1	E
19	0	0	0	0	1	1	E
20	0	0	0	0	0	0	F

Thus:

1. A score of 5 means the review paper is clearly reported
2. A score of 4, the review paper is mostly clearly reported
3. A score of 3, the review paper is average reported
4. A score of 2, the review paper is mostly unclearly reported
5. A score of 1, the review paper is unclearly reported
6. A score of 0, the review paper is poorly reported

For each review paper, then scoring was given as shown in Table 4.

After reviewing 20 review-based papers, it is found that there the paperre none of the papers falling in the category of A rated paper and B rated paper. There the paperre 5 C rated paper, 5 D rated paper, 5 E rated papers and 5 F rated papers.

Findings

Based on our umbrella review of review-based papers, it was found that

- Out of 20 review-based paper, 5 papers did not used any term in their title; 5 used the term 'systematic literature review'; 4 used the term survey and 2 used the term review. There the paperre only 1 paper each using the term 'state-of-the-art' and comprehensive review.
- None of the review-paper resulted into development of a new theory.
- None of the review paper defined research problem and research objective was defined by only 3 review paper. Furthermore, it is observed that research questions the paperre defined in 4 review papers but source of database was clearly defined in 9 review papers. The most important thing is that 14 review papers out of 20 described the method of analyzing the findings.
- None of the papers fell in the category of A rated paper, B rated paper and 5 paper in category of C,D & E rated.
- Analysis used in the paper are – Bibliometric analysis is used in 3 papers and Meta-analysis is used in 2 papers, comparative analysis is used in 2 papers,

CONCLUSION

The current study concludes that the reviewed papers in the field of 'Blockchain, DLT and banking' require to be more clearly defined to identify the research gap in the field. In particular, review paper should provide research methodology used in the paper for better understanding. Additionally, with most of the reviews based on meta-analysis and bibliometric analysis, other forms of analyzing a review paper is required to be explored. Thus, a review paper should provide transparent and clearly defined research methodology including the research problem dealt in the paper, research objective, research questions, source of data base and method of analysis used in the paper. The findings of a review paper should be verifiable.

In the current umbrella review of review paper, it was found that there is heterogeneity with respect to clarity in method used to review the paper and the research objectives of the review paper are not clearly defined. Additionally, the present umbrella review paper, clearly defines the method used for reviewing the paper which can be used as a framework by review papers for conducting or reviewing literature.

The current umbrella review has limitation also as there are few review papers in the field of blockchain, DLT and banking. Also, only one database was explored to conduct the umbrella review. Thus, in quantitative terms, reviewing 20 review-based paper is an unsatisfactory number to be reviewed.

IMPLICATION FOR FUTURE RESEARCH

The future studies in the field of blockchain, DLT and banking may consider the use cases of blockchain in banking, may provide a framework for implementing blockchain in unexplored areas of banking, the already defined frameworks in the previous papers can be tested in sample banks, etc. Also, based on the limitations and challenges faced in implementing blockchain in banking, the future research can provide suggestions and recommendations to improve the applicability of blockchain in banking. The research methodology explained in the given umbrella review paper can be used by future review-based papers to explain their methodology. The scoring and ranking of review papers given in this umbrella review can be used in other forms of research papers also.

REFERENCES

Adams, R., Kewell, B., & Parry, G. (2018). Blockchain for good? Digital ledger technology and sustainable development goals. In *Handbook of sustainability and social science research* (pp. 127–140). Springer. doi:10.1007/978-3-319-67122-2_7

Aggarwal, S., Chaudhary, R., Aujla, G. S., Kumar, N., Choo, K. K. R., & Zomaya, A. Y. (2019). Blockchain for smart communities: Applications, challenges and opportunities. *Journal of Network and Computer Applications*, *144*, 13–48. doi:10.1016/j.jnca.2019.06.018

Al-Hashedi, K. G., & Magalingam, P. (2021). Financial fraud detection applying data mining techniques: A comprehensive review from 2009 to 2019. *Computer Science Review*, *40*, 100402. doi:10.1016/j.cosrev.2021.100402

Ali, O., Ally, M., & Dwivedi, Y. (2020). The state of play of blockchain technology in the financial services sector: A systematic literature review. *International Journal of Information Management*, *54*, 102199. doi:10.1016/j.ijinfomgt.2020.102199

Ante, L. (2020). Smart contracts on the blockchain–a bibliometric analysis and review. *Telematics and Informatics*, 101519.

Aromataris, E., Fernandez, R., Godfrey, C. M., Holly, C., Khalil, H., & Tungpunkom, P. (2015). Summarizing systematic reviews: Methodological development, conduct and reporting of an umbrella review approach. *JBI Evidence Implementation*, *13*(3), 132–140. PMID:26360830

Arslan, S. S., Jurdak, R., Jelitto, J., & Krishnamachari, B. (2020). *Advancements in distributed ledger technology for Internet of Things*. Academic Press.

Arslanian, H., & Fischer, F. (2019). Blockchain as an enabling technology. In *The Future of Finance* (pp. 113–121). Palgrave Macmillan. doi:10.1007/978-3-030-14533-0_10

Beck, R., Avital, M., Rossi, M., & Thatcher, J. B. (2017). *Blockchain technology in business and information systems research*. Academic Press.

Brandão, A., São Mamede, H., & Gonçalves, R. (2018, March). Systematic review of the literature, research on blockchain technology as support to the trust model proposed applied to smart places. In *World conference on information systems and technologies* (pp. 1163-1174). Springer. 10.1007/978-3-319-77703-0_113

Casino, F., Dasaklis, T. K., & Patsakis, C. (2019). A systematic literature review of blockchain-based applications: Current status, classification and open issues. *Telematics and Informatics*, *36*, 55–81. doi:10.1016/j.tele.2018.11.006

Cucari, N., Lagasio, V., Lia, G., & Torriero, C. (2021). The impact of blockchain in banking processes: The Interbank Spunta case study. *Technology Analysis and Strategic Management*, 1–13.

Efanov, D., & Roschin, P. (2018). The all-pervasiveness of the blockchain technology. *Procedia Computer Science*, *123*, 116–121. doi:10.1016/j.procs.2018.01.019

Frizzo-Barker, J., Chow-White, P. A., Adams, P. R., Mentanko, J., Ha, D., & Green, S. (2020). Blockchain as a disruptive technology for business: A systematic review. *International Journal of Information Management*, *51*, 102029. doi:10.1016/j.ijinfomgt.2019.10.014

Gleim, M. R., & Stevens, J. L. (2021). Blockchain: A game changer for marketers? *Marketing Letters*, *32*(1), 123–128. doi:10.100711002-021-09557-9

Hassani, H., Huang, X., & Silva, E. (2018). Banking with blockchain-ed big data. *Journal of Management Analytics*, *5*(4), 256–275. doi:10.1080/23270012.2018.1528900

Hewa, T., Ylianttila, M., & Liyanage, M. (2020). Survey on blockchain based smart contracts: Applications, opportunities and challenges. *Journal of Network and Computer Applications*, 102857.

Kewell, B., Adams, R., & Parry, G. (2017). Blockchain for good? *Strategic Change*, *26*(5), 429–437. doi:10.1002/jsc.2143

Klarin, A. (2020). The decade-long cryptocurrencies and the blockchain rollercoaster: Mapping the intellectual structure and charting future directions. *Research in International Business and Finance*, *51*, 101067. doi:10.1016/j.ribaf.2019.101067

Kołodziej, M. (2021). Development Factors of Blockchain Technology Within Banking Sector. In *Contemporary Trends and Challenges in Finance* (pp. 125–138). Springer. doi:10.1007/978-3-030-73667-5_8

Krezmien, M. P., Camacho, K. A., & Travers, J. C. (2017). Using methodological reviews and meta-analyses to identify current best practices in school-based counseling. In *International handbook for policy research on school-based counseling* (pp. 105–120). Springer. doi:10.1007/978-3-319-58179-8_8

Le Gear, A. (2020). A Blockchain Supported Solution for Compliant Digital Security Offerings. In *Blockchain and Distributed Ledger Technology Use Cases* (pp. 113–131). Springer. doi:10.1007/978-3-030-44337-5_6

Lele, A. (2019). Blockchain. In *Disruptive Technologies for the Militaries and Security* (pp. 197–202). Springer. doi:10.1007/978-981-13-3384-2_12

Lemieux, V. L. (2016). Trusting records: Is Blockchain technology the answer? *Records Management Journal*, *26*(2), 110–139. doi:10.1108/RMJ-12-2015-0042

Lipton, A. (2018). Blockchains and distributed ledgers in retrospective and perspective. *The Journal of Risk Finance*, *19*(1), 4–25. doi:10.1108/JRF-02-2017-0035

Liu, X., Farahani, B., & Firouzi, F. (2020). Distributed ledger technology. In *Intelligent Internet of Things* (pp. 393–431). Springer. doi:10.1007/978-3-030-30367-9_8

Lu, Y. (2019). The blockchain: State-of-the-art and research challenges. *Journal of Industrial Information Integration*, *15*, 80–90. doi:10.1016/j.jii.2019.04.002

Matzutt, R., Hiller, J., Henze, M., Ziegeldorf, J. H., Müllmann, D., Hohlfeld, O., & Wehrle, K. (2018, February). A quantitative analysis of the impact of arbitrary blockchain content on bitcoin. In *International Conference on Financial Cryptography and Data Security* (pp. 420-438). Springer. 10.1007/978-3-662-58387-6_23

Maull, R., Godsiff, P., Mulligan, C., Brown, A., & Kewell, B. (2017). Distributed ledger technology: Applications and implications. *Strategic Change*, *26*(5), 481–489. doi:10.1002/jsc.2148

Merediz-Solà, I., & Bariviera, A. F. (2019). A bibliometric analysis of bitcoin scientific production. *Research in International Business and Finance*, *50*, 294–305. doi:10.1016/j.ribaf.2019.06.008

Mohanta, B. K., Jena, D., Panda, S. S., & Sobhanayak, S. (2019). Blockchain technology: A survey on applications and security privacy challenges. *Internet of Things*, *8*, 100107. doi:10.1016/j.iot.2019.100107

Moyano, J. P., & Ross, O. (2017). KYC optimization using distributed ledger technology. *Business & Information Systems Engineering*, *59*(6), 411–423. doi:10.100712599-017-0504-2

Narayan, R., & Tidström, A. (2020). Tokenizing coopetition in a blockchain for a transition to circular economy. *Journal of Cleaner Production*, *263*, 121437. doi:10.1016/j.jclepro.2020.121437

Nguyen, Q. K. (2016, November). Blockchain-a financial technology for future sustainable development. In *2016 3rd International conference on green technology and sustainable development (GTSD)* (pp. 51-54). IEEE. 10.1109/GTSD.2016.22

Niranjanamurthy, M., Nithya, B. N., & Jagannatha, S. (2019). Analysis of Blockchain technology: Pros, cons and SWOT. *Cluster Computing*, *22*(6), 14743–14757. doi:10.100710586-018-2387-5

Ølnes, S., Ubacht, J., & Janssen, M. (2017). *Blockchain in government: Benefits and implications of distributed ledger technology for information sharing*. Academic Press.

Ozbayoglu, A. M., Gudelek, M. U., & Sezer, O. B. (2020). Deep learning for financial applications: A survey. *Applied Soft Computing*, *93*, 106384. doi:10.1016/j.asoc.2020.106384

Quatrini, S. (2021). Challenges and opportunities to scale up sustainable finance after the COVID-19 crisis: Lessons and promising innovations from science and practice. *Ecosystem Services*, *48*, 101240. doi:10.1016/j.ecoser.2020.101240 PMID:36568712

Reedy, P. (2020). Interpol review of digital evidence 2016-2019. *Forensic Science International: Synergy*.

Sanka, A. I., Irfan, M., Huang, I., & Cheung, R. C. (2021). A survey of breakthrough in blockchain technology: Adoptions, applications, challenges and future research. *Computer Communications*, *169*, 179–201. doi:10.1016/j.comcom.2020.12.028

Saxena, S., Bhushan, B., & Ahad, M. A. (2021). Blockchain based solutions to secure IoT: Background, integration trends and a way forward. *Journal of Network and Computer Applications*, *181*, 103050. doi:10.1016/j.jnca.2021.103050

Shermin, V. (2017). Disrupting governance with blockchains and smart contracts. *Strategic Change*, *26*(5), 499–509. doi:10.1002/jsc.2150

Sunyaev, A. (2020). Distributed ledger technology. In *Internet Computing* (pp. 265–299). Springer. doi:10.1007/978-3-030-34957-8_9

Taylor, P. J., Dargahi, T., Dehghantanha, A., Parizi, R. M., & Choo, K. K. R. (2020). A systematic literature review of blockchain cyber security. *Digital Communications and Networks*, *6*(2), 147–156. doi:10.1016/j.dcan.2019.01.005

Tian, Y., Lu, Z., Adriaens, P., Minchin, R. E., Caithness, A., & Woo, J. (2020). Finance infrastructure through blockchain-based tokenization. *Frontiers of Engineering Management*, *7*(4), 485–499. doi:10.100742524-020-0140-2

Tricco, A. C., Langlois, E., Straus, S. E., & World Health Organization. (2017). *Rapid reviews to strengthen health policy and systems: a practical guide*. World Health Organization.

Venegas, P. (2020, July). Trustable Risk Scoring for Non-bank Gateways in Blockchain and DLT Financial Networks. In *International Conference on Complex Systems* (pp. 165-178). Springer.

Vial, G. (2019). Understanding digital transformation: A review and a research agenda. *The Journal of Strategic Information Systems*, *28*(2), 118–144. doi:10.1016/j.jsis.2019.01.003

Vranken, H. (2017). Sustainability of bitcoin and blockchains. *Current Opinion in Environmental Sustainability*, *28*, 1–9. doi:10.1016/j.cosust.2017.04.011

Chapter 3
Green Financing Strategies Adopted in Zimbabwe Towards Attainment of Sustainable Development Goals

Mufaro Dzingirai
https://orcid.org/0000-0002-1518-8275
Midlands State University, Zimbabwe

Kudakwashe Zvitambo
Midlands State University, Zimbabwe

Herbert Masukume
Midlands State University, Zimbabwe

ABSTRACT

The issue of green financing has increasingly become more relevant in the 21st century. Accordingly, scholars, researchers, and policymakers are now interested in how green finance can accelerate the attainment of the Sustainable Development Goals (SDGs) across the world. Surprisingly, there is scant evidence in the development mainstream literature that addresses the issues of green financing strategies, particularly in African countries. This study established eight green financing strategies that have been employed in Zimbabwe towards attaining SDGs, namely the national climate change fund strategy, IDBZ climate finance facility strategy, domestic public finance strategy, domestic private finance, public-private partnerships (PPPs) financing strategy, foreign investment strategy, and development finance strategy. These results can help the Zimbabwean government, NGOs, financial institutions, and society at large as well as educators and researchers.

DOI: 10.4018/978-1-6684-8361-9.ch003

INTRODUCTION

Recently, green financing is gaining traction in the development literature. After the announcement of Sustainable Development Goals SDGs in March 2016 by the United Nations, a plethora of different economies began to execute new financing strategies tailor-made to suit the needs of inclusive green growth (Desalegn & Tangl, 2022). It is worth noting that the green finance strategy captures the various ways that can be executed to increase financial inflows from the private, public, and non-profit-making sectors in promoting and supporting sustainable development interventions, projects, and initiatives. With this in mind, it is, therefore, not surprising to observe that green finance is influential in promoting a green economy whereby inclusive green growth helps to deal with the negative consequences associated with climate change (Desalegn & Tangl, 2022). Financial institutions across the world are expected to offer various financial products and services aimed at promoting environment-friendly projects and interventions. This can be in form of facilitating money transfers, savings, insurance, savings, and financial technology that promote a green economy. As such, the financial products and services must promote a paradigm shift towards a green economy by ensuring the attainment of SDG 1 (no poverty), SDG 7 (affordable and clean energy), and SDG 13 (climate action), all of which intentionally enrich inclusive green growth.

In light of the above, green finance calls for both national and international interventions. Nationally, several countries like Japan, the United Kingdom, Mexico, and Canada managed to come up with a myriad of policies to increase the citizens' consciousness about the negative consequences of fossil fuel emissions in the context of climate change risks (Ozili, 2022). From an international perspective, many countries are a signatory to the Paris Agreement which focus on climate change mitigation at an international level (Blau, 2017; Ozili, 2022). The sole purpose of this agreement is to minimize global warming levels to below 1.5 or 2 degree Celsius which is a mammoth task for several developing countries (Hoegh-Guldberg et al., 2018). To effectively address the Paris Agreement goal and the COP26 mandate, there is a dire need for strong financial muscle both at national and international levels (Tollefson, 2018). The various financial sources are widely known in the mainstream literature as green financial instruments, sustainable finance, climate finance, or green finance. This implies that environment-friendly demands novel financing strategies to arrest the green economy challenges (Dikau & Volz, 2021; Jia, 2023; Jiakui et al., 2023; Sachs et al, 2019; Tan et al., 2023).

In the context of China, green finance has been widely acknowledged by the Chinese government as an effective approach to reducing carbon emissions. It has been in the public domain that China is at the top of all the countries when it comes to carbon emissions given that it is the second-largest economy in the world (Bai et al., 2022; Quin et al., 2023). According to Bai et al. (2022), the Chinese government proposed a policy known as "Carbon Peak and Carbon Neutral" as a concerted effort to arrest the challenges linked to global climate deterioration. This policy has a far-reaching effect on the economic structure, production and consumption, and energy structure of China (Liang et al., 2020; Hasnaoui et al., 2021).

In terms of Africa, it has been noted that limited efforts to promote green economies have been observed as substantiated by limited investment in green infrastructure and renewable energy. In this regard, Shipalana (2020) concluded that many African governments are struggling to execute robust green fiscal reforms whereby the development of the green finance sector and green segments must be promoted as well as redirecting existing funding towards green economy initiatives. Although African economies are starting to experiment with green finance packages, the African Development Bank (AfDB) estimates that Africa's financial requirements to adapt to climate change range from $20–$30 billion per year until 2030 (Shipalana, 2020). This implies that green banks must be witnessed if the African governments are serious about the issues pertaining to green financing. Worryingly, there is fragmented literature related to green financing in developing countries. Moreover, not much is known about the green financing strategies in Zimbabwe. To cover these knowledge gaps, this study serves to analyze the green financing strategies adopted in Zimbabwe toward the attainment of SDGs.

The study begins by explaining the background of the study justifying the study, explaining the research problem, and presenting the objectives of the study in the introduction section. It further presented a review of the literature of themes derived from the research objectives, namely, green financing and SDGs, the contribution of finance technology to green financing, green financing in developed countries, green financing in Sub-Saharan Africa, benefits of green financing in Sub-Saharan Africa, and challenges faced by Zimbabwe in implementing green financing strategies. In addition, the chapter presents research methodologies used in collecting data, results, discussions, and recommendations.

BACKGROUND

There are some controversies linked to green financing and SDGs (Desalegn & Tangl, 2022). Notably, there is no unequivocal meaning of green finance given that there is a myriad of definitions of green finance from different authors from different academic fields such as economics, development, law, and sociology as well as finance and management (Ozili, 2022). To make matters worse, the terminology used for green finance is varied as it may be known as sustainable finance, climate finance, and environmental finance (Bai et al., 2022). Put simply, various scholars provide different definitions of green finance. Generally speaking, green finance demands the need for innovative finance solutions to cater for low carbon emissions and green activities and initiatives (Huang et al, 2019). In the same vein, Cui et al. (2020) view green finance as a policy aimed at coordinating economic development to support solving physical environmental problems. According to these scholars, green finance becomes an innovative way of providing financial support to entities in green.

On the other hand, Sheryani and Nobanee (2020) adamantly regard green finance as a concept that integrates the use of business processes with sensitivity issues affecting society. This definition emphasizes solving community challenges by business entities. It does not specify the physical environment making it broad. In addition, Sheryani and Nobanee (2020) articulate that the behavior of parties involved in the supply chain of goods and services, and the consumers of those goods and services determine the nature of green finance. Contributing to the discourse of green finance, Dziwok and Jager (2021) describe it as a term that includes social issues, while climate finance is considered as a narrower element of it. These scholars regard green finance as an element of sustainable finance. In other words, Dziwok and Jager (2021) allude that green finance contributes to sustainable development goals. In that context, green finance aims to make countries achieve sustainable development goals by funding well-designed initiatives to arrest environmental challenges which go a long way in climate resilience and poverty reduction.

More interestingly, United Nations drafted and endorsed 17 SDGs, 165 goals, and 330 indicators intended to be accomplished by 2030 (Hak, Janouskova, & Moldan, 2016). The SDGs apparently address the widely acknowledged humanity's desire for good life whilst observing the challenges imposed by nature (Fonseca, Domingues, & Dima, 2020). However, funding the operationalization of these SDGs poses acute challenges. It is within this context that Zeb et al, (2021) recommended the private sector fund for SDGs through robust interventions such as corporate social responsibility programs. Unfortunately, the study by Zeb et al. (2021) established that the private sector lacked the coordination to fund these programs. On the other hand, Debrah, Chan, and Darko (2022) argued that government and international organizations need to make strategic collaborations with academia with the purpose to increase research on funding SDGs through green finance. This acknowledgment of the absence of a model differs from other scholars who recommend green strategies that fail to work in developing countries. Therefore, the literature indicates that funding SDGs remain a challenge. It is, therefore, the aim of this study to analyze the green finance strategies that can be used to finance SDGs.

Scholars like Dziwok and Jager (2021) classified green finance into various categories, namely, neoliberal forms of green finance, laissez-faire new liberal green finance, standard new liberal green finance, and market-making neoliberal green finance. In addition, Dziwok and Jager (2021) mentioned reformist forms of green finance, tax-based reformist public finance, and command and control policies in green finance. The categorization of green finance helps to understand the models that could be used to source green finances. However, the application of this categorization model to the funding of SGDs needs further research.

Similarly, Cui et al. (2020) adamantly argued that the green financing system directly influences sustainable development and cleaner production. However, the study recommended the strengthening of government regulations, slashing of financial institutions and enterprises' green finance production costs, an increase of compensation for consumer pollution, and a reduction in the supervision cost of government as a prerequisite for implementing green finance strategies. These issues mentioned above are associated with serious challenges when it comes to implementation in various contexts, especially in developing countries like Zimbabwe (Debrah et al., 2022). Literature reveals that scholars recommended the application of artificial intelligence when applying green finance to SDGs (Debrah, Chan, & Darko) which contradicts Dziwok and Jager's (2021) green finance categorization model. It shows that scholars fail to agree on the funding model for green finance that fund SDGs.

It is important to note that Sheryain and Nobanee's (2020) results established different views. In this regard, the study showed that different sectors adopt sustainability to ensure compliance with various environmental regulations in their policies governing production operations. It means companies applying green financing at their level without submitting the funds to third parties. The literature further indicates that the financial sector puts in place policies for funding companies that work towards the achievement of SDGs. The study established that research and modeling of green finance failed to be integrated with the planning and implementation of green projects.

Similarly, Wu et al., (2021) revealed that climate change mitigation indicators affect the Gross Domestic Product (GDP) of G7 countries. In addition, it shows that green financing strategies, if implemented, cleaner the environment. Results of this study showed that a 1% rise in the green financing index increases the environmental quality by 0.375%, whilst purifying 0.3925% environment. However, these theoretical results lack practical implementation. It becomes difficult to measure the effects of green financing strategies used in achieving SDGs in developing countries. The theoretical propositions that green finance strategies used in SDGs yield results remain unproven.

Contribution of Finance Technology to Green Financing

A thorough scanning of the literature shows that the concept of finance technology is still new within the context of the development community, especially in developing countries (Hunjra et al., 2023; Liu & Wang, 2023; Suryomo et al., 2020). Notably, finance technology integrates customers, and machines, including information and communication technologies to achieve rapidly changing governing and controlling of company processes (Anshari et al., 2020). However, literature research showed that the majority of studies were theoretically done without practical implementations, based on secondary data rather than primary data.

Nevertheless, Akomea-Frimpong et al. (2021) and Huang et al., (2023) indicated that green securities, green investments, climate finance, carbon finance, green insurance, green credit, and green infrastructure bonds contribute to green financing of SDGs. In the same study, the authors established that environmental and climate change policies, interest rates, religion, risk and social inclusion, social justice, and banking regulations influence green financing that leads to the funding of SDGs using finance technology. However, these scholars reached these conclusions through desk-top research without practical empirical evidence. Hence, these finance technology systems need to be tested practically.

Literature on the intersection of technological finance and green finance was scarce. Searching on different search engines, like Google-scholar and e-journals, reveal only green finance separate from technological finance. However, Schulz and Feist (2021) results show that international climate finance stands to benefit from financial technology. They argue that distributed ledger technologies could be leveraged to support climate actions. Conversely, the same study pointed to limitations of technology financing-driven solutions, namely, they cannot stand alone without resourcing and governance. This becomes a major challenge in developing countries because they lack resources and have poor governance measured by high corruption indexes.

Green Financing in Developed Countries

After capturing the contribution of finance technology to green financing, it is deemed most appropriate to interrogate the state of affairs when it comes to green financing in developed countries. Green finance has grown rapidly in recent years around the world, becoming a new form of environmental governance. In the context of developed countries, Batrancea et al., (2020) conducted a quantitative study on the green financing system in Brazil, Canada, and the USA by applying panel data analysis with a special focus on key components of the financial system during and post-2008 financial crisis. In this regard, the components such as CO2 emissions,

N2O, and GDP as well as the forest and fishing activities we examined and they observed that domestic credit finance from formal banks was not adequate to cater for green financing in these developed countries. In addition, their results proved that CO2 emission was still a challenge despite the implementation of domestic credit facilities. Interestingly, their findings supported the idea that global warming and policies targeting climate change contribute to green financing.

It is important to capture that Brazil has witnessed 19 bonds that were issued by 13 companies giving a total amount of $1.5 billion whilst few bonds were channeled toward forestry and agriculture projects (Batrancea et al., 2020). In this regard, the Inter-American Development Bank offered financial assistance to the government of Brazil whereby the simplified procedure for accessing green bonds was assured. This implies that there is a dire need for both local and international financial institutions to offer unique green bonds. Interestingly, Brazil is the leader when it comes to the issuance of green bonds. Therefore, it is an open secret that different development banks can serve different American clients in a different manner depending on the capacity to repay. As such, Brazil is now regarded as the most popular debtor owing to the fact that it is receiving loans from a multitude of banks except the US EXIM bank, and Caribbean development bank (Gallagher & Irwin, 2015).

In the case of the US, it is worth mentioning that it is one of the developed countries that have the largest economy worldwide as measured by GDP. With this in mind, it is not surprising that it is the major contributor to global warming (Batrancea et al., 2020). In terms of Canada, it is widely acknowledged that it is the second largest country by area of which 49.24%b of the area is covered by forests. Notably, the US produced 16% of the world's carbon dioxide and Canada produced nearly 2% whilst Brazil produced 1% (Batrancea et al., 2020). Although many people encourage development banks to increase the proportion of climate finance, a number of developed countries managed to establish green banks, especially in Australia, the UK, and Japan. It is interesting to observe that the North American Development Bank (NADB) engaged in an exclusive green project for more than 20 years which is even before the concept of green finance was coined (Yuan & Gallagher, 2015). It is in the public domain that NADB provided grants and loans of $2.7 billion targeted for green projects that were implemented in Mexico and the US. In terms of the portfolio in Mexico, the amount of $1.5 billion was used towards green projects related to waste management, public transportation, water supply, basic infrastructure, and air quality whereby more than 15 million people benefited from these green projects (Yuan & Gallagher, 2015). Furthermore, it has been reported that the Global Alliance for Sustainable Investment which focuses on five regions from Australia to the US provided more than US$30.7 trillion dedicated to green or sustainable projects (Niyazbekova et al., 2021).

In terms of the Europe Greenhouse Gas Emission Trading Scheme, the cap-and-trade trading scheme is used to regulate and govern the carbon emission allowances distributed by auction or free in each prescribed period. Enterprises that receive emission allowances may reduce their emissions and sell excess allowances, or increase their emissions and purchase additional allowances, but at the end of the period, they must submit to the regulatory a quota equal to the actual emissions during the period (Weber & Cabras 2017). Because businesses can sell their emissions allowances and use forward contracts to repurchase them, the amount for trading can be so large and the available time so long that it can be used to finance. It is permissible for businesses to use emission credits other than Europe Emission Trading Scheme; however, the credits can only be Certified Emission Reductions (CERs) or Emission Reduction Units (ERUs) (Tong et al., 2018).

Going forward, Britain was the world's first country in the world to develop and executed a greenhouse gas trading system (Burtraw, 2002). Britain launched an emissions trading system for six types of greenhouse gases in 2002. The UK uses a baseline-and-credit trading system in which the authority issues emission credits to companies whose actual emissions are less than the highest emission baseline set by the authority by the end of one period and requires companies that exceed the standard emissions to submit excess credits. Only after the balance is settled in the system can the quota be traded, so the amount for trading is small and the available time is limited. The annual allowance is calculated by subtracting the average emissions from 1998 to 2000 from the voluntary reductions committed by businesses each year.

The Need for Green Financing in Developing Countries

It is worrisome to observe that many developing countries are at a crossroads since they are the most vulnerable to the negative outcomes of climate change. To make matters worse, they heavily depend on developed-country climate finance to fund climate adaptation and mitigation projects which may come in form of donor funding (Bowman & Minas, 2019). This is a danger if not immediately addressed because challenges faced in developing countries must be addressed by people and organizations from such countries not just relying on developed countries. This is evident whereby the Climate Funds Update is one of the most comprehensive databases on multilateral climate finance initiatives, and the Green Climate Fund, established by the United Nations Framework Convention on Climate Change (UNFCCC) in 2010, is now the largest climate fund for developing regions such as Sub-Saharan Africa, Asia, and the Middle East (Fonta et al., 2018). However, many developing countries that have attempted to access this finance have encountered difficulties.

These difficulties arise as a result of developing countries' difficulties in project design and coordination due to a lack of effective institutions and expertise.

Recently, China is one of the fastest-growing economies which is substantiated by the growth of manufacturing industries. As such, the emission of carbon dioxide in the air is the order of the day. As such, green finance development in China is mainly improving market mechanisms which are key to its development. According to Peng et al. (2018), in the face of harsh and acute environmental problems, China has entered a critical period for altering its path towards sustainable development. Green finance has emerged as a new trend as a result of the increasing demand for finance from the development of green industries and the green improvement of traditional industries. Nishimura (2017) adamantly pointed out that the development of green finance not only reflects financial institutions' sense of social responsibility, but it is also an unavoidable choice for the development of green financial institutions themselves. However, in comparison to developed countries' green financial markets, China started relatively late, and the improvement of the green financial system and the enhancement of green financial capabilities have yet to be addressed.

According to Chien et al., (2021) in the United Arab Emirates small to medium enterprises have been referred to as the backbone of the economy due to their ability to improve social development and foster financial growth. This is so because customers there have become more conscious of their purchase preferences and choices and their consequences to the environment. Therefore this pushes SMEs in The United Arab Emirates to find financial opportunities to adopt green innovation techniques to cater for the potential hindrances to increasing green goods, management, and processes.

It has been observed that there is a need to increasingly focus on green sectors in Sub-Saharan Africa (SSA) given that climate change is thwarting its potential to gain from socio-economic transformations in recent years. According to AFDB (2018), SSA has experienced an exponential upsurge in coastal floods, increased risks to human health, reduced agricultural productivity, droughts and famine, and unexposed to extreme negative climatic events. The region also suffers from some serious environmental problems, including deforestation, soil erosion, water scarcity, ineffective waste management, and water, land, and air pollution, prompting policymakers to pursue growth in a manner that does not endanger the region's natural environment. As such, it appears to be the right time to critically scrutinize the financing strategies adopted by the region in trying to arrest the environmental challenges.

There is an urgent call for developing countries to increase the issuance of green bonds in an attempt to reduce the negative effects of climate change. Green bonds are widely known as one of the most innovative and promising financing strategies for the reduction of climate change worldwide (Ngwenya 2019). The green bond market has exponentially grown at a 92% annual rate in terms of the last decade, from a few green bonds purchased in 2007 to more than USD200 billion in green bonds purchased in 2018.

Climate change has had an impact on South African society and the economy as a whole (Le-Page, 2019). Figures show that the prolonged drought from 2014 to 2017 decreased GDP due to the impact on agricultural production (Baudoin, 2017). Furthermore, and this is still being debated in policy circles, the consequences of climate change have accelerated the need to implement national policies and consider strategies to build social, environmental, and economic resilience. Various policies and strategies, such as the Draft National Climate Change Adaptation Strategy (2019) and the National Climate Change Response (2011) were formulated with the agenda to curb the negative effects of climate change.

It is well-accepted that the chief goal of sustainable development initiatives is to strike a balance between environmental, social, and economic sustainability (Darko & Chan, 2017). Many developing countries engaged in massive awareness has been with the purpose to reduce the negative and deadly environmental effects of environmentally unfriendly construction activities (Chan et al., 2016). With this in mind, there is no doubt that the increase in demand for construction products and services has put an enormous strain on resources and the environment (Darko & Chan, 2017). Accordingly, it has been witnessed that acid rain and global warming have occurred which produce more harm than good when it comes to sustainable development (Asadollahfardi et al., 2016). However, there have been some concerted efforts whereby green building initiatives have been adopted as one of the unique and innovative ways to stimulate sustainable development to address the unsustainable development activities in the context of the construction industry (Darko & Chan, 2017). Some of the advantages of green finance include improved health and well-being, environmental protection, and energy efficiency (Chan et al., 2016). It has been claimed that the initial cost of design and construction is high when compared to conventional buildings (Dwaikata & Ali, 2016).

The construction industry is growing in a plethora of developing countries since there is a high rate of rural-to-urban migration in these countries. Therefore, given the cost of building maintenance, having a green finance initiative can help developing countries in addressing climate change in the most cost-effective manner. This is because less money is spent on operations and maintenance, as well as the long-term costs of reducing pollution (Dwaikata and Ali, 2018). According to Olubunmi et al. (2016), green building initiatives, projects, and interventions create avenues of new job opportunities for stakeholders as new construction materials, construction methods, and designs are developed and executed. In spite of these notable economic advantages, the adoption of green financing remains elusive (Darko & Chan, 2017). Cobbinah et al. (2015) argued that the approach to sustainability should put into consideration the consequences of poverty and urbanization in a number of developing countries.

Challenges Faced by Zimbabwe in Implementing Green Financing Strategies

Although the Zimbabwean government is at the forefront of promoting sustainable development, it has been observed that it is facing a myriad of climate-financing challenges just like any other developing country. According to Chirisa et al. (2021), Zimbabwe like the rest of Southern Africa is suffering from severe climate-related disasters. This has a significant impact on the country because it is dependent on climate-sensitive industries such as farming. The Zimbabwean government has made efforts to reduce vulnerability to climate change and improve communities' long-term coping capacities in dealing with climatic impacts. However, the following climate financing challenges were observed:

Overreliance on Global Finance Mechanisms

It is important to mention that the Zimbabwean government primarily relies on global finance mechanisms when it comes to climate finance (Chirisa et al., 2021). As such, this means that multilateral financial institutions such as World Bank and International Monetary Fund offer the terms and conditions that allow them to achieve their agenda at the expense of Zimbabwe (Dzingirai & Ndava, 2022). Moreover, the climate finance packages that are offered by these global financial institutions are not linked to home-grown solutions which then inhibits the success of such packages because Zimbabwe is associated with a unique socio-economic and political context. Despite the fact that Zimbabwe is so rich in terms of natural resources, it is quite disturbing to note that it still relies on global finance to fund green projects and interventions, especially when dealing with issues concerning electricity, water supply, and other basic infrastructure.

Decline in Foreign Direct Investment

For the past three decades, Zimbabwe as a country was exposed to a sharp decline in foreign direct investment which can limit the capacity of the government to generate revenue through taxes. Consequently, this implies that the government faces an acute financial crisis which weakens the capacity of the Zimbabwean government to efficiently and effectively fund green projects and initiatives. Notably, after registering US$745 million in 2018 when it comes to foreign direct investment, the country severely suffered from significant declines in foreign direct investment

(International Trade Administration, 2022). Worryingly, foreign direct investment in Zimbabwe declined sharply from US$280 million (2019) to US$194 million (2020).

Lack of a Clear Climate Finance Roadmap

It is of utmost importance to note that there is no clear climate finance roadmap in Zimbabwean which then compromises the effectiveness of all fragmented climate finance initiatives to deliver the expected outcomes. Although Chirisa et al. (2021) observed that the Infrastructure Development Bank of Zimbabwe was trying its level best to offer climate finance facilities targeted for green projects, the domestic financial base is very weak in Zimbabwe.

Absence of a Green Economy Legislative Framework

According to the International Labour Organization, a lack of incentives discourages businesses from investing in greening their business processes or participating in environmental certification programs to reduce their carbon footprint. As a result, there is a scarcity of data and information on the carbon footprint of businesses and economic sectors. According to ZIMASSET, "despite Zimbabwe's abundance of natural resources, the country continues to face multiple environmental management challenges such as pollution, poor waste management, deforestation, land degradation, veld fires, poaching, and biodiversity loss."

Going forward, many businesses in Zimbabwe have yet to implement integrated waste management. Due to high waste generation rates, a lack of effective waste management technologies, and a lack of world-class disposal sites, many businesses dispose of waste in water bodies and undesignated sites. The Zimbabwean industry currently generates 442 839 tonnes of waste per year. Hazardous waste from industry, including used oil, is a major problem at disposal sites such as Harare's Golden Quarry, according to the Zimbabwe Integrated Solid Waste Management Plan (2011). Due to limited access to capital and technical assistance, industries are generally unable to fully invest in wastewater treatment technologies, resulting in some industries facing potential closure by environmental management authorities. However, a lack of a clear strategy and effluent management technologies has resulted in high levels of pollution in water bodies such as Lake Chivero and the Manyame River. Several studies have found that water hyacinth is growing at an unprecedented rate in Lake Chivero, which could have an impact on the lake's water treatment works as well as its aesthetic functions. Water treatment costs in Lake Chivero are already estimated to be around US$4 million, and as pollution levels rise, this figure will rise further.

Huge External Debt

It is in the public domain that Zimbabwe has a huge external debt. With this in mind, it is very cumbersome for the Zimbabwean government to come up with robust climate finance initiatives whilst servicing the external debt at the same time. According to International Trade Administration (2022), Zimbabwe has an external debt of about US$14.4 billion which accounts for 71% of the Zimbabwean GDP. With this huge debt in mind, it is very difficult to fund green projects and interventions that are locally based. This is so because this huge external debt can act as the stumbling block when it comes to the capacity of the Zimbabwean government to access development and climate finance from international financial institutions. The Government of Zimbabwe (2021) apparently indicated that the initiatives for mitigation and adaptation will cost about US$4 834.47 million. Given such a figure, it means international climate finance is much needed to promote the effectiveness of climate adaptation and mitigation interventions and projects.

Lack of Financial Support From Financial Institutions in Zimbabwe

Most financial institutions have not made the necessary investments for the transition to a green economy. In short, the market in Zimbabwe for any type of business loan or credit is small and constrained by low incomes, a declining corporate sector, shrinking formal sector employment, high levels of non-performing loans, and increased informality (Zimbabwe Financial Inclusion Report, CENFRI, 2016). ILO consultations with a Technical Assistance (TA) service provider to a multi-million dollar credit guarantee scheme with one of Zimbabwe's largest commercial banks revealed how SMEs, particularly youth and women-owned SMEs, find it virtually impossible to access loans despite the existence of a credit guarantee facility with a 50% risk sharing. Bank culture and credit risk assessments continue to favor lending to larger firms with collateral, fixed assets, and a track record, rather than young entrepreneurs and businesses with no movable assets and no personal or business banking track record. The scheme in question only made four loans over a two-year period, demonstrating that using credit guarantees does not provide a quick fix for increasing SMEs' access to credit.

Limited Capacity to Develop Prerequisite Skills for Implementing Green Economy

Because there is no comprehensive green economy policy framework, there are no financial incentives to encourage the transition to cleaner production and a green economy. Furthermore, Zimbabwean businesses are not required to obtain environmental certification, such as ISO 14001, or to set up internal environmental management systems (Akesson et al., 2016). If properly resourced, the Environmental Management Authority could play an important role in assisting government and private sector climate change adaptation and mitigation activities. In order to achieve this goal, the Zimbabwean government established an ambitious but attainable goal of "reducing solid waste generation by maximizing resource use at source through sustainable consumption and cleaner production" (Government of Zimbabwe, 2021).

Unfathomable Illicit Financial Flows

There are notable financial leakages in the Zimbabwean context in form of unfathomable illicit financial flows which compromise the ability to fund climate change initiatives. These initiatives can be in form of adaptation and mitigating measures. It is within this context that Slany et al., (2020) documented that Sub-Saharan Africa has the highest level of illicit financial flows which go a long way in hampering the success of sustainable development projects. This suggests that Zimbabwe is not an exception to these financial shenanigans. More interestingly, Kurebwa (2021) adamantly stated that unfathomable illicit financial flows are as cancerous in Zimbabwe as it is limiting the effective and efficient allocation of financial resources towards development programs. Worryingly, Kurebwa (2021) found that US$32.179 billion has been attributed to illicit financial flows in Zimbabwe. Given this high figure of financial leakage, it is not surprising to note that the government is failing to provide climate finance. This state of affairs manifests owing to people in offices of authority who have the highest affinity for hiding wealth in other countries and also evading taxes (Kurebwa, 2021). This is surprising because the country has some laws that deal with laundering offenses however the cases of money laundering are so high in Zimbabwe. According to Nyarugwe (2020), the country lost about US$1.8 billion in 2013 which represents a portion of 13% of the Zimbabwean GDP for the same year.

Mismatch Between the Skills Being Taught in Formal Systems and the Demands of the Labor Market

According to a 2017 UNESCO report, "the transition to a green society and economy is expected to drive new developments, new jobs, and new skill requirements." As a result, a new way of thinking is required, particularly from sectors with direct responsibility for producing skilled labor that can be absorbed in the labor market." Thus, one of the first steps in 'greening' Zimbabwe's economy is to 'green' vocational training centers by introducing green curricula to produce skilled green-collar workers. This would also aid in aligning training centers with emerging market demands, bridging the gap between vocational training and industry, and increasing the employability of Zimbabwean youths who graduate from vocational training centers. Skill shortages are impeding transitions to a greener economy, and post-secondary curricula are largely devoid of greening strategies and technologies.

Economic Fragility

Economic fragility is another great challenge that is limiting the effectiveness of green finance in Zimbabwe. It is widely known that the Zimbabwean economy is very fragile as compared to other countries in Southern Africa given that the Zimbabwean economy is associated with high-interest rates of about 200% and high levels of exchange rate fluctuations. As such, it is really hard to expect robust climate finance products and services in a country that is experiencing economic turmoil. In spite of the fact that the government inherited a robust economy in 1980, it is discouraging to observe that it has grappled with low capacity utilization, failure to export, high unemployment rates, massive liquidation of firms, high poverty levels, and acute economic recession (Nyemba & Mbohwa, 2018). Therefore, the sources of government revenues are dwindling at an alarming rate which then forces the government to come up with ineffective climate finance interventions and initiatives.

RESEARCH METHODOLOGY

This study adopted a systematic literature review methodology on the green financing strategies adopted in Zimbabwe towards the attainment of SDGs. This methodology permitted the researcher to carry out a comprehensive and robust analysis of the existing fragmented literature when it comes to the linkage between green financing strategies and SDGs. The databases such as Scopus, Web of Science, and Google scholar were used in searching the literature. Notably, other grey literature such as government documents, and organization reports were also considered given that there are very limited studies on green finance within the context of Zimbabwe (Chirisa et al., 2021; Kurebwa, 2021; Nyemba & Mbohwa, 2018). With the interest to instill rigor, a literature search strategy was effectively adopted as advocated by Page (2008). Thematic analysis was applied as the data analysis strategy whereby the themes were extracted from the existing literature on green financing strategies in Zimbabwe.

RESULTS AND DISCUSSION

The results related to the green financing strategies are presented in this section. Moreover, the researchers went further to discuss the results in line with the existing body of knowledge as follows:

National Climate Change Fund Strategy

It emerged that the national climate change strategy was one of the strategies that were adopted in Zimbabwe in an attempt to achieve the SDGs. This strategy was designed by the government whereby the financial resources collected from both private, international, public, and domestic financial resources are pooled together so as to support climate or green interventions and programs in Zimbabwe (Government of Zimbabwe, 2021). This implies that financial products and services are given in form of concessional loans and grants interventions linked to climate change adaptation and mitigation.

IDBZ Climate Finance Facility Strategy

In the quest for financing green projects, the Zimbabwean government put in place the Infrastructure Bank of Zimbabwe (IDBZ) which oversees the climate finance facility. More interestingly, this strategy is mainly used for the mobilization of financial resources and then channeling them towards green initiatives and projects (Government of Zimbabwe, 2021). The money for funding the climate finance facility is generated from various taxes for green programs. This funding strategy is supported by a robust legal framework that governs how the Trust Deed Fund is operationalized while the administration procedures are espoused in the Fund Administration. Put simply, the climate finance facility strategy allows IDBZ to finance green projects in Zimbabwe that are aligned to transport, water and sanitation, waste, and energy (Zvirevo, 2019).

Domestic Public Finance Strategy

The Zimbabwean government embarked on increasing the volume of public funds towards green projects in the country. In this regard, public finance is channeled towards climate-resilience components in energy, water and sanitation, waste, and agriculture. According to the Government of Zimbabwe (2021), the government managed to take bold steps towards supporting green projects through domestic public expenditure as substantiated by the development of climate-sensitive public investment management guidelines. For example, the Zimbabwean government offered a grant of US$7 million for the maintenance of irrigation schemes (Zvirevo, 2019). This development is a clear indication of the commitment of the Zimbabwean government towards financing climate-sensitive interventions in the areas of adaptation, climate risk, and mitigation. This implies that the central government disburses money towards climate adaptation and mitigation through the budget process.

Domestic Private Finance Strategy

It is interesting to observe that private players like banks are now showing their interest in funding green projects in Zimbabwe. This has ensured private investment in renewable energy in the country since many solar projects are being funded by financial institutions. In this regard, according to Ndlovu (2022), CBZ Holding is at the advanced stage in financing green projects as cemented by its plan to invest 2% of its profit towards green projects in Zimbabwe. Moreover, the National Building Society (NBS) is also providing Solar Energy Loan Fund (SELF) with a tenure of 3 to 12 months. This is interesting in the sense that private financial institutions like CBZ Holding and NBS are complementing the government's efforts towards a green economy in the context of Zimbabwe. It is widely accepted that private players must be supporting the initiatives that are tailor-made to a green economy.

Public-Private Partnerships (PPPs) Financing Strategy

The public-private partnership is one of the green financing strategies that has been adopted in Zimbabwe in an effort to stimulate a green economy (Zvirevo, 2019). This is a situation whereby the public institutions are working hand in hand with the private player with the purpose to ensure that the green programs or projects are adequately funded.

Foreign Investment Strategy

The government is trying its level best to attract foreign direct investment in the areas related to a green economy. By attracting foreign investors, it is not surprising that climate mitigation and adaptation projects can bear the expected fruits. As we know that big projects in areas like renewable energy and waste management require huge amounts of capital. This means that foreign investors have the strong financial muscle to take these green projects on board.

Development Finance Strategy

Development finance strategy is one of the green financing strategies that has delivered the expected outcomes within the Zimbabwean context. It has been observed that the developmental partners especially non-governmental organizations (NGOs) were at the forefront of financing green projects. For example, Green Climate Fund gave a grant (US$3 million) towards the National Adaptation plan and capacity building, GEF Trust, UNDP, and UNV offered a grant of US$33 million towards Supporting Enhanced Climate Action for Low Carbon and Climate Resilient Development Pathway (SECA-LCCRDP) (Zvirevo, 2019). Moreover, development finance has been used for the capacity building when it comes to up-skilling in terms of designing and implementing green projects.

SOULUTIONS AND RECOMMENDATIONS

In order to ensure a green economy in the Zimbabwean context, the study recommends the following:

Green Bonds and Notes: The study recommends that financial institutions should issue green bonds and notes so as to increase the volume of private finance towards green projects. It has been observed that financial institutions are currently offering short-term loans towards green projects. With this in mind, long-term sources of green finance should be put in place.

Robust Green Finance Policy: The government of Zimbabwe is recommended to put in place a robust green finance policy that incentivizes green projects by giving subsidies and tax holidays. This could go a long way in promoting investment in green projects such as solar energy and biogas.

Intensify Development Finance: The study hereby suggests that the NGOs should increase funding towards renewable energy in Zimbabwe since the country is facing an acute energy crisis. The international NGOs have strong financial muscle when it comes to the execution of green projects in Zimbabwe.

Green Economy Awareness Campaign: The study recommends that the government and the media to embark on massive green economy awareness campaigns in Zimbabwe. This could help to educate the people which can lead to behavioral change towards green energy in Zimbabwe.

Funding Green Economy Research: In order to ensure evidence-based policy-making when it comes to a green economy, the study recommends that the government should invest in research. It is worrisome to observe that most of the green projects that have been implemented in Zimbabwe were just copied from other countries without empirical evidence from the Zimbabwean context. This is the primary reason why most of these projects are not delivering the expected outcomes.

FUTURE RESEARCH DIRECTIONS

This study focused on Zimbabwe as the context of study which opens new avenues for comparative study with other African countries such as South Africa and Kenya. Moreover, studies are welcomed when it comes to the financial management of green projects in Zimbabwe especially those funded through public finance. Interestingly, a comparative study between developed and developing countries is welcomed when it comes to green financial strategies.

CONCLUSION

This study focused on the green financing strategies adopted in Zimbabwe towards the attainment of SDGs. As such, it adds value to ongoing debates on green financing strategies in developing countries by capturing the Zimbabwean perspective. It has been observed that most of the studies have been conducted in more advanced countries and developing countries have been neglected when it comes to green financing. This study established eight green financing strategies that have been employed in Zimbabwe towards attaining SDGs, namely, the national climate change fund strategy, IDBZ climate finance facility strategy, domestic public finance strategy, domestic private finance, public-private partnerships (PPPs) financing strategy, foreign investment strategy, and development finance strategy. These results can help the Zimbabwean government as the policy maker, NGOs, financial institutions, and society at larger as well as educators and researchers. Notably, the future research directions are unearthed herein. Therefore, the study concludes that green finance strategies play a fundamental role in promoting a green economy in Zimbabwe.

REFERENCES

AfDB. (2018). *African Development Bank, Nordic Development Fund, Global Environment Facility and Calvert Impact Capital partner in US $55-million investment into Off-Grid Energy Access Fund*. Retrieved December 10, 2022, from https://www.afdb.org/ar/news-and-events/african-development-bank-nordic-development-fund-global-environment-facility-and-calvert-impact-capital-partner-in-us-55-million-investment-into-off-grid-energy-access-fund-17743

Akesson, U., Wingqvist, G. Ö., Ek, G., & César, E. (2016). *Environmental and climate change policy brief Zimbabwe.* Gothernburg: Sida's Helpdesk for Environment and Climate Change. Retrieved December 1, 2022, from https://sidaenvironmenthelpdesk.se/digitalAssets/1725/1725303_zimbabwe_environment-cc_policybrief-2016-04-13.pdf

Akomea-Frimpong, I., Adeabah, D., Ofosu, D., & Tenakwah, E. J. (2021). A review of studies on green finance of banks research gap and future directions. *Journal of Sustainable Finance and Investment*, *12*(4), 1241–1264. doi:10.1080/20430795.2020.1870202

Al-SheryaniK.NobaneeH. (2020). *Green Finance: A Mini-Review.* Available at SSRN 3538696.

Anshari, M., Almunawar, M. N., & Masri, M. (2020). An overview of financial technologies in Indonesia. *The Financial Technology and Disruptive Innovation in ASEAN,* 216-224.

Asadollahfardi, G., Panahandeh, A., Khalvati, A. A., & Sekhavati, A. (2017). Life cycle assessment of construction phase of monorail project in Qom, Iran. *Pollution*, *3*(1), 81–99.

Bai, J., Chen, Z., Yan, X., & Zhang, Y. (2022). Research on the impact of green finance on carbon emissions: Evidence from China. *Economic Research-Ekonomska Istraživanja*, *35*(1), 6965–6984. doi:10.1080/1331677X.2022.2054455

Batrancea, I., Batrancea, L., Maran Rathnaswamy, M., Tulai, H., Fatacean, G., & Rus, M. I. (2020). Greening the financial system in USA, Canada and Brazil: A panel data analysis. *Mathematics*, *8*(12), 2217. doi:10.3390/math8122217

Baudoin, M. A., Vogel, C., Nortje, K., & Naik, M. (2017). Living with drought in South Africa: Lessons learnt from the recent El Niño drought period. *International Journal of Disaster Risk Reduction*, *23*, 128–137. doi:10.1016/j.ijdrr.2017.05.005

Blau, J. (2017). *The Paris Agreement: climate change, solidarity, and human rights.* Springer. doi:10.1007/978-3-319-53541-8

Bowman, M., & Minas, S. (2019). Resilience through interlinkage: The green climate fund and climate finance governance. *Climate Policy*, *19*(3), 342–353. doi:10.1080/14693062.2018.1513358

Burtraw, D., Palmer, K., Bharvirkar, R., & Paul, A. (2002). The effect on asset values of the allocation of carbon dioxide emission allowances. *The Electricity Journal*, *5*(5), 51–62. doi:10.1016/S1040-6190(02)00316-0

Chan, A.P.C., Darko, A., Ameyaw, E.E., & Owusu-Manu, D.G. (2016). Barriers affecting the adoption of green building technologies. *Journal of Management in Engineering*, *33*(3). doi: ME.1943-5479.0000507. doi:10.1061/(ASCE)

Chien, F., Ngo, Q. T., Hsu, C. C., Chau, K. Y., & Iram, R. (2021). Assessing the mechanism of barriers towards green finance and public spending in small and medium enterprises from developed countries. *Environmental Science and Pollution Research International*, *28*(43), 60495–60510. doi:10.100711356-021-14907-1 PMID:34156623

Chirisa, I., Gumbo, T., Gundu-Jakarasi, V. N., Zhakata, W., Karakadzai, T., Dipura, R., & Moyo, T. (2021). Interrogating climate adaptation financing in Zimbabwe: Proposed direction. *Sustainability*, *13*(12), 6517. doi:10.3390u13126517

Cobbinah, P. B., Erdiaw-Kwasie, M. O., & Amoateng, P. (2015). Rethinking sustainable development within the framework of poverty and urbanisation in developing countries. *Environmental Development*, *13*, 18–32. doi:10.1016/j.envdev.2014.11.001

Cui, H., Wang, R., & Wang, H. (2020). An evolutionary analysis of green finance sustainability based on multi-agent game. *Journal of Cleaner Production*, *269*, 121799. doi:10.1016/j.jclepro.2020.121799

Darko, A., & Chan, A. P. C. (2017). Review of barriers to green building adoption. *Sustainable Development*, *25*(3), 167–179. doi:10.1002d.1651

Debrah, C., Chan, A. P. C., & Darko, A. (2022). Green finance gap in green buildings: A scoping review and future research needs. *Building and Environment*, *207*, 108443. doi:10.1016/j.buildenv.2021.108443

Desalegn, G., & Tangl, A. (2022). Enhancing green finance for inclusive green growth: A systematic approach. *Sustainability*, *14*(12), 7416. doi:10.3390u14127416

Dikau, S., & Volz, U. (2021). Central bank mandates, sustainability objectives and the promotion of green finance. *Ecological Economics*, *184*, 107022. doi:10.1016/j.ecolecon.2021.107022

Dwaikat, L. N., & Ali, K. N. (2018). Green buildings life cycle cost analysis and life cycle budget development: Practical applications. *Journal of Building Engineering*, *18*, 303–311. doi:10.1016/j.jobe.2018.03.015

Dzingirai, M., & Ndava, R. (2022). Global institutional role to promote achievement of the sustainable development goals in Zimbabwe. In N. Baporikar (Ed.), *Handbook of Research on Global Institutional Roles for Inclusive Development* (pp. 99–117). IGI Global. doi:10.4018/978-1-6684-2448-3.ch006

Dziwok, E., & Jager, J. (2021). A classification of different approaches to green finance and green monetary policy. *Sustainability, 13*(21), 11902. doi:10.3390u132111902

Fonseca, L. M., Domingnes, J. P., & Dima, A. M. (2020). Mapping the SDGs relationships. *Sustainability*, *12*(8), 3359. doi:10.3390u12083359

Fonta, W. M., Ayuk, E. T., & van Huysen, T. (2018). Africa and the Green Climate Fund: Current challenges and future opportunities. *Climate Policy*, *18*(9), 1210–1225. doi:10.1080/14693062.2018.1459447

Gallagher, K. P., & Irwin, A. (2015). China's economic statecraft in Latin America: Evidence from China's policy banks. *Pacific Affairs*, *88*(1), 99–121. doi:10.5509/201588199

Government of Zimbabwe. (2021). *Zimbabwe Revised Nationally Determined Contribution*. Retrived November 25, 2022, from https://unfccc.int/sites/default/files/NDC/2022-06/Zimbabwe%20Revised%20Nationally%20Determined%20Contribution%202021%20Final.pdf

Hak, T., Janoušková, S., & Moldan, B. (2016). Sustainable Development Goals: A need for relevant indicators. *Ecological Indicators*, *60*, 565–573. doi:10.1016/j.ecolind.2015.08.003

Hasnaoui, J. A., Rizvi, S. K. A., Reddy, K., Mirza, N., & Naqvi, B. (2021). Human capital effi-ciency, performance, market, and volatility timing of Asian equity funds during COVID-19 outbreak. *Journal of Asset Management*, *22*(5), 360–375. doi:10.105741260-021-00228-y

Hoegh-Guldberg, O., Jacob, D., Bindi, M., Brown, S., Camilloni, I., Diedhiou, A., . . . Zougmoré, R. B. (2018). Impacts of 1.5 C global warming on natural and human systems. Global warming of 1.5 C. An IPCC Special Report.

Huang, Y., Duan, K., & Urquhart, A. (2023). Time-varying dependence between Bitcoin and green financial assets: A comparison between pre-and post-COVID-19 periods. *Journal of International Financial Markets, Institutions and Money*, *82*, 101687. doi:10.1016/j.intfin.2022.101687

Huang, Z., Liao, G., & Li, Z. (2019). Loaning scale and government subsidy for promoting green innovation. *Technological Forecasting and Social Change*, *144*, 148–156. doi:10.1016/j.techfore.2019.04.023

Hunjra, A. I., Hassan, M. K., Zaied, Y. B., & Managi, S. (2023). Nexus between green finance, environmental degradation, and sustainable development: Evidence from developing countries. *Resources Policy*, *81*, 103371. doi:10.1016/j.resourpol.2023.103371

International Trade Administration. (2022). *Zimbabwe - Country Commercial Guide*. Retrieved December 5, 2022, from https://www.trade.gov/country-commercial-guides/zimbabwe-investment-climate-statement

Jia, Q. (2023). The impact of green finance on the level of decarbonization of the economies: An analysis of the United States', China's, and Russia's current agenda. *Business Strategy and the Environment*, *32*(1), 110–119. doi:10.1002/bse.3120

Jiakui, C., Abbas, J., Najam, H., Liu, J., & Abbas, J. (2023). Green technological innovation, green finance, and financial development and their role in green total factor productivity: Empirical insights from China. *Journal of Cleaner Production*, *382*, 135131. doi:10.1016/j.jclepro.2022.135131

Kurebwa, J. (2021). Implications of illicit financial flows on Zimbabwe's development. *International Journal of World Policy and Development Studies*, *7*(2), 27–34. doi:10.32861/ijwpds.72.27.34

Le Page, D., Tyler-Davie, G., & Hamilton, G. (2019). Climate change must be a central pillar of SA's economic growth. *Business Day*, *6*, 1–2.

Liang, C., Wei, Y., & Zhang, Y. (2020). Is implied volatility more informative for forecasting realized volatility: An international perspective. *Journal of Forecasting*, *39*(8), 1253–1276. doi:10.1002/for.2686

Liu, S., & Wang, Y. (2023). Green innovation effect of pilot zones for green finance reform: Evidence of quasi natural experiment. *Technological Forecasting and Social Change*, *186*, 122079. doi:10.1016/j.techfore.2022.122079

Ndlovu, R. (2022). *CBZ to invest two percent of income in green projects*. Retrieved December 10, 2022, from https://vicfallslive.co.zw/cbz-to-invest-two-percent-of-income-in-green-projects/

Ngwenya, N. (2019). *South Africa's green bonds show there are massive opportunities for growth*. Retrieved December 12, 2022, from https://www.businesslive.co.za/bd/opinion/2019-06-20-sas-green-bonds-show-there-are-massive-opportunities-for-growth/

Nishimura, M. (2017). Business Model for a Low-Carbon Economy. *Journal of International Management*, *1*, 112–122.

Niyazbekova, S., Jazykbayeva, B., Mottaeva, A., Beloussova, E., Suleimenova, B., & Zueva, A. (2021). The Growth of "Green" finance at the global level in the context of sustainable economic development. In E3S Web of Conferences (Vol. 244, p. 10058). EDP Sciences. doi:10.1051/e3sconf/202124410058

Nyarugwe, R. T. (2020). *An analysis of the Zimbabwean money laundering and proceeds of crime amendment act of 2018*. Retrieved December 2, 2022, from https://etd.uwc.ac.za/handle/11394/8057

Nyemba, W. R., & Mbohwa, C. (2018). Challenges and opportunities in adopting and implementing sustainability plans in engineering, mining and processing companies in Zimbabwe. *Procedia Manufacturing*, *21*, 181–188. doi:10.1016/j.promfg.2018.02.109

Olubunmi, O. A., Xia, P. B., & Skitmore, M. (2016). Green building incentives: A review. *Renewable & Sustainable Energy Reviews*, *59*, 1611–1621. doi:10.1016/j.rser.2016.01.028

Ozili, P. K. (2022). Green finance research around the world: A review of literature. *International Journal of Green Economics*. Retrieved October 30, 2022, from https://papers.ssrn.com/sol3/papers.cfm?abstract_id=4066900

Page, D. (2008). Systematic literature searching and the bibliographic database haystack. *Electronic Journal of Business Research Methods*, *6*(2), 199–208.

Peng, H., Feng, T., & Zhou, C. (2018). International experiences in the development of green finance. *American Journal of Industrial and Business Management*, *8*(02), 385–392. doi:10.4236/ajibm.2018.82024

Qin, M., Zhang, X., Li, Y., & Badarcea, R. M. (2023). Blockchain market and green finance: The enablers of carbon neutrality in China. *Energy Economics*, *118*, 106501. doi:10.1016/j.eneco.2022.106501

Sachs, J., Woo, W. T., Yoshino, N., & Taghizadeh-Hesary, F. (2019). Importance of green finance for achieving sustainable development goals and energy security. Handbook of green finance: Energy security and sustainable development, 3-12.

Schulz, K., & Feist, M. (2021). Leveraging blockchain technology for innovative climate finance under the Green Climate Fund. *Earth System Governance*, *7*, 100084. doi:10.1016/j.esg.2020.100084

Shipalana, P. (2020). *Green finance mechanisms in developing countries: Emerging practice*. Retrieved November 2, 2022, from https://cer.org.za/wp-content/uploads/2021/07/Shipalana-Policy-Briefing-.pdf

Slany, A., Cherel-Robson, M., & Picard, L. (2020). *Economic development in Africa Report 2020 tackling illicit financial flows for sustainable development in Africa*. Retrieved December 5, 2022, from https://unctad.org/system/files/official-document/aldcafrica2020_en.pdf

Suryono, R. R., Budi, I., & Purwandari, B. (2020). Challenges and trends of financial technology (Fintech): A systematic literature review. *Information (Basel)*, *11*(12), 590. doi:10.3390/info11120590

Tan, J., Su, X., & Wang, R. (2023). The impact of natural resource dependence and green finance on green economic growth in the context of COP26. *Resources Policy*, *81*, 103351. doi:10.1016/j.resourpol.2023.103351

Tollefson, J. (2018). IPCC says limiting global warming to 1.5 C will require drastic action. *Nature*, *562*(7726), 172–173. doi:10.1038/d41586-018-06876-2 PMID:30301994

Tong, D., Zhang, Q., Davis, S. J., Liu, F., Zheng, B., Geng, G., Xue, T., Li, M., Hong, C., Lu, Z., Streets, D. G., Guan, D., & He, K. (2018). Targeted emission reductions from global super-polluting power plant units. *Nature Sustainability*, *1*(1), 59–68. doi:10.103841893-017-0003-y

Weber, G., & Cabras, I. (2017). The transition of Germany's energy production, green economy, low-carbon economy, socio-environmental conflicts, and equitable society. *Journal of Cleaner Production*, *167*, 1222–1231. doi:10.1016/j.jclepro.2017.07.223

Wu, X., Sadiq, M., Chien, F., Ngo, Q. T., Nguyen, A. T., & Trinh, T.-T. (2021). Testing role of green financing on climate change mitigation: Evidences from G7 and E7 countries. *Environmental Science and Pollution Research International*, *28*(47), 66736–66750. doi:10.100711356-021-15023-w PMID:34235703

Yuan, F., & Gallagher, K. P. (2015). *Greening development finance in the Americas*. Global Economic Governance Initiative, Boston University. Retrieved November 28, 2022, from https://www.bu.edu/pardeeschool/files/2014/12/Greening.Development.Final_.pdf

Zeb, S., Shah, I. A., Rashid, A., & Raza, H. (2021). Impact of corporate social responsibility and corporate governance on firm performance. *Journal of Business and Economics*, *13*(1), 18–34.

Zimbabwe Financial Inclusion Report C. E. N. F. R. I. (2016). *Making Access Possible*. Retrieved November 27, 2022, from https://cenfri.org/wp-content/uploads/2016/01/MAP-Zimbabwe_Synthesis-report_Cenfri-FinMark-Trust-UNCDF_October-2016.pdf

Zimbabwe Integrated Solid Waste Management Plan. (2011). *Zimbabwe Integrated Solid Waste Management Plan statistics for the year 2011, (IES, 2014)*. Retrieved December 6, 2022, from https://www.yumpu.com/en/document/view/62915014/zimbabwe-integrated-solid-waste-management-plan

Zvirevo, W. (2019). *Green Financing in Zimbabwe: Case of the Infrastructure Development Bank of Zimbabwe*. Elephant Hills Hotel.

ADDITIONAL READING

Dörry, S., & Schulz, C. (2018). Green financing, interrupted. Potential directions for sustainable finance in Luxembourg. *Local Environment*, *23*(7), 717–733. doi:10.1080/13549839.2018.1428792

KEY TERMS AND DEFINITIONS

Green Bond: This refers to a long-term debt financial instrument aimed at financing green projects, initiatives, or interventions which offer investors regular income payments.

Green Economy: It refers to an economy that aims at low carbon, socially inclusive, and improved resource efficiency whilst significantly eliminating ecological and environmental risks.

Green Finance Strategy: It refers to the method or approach used to fund green projects, initiatives or interventions with the purpose to promote a green economy.

Green Note: It describes a fixed-income long-term financial instrument designed to provide financial support to environmentally-friendly projects or interventions.

Green Project: It is described as the intervention that aims to produce products and services that support the adoption of clean energy and reduce greenhouse gas emissions.

Sustainable Development: It is the approach to development that support the designing of a robust strategy that ensures efficient utilization of resources in such a way that the needs of the future generation are not compromised.

Chapter 4
Sustainable Approaches of Blockchain Tech, Artificial Intelligence, and Climate Finance in the 4&5IR:
Low Emission Technologies and Economy

Amitab Bhattacharjee
https://orcid.org/0000-0003-3765-7412
Sophia University, Japan

Vikram Bansal
Jawaharlal Nehru University, India

ABSTRACT

Save the green and live in the green should be the mottos of the modern high-tech world. Industry 4.0 introduces the most advanced automated technologies, but many of them cause high CO_2 emissions around the globe that need strong compelling force because any catastrophic changes in the climate causes dreadful vandalization in the economy and society. This chapter discusses the climate-friendly economic and low-emission technological developments in the 4IR and 5IR by using the practical-sense mechanism. Reading this chapter will therefore increase the knowledge of blockchain technology (BT), artificial intelligence (AI), and climate finance in the low carbon economic sustainability. Furthermore, the proposed green development themes (i.e., hybrid green city and industrial layout, hybrid low emission agriculture farm) affirms the sustainable low carbon economic developments in the forthcoming Industry 5.0. Finally, the strategic recommendations will assist in developing the low carbon economy with the perfection of BT, AI, and global climate finance in the world.

DOI: 10.4018/978-1-6684-8361-9.ch004

INTRODUCTION

The eco-epoch of the Anthropocene has begun with the industrial revolution. Consequently, a different level of eco-crisis has sparked nowadays and been gradually accelerating day by day. Surge in CO_2 and other greenhouse-emission significantly structured ecological imbalance that causes developing threats in the human welfare, animal-welfare etc. Manufacturing factories i.e., oil filters for cars, plastic materials, color dying units are largely producing harmful gas emissions. In a result, the highly matured economy becomes a high-carbon economy with future uncertainties because all countries and businesses are implicitly or explicitly dependent on the environment. Investing in these sectors may excel the eco-crisis. Thus, any concern in the business activities would relate to environmental issues or crises. As few processes are natural that we couldn't stop or fully protect from the eco-crisis, but they might be reduced through increasing green investments. To reduce the high-CO_2 risk, the Paris agreement has formed the formal legislation of the climate finance (CF) policy (Giglio et al., 2021; Geddes et al., 2020). The concessional funds of the CF policy have accumulated to support the low-carbon industrial developments and green business practices in industry 4.0 and industry 5.0 around the world.

In the low carbon industrial improvements, developing and poorest regions need billions of green financing dollars. Developments and executions of green technologies i. e., BT or AI based low emission industrial devices or tools require a bulk amount of fixed costs. Even if the implementation of those climate friendly industrial technologies has done prominently then it may significantly expand the economic burden that many countries or firms don't afford (i. e., countries lacking green funds may be unsuccessful in climate friendly industrial developments without sufficient liquidity support from global climate finance). Admittedly, in many industrial sectors, changing existing technologies and infrastructure will dramatically increase the disposal costs and green technological costs. Global climate finance therefore becomes the major source of green financing to build the low carbon industrial developments in the 5IR.

Recent studies disclose that using global climate finance in developing and establishing blockchain and artificial intelligence based industrial technologies in the poorest regions would assist to achieve the zero global emission targets by 2050 (Qerimi & Sergi, 2022; see also Schulz & Feist, 2021). By green technological approaches, different research finds a promising impact of AI technologies on green business practices and emission free climate (Qerimi & Sergi, 2022). Another study explores that blockchain technology has positive association with climate friendly technological developments (Schulz & Feist, 2021). These statements affirm that

BT and AI based technologies are eco-friendly. Both technologies will be promising to decrease high emission industrial burden in the 5IR.

To eradicate the environmental burden, machine readable (MR) technologies have impressively modified business practices in the fourth-grade industrial revolution (4IR). Encrypted-digital developments e. g. blockchain technology (BT), artificial intelligence (AI) architectures are rapidly growing with trust to serve the digital business globe in a better way (French et al., 2021). Tangible documentation process and real time access become digital encrypted form by those MR technologies, which cuts off more than 25% of CO_2 emissions around the earth (Kouwenberg & Zheng, 2023). The eco-economic concern then provides another advantage to the globe by introducing low emission business practices with climate finance that interlinked with green environmental issues. Nowadays, many enterprises are literally accepting or changing their existing investment plans to make eco-friendly business practices or green business-solutions that impact lower emissions in the world. Such climate friendly investment concerns indicate that the acceptance of climate finance policy will be growing in industry 5.0. Basically, the concept of climate finance (CF) has developed to protect the green environment (Buchner et al., 2019). This CF concern increases green financing consciousness among investors. As a result, the growing awareness of green financing impacts on the investor's consideration and now they have been gradually adopting the green environmental consideration when investing for a business concern.

However, by methodological orientation, authors applied systematic review and meta-synthesis techniques in this chapter writings due to the qualitative approach. This technique allows to demonstrate the issues by practical orientation (Jahanshahi et al., 2021; Jones, 2004). This chapter therefore followed a practical sense mechanism to provide real time knowledge of blockchain technology (BT), artificial intelligence (AI), and climate finance (CF). Adopting these techniques ensures the detailed narrative explanations of the facts in original form that helps readers to understand the theme of this chapter i. e., ongoing process and changes of BT, AI & CF along with the potential developments and shortcomings in the future world.

In this chapter, authors integrate a wide range of directions to articulate how blockchain technology accelerates green entrepreneurial concerns and climate finance activities in the 4IR & 5IR around the globe. This chapter includes realistic demonstrations regarding the strategic directions of blockchain and artificial intelligence technologies in the low-CO_2-industrial developments. The further description affirms that the eco acceleration can sustainably improve by using the most precious, secure, reliable, and trustworthy technologies i.e., blockchain technology and artificial intelligence in the forthcoming industrial revolution (e.g., industry 5.0). Moreover, the discussion about the impacts of the adoption of blockchain technology and artificial intelligence in the micro, small and medium enterprises (MSMEs) are accordingly explained with the economic progress-based examples to develop financial sustainability.

Furthermore, this chapter articulately explains about the potential scopes of the low-emission investments and climate friendly low CO_2 emission models (proposed) to increase the sustainability in the forthcoming low carbon economy. In the last part, this chapter depicts strategic recommendations, implications, and conclusion. The contribution of this chapter would therefore enrich the knowledge and practices about the high emission climate-crisis management, the adoption of BT & AI, global & domestic climate finance, and global sustainability in the low carbon economy, society & green environment in industry 4.0 and industry 5.0.

BLOCKCHAIN TECHNOLOGY AND ARTIFICIAL INTELLIGENCE

Blockchain Technology

The blockchain coding framework was developed by '*Satoshi Nakamoto*' for solving distributed digital currency ledger systems in the year of 2008. The architecture of digital currency ('*cryptocurrency*') transactions was firstly designed and constructed by blockchain technology (BT) but thereafter this technology has started being used to reform different digital platforms of economy (Ebekozien et al., 2022) and other sectors around the world. Following the blockchain technology, completed boxes of data files are encrypted with *'no alteration term'* that ensures technological security against third party modification (e. g. remote hacking) and unique coding box-pattern for every user. Blockchain technological framework, is therefore, highly secure, flexible, and transparent.

Artificial Intelligence

Artificial intelligence or AI is the highly developed coding framework that enables mechanical devices to simulate promising human-intelligence. Using AI technologies is literally efficient to perform macro basis complex tasks that may be difficult in processing by individuals. Some innovative AI systems are quantum artificial intelligence of NASA, Crysta-Apex S (inspection machine), virtual assistant, automated weather forecasting, speech and visual recognition system, humanoid robots, industrial robots.

Blockchain Technology and Artificial Intelligence in Business

The new alliance between blockchain-technology and artificial intelligence further improved the incremental advancement to the economy, society, environment, and even sustainable industrial revolution. Artificial intelligence (AI) facilities and BT are significantly resolving many secure-data processing and eco challenges in the fourth industrial revolution (4IR). Ensuring safety on data transmission, processing, digital data archive, and environmental crisis are now the most complex challenges in the 4IR. Because data is a more valuable item than money in the modern economy. For example, hackers use '*digital web coding*' to transfer or modify banking data to hack reserved liquidity or copyright protected blueprints data to make money. The process of digitalization is therefore crucial to develop a sustainable and secure-digital transformation system in the industry 4.0 and 5.0.

After the year of 2019, the safety challenges of the digitalization in the 4IR have been gradually reduced by the AI-facilities (Loureiro et al., 2021; Di Vaio et al., 2020) and BT. Although the initial fixed cost of adopting blockchain and artificial intelligence technologies is literally high, it will increase the firm's revenue performance and decrease the variable costs in the long run. In Japan, there are micro-block digital communication systems that many Japanese firms use to reduce the potential risk of cybercrime. In this procedure, firms build home and remote accessing digital-data modules with blockchain technique, so that third party or remote/guest users will never access their archive files. However, in the environment crisis, AI and BT are impressively changing concerning issues for example developing low-carbon manufacturing systems, eco- friendly hybrid-supply-chain management, and green energy distribution systems. Artificial intelligence software (AIS) integrates with eco-friendly management systems and green business/investment operating platforms that surprisingly decrease harmful gas emissions and higher consumption of natural resources. AIS-platform allows individuals or entities real time accessing into the digital financial markets (Di Vaio et al., 2020), good's market for daily necessity things, business management, financial management, web-based digital office work, robotic applications that reduce the drive-need (saves fuels and times), less-tangible paper-works (saves natural resources like trees, less production of items of paper-work facilities), reduce the office-space, increasing the diversification, eco-friendly production (eco-drive cars), increasing renewable energy generation system from natural resources and so on. Therefore, adopting artificial intelligence approaches would be highly effective to ease the complex procedures with minimum physical labor while blockchain technology ensures secured data infrastructure of the modern economy in the 4IR & 5IR.

Attributes of BT and AI

Developing blockchain tech (BT) and artificial intelligence (AI) based technological platforms will be sustainable due to having real time tech-resistance. The user resistance of the BT and AI has an anti-cybercrime protocol system when using the internet of things (IoT). Both technologies have few similar working-attributes. The major attributes of BT and AI are depicted as six, namely verifiable, inconspicuousness, immutable, fragmentation, transparency, and perseverance (see Figure 1).

Figure 1. Six major attributes of blockchain and artificial intelligence technology
Source: Author's elaboration.

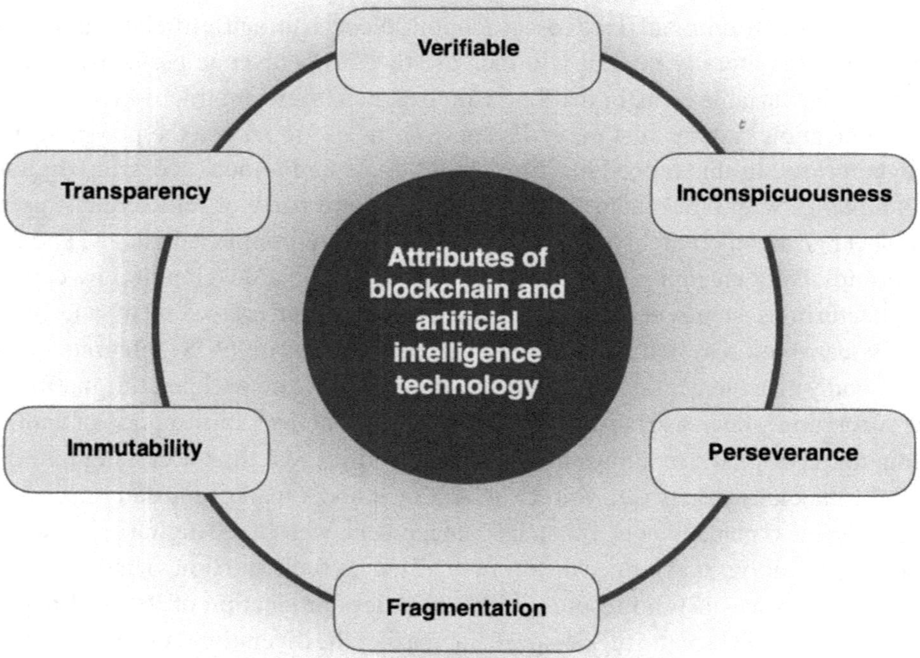

Verifiable

This attribute depicts that every BT block has a secure established code-link technology with the permanent or previous BT block in the block-coding system. This BT-coding architecture enables high speed easy-verification and tracking facilities of every single transaction or communication through the artificial intelligence-based application system. AI-based applications even have a real time screening and verification system that can identify and record all data communication between users within nanoseconds.

Inconspicuousness

In the BT and AI based platform, every time, the communication system with the BT and AI generates unique and individual identity code virtually that encloses the original identical information of the user. Therefore, illegal accessing for identical data stealing into the system won't be possible by the server hacking system.

Perseverance

In the blockchain-technology (BT) system, any identified data transmission is impossible to rollback or deduct from the source, if the identified dada adds into a coding-block of the BT system. Additionally, using the real time data (e.g., any transaction code-protocol) blocking system can immediately identify the invalid or false data transmission. In this platform, artificial intelligence will provide an autonomous facility that increases competitive advantages for the participants.

Fragmentation

The peer to peer (P2P) networking platform is used to host the distributed digital-ledger system that verifies as well as process each set of data transmission. This technology in blockchain eliminates the third party or middle trusted merchant between the participants or users because all the nodes act jointly peer to peer basis to add as well as verify the data transmission. The autonomous AI applications allow primary users to design and execute direct communication or data transfer systems that don't require any intermediaries. This autonomous AI system is time and cost effective.

Immutability

The combination of blockchain and artificial intelligence technologies allow data to flow in or out through end-to-end encrypted permanent blocks. Therefore, once the network module builds, the data architecture alteration won't be possible, which ensures the anti-cyber security at the trusted level.

Transparency

Artificial intelligence (AI) and blockchain tech (BT) can be the precious combination to develop a decentralized block framework. In this BT-block technology, the data-block securely stores the profile-based detail information of all participants and all transferred data records that literally ensure the transparency to all users. The viewable feature of the permanent BT-block shows all changes in the data on a real time basis that concretes the transparent mechanism of AI and BT.

Necessities of BT and AI Adoption

Technological development is an ongoing process to ensure safety and increase flexibility, but all technological platforms won't have sophisticated advantages nowadays. This consideration raises a question, *"What type of technological framework applications will be sophisticated in business in the following periods?"* With climate friendly and high-tech resistance benefits, blockchain technology (BT) and artificial intelligence (AI) will be sophisticated in the future. As risk friendly cyber threats have dramatically increased the last couple of years around the world because a large portion of global business activities are now operating virtually. Therefore, all firms badly need blockchain technology (BT) and artificial intelligence (AI) based technological tools and devices to enhance low-emission business practices and business resistance against potential cyber-threats. In the developing and developed countries, the micro, small and medium enterprises (MSMEs) are literally a good choice to snatch out financial data or other valuable information like blueprint of product design and manufacturing technology by a risk friendly group. Moreover, the financial budget for technological hubs (cyber-attacks protocol technologies) is mostly limited in the developing countries and continents (e.g., Africa). After that another reason heads up as an environmental crisis. In the agriculture industry, farming research data, weather forecasting data, renewable energy data have been growing rapidly, which would be complex and difficult to analyze without an artificial intelligence platform (machine readable technology).

Furthermore, the controlling, monitoring, justification, communication systems in industry 4.0 have been changed by hybrid technologies (Di Vaio et al., 2020) that reduces physical labor but increases efficiency and productivity with higher impact on reducing CO_2 emissions. In the forthcoming years, the necessity of basic food production will be higher than now. Reasonably, many agro farms have been involved in the innovation of hybrid plant versions to supply the increasing demand of basic foods e.g., rice, wheat, green veggies, corn. This innovation process needs to analyze a large volume of data and then the output details of the analyzed data will draw new production mechanisms that would be sensitive to fully disclose to other competitors or third parties. Similar complexity may also have in the other technological industry i.e., microchip industry has similar sensitive information issues that require higher technological protocols.

Many firms in MSMEs sector jointly developed new chip architecture with higher efficiency but there may have potential unethical interests by others (shadow merchants in the same or different regions) on those architectures of newly invented chips to make money or autonomy power in the industry. These potential uncertainties have developed reliable, secure, and environment-friendly business operating channel challenges. In this circumstance, blockchain and artificial intelligence bring unique advantages for most of the MSMEs firms as well as other industries. Blockchain would have promising flexibility and security to protect highly sensitive data transactions and devices from unauthorized access by risk friendly targets while artificial intelligence provides a base platform for off-cloud or cloud server technologies that would ensure real time user interaction with minimum physical labor.

Adoption Techniques

To enhance real time cyber security and reliable communication systems, the adoption interest of blockchain and artificial intelligence technologies have been growing in the industry 4.0. Many manual/physical works have been automated by utilizing those technologies that highly benefited the large, medium, and small firms (Ebekozien et al., 2022; Di Vaio et al., 2020). The large companies have already started adopting BT and AI technologies because of cyber guard perspectives and controlling potential fraudulent scams (Ebekozien et al., 2022; French et al., 2021). Although the blockchain and artificial intelligence are young tech architecture, these technologies would be prominent in the forthcoming industry 5.0 or further industrial revolution. The micro, small and medium firms should therefore need to adopt BT and AI technological advances to increase entrepreneurial sustainability. These technologies can be adopted in several ways. Among them, hybrid BT and AI, hybrid smart contact, BT and AI for energy supply system, BT and AI for supply chain management, BT and AI based peer to peer (P2P) financial transactions system, BT and AI based cloud ledger and accounting system would be significant for MSMEs industry in the developing countries. All-business industries are therefore indeed to adopt blockchain tech with artificial intelligence architecture to enhance secure and authentic transmissions of data, communication systems and future sustainability.

Challenges and Voids

Employment Scarcity

Blockchain and AI technologies may aggregate the eco-friendly automation system development because all hybrid industrial technologies are built with automation systems to increase the efficiency and reduce the time & costs. Even, presupposed technologies in the transportation sector will systematically need to be installed with automation systems that significantly reduce the physical labor worldwide in the coming future. For example, in Japan, replacing gas and oil fuel technological vehicle manufacturing into hybrid technologies (e. g., electric vehicles) will dramatically reduce the physical labor necessity. As a result, many front-line workers and professionals may have to struggle with unemployment uncertainty.

Data-Sensing

This problem occurs because of sensor based data transmission within the IoT system. To enhance the real time data networking, all IoT-sensors installed in the machine or operating devices will emit a data signal continuously that causes increased data traffic error (i. g., data-sensing obstacle) in the project network.

Complex-Networking

In the eco-friendly blockchain and artificial intelligence framework real time data transmission system, the IoT facilities are used to ensure error free communication and technological facilities. To connect every device (including machines, vehicles, mobile, etc.) with IoT facilities, the network system develops based on heterogeneous networking design that increases inter-network complexity.

Consumptions of High Energy

To build the low CO_2 emission system, IoT networking communication systems (without energy distribution framework) in the industrial sector (including hybrid agriculture sector) need to run 24/7 based to maintain real time outputs that increase energy consumption and energy transmission loss. By the data transmission network, the wireless technology consumes higher energy than wired technology (e.g., Fiber line). The growing dependency on 5G technology is also one of the major causes of high energy consumption. Therefore, implementing IoT networking channels without a proper energy distribution framework will lead to enormous energy loss and expenses.

Institutional Voids

The technological developments have been spreading out for digitalization around the world, but many places are still not included in the smart network. Additionally, lack of financial intermediaries, minimum technological developments, real time transaction system, infrastructure creates obstacles in doing virtual business activities with real time communication system, potential financial transaction barriers between buyer and sellers etc. In these areas, developing low CO_2 emission industrial or technological developments may be time consuming as well as costly, but this type of immature markets is emerging for win-win situations.

CLIMATE FINANCING IN GREEN DEVELOPMENTS

Climate Finance

Climate finance (CF) affirms the international or domestic concessional liquidity that only utilises for investing or supporting in low-emission economic developments. The global CF policy has been implemented in the Paris climate agreement for zero emission targets and zero or low emission economic developments in the world. The global CF funds are mainly accumulated by CF member countries on a voluntary basis, but the domestic CF funds are collected from both public and private sources. Thus, the activity of CF policy is divided into two major segments, namely international CF funds and domestic CF funds. Both sources are actively supporting the climate friendly concerns at the country level and firm level.

Mechanism of Climate Finance

The climate finance (CF) mechanism aggregates the green transition in industry 4.0 and will be sustainability growing in industry 5.0 around the world. Following this green mechanism, the concessional funds of climate concern have accumulated by mainly five major countries e.g., United States, Japan, France, Canada, Australia, international financial giants such as World Bank, development banks and more on in the recent years (Kouwenberg & Zheng, 2023; Buchner et al., 2019). Arranging concessional funds for the green investment program will be difficult because of large scale financial scarcity in the developing or underdeveloped countries around the world. Climate finance mechanism (CFM) has two core considerations. First consideration is to accumulate sufficient concessional funds for green environmental concern, and another is to make available those funds for climate friendly investments to reach 'net-zero emission' target by next few years.

Figure 2 shows the activity channels of international and domestic climate finance that is divided into several activity-channels. The practical action starts from the decision made by the higher authorities and legislation-bodies of climate finance (CF) globally that apply in a similar manner in all regions (having high-risk gas emission). Therefore, the variation of discriminant facts is almost zero. In the upper channel, the founder authorities of the CF reserve the right to make necessary legislation and decisions on providing low-CO2 investment support to the country level as well as the firm level internationally. The next level activity-channel involves accumulating the concessional funds for the low-carbon economy. In the next channel, there are included three major CF activities, receiving concessional liquidity funds from the CF members, arranging distribution of available CF funds based on project authorization, and collecting receivables schedule basis from the CF funds borrowing countries or firms. This channel has two different activity flows, international and local low-CO2 management systems. The global climate-finance (GCF) works to support internationally while the domestic climate-finance (DCF) acts to support locally or within the country. Although the GCF and DCF are involved to support the low-CO2 economy by the concessional liquidity of CF but their CF fund distributing zones are different by country level and firm level. In the following channel, the low-carbon development proposal, evaluation of the eco-development necessity, and formal acceptance of CF supports into the green concern have rolled out.

After that, the new presuppose developments of the low-carbon projects must execute with essential monitoring. The last channel works out to determine the timely payback of distributed CF funds (principal amount) with minimum interest amount. The imposed interest rate on the concessional CF funds will be always lower than the existing market rate that is promised by the CF founder members in the Paris agreement. Therefore, each low CO_2 emission project financed by the CF concessional liquidity should be paid both principal and interest amounts within the predetermined periods by the borrower country or projected organization. The competitive facilities of climate finance for example lowest interest rate and long pay-back duration may encourage the implementation of eco-friendly industrial and infrastructural changes at the country level.

Figure 2. The activity channels of international and domestic climate finance
Source: Author's elaboration.

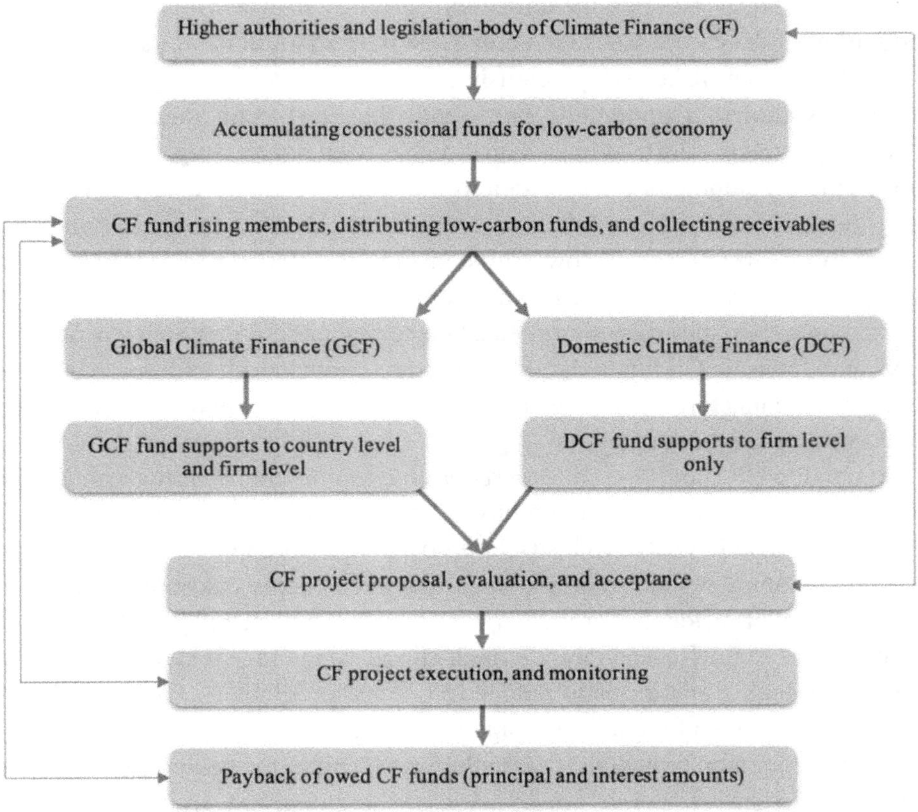

Climate Finance and Blockchain Technology

In the most recent modern tech, Blockchain technology (BT) is flourishing as a reliable and secure digital mechanism to ensure transparency and safety in many sectors. Blockchain tech was introduced to build the digital currency e.g., Crypto currency but later this young technology became sophisticated because of its block-based architectures. Each data block has formed an end-to-end encrypted system that couldn't be overwritten or overlapped by risk friendly parities. This advantage signifies the blockchain tech extremely anti-cyber-crime coding technology and long-term sustainability. This technology also has a low-emission impact in the green environment. Researchers in different studies show that blockchain based technologies need to be made available for green environmental safety (Schulz & Feist, 2021). Admittedly, these reasons focus on sufficient climate financing in BT based industrial developments. By cost effective terms, small and large firms can adopt BT based industrial or business technologies because BT has many inexpensive adoption techniques. Besides, the source code of blockchain tech is available as open mode and all codes can be used to re-coding new micro data blocks for every different user or device that makes BT preciously unique than other existing technologies. This facility allows a firm to build eco-friendly business technologies.

Although green industrial transformation has been progressing, but most of the firms in the developing or poorest regions don't have required funds for executing green industrial technologies (Schulz & Feist, 2021). So, global CF funds can support those firms to adopt low emission industrial technologies. By the *data management orientation*, the large volume of data can be analyzed in a moment that increases the data-processing speed. Due to higher data-processing efficiency, global and domestic CF funds should invest in blockchain tech to develop the most secure data architecture of the *sensitive green data and device management network* in the low emission industry.

Eventually, CF should go for *blockchain based climate friendly technological developments* in the developing regions because BT can be used as *'presupposed technology'* in the low-CO2-industrial improvements e. g., large data analyzing of the weather/natural resources or low-emission green energy distribution system in the agriculture or residential or industrial sectors and establishing IoT based green supply-chain system. Reasonably, CF funds should be invested to develop BT based green technological platforms to reduce CO_2 emission globally. Furthermore, the successful execution of the low emission industrial investment needs *transparency and safety* rather than only digital technologies. Specifically, geo-politics may play a great role in the *'corporate governance'* of the global low emission industrial developments that increases the *'data communication sensitivity'*. Any CF funding developments by country or large organization will be vulnerable if the *'risk friendly parties'* have unofficial access into the confidential global data. Therefore, climate finance should be used to establish a BT based secure and sustainable *'data communication system'*. Thus, the green execution target of CF will be worked out with extremely fewer potential errors and minimum development challenges.

Climate Finance and Artificial Intelligence

In today's precious economy, financing is the fuel of industrial technological developments while the industrial advancement holds the growth of the economy. This assumption indicates that Industrial technological progress (ITP) and economic progress are dependent on each other. From earlier decades to present, the industrial technological sector promotes mostly revenue-oriented developments rather than climate friendly technologies. Following this IR strategy significantly develops environmental threats by risk friendly CO2 emission worldwide that spreads out red alarm for economic sustainability. The ongoing high-risk emission industrial system can be changed by green investment considerations around the globe. This concern is constructed by global climate finance policy. But there is a debate on "*how does the climate financing progress eco-friendly industrial developments*?" The strategic answer of this argument is to invest climate financing in developing zero or low emission industrial technologies.

Few recent studies showed evidence that artificial intelligence-based technologies will be sustainable solutions for high tech climate friendly industrial developments in the 4IR and 5IR (Leal Filho et al., 2022; Qerimi & Sergi, 2022). AI based mechanical devices and intelligence tools would be low-emission types, highly efficient and eco-friendly (Leal Filho et al., 2022; Qerimi & Sergi, 2022). Besides, using AI technologies in business will improve the firm's internal capabilities i. e., revenue performance, manufacturing efficiency (Jahanshahi et al., 2021). Research scholars even explain that AI based technologies can efficiently simulate human-intelligence techniques (Leal Filho et al., 2022). Therefore, investing climate finance in AI based industrial developments will support the global low-carbon economy. In addition, the concessional liquidity of global climate finance would be a beneficial source for the firms or countries with insufficient green funds.

In the agriculture sector, investing in climate finance for developing AI-applications (e. g., tools and machines for hybrid farming research, planting machines, automated soil testing system, water purifying system) will improve the hybrid agriculture system. Similarly, if climate financing invests in AI technologies for the green manufacturing sector, green transportation sector and gas distribution sector will increase the low-emission industrial progress (Leal Filho et al., 2022; Qerimi & Sergi, 2022). In the developed countries, some companies have already started executing AI based low emission technologies e. g., Johnson Matthey Japan, Johnson Matthey Germany, Mitutoyo Corporation Japan, Japanese LPG distributing firms, and quantum AI system of NASA in the United States.

Climate-Friendly Financial Sustainability

The emerging concern of the green environment has been framed to improve eco-friendly business practices all around the world. Since it has been affecting the industrial revolution by emphasizing the eco-friendly innovations for the green business practices. Today's automated machine-readable system development i.e., AI based Fanuc robot used in the car parts manufacturing industry in Japan, could be a good example that makes complex tasks easy in industry 4.0.

The climate financing system has therefore developed to ensure environmental safety not only in the developed countries but also all countries in every region (Kouwenberg & Zheng, 2023). Although automated metallic industries are a fast-growing concept, the future sustainability could be less profitable due to rising green environmental issues. So, the climate or environment friendly green investments would be sustainable in the future generations industries. The financial sustainability in the business sector will be sustainable if the business operating activities and technological developments are eco-friendly, but going green technologies will need initial investment that many companies or countries don't have. In this friction, climate finance is the only solution to implement eco-friendly technologies.

Climate finance is fully reserved for supporting green environmental improvement projects all over the world. There are several ways to change or adopt an eco-friendly business model by a climate financing system for financial sustainability. For example, a firm may use renewable energy e.g., solar energy system or wind power energy in the selected section or areas. To manage the eco-friendly improvement, firms would collect and use the climate finance funds at a minimum interest rate (below market rate facility). After the successful execution, the variable cost (utility expenses) would be significantly reduced and even increase the firm's longevity in the long-run. These facilities will improve the financial sustainability of the eco-friendly organizations at the firm level.

Specific Climate Finance

The specific climate finance (SCF) refers to the concessional liquidity that reserves for investing in the selected high-emission sectors or regions. In the country level, specific CF is used to support eco-friendly development in the large area or region while at the firm level, specific CF utilizes either going green business upgrading or selected eco-friendly conversion. In both ways the main aim of the SCF is to support high emission sectors to reduce the potential climate risk all over the world. In the industry 4.0, the specific CF focuses dedicatedly five different sectors i.e., energy, finance & IT, infrastructure, transportation, and manufacturing (including agriculture) have been improving as green energy system, green financing and information technologies, green infrastructure development, green transportation system, and green manufacturing technologies respectively (see Figure 3).

One of the real time examples of specific climate finance (SCF) has been included here. The specific climate finance (SCF) project has started execution in Canada. In this country, the low-CO2 emission fund invests to eradicate the manufacturing or importing of any plastic bags, items of plastic cutlery or food-service ware (e. g., plastic spoon, coffee cups, drinking straws) and many more from December in the year of 2022. This prohibition has been formally implemented with new legislation throughout the country. Now, the specific CF has been supporting the local manufacturers to use disposable materials (i. e., paper cups, straws) instead of plastic material. This eco-friendly changes in the manufacturing industry significantly impacts to reduce CO2 emission in the country as well as globally.

Figure 3. Five major sectors of SCF by the country level and firm level
Source: Author's elaboration.

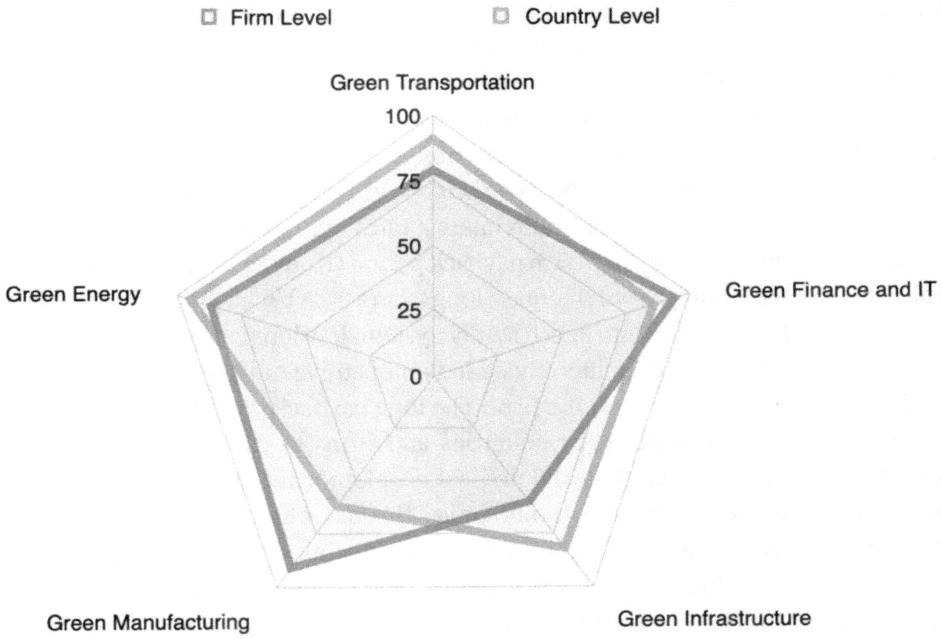

Benefits of Climate Finance

Many firms around the world don't have sufficient liquidity reserves or support for the low-emission developments. This reason, the implementation progress of the '*low-carbon green economy*' (LCGE) would be time consuming or might be vulnerable without liquidity support. To ensure '*climate safety and sufficient liquidity support*' for eco-friendly business at the country level as well as at the firm level, the climate finance policy has been formed with legislation (Giglio et al., 2021). The execution of the climate finance (CF) policy has been widely excelling the global goal of a low-carbon green economy that widens numerous advantages for the *environment, economy, society,* country level and firm level.

One of the prime benefits of CF policy is the '*development of a low-carbon green economy*' in the world. The CF funds significantly increase eco-friendly business practices by changing the existing high-emission industrial system. The climate threats will be reduced if most of the firms accept the *low-carbon business practices*. Hence, it would surplus the potential *green environmental protection* too. Sustainable economic progress is interlinked with a green environment because all the material sources are centered in the environment (Giglio et al., 2021). At the country level, any country could now borrow from the global CF funds to change high-risk-carbon emission sources around the country. Each successful execution of eco-friendly changes will *decrease the high-risk carbon emission* worldwide. As a result, low-carbon business practices will ensure a green environment or climate safety and sustainable *low-carbon green economic developments* in industry 4.0 and next industrial revolutions (e.g., 5IR, 6IR).

Next potential benefit would be '*monetary gain*'. Firms or countries may collect any required CF funds with minimum interest rates (extremely lower than existing market rate of interest) and long-term payback period (Kouwenberg & Zheng, 2023). These financial advantages will increase long term assets because countries or firms would invest the CF funds into eco-friendly system developments. Establishing the low-carbon industrial system literally added competitive advantages for long term fresh revenues of the country or the firm. The long payback period with low interest rate may highly encourage many countries and firms to execute the low-carbon infrastructure and ecofriendly technological developments. It will even accelerate the green innovations in business technologies. Besides, climate finance will be used to reform the modern agriculture system by introducing low-carbon technologies. The existing agriculture technologies have potential high-emission threats for the climate. Therefore, the agriculture sector will be benefited by the global CF policy.

Another transforming CF scope will be the '*green energy generation system*' that may fulfill the emerging demand of energy in the *5IR*. The global and domestic CF funds will be used to develop new renewable green energy plants around the world that may significantly fulfill the energy demand in the future. Additionally, the support of CF funds to the country level and firm level will sustainably increase the green projects all over the world that reasonably raises the '*new employment opportunities*' for large numbers of people around the world. The eco-friendly changes all around are therefore improved green lifestyle practices in the society. Thus, the society will be benefited by the implementation of the CF policy.

Low Emission Investments and Entrepreneurial Sustainability

The high emission industrial revolution and modernizing all around the world have been tremendously increasing the climate threat that causes developing unexpected environmental crises day by day. The emission of *CO2, CH4, N2O* and other harmful gas has been influencing business activities, living things and climate especially in agriculture, shipping, wildlife, human health safety, ice shelf safety, ozone-shield safety, and green environmental safety. To reduce the high amount of emission of greenhouse gasses (EGHG), the low-emission investment policy has been introduced under climate finance (Kouwenberg & Zheng, 2023). Investments with a purpose of reducing EGHG impact affirms the low-emission investments. Investing or reinvesting for developing the low-carbon business is the epic purpose of climate finance. Most of the firms in the developing and under developing countries need liquidity support for switching into *low-carbon technologies (LCT)*. Firms can therefore collect the required switching funds for LCT development from the emission investment funds of climate finance policy (Kouwenberg & Zheng, 2023). Furthermore, to gain entrepreneurial sustainability through proper utilization of green investments, firms obviously need to follow strategies. Because any investment decision in the business comes up with a strategy.

Time oriented strategy for new and reinvestments literally develops entrepreneurial sustainability in the long run but never all investments bring expected long term monetary and environmentally friendly benefits with the purposes if the investment executes without proper strategic drive and eco-ethics. The new firm (public or private concerns) begins with its initial start-up investments, and the existing firm goes for reinvestments. There is another type of time lapse investments by shadow entrepreneurs in the private sector. Therefore, any concern of the investments regardless of the public or private sector should have time oriented strategic drive. For example, '*artificial landscape strategy*' or *ALS* would be beneficial for achieving entrepreneurial sustainability through utilizing low-emission investments (Bhattacharjee & Jahanshahi, 2021). Applying ALS, firms can gain competitive advantages with the emission funds i.e., building used water purification systems and waste disposal plants with alliance based rather than a single project. The alliance based large project will reduce both the *fixed costs* and *variable costs* with excess burdens for each firm. Other green strategic approaches would be '*time block strategy*' for the commercial or renewable energy distribution sector, and '*cost-leadership*' in the long run after the green technological transformation period.

Many micro, small and medium enterprises (MSMEs) can alliance together to establish low-carbon renewable energy systems e.g., eco-solar plants and biogas plants. The energy supplying system needs to be built with blockchain technology to reduce the energy transmission loss and efficient energy supply with costs. The produced energy will be shared between firms in the alliance group. In Japan and Australia, many industrial/urban areas have started using this strategy to implement low-carbon energy supply. Another example of emission investments, CO_2 emission free fuel cell technology developed by Japan that is specifically designed for household purposes. This eco-friendly energy generation product has been named as '*ENE-FARM TYPE S*'.

Challenges of Climate Finance

Even though climate finance has been flourishing in the developed countries, it would be challenging to implement the low-carbon industrial development successfully in the developing or underdeveloped regions. One of the conflicting challenges for climate finance is the geopolitical friction (*e. g., Cold regional conflict*) between the regions (Geddes et al., 2020). The most critical challenges of climate finance (CF) are COVID-19 pandemic, equal distribution, cold regional conflicts, and systematic monetary loss. They are followings:

COVID-19 Pandemic

The *COVID-19* pandemic has changed the economic and social networking system that is affecting vastly in the global climate friendly investments. The additional government expenses for eradicating pandemic losses have claimed a large amount of reserved government funds globally. This pandemic causes a surge in the economic constraints in many countries, but on the other side, it develops the virtualization necessity in the business. Although many obligations due to the COVID-19 pandemic have been withdrawn, the ongoing pandemic recovery is still wiping out lots of money (i. e., expenses for the COVID-19 vaccinations). Therefore, many countries including developing countries may not have sufficient funding for climate financing.

Equal Distribution

Next challenge might be the equal distribution of climate financing in all regions at the same time. As the accumulated amount of concessional liquidity of CF may not reach a sufficient level yet because of the volunteer participation and few CF policy friendly members but the hope is it's growing. Therefore, the unexpected equal distribution challenge may have in the establishing low carbon technologies (for example blockchain and artificial intelligence-based energy distribution networking system, blockchain framework supply-chain with IoT facilities, eco-friendly transportation system with IoT and sufficient renewable energy generation plants) in few regions (Geddes et al., 2020). To reach the global climate friendly low emission target, the climate finance should go for high priority regions (e.g., West African region, Southern Salamat region and South Asian region) rather than developed regions.

Cold Regional Conflicts

The emerging cold conflicting situation between different regions would literally increase the competitive barriers in equal distribution of natural resources (e.g., natural gas and oil). Many early decisions have come to be implemented in immature situations because of cold conflicts. This issue may therefore impact the successful implementation of the Paris climate friendly targets.

Systematic Monetary Loss

To build the low CO_2 emission industrial setups, the existing infrastructure with less than 50% depreciation may have to be renovated or demolished. Therefore, if a project needs renovation or demolition or completely new constructions then it will highly increase systematic monetary or asset losses in many low CO_2 industrial developments. This problem will develop difficulty to implement low-emission renovation and new establishments in the developing countries where newly industrial infrastructures are developing.

Green Development Themes

This part demonstrates several proposed climate-friendly green development themes (i. e., hybrid green energy home, hybrid green city and industrial layout, hybrid low-emission agriculture farm), in which international and domestic CF funds can be invested to reduce the global GHG emission (e. g., CO_2) in industry 5.0. This type of climate friendly green development themes will enhance sustainable low carbon economic and environmental developments globally.

Hybrid Green Energy Home

Figure 4 demonstrates the proposed model of hybrid green energy home (HGE home). This type of HGE home would be climate friendly because of the low CO_2 emission system. The energy source of this home is divided into two different types, direct energy source (e. g., commercial electricity) and renewable energy source (e. g., *photovoltaic power-generation technology, waste heat-fuel cell system*). Both energy sources are installed with heat resistant systems to reduce residential heat or CO2. As seen in Figure 4, the red color wired directions show the energy supply from the eco-friendly low-carbon residential photovoltaic power-generation (*solar energy systems*) while the black color wire indicates the energy flows from commercial electricity. The solar energy system should have to be installed based on fulfilling 50% of the daily energy consumptions in the *home* and *electric vehicle charging*. To improve the energy utilization, the waste energy or biogas residential plant can be used. The smart LED lighting with low heat transmitting facility device decreases the residential heat and low consumption of energy. Furthermore, eco-friendly electric cars would be the time worthy investment in the future to reduce carbon emission. Thus, investing in hybrid green energy homes would have a competitive advantage to decrease residential carbon emission.

Figure 4. Proposed model of hybrid green energy home
Source: Author's elaboration.

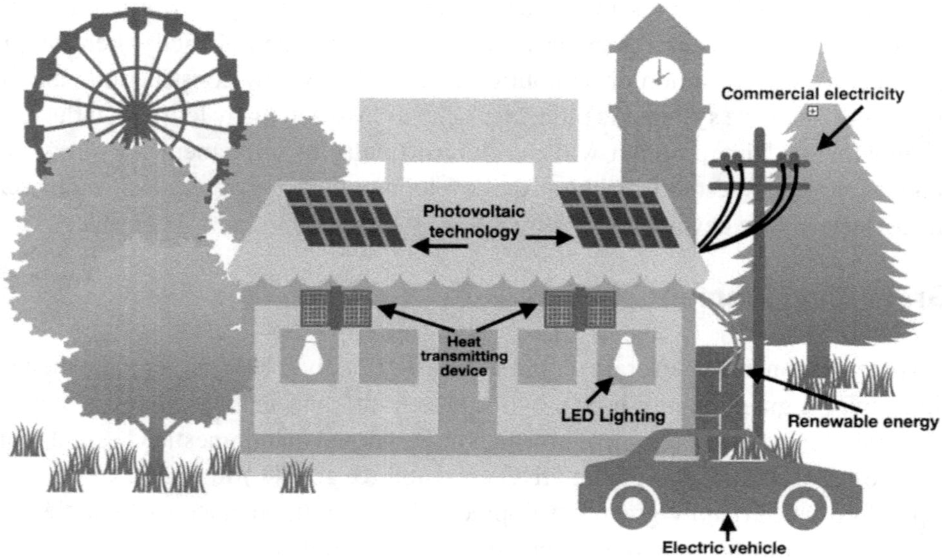

Hybrid Green City and Industrial Layout

The hybrid green city and industrial layout (HGCI layout) is the second climate friendly proposed model. Figure 5 shows the detailed architecture of HGCI layout. According to the hybrid green city and industrial layout, it suggests that the energy distribution system should use blockchain and artificial intelligence-based technologies for increasing sustainability as well as low emission facilities. Secondly, renewable energy sources (i. e., *Photovoltaic power-generation technology, Wind power-generation technology*) should have to be established to supply energy in the selected areas during the specific time blocks. For example, in a specific industrial zone, all firms use *renewable energy* for office lighting, heating, and cooling systems. Another example, all residential outdoor lightings and street lightings of a hybrid smart city should use the renewable energy system from 6:30 PM to 5:30 AM. Therefore, every area should be connected to both the '*commercial electricity*' supplying network and *renewable energy* supplying network. Furthermore, every hybrid smart zone should have a '*hybrid heating & cooling system*', and one or more '*cogeneration system*' regardless of the city area or the industrial area. The *electric vehicle charging station* should have both renewable & commercial energy sources to reduce utility costs.

Figure 5. Proposed model of hybrid green city and industrial layout
Source: Author's elaboration.

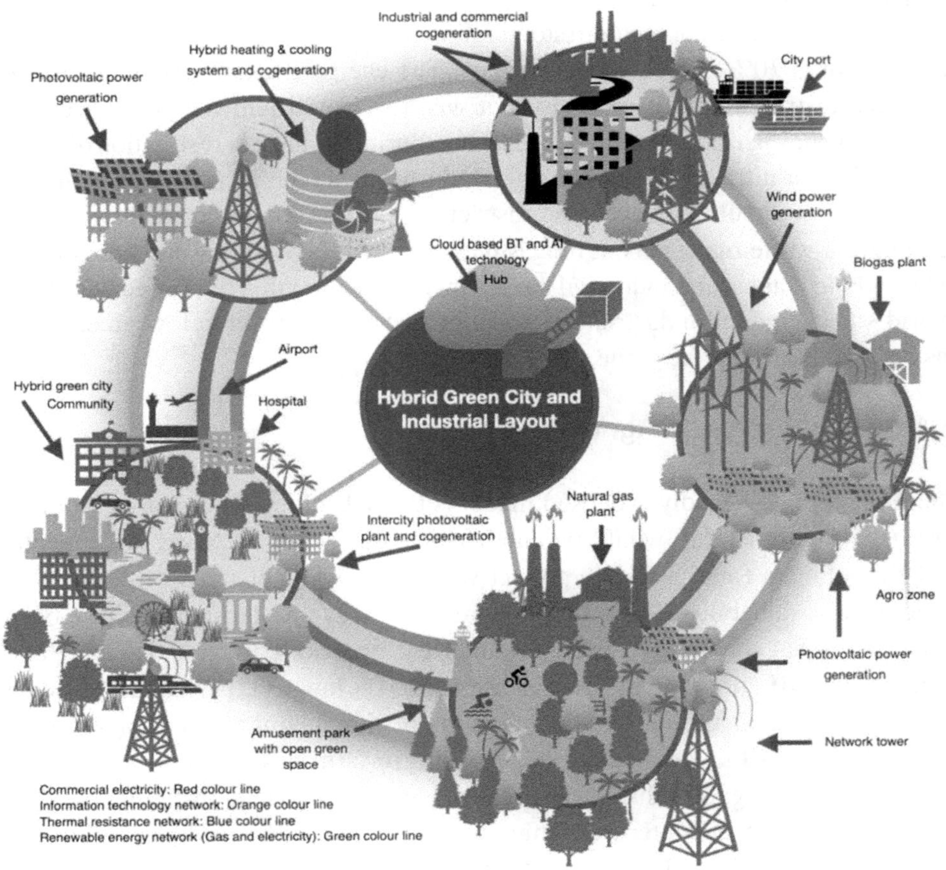

In the hybrid smart zone (city or industrial area), the networking channels should be divided into four different networking systems: information or data networking channel, renewable energy networking channel, commercial electricity networking channel and thermal-resistant networking channel. After that the consumption level of energy should be specified based on the using purposes. For example, the residence area should have a maximum 50% commercial electricity supply and minimum 50% renewable energy supply. Similarly, the amusement park and shopping malls should have a maximum 30% commercial electricity supply and minimum 70% renewable energy supply. In the industrial area, each factory should have 40% renewable energy backup with 60% (can be increased up to 70%) commercial electricity supply.

Daylight working organizations (meaning working hours during the day only or open in the morning and closed by early evening i. e., schools, training institutions, different offices, small or medium stores) should use 80% renewable energy sources and maximum 30% commercial electricity. The energy backup system should be developed district wise rather than division wise that would help to supply electricity in an emergency period (e. g., sudden blackout, during damage or restoration of a city energy plant or infrastructure). Next, the industrial and commercial '*cogeneration infrastructure*' should be developed district wise. Furthermore, each hybrid zone must have a waste management biogas plant that will be used to supply green gas to household's areas and industrial areas. So, establishing this type of eco-friendly hybrid smart city and industrial zone would sustainably develop low greenhouse gas emissions around the globe.

Hybrid Low Emission Agriculture Farm

The third climate friendly proposed model is the hybrid low emission agriculture farm (see Figure 6) that would be another precious scope of green investments. Utilizing climate finance in this project would bring lots of fresh revenues with ecological sustainability. Since long before the energy and technology have been using traditional way in the agriculture industry, especially in the developing and underdeveloped regions (e. g., Africa, South Asia). The low-CO2 agriculture farm can develop by investing the concessional liquidity of climate finance in the agriculture sector. The low CO2 architecture of hybrid agro farm has four major segments such as landscaping, establishing the renewable energy source, installing the data networking system, and internet of things applications (IoTA). By landscaping, the farming land should be a large area rather than a small area. If there are many small size individuals farming lands, then two or more farming houses need to connect each other to implement the hybrid facilities. Developing a hybrid agriculture networking system, every farm in a large area can access the facilities. In the hybrid low-carbon agriculture farm, firstly need to develop renewable electricity and gas sources.

Figure 6. Proposed model of hybrid low-emission agriculture farm
Source: Author's elaboration.

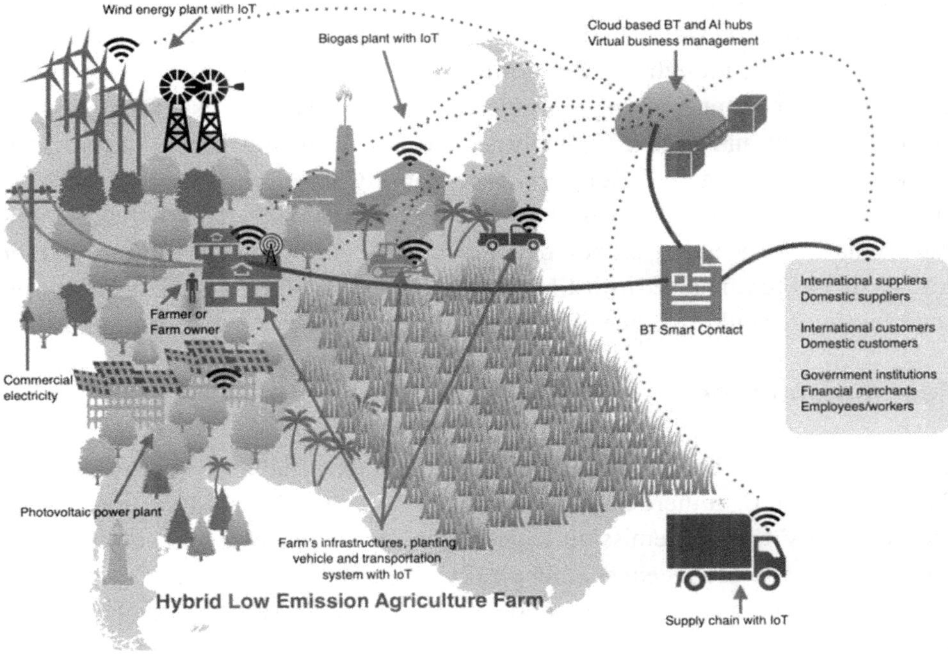

The renewable electricity source refers to the green energy generation plants (i. e., photovoltaic power-generation technology, wind power-generation technology) and renewable gas source depicts the biogas plant. In the small farming-land, photovoltaic energy generation would be worthwhile, but biogas plants can develop in any type of land. So, one portion of the agricultural land needs to be used for green energy setup and another side for biogas. It should be considered that the green energy production must meet the daily need including *electric vehicle charging facility*. If a firm uses 200kWh then the energy generation plant should be installed for a minimum 220kWh (200 + 10% extra) basis. This hybrid agro farm also has commercial electricity supply but not more than 30% of daily consumption. Next, the biogas plant should develop for managing waste of the farm and residential sources. By data networking setup, blockchain and artificial intelligence technologies should be used to make automated data communication systems and include internet of things application (IoTA) facilities with farm's infrastructures, planting vehicles, energy distribution system, and product supplying vehicles. The farmer or farm owner uses this system to maintain communication with suppliers and customers, virtual business, supplying goods, virtual transactions (M2M system), and weather forecasting.

The highly efficient BT based smart contact system should be built to enhance better real time communication systems. In every division, one agro research house should have to develop for providing the soil, weather, planting related information and green innovation facilities. The divisional agriculture research house will have direct connection (through IoTA system) with all agro farms in the division. In the farm, the water pump running activities, security survey lenses, flooding alert, earthquake alarm and electricity supply network should use blockchain and artificial intelligence technologies for long-run sustainability. The farm owner should have IoT facilities to ensure an eco-friendly and real time supply chain that eliminates intermediaries. Receiving orders, delivery trucks, green energy grid and indoor devices should be connected by IoT facilities. This eco-friendly architecture of hybrid low emission agriculture farm will reduce the greenhouse gas-emission remarkably.

Recommendations

Any prosperity may be shining through overcoming the challenges. If the potential challenges exist, then there may be solutions too but need to find the appropriate ones. Similarly, the zero-emission target of the Paris climate agreement may need to medicate potential challenges strategically to achieve sustainable outcomes in the industry 4.0 or industry 5.0. Here, based on the potential barriers of technological improvements and climate finance, some strategic recommendations have been demonstrated to make the climate finance sustainable with the climate friendly technological developments globally. In the high priority sector (e. g., energy sector), the sufficient concessional funds of climate finance should go for sustainable green energy generation plants developments in every region. Then, the climate friendly financing should increase in the poorest regions (i. e., Chad and Burkina Faso) where institutional voids exist as well as costly developments that are impossible to establish by the regional monetary sources.

In the developed and developing countries, domestic level climate financing should be arranged around 60% funds of the necessary developments by public and private sources of the country while the rest of the amount should be supported by the reserve of the global climate finance. The business technologies have been changing to automation and virtual business systems by blockchain and artificial intelligence applications that enormously decreases the physical labor but the potential unemployment problem would be short-term basis. The employment opportunities will be increased with the adoption of blockchain and artificial intelligence (AI) technologies in the long term. Therefore, the direct and indirect subsidiaries of AI-based technologies should be extended as much as possible. This process will let the employed people in the job and new employment opportunities for fresh candidates. Furthermore, the CF policy implication should have to follow some strategies to avoid future uncertainties in the global employment sector. The competitive strategic drive such as applying artificial landscape strategy in the climate financing will significantly improve the assets utilizing the alliance.

Using IoTA (internet of things application) will decrease the data sensing complexity. The IoTA has been newly introduced but its efficiency is extremely high to manage complex data processing within BT and AI based networking systems. In the manufacturing sector, climate finance should invest in developing a *climate resilient manufacturing system* to decline carbon emissions. Using technology such as artificial intelligence applications can increase the technological sustainability and reduce both fixed & variable costs of the firms.

The financial transaction in the virtual business is a critical process that requires safety and financial merchants. Around the world, there are many emerging business places where the financial merchants may not be available yet that creates institutional voids for the firms operating in those places. To overcome such void, firms can use the M2M transaction system because any financial transactions by M2M doesn't need any intermediator. Thus, firms having financial merchant's problems would achieve competitive advantages in the virtual economic market.

By the sustainable energy distribution system, the time block strategy would be beneficial for the developing and underdeveloped regions. Climate friendly technologies have already progressed in the developed nations, but developing and poorest regions are still behind. So, the richest nations having competitive advantages in the low carbon technological developments should bring to developing and underdeveloped countries. Thus, the global zero emission targets and climate friendly industrial revolution will be successful and sustainable in the future world.

Implications

This chapter reiterates significance of the climate friendly technological and financial aspects for a sustainable low-emission economic and industrial development in the 4IR and forthcoming industrial revolutions (e.g., 5IR). Admittedly, *by 'implications for academia'*, the climate friendly technological demonstrations of this chapter would unfold benefits for the professionals in the academia, especially researchers may find excellent research scopes on low-emission industrial technological and architectural innovations in the 5IR. Additionally, the detailed elucidation of climate financing for green technological developments would provide the construct execution idea of green environmental improvements (i. e., climate financing for numerous low-CO2 emission prospects, blockchain and artificial intelligence-based green technologies) to academic practitioners and students. However, *by 'green economic and technological implications'*, at the industrial level, business entrepreneurial, managerial, governmental, and non-governmental policy makers will be benefited by following the eco-friendly directions, such as developing the climate friendly hybrid smart zone system for long-run economic and green environmental sustainability.

Hybrid green smart zone indicates low-emission design and facilities rather than geographical scope. Therefore, hybrid green facilities can be established in a small area or large area and even at a firm level. Similarly, investors, nascent entrepreneurs, established entrepreneurs and business managers would gain competitive advantages by adopting the low-emission technologies and green investment concerns (e. g., green manufacturing system, eco-friendly supply chain system) with strategic drives while public and private level monetary support for climate finance excels the green investments (e. g., funding for renewable energy generation, green city and industrial developments) at the country level and firm level.

In the agriculture industry, farmers and farming owners will achieve green sustainability by adopting renewable energy generation systems, blockchain and IoTA based networking systems. Establishing these green facilities will significantly reduce variable costs in the short-term and fixed costs in the long-term. As a result, any agro farm with hybrid low emission facilities will gain cost leadership advantage with higher revenues. The renewable energy generation and intercity cogeneration sectors should use blockchain and AI based applications to reduce costs and increase expected efficiency. Furthermore, climate friendly green development themes would encourage developers to build green city and industrial developments.

Finally, this chapter articulately addresses the emerging necessities of reforming industrial and business practices with different innovative green project themes. The idea and architecture of hybrid green city and industrial developments, hybrid green energy home, hybrid agriculture system will therefore provide practical sense guidance for green environmental and low-carbon economic sustainability in the fifth-grade industrial revolution (5IR).

CONCLUSION

This chapter elucidates the sustainable green phenomenon as "the synthesis of green technologies (e.g., *blockchain and AI*) and green investments (e.g., *climate financing*)". The concessional funds of climate financing and climate friendly blockchain & AI technological developments are yet insufficient for the 4IR and forthcoming industrial revolution i. e., 5IR. Many countries except developed nations have been struggling for eco-friendly technological adoption due to the initial bulk amount of costs. In this phenomenon, climate finance (CF) policy raises the bright sunshine for all but still has noteworthy debates regarding the equal opportunity of climate financing in the 4IR & 5IR. Therefore, this chapter discusses the wide range of promising techniques of green financing and green technological developments in the different perspectives in the 4IR & 5IR.

Nevertheless, emphasizing on industrial modernizing only won't be sustainable if it increases high risk of emission 5IR. Similarly, forced digitalization in the traditional way won't be effective because of existing risk friendly targets. To overcome these challenges, the narrative demonstrations of this chapter on blockchain, artificial intelligence and climate finance policy would be beneficial for achieving sustainable low-carbon economic, technological, and green environmental developments around the world. In addition, the practical sense recommendations will provide strategic opportunities in the actual execution stages of green financing (i. e., climate financing, low-emission investments) and green industrial technological prospects (i. e., blockchain and AI) in the 4IR as well as 5IR.

Finally, by strategic orientation, applying artificial landscape strategy, time block strategy will significantly reduce opportunity costs and potential reformation loss in the green business practices or legacy period. However, the distribution of climate finance among developed, developing, and under-developed countries for climate friendly developments (e.g., renewable energy generation, green transportation, hybrid green city & industrial zone, hybrid low-emission agriculture system, green manufacturing, green finance, blockchain and artificial intelligence based eco-friendly technologies) should go with equal priority basis rather than inequality. Only then the vision of low carbon industrial and economic developments may come true, where *green society and green business practices begin with a sustainable green environment*. Thus, a peaceful, and green world may enjoy the green sustainable growth forever.

REFERENCES

Bhattacharjee, A., & Jahanshahi, A. A. (2021). Artificial landscape strategy: A business growth recovery plan in the post pandemic world. *Academia Letters*. Advance online publication. doi:10.20935/AL2311

Buchner, B., Clark, A., Falconer, A., Macquarie, R., Meattle, C., & Wetherbee, C. (2019). *Global landscape of climate finance 2019*. http://119.78.100.173/C666/handle/2XK7JSWQ/242591

Di Vaio, A., Palladino, R., Hassan, R., & Escobar, O. (2020). Artificial intelligence and business models in the sustainable development goals perspective: A systematic literature review. *Journal of Business Research*, *121*, 283–314. doi:10.1016/j.jbusres.2020.08.019

Ebekozien, A., Aigbavboa, C., & Samsurijan, M. S. (2022). An appraisal of blockchain technology relevance in the 21st century Nigerian construction industry: perspective from the built environment professionals. *Journal of Global Operations and Strategic Sourcing*. doi:10.1108/JGOSS-01-2022-0005

French, A., Shim, J. P., Risius, M., Larsen, K. R., & Jain, H. (2021). The 4th Industrial Revolution powered by the integration of AI, blockchain, and 5G. *Communications of the Association for Information Systems*, *49*(1), 6. doi:10.17705/1CAIS.04910

Geddes, A., Schmid, N., Schmidt, T. S., & Steffen, B. (2020). The politics of climate finance: Consensus and partisanship in designing green state investment banks in the United Kingdom and Australia. *Energy Research & Social Science*, *69*, 101583. doi:10.1016/j.erss.2020.101583

Giglio, S., Kelly, B., & Stroebel, J. (2021). Climate finance. *Annual Review of Financial Economics*, *13*(1), 15–36. doi:10.1146/annurev-financial-102620-103311

Jahanshahi, A. A., Bhattacharjee, A., & Maghsoudi, T. (2021). Internal capabilities as the source of achieving competitive advantage in small-sized businesses. *International Journal of Business Innovation and Research*, *26*(2), 141–162. doi:10.1504/IJBIR.2021.118446

Jones, M. L. (2004). Application of systematic review methods to qualitative research: Practical issues. *Journal of Advanced Nursing*, *48*(3), 271–278. doi:10.1111/j.1365-2648.2004.03196.x PMID:15488041

Kouwenberg, R., & Zheng, C. (2023). A Review of the Global Climate Finance Literature. *Sustainability*, *15*(2), 1255. doi:10.3390u15021255

Leal Filho, W., Wall, T., Mucova, S. A. R., Nagy, G. J., Balogun, A. L., Luetz, J. M., ... Gandhi, O. (2022). Deploying artificial intelligence for climate change adaptation. *Technological Forecasting and Social Change*, *180*, 121662. doi:10.1016/j.techfore.2022.121662

Loureiro, S. M. C., Guerreiro, J., & Tussyadiah, I. (2021). Artificial intelligence in business: State of the art and future research agenda. *Journal of Business Research*, *129*, 911–926. doi:10.1016/j.jbusres.2020.11.001

Qerimi, Q., & Sergi, B. S. (2022). The case for global regulation of carbon capture and storage and artificial intelligence for climate change. *International Journal of Greenhouse Gas Control*, *120*, 103757. doi:10.1016/j.ijggc.2022.103757

Schulz, K., & Feist, M. (2021). Leveraging blockchain technology for innovative climate finance under the Green Climate Fund. *Earth System Governance*, *7*, 100084. doi:10.1016/j.esg.2020.100084

KEY TERMS AND DEFINITIONS

Concessional Liquidity: Concessional liquidity means the accumulated funds that are used to support the climate friendly economic developments around the world.

Daylight Working Organization: This term describes how the firm or organization operates its business operations (e. g., office activity hours,) during the '*daylight period or sunlight hours*' for example the office working schedule of ABC company is from morning 8:00 AM to evening 5:00 PM. Another example, the working hour of a training center is from morning to noon.

Domestic Climate Finance (DCF): The fund of climate friendly developments accumulated by the public and private sources of the country is defined as the domestic climate finance in this chapter. Domestic climate finance (DCF) mostly supports the low-CO2 emission projects within the country only.

Existing Market Rate of Interest: The existing market rate of interest indicates the present interest rate on loan amount in the financial market (e.g., interest rate on bank loan).

Fixed Cost: In this chapter, the fixed cost term is used to define the different long term assets costs of the climate friendly project or new developments. Fixed cost refers to the expenses on any long-term assets purchase or developments (e. g., land purchases, green technology purchase). This cost will never change within a year or more than a year for example, land or office rent.

Global Climate Finance: After the Paris climate agreement, the government level parties of developed countries formally formed new concessional funding sources for financing climate friendly improvements around the world. This formation of climate finance is defined as the global climate finance in this chapter. In other words, when two or more countries jointly form a source of fund only for climate friendly investments is also called the global climate finance (GCF). For example, the U.S., Paris, Japan, Canada, and Australia are unitedly forming a global climate finance to support low carbon economies in the world.

IoTA: The internet of things application (IoTA) is a completely automated sensor-based networking system that enables real time data communication using the blockchain and artificial intelligence technologies. In this chapter, IoTA application is used to develop BT and AI based hybrid technologies in different sectors, for example the energy distribution system, hybrid agriculture system.

Low Carbon Economy: The economic development causes zero or low greenhouse gas emission around the world affirms the low carbon economy. Any eco-friendly investment is part of a low carbon economy. At present the large number of high-tech industrial technologies emit high carbon in the air that causes global warming. Therefore, the present financial market is a high-carbon economy. The high-risk CO2 emission has been gradually destroying the climate harmony that needs to be reduced as soon as possible through taking effective measures. In this mechanism, the new industrial or business developments must follow eco-friendly measures. So, the forthcoming economic development will reduce the CO2 emission at zero or low level that is called the low-carbon economy.

M2M Transaction: The term M2M is basically the transaction between machines or system devices. The information of e-transaction can be done easily by using the M2M (machine to machine) autonomous system. This technology reduces the transaction costs by eliminating intermediaries and time.

Variable Cost: The accounting term variable cost is used to explain the schedule expenses of the project in the chapter. This cost changes regularly or less than a year (i.e., energy expenses because this cost will increase or decrease depending on the energy used).

Chapter 5
The New Architecture of Smart Contracts and Its Impact on Performance, Vulnerability, Pollution, and Energy Saving

Rinat Galiautdinov
https://orcid.org/0000-0001-9557-5250
Independent Researcher, Italy

ABSTRACT

The main purpose of the research is to provide a solution that can resolve the well-known issues in the current smart contract concept and fully change the architecture used in smart contracts and blockchain. For this purpose, the author lists the issues, analyzes them, and provides the solution explaining how it will change the situation and what kind of positive impact it will have not only on the performance of smart contracts and their extensibility but also the impact on pollution and saving of energy.

INTRODUCTION

During over 10 years blockchain is known as a technology which is used as distributed database (Bernstein & Lange, 2016) which keeps the track of financial transactions of different types of cryptocurencies (Brown, 2016), such as BTC, ETH, etc. All the payments or financial transactions go via P2P (peer –to- peer) network which allows to decentralized the participants of the network granting them equal, from the network point of view, privileges and consequently such the network architecture is different from a regular client-server architecture where all the clients depend on

DOI: 10.4018/978-1-6684-8361-9.ch005

the server: in the other words, if server is down then no client can connect to it and consequently make any type of transaction (Heuvel, 2014).

Bitcoin officially was the first globally known crypto-currency, although the very first one appeared in the beginning of 90s (Li et al., 2017). The Bitcoin blockchain contains only financial transactions and nothing else. The second well known cryptocurrency in this sphere was ETH which additionally introduced the term "smart contracts" into the blockchain world. A smart contract can be considered as a small program running on a blockchain when it receives a request (Nguyen, 2019). With the help of smart contracts the users could add additional logic not only to the financially related logic but also create very primitive games. At the same time, from the technical prospective, a smart contract is considered as a user who can receive and send transactions. This "user" has a record of different states, also known as variables and these variables stored in a blockchain can be changed and/or read. Reading a blockchain data is free for the users (however is still very slow) however the change of variables (also called as a state change) is expensive (Zhang Rong, 2020). Every state change consumes funds (in Ether world known as gas), it also consumes quite a lot of time necessary for: a) making a transaction (a request for a state change), b) for processing such the transaction c) for building a transaction block which contains a new value for a smart contract. Thus in the Ether world, before the hard fork, the time for building a new block was 21 seconds, after the hard fork it still takes 12.5 seconds which is a lot in the world of IT (Mkrttchian et al., 2019).

An example of a smart contract could be a piece of code (a smart contract) which verifies that both parties of some deal successfully committed their obligations (Nofer et al., 2017), as an example: a buyer sent a transaction and a seller sent a purchased item. Another example of a smart contract from the gaming sphere could be some piece of code (a smart contract) within the gambling sphere: the players make the bets and a smart contract(the code) "runs the roulette" and selects a winner after which the smart contract sends the won funds to the account of the winner. A smart contract could also be used in the other spheres more related to the government (Kongmanee et al., 2019), for example it could be used for different types of elections or collection of different types of opinions, etc. However here we can note that the role of an intermediate judge in the payment process can be done by any of the existing third-party organizations; with regards to the games: the power and ability of the smart contracts are enough only for extremely primitive games; and no government will ever use honest and controlled smart contracts for elections.

Smart contracts are also subjected to attacks, so in 2016 when the Decentralized Autonomous Organization (DAO) smart contract was manipulated to steal around 2 Million ETH (50 Million USD on the time) because of its re-entrancy vulnerability

(Tasca Paolo, 2019). In addition to the vulnerability problem, smart contracts face several challenges including privacy, legal, and performance issues.

Below is one of the examples of re-entrancy attacks on a smart contract:

```
// SPDX-License-Identifier: MIT
pragma solidity ^0.8.0;
contract Auction {
    mapping(address => uint) public bidders;
    bool locked;
    function bid() external payable {
        bidders[msg.sender] += msg.value;
    }
    function refund() external {
        uint refundAmount = bidders[msg.sender];
        if (refundAmount > 0) {
            (bool success,) = msg.sender.call{value:
refundAmount}("");
            require(success, "failed!");
            bidders[msg.sender] = 0;
        }
    }
    function currentBalance() external view returns(uint) {
        return address(this).balance;
    }
}
```

From the first glance at the smart contract the refund method has to get the value of the funds of a user and send him back his funds: (bool success,) = msg.sender. call{value: refundAmount}("");

After which the line bidders[msg.sender] = 0; marks that his current balance is 0.

And it seems to be ok and it was a regular application (not a smart contract of Etherium) it would work fine. But not in the world of Etherium.

Below is another smart contract which makes a re-entrancy attack on the Auction contract:

```
contract AuctionAttack {
    uint constant BID_AMOUNT = 1 ether;
    AuctionHacked auction;
    constructor(address _auction) {
        auction = AuctionHacked(_auction);
```

```
    }
    function proxyBid() external payable {
        require(msg.value == BID_AMOUNT, "incorrect");
        auction.bid{value: msg.value}();
    }
    function attack() external {
        auction.refund();
    }
    receive() external payable {
        if(auction.currentBalance() >= BID_AMOUNT) {
            auction.refund();
        }
    }
    function currentBalance() external view returns(uint) {
        return address(this).balance;
    }
}
```

What happens here is: an intruder first calls for a proxyBid() function to send some funds to the Action contract. Then the Action contract will receive this money and will make a record that a new user made a bid equal to some amount of the money. But then intruder calls for a attack() function which automatically calls a refund() function of the Action smart contract. The Action smart contract checks whether the user has the funds (yes) and tries to send them: (bool success,) = msg. sender.call{value: refundAmount}(""); However in the world of smart contract of Etherium instead of making an update on the user's record making it 0, it will run the receive() function of an intruder which contains another request for the Action smart contract: action.refund() and as a result, the intruder will get all the money possessed by Auction smart contract.

This attack can be avoided if we make some changes in the Action smart contract:

```
    modifier noReentrancy() {
        require(!locked, "no reentrancy!");
        locked = true;
        _;
        locked = false;
    }
    function refund() external noReentrancy {
        uint refundAmount = bidders[msg.sender];
        if (refundAmount > 0) {
```

```
            bidders[msg.sender] = 0;
            (bool success,) = msg.sender.call{value:
refundAmount}("");
            require(success, "failed!");
        }
    }
```

However it's not obvious for the developers who came into the smart contracts world from the other spheres of software development.

However the problems with smart contracts are not limited by different types of attacks. Smart contracts have too many limitations which dramatically reduce their potential. Additionally to this smart contracts now are considered as a part of a payment system (for example in ETH blockchain) which is logically incorrect because logic on how exactly to process any financial transaction should have nothing to do with the blockchain where it stores the data. The current architecture negatively reflects on pollution, the cost of transaction, energy cost and all this could be easily changed. And speaking of pollution the problem is obvious: the calculation of some simple and primitive things using smart contract in its current architecture consumes lots of computing resources not only from the viewpoint of calculation (the calculation on a blockchain is more expensive than calculation on a local machine) but also from the viewpoint of a miner/miners which consume(s) lots of electricity and it means that consuming lots of electricity effects on consumption of more oil/gas to produce this electricity and as a final result it leads to consumption of much more of non-renewable natural resources and also it leads to extra pollution of nature on all the stages of the technology process.

Literature Review

This work is related to several crucial problems in smart contract world and includes the following aspects: the efficient work of smart contracts, the competition of smart contracts with the other software programs running on the servers, the computing infrastructure of smart contracts vs the infrastructure of the other software programs running on the servers (Chohan, 2022), the computer languages used in smart contract development (as an instrument of making them more efficient), the influence on natural environment and pollution. And there is no article which covers it all. There are multiple articles which explain the difference between pros and cons of Proof of Stake and Proof or Work (Rouhani S., 2019), there are some articles related to pros and cons of different computer languages used in the different blockchains, but there is no article which provides solution or suggests the ways to resolve the number of issues related to smart contracts which could make them comparable with the centralized apps running on the servers, and there is no article which shows the negative aspects of how smart contracts and miners effect on the pollution of natural environment.

Although there are some articles which make a simple comparison of smart contracts vs centralized apps. This comparison is obvious and it does not really makes sense to dive into its details.

There are some works (Sreehari et al. 2017) which compare Ethereum, IBM Open Blockchain (Hyperledger project), Intel Sawtooth lake, BlockStream Sidechain Elements and Eris platforms. This study suggests Ethereum to be the primary choice of platform in terms of scalability, development, documentation and maintenance. As Intel Sawtooth Lake wasn't fully implemented at the time, the authors come to conclusion that Ethereum is a better solution for developers as it has no security issues known at the time.

In another work (Wang et al., 2021) the authors analyze the usage of smart contracts platforms from various perspectives. The study examines a sample of 6 smart contract platforms such as Bitcoin, Ethereum, Counterparty, Stellar, Monax and Lisk and highlights some of the key differences in terms of blockchain types, smart contract language and volume of daily values transfers. A sample of 834contracts was studied for the 2 platforms — Bitcoin and Ethereum, categorizing each of them by application domain, and measuring the relevance of each of these categories.

They concluded that about 80% of the Ethereum contracts use at least one of the nine design patterns presented in the paper. There are also listed several assessments related to the principals of works that study different blockchain technologies. So Anderson compared three types of blockchains: Ethereum, Namecoin, and Peercoin. For Ethereum, the author analyzed the problems which were introduced by the negligent design of smart contracts. In the case of Namecoin the focus was on the name registration which was used and had developed over time. For Peercoin the focus was on the use of proof-of-stake. Similarly, Fahad (2021) compared a variety of smart contract platforms. The work offers an overview of the scripting languages used in blockchains, particularly scripting languages used in Bitcoin scripts, Nxt and Ethereum. The study covers technologies which might be used to underpin extensions and innovations in scripting and contracts, including technologies for verification (e.g., zero-knowledge proofs, proof-carrying code and static analysis), as well as approaches to making systems more efficient, e.g., Merkelized Abstract Syntax Trees. The works which analyze the security of Ethereum smart contracts have been growing a lot during the last period of time.

Another very important aspect is the influence of miners and consequently the smart contracts on the pollution of natural environment.

Though skeptics may characterize cryptocurrency as "fake money", it is a very real business. The market capitalization of almost 19,000 cryptocurrencies in circulation is currently around $1.75 trillion.

But crypto has a huge negative effect on the real world: it uses a lot of energy. For example, Bitcoin currently consumes an estimated 150 terawatt-hours of electricity annually—more than the entire country of Argentina, population 45 million. Producing that energy emits some 65 megatons of carbon dioxide into the atmosphere annually—comparable to the emissions of Greece—making crypto a significant contributor to global air pollution and climate change.

"Bitcoin mining operations are in an arms race between time, the volume of miners, and the efficiency of the machines they use," said Joshua D. Rhodes of the Center on Global Energy Policy. "When it comes to Bitcoin's energy use, it's currently something of a 'wildcatter' market. The Texas grid operator ERCOT estimates that crypto miners may increase energy demand by up to 6 gigawatts by mid-2023, roughly the equivalent of adding another Houston to the grid."

As Bitcoin mining increasingly comes under fire for its growing energy use, the phenomenon may be approaching a tipping point where, in order to prove to be a true game changer, crypto will need to come clean and go green.

Today, Bitcoin mining is a highly competitive business, with sprawling, climate-controlled facilities that house tens of thousands of high-tech computers operating around the clock.

However China's crackdown on digital currencies appears to have made crypto mining even dirtier. Some mining operations in China had reduced their carbon emissions by taking advantage of cheap and abundant hydropower—a renewable energy source—during the rainy season. But after China's crackdown, the share of natural gas used in Bitcoin's electricity mix doubled to 31%. And Kazakhstan, now the world's second largest Bitcoin hub, gets about 50% of its energy from high-emissions coal-powered plants. Soon the first place in this "competition" might take Russia where all types of pollution control in fact have been cancelled, as an example they allow engine standards of Euro 0 for the cars now due to the sanctions, but the Earth is for everyone so eventually it will have a negative effect on the whole planet.

Perhaps even more concerning, some companies in the U.S. are now bringing retired power plants back online in order to cash in on crypto. Greenidge Generation, a natural gas-powered Bitcoin mining plant in the picturesque Finger Lakes region of upstate New York, is a controversial example of this trend. Local groups point out that the plant not only pollutes the air, but also harms the Seneca Lake ecosystem by discharging up to 134 million gallons of hot water a day into New York's deepest glacial lake. More broadly, there are concerns the plant may be a canary in the crypto mine both for New York State and the nation.

Like other disruptive new technologies, cryptocurrency has caught governments unprepared and unsure how to regulate the explosive new market. Though Plattsburgh, NY became the first U.S. city to temporarily ban cryptocurrency mining in 2018, currently there is no federal legislation that specifically focuses on crypto mining. At the state level, the New York State Assembly passed a bill that would impose a two-year moratorium on energy-intensive proof-of-work cryptocurrency mining facilities that receive behind-the-meter power from fossil fuel power plants.

A corresponding bill currently awaits approval in the state Senate, where it faces fierce opposition from the crypto industry.

"Some of my research has shown that, if the mines are willing to be flexible, they can pair well with renewables by quickly adjusting their energy use depending on current grid conditions," said Rhodes. "However, it is not a given that they will do so. It is important for crypto mining to support the development of renewable (or other zero-carbon) energy because otherwise it will just be another industry contributing to the climate crisis."

Like other industries, the cryptocurrency space will face many challenges if it attempts to go green, such as acknowledging its impact on the environment, integrating truly sustainable practices (such as the proof-of-stake consensus mechanism) into its operations, and ultimately eschewing the pursuit of profit at any cost.

TECHNICAL PROBLEMS OF SMART CONTRACTS

The existing approach to the architecture of the smart contracts provides lots of disadvantages, such as:

- Slow speed
- Unable to horizontally scale
- Can't have multiple run time environment for the running Smart contracts
- SOLID
- Can't use external services, databases, etc.
- Expensive to run a smart-contract
- Very limited number of the operation inside of a contract
- Limited typess

Officially, the advantages of sand-box specify:

A smart contract can't be modified.

However, this is not fully true.

Since smart contracts in most cases (we all remember many cases where blockchains of ether and the other currencies were rolled back because it was not profitable for some of the groups) can't be modified (Almakhour et al., 2019), developers use a programming pattern which allows to switch between different versions of smart contracts. As an example, such the implementation could be done in the following way:

```
 //SPDX-License-Identifier:MIT
pragma solidity ^0.8.13;
contract Proxy {
    address public implementation;
    uint public x;
    function setImplementation(address _imp) external {
        implementation = _imp;
    }
    receive() external payable {
    }
    function _delegate(address _imp) internal virtual {
        assembly {
            calldatacopy(0, 0, calldatasize())
            let result:= delegatecall(gas(), _imp, 0,
calldatasize(), 0, 0)
            returndatacopy(0, 0, returndatasize())
            switch result
            case 0 {
                revert(0, returndatasize())
            }
            default {
                return (0, returndatasize())
            }
        }
    }
    fallback() external payable {
        _delegate(implementation);
    }
}
contract V1 {
    address public implementation;
    uint public x;
    function inc() external {
            x+=1;
    }
```

```
    function enc() external pure returns (bytes memory) {
        return abi.encodeWithSelector(this.inc.selector);
    }
    function encX() external pure returns (bytes memory) {
        return abi.encodeWithSelector(this.x.selector);
    }
}
contract V2 {
    address public implementation;
    uint public x;
    function inc() external {
            x+=10;
    }
    function dec() external {
            x-=1;
    }
    function enc1() external pure returns (bytes memory) {
        return abi.encodeWithSelector(this.inc.selector);
    }
    function enc2() external pure returns (bytes memory) {
        return abi.encodeWithSelector(this.dec.selector);
    }
    function encX() external pure returns (bytes memory) {
        return abi.encodeWithSelector(this.x.selector);
    }
}
```

Are there other advantages of placing the smart contracts to blockchain? Highly likely the answer is No.

At the same time the list of disadvantages is quite big:

- Slow speed

A smart contract is running on a miner's machine and consequently is additionally limited by the speed of its computer.

- Unable to horizontally scale

A smart contract can't be horizontally scaled, which means a miner's machine can't create multiple instances of a smart contract to speed up its work and/or to accept multiple incoming requests. At the same time a smart contract can't be stateless (if it's doing something meaningful) and it also creates the additional issues because currently there is no way to split data from logic.

- Can't have multiple run time environment for the running smart contracts

A smart contract does not support a situation where multiple smart contracts run in their own (isolated) runtime environments

A smart contract does not support creation of a separate processes and/or even threads which eventually have a negative effect on smart contract's performance.

- SOLID

SOLID is a very well-known paradigm in software development where S stands for Single Responsibility, meaning that each service should be responsible only for its own business entity. However this approach should be applied to the crypto-currency sphere and it demonstrates that smart contracts should never be a part of blockchain.

- Can't use external services, databases, etc.

Smart contracts can't use any external services, databases, etc. and all this dramatically limits the abilities of smart contracts.

- Expensive to run a smart contract

One of the critical issue related to smart contracts is enclosed in the fact that consumer of a smart contract (meaning that consumer makes some operation which lead to the state change of a smart contract and consequently makes a transaction) has to pay for every operation and it reflects on the complexity of the smart contracts: you can't really apply quite complex and extended logic also because of this limitation.

- Very limited number of the operation inside of a contract

Smart contract charges coins for operations and by default have lots of limitations on the number of the cycles inside of a smart contract, the number of operations, etc. All this limits the abilities of smart contracts.

- Limited types

Smart contracts have quite limited list of the allowed types.

Thus, all these issues clearly demonstrate the poor side of smart contracts and the absence of any progress in this direction.

SOLUTION

Considering all such the issues we can come to conclusion that it's necessary to split smart contracts into 2 parts: the data and the services. In software development such the principal is used in several design patterns, for example in the Visitor pattern, where Visitor traverses the Data objects and performs some operations on them. The same is obviously required in the Smart Contract world: the contract should be split. However although this is a necessary part it's not the full solution (Galiautdinov & Mkrttchian, 2019a).

The next step in resolving the mentioned earlier issues related to smart contracts would be to get rid of smart contract logic from blockchain. This is a huge mistake and dead end from the technology prospective to store smart contract logic in blockchain (Galiautdinov & Mkrttchian, 2019b). The best option for this would be to store the logic in the cloud platforms, such as AWS, Azure, etc.

Finally, we can introduce the new terms for the new smart contracts and some features:

A smart contract from now could be one of the following 2 types: Data Contract, Service Contract.

A service contract should be stateless which means it could not contain any state which has to be stored inside of a service contract and consequently reflect on its logic: the result of this will lead to ability to horizontally scale such the service contract in order to process multiple requests simultaneously.

Doing so we'll allow to resolve the following issues:

- Slow speed

Smart contract will become fast since it's running on a cloud platform.

- Unable to horizontally scale

A smart contract could easily become horizontally scaled; it will also make developers to make smart contract services stateless.

- Can't have multiple run time environment for the running smart contracts

Each smart contract will have its own run time environment, there will be the possibilities to use threads or light threads (similar to Go Routins in Golang), separate processes, etc.

- SOLID

The extrapolation of SOLID principals will make blockchain and financial system more logical and stable.

- Can't use external services, databases, etc.

The Service contracts could easily use any type of external databases relational and/or non-relational. Which will allow to use big data and apply it to blockchain.

- Expensive to run a smart contract

Running a smart contract will become cheap, it will cost the same as the cost of an ordinary request to a web service. The result of this will be a positive effect reflecting on natural environment and saving the energy.

- Very limited number of the operation inside of a contract

A Smart contract running on a cloud platform as a service will be able to extend its functionality and remove the limits on the number and the types of allowed operations.

- Limited types

Having a smart contract running on a cloud platform will also allow to introduce the new types which now can't be used.

The only type of disagreement with such the approach could be based on opinion that going this way will make smart contracts changeable and consequently there will be no guarantee that the logic was not changed (Galiautdinov, 2020). And that's true, however in the beginning of the article the author showed the pattern which is used by smart contract developers which allows to apply different logic depending on the version of a smart contract which means it does not make any difference. And as a result of such the approach a blockchain will contain only Data related to Data Contracts and the version number of a Service Contract used to process the data. The Service Contract will b located on a Cloud Platform, will have its own version and will work on the principals of Proof-of-Stake.

Proof-of-stake is a cryptocurrency consensus mechanism for processing transactions and creating new blocks in a blockchain. A consensus mechanism is a method for validating entries into a distributed database and keeping the database secure. In the case of cryptocurrency, the database is called a blockchain—so the consensus mechanism secures the blockchain.

Speaking of POS benefits:

- With proof-of-stake (POS), cryptocurrency owners validate block transactions based on the number of staked coins.
- Proof-of-stake (POS) was created as an alternative to Proof-of-work (POW), the original consensus mechanism used to validate a blockchain and add new blocks.
- While PoW mechanisms require miners to solve cryptographic puzzles, PoS mechanisms require validators to hold and stake tokens for the privilege of earning transaction fees.
- Proof-of-stake (POS) is seen as less risky regarding the potential for an attack on the network, as it structures compensation in a way that makes an attack less advantageous.
- The next block writer on the blockchain is selected at random, with higher odds being assigned to nodes with larger stake positions.

Additionally to this, as it was mentioned earlier: POS will have a positive impact on saving the energy and will surely reduce the pollution which is especially important nowadays.

Having POS concept it's necessary to compare it against the POW:

Both consensus mechanisms help blockchains synchronize data, validate information, and process transactions. Each method has proven to be successful at maintaining a blockchain, although each has pros and cons. However, the two algorithms have very differing approaches.

Under PoS, block creators are called validators. A validator checks transactions, verifies activity, votes on outcomes, and maintains records. Under PoW, block creators are called miners. Miners work to solve for the hash, a cryptographic number, to verify transactions. In return for solving the hash, they are rewarded with a coin.

To "buy into" the position of becoming a block creator, you need only own enough coins or tokens to become a validator on a PoS blockchain. For PoW, miners must invest in processing equipment and incur hefty energy charges to power the machines attempting to solve the computations.

The equipment and energy costs under PoW mechanisms are expensive, limiting access to mining and strengthening the security of the blockchain. PoS blockchains reduce the amount of processing power needed to validate block information and transactions. The mechanism also lowers network congestion and removes the rewards-based incentive PoW blockchains have.

Table 1. Demonstrates comparison between proof of stake and proof or work

Proof of Stake	Proof of Work
Block creators are called validators	Block creators are called miners
Participants must own coins or tokens to become a validator	Participants must buy equipment and energy to become a miner
Energy efficient	Not energy efficient
Security through community control	Robust security due to expensive upfront requirement
Validators receive transactions fees as rewards	Miners receive block rewards

Smart contracts can be created and maintained in multiple available blockchain implementations. Bitcoin is a solution that aims at the transfer of funds (also known as cryptocurrency), in a decentralized manner, using a public blockchain that registers in the ledger all the transactions that have happened. Bitcoin's infrastructure allows the use of a scripting language with limited resources; however its open model and data immutability have guided the development of other protocols that allow the creation of very primitive versions of smart contracts. There is also another platform that runs on its own blockchain and has a consensus algorithm very close to Bitcoin – it's Ethereum, whose cryptocurrency is called Ether. Ethereum allows the development of smart contracts using programming languages such as Solidity which is pretty much close to JavaScript. The contracts are triggered when transaction is sent to the blockchain and then it's validated by the network. In the Ethereum eco-environment both users and smart contracts can send and receive cryptocurrencies ether among themselves. The Stellar platform, which also has its own blockchain, uses a consensus algorithm based on the Byzantine Agreement Protocol (De Graaf, 2019), which provides slower resource consumption to validate blocks of data in relation to the cryptographic puzzle required by Bitcoin in its validation and mining operations. Unlike Ethereum, Stellar does not have its own language for the creation of smart contracts, but allows contracts of this type to be made using the transactions that occur in its network. Besides those mentioned above, there is Lisk, which also has its own cryptocurrency and allows the creation of private blockchains, where their owners can define access privileges for third parties.

However even this is not the end of the story as crypto-currencies contain the number of the other weak sides which sometimes are not obvious.

All the crypto-currency concept is based on the hash functions which, according to the number of testimonies, can't have collisions (or more exactly: almost no collisions during some obvious period of time). Unfortunately there is no publicly published theorem proving this concept.

But there is still another issue: most of the crypto-currencies, including BTC, have so called self-destroyed mechanism, represented by a special command or programming instruction. That could be the answer to the question how crypto-world will blow up.

CONCLUSION

In the article the author made a research and provided a solution which can resolve the well known issues in the current smart contract concept and fully change the architecture used in smart contracts and blockchain. The author listed well known issues related to smart contract, analyzed them and provided the solution explaining how it will change the situation and what kind of positive impact it will have not only on the performance of smart contracts and their extensibility but also the impact on pollution and saving of energy.

REFERENCES

Almakhour, M., Sliman, L., Samhat, A., & Mellouk, A. (2020). *Verification of smart contracts: A survey* (Vol. 67). Pervasive and Mobile Computing.

Bernstein, D. J., & Lange, T. (2016). *SafeCurves: Choosing safe curves for elliptic-curve cryptography.* https://safecurves.cr.yp.to/

Brown. (2016). *SECG SEC 1: Elliptic Curve Cryptography (Version 2.0).* https://www.secg.org/sec1-v2.pdf

ChohanU. W. (2022). Web 3.0: The future architecture of the internet? doi:10.2139/ssrn.4037693

Galiautdinov, R. (2020). Brain machine interface: The accurate interpretation of neurotransmitters' signals targeting the muscles. *International Journal of Applied Research in Bioinformatics*, *10*(1), 26–36. Advance online publication. doi:10.4018/IJARB.2020010102

Galiautdinov, R., & Mkrttchian, V. (2019a). Math model of neuron and nervous system research, based on AI constructor creating virtual neural circuits: Theoretical and Methodological Aspects. In V. Mkrttchian, E. Aleshina, & L. Gamidullaeva (Eds.), *Avatar-Based Control, Estimation, Communications, and Development of Neuron Multi-Functional Technology Platforms* (pp. 320–344). IGI Global. doi:10.4018/978-1-7998-1581-5.ch015

Galiautdinov, R., & Mkrttchian, V. (2019b). Brain machine interface – for Avatar Control & Estimation in Educational purposes Based on Neural AI plugs: Theoretical and Methodological Aspects. In V. Mkrttchian, E. Aleshina, & L. Gamidullaeva (Eds.), *Avatar-Based Control, Estimation, Communications, and Development of Neuron Multi-Functional Technology Platforms* (pp. 345–360). IGI Global. doi:10.4018/978-1-7998-1581-5.ch016

Graaf, T. J. de. (2019). *From old to new: From internet to smart contracts and from people to smart contracts.* Academic Press.

Heuvel, S. (2014). The demand for short-term, safe assets and financial stability: Some evidence and implications for central bank policies. *Introduction to web3.* Available: https://ethereum.org/en/web3

Kongmanee, J., Kijsanayothin, P., & Hewett, R. (2019). Securing smart contractsin blockchain. In *2019 34th IEEE/ACM International Conference on Automated Software Engineering Workshop (ASEW).* IEEE.

Li, W., Andreina, S., Bohli, J.-M., & Karame, G. (2017). Securing Proof-of-Stake Blockchain Protocols. In J. Garcia-Alfaro, G. Navarro-Arribas, H. Hartenstein, & J. Herrera-Joancomartí (Eds.), *Data Privacy Management, Cryptocurrencies and Blockchain Technology* (pp. 297–315). Springer International Publishing., doi:10.1007/978-3-319-67816-0_17

Mkrttchian, V., Gamidullaeva, L., & Galiautdinov, R. (2019). Design of Nano-scale Electrodes and Development of Avatar-Based Control System for Energy-Efficient Power Engineering: Application of an Internet of Things and People (IOTAP) Research Center. *International Journal of Applied Nanotechnology Research*, *4*(1), 41–48. Advance online publication. doi:10.4018/IJANR.2019010104

Nguyen, C. T., Hoang, D. T., Nguyen, D. N., Niyato, D., Nguyen, H. T., & Dutkiewicz, E. (2019). Proof-of-Stake Consensus Mechanisms for Future Blockchain Networks: Fundamentals, Applications and Opportunities. *IEEE Access : Practical Innovations, Open Solutions*, *7*, 85727–85745. doi:10.1109/ACCESS.2019.2925010

Nofer, M., Gomber, P., Hinz, O., & Schiereck, D. (2017). Blockchain. *Business & Information Systems Engineering*, *59*(3), 183–187. doi:10.100712599-017-0467-3

Rouhani & Deters. (2019). Security, performance, and applications of smart contracts: A systematic survey. *IEEE Access, 7*(50), 759–779.

Saleh, F. (2021). Blockchain without Waste: Proof-of-Stake. *The Review of Financial Studies, 34*(3), 1156–1190. doi:10.1093/rfs/hhaa075

Sreehari, P., Nandakishore, M., Krishna, G., Jacob, J., & Shibu, V. (2017). Smartwill converting the legal testament into a smart contract. In *2017 Interna-tional Conference on Networks & Advances in Computational Technolo-gies (NetACT)*. IEEE.

Tasca, P., & Tessone, C. J. (2019). A Taxonomy of Blockchain Technologies: Principles of Identification and Classification. *Ledger, 4*. doi:10.5195/ledger.2019.140

Wang, Q., Li, R., Wang, Q., & Chen, S. (2021). *Non-fungible token (nft):Overview, evaluation, opportunities and challenges*. arXiv *preprintarXiv*:2105.07447. doi:10.5195/ledger.2019.140

Zhang, R., & Chan, W. K. (2020). Evaluation of Energy Consumption in Block-Chains with Proof of Work and Proof of Stake. *Journal of Physics: Conference Series, 1584*(1), 012023. doi:10.1088/1742-6596/1584/1/012023

Zhang, Y., Ma, S., Li, J., Li, K., Nepal, S., & Gu, D. (2020). Smartshield: Automatic smart contract protection made easy. In *2020 IEEE 27thInternational Conference on Software Analysis, Evolution and Reengi-neering (SANER)*. IEEE.

Chapter 6
Cryptocurrency Adoption Behaviour of Millennial Investors in India

Renuka Sharma
https://orcid.org/0000-0002-6514-3411
Chitkara Business School, Chitkara University, India

Kiran Mehta
Chitkara Business School, Chitkara University, India

Ritik Rana
Chitkara Business School, Chitkara University, India

ABSTRACT

Young investors, fuelled by the hype and ads, are rushing to cryptocurrency exchanges with the hopes of generating rapid riches, and investors of the millennial generation especially believe cryptocurrency can make them billionaires. Crypto Research and Intelligence Business found that over 15 million Indians had accepted cryptocurrencies and invested close to $10 billion in crypto assets. Because of the ongoing changes over the last few years, changing from paper to virtual currency, a new type of currency, namely cryptocurrency, has emerged. Shorter transaction times and lower transfer fees are two of the advantages that cryptocurrencies offer to their potential users. The concept of cryptocurrency is underpinned by decentralised technology, which has captivated the interest of a variety of stakeholders. This research examines millennial cryptocurrency adoption behaviour in India.

DOI: 10.4018/978-1-6684-8361-9.ch006

INTRODUCTION

In the last several years, many technical developments have occurred, including digital payments, electronic commerce and the internet of things. These changes may be noticed in how individuals connect and use the money to exchange goods and services (Poongodi et al., 2020). Because of the ongoing changes in things over the last few several years, with the rise of virtual currency, a new form of money called cryptocurrency has emerged. This type of currency is different from traditional paper currency. It is based on complex cryptographic algorithms that allow it to be securely transferred and verified without a central authority. According to ((Mazambani & Mutambara, 2020), it is a digital currency that uses the technologies of blockchains to perform various numbers of financial transactions. These blockchain-based cryptocurrency operations aim to provide anonymity, transparency and security (Al-Amri et al., 2019; Winter & Davidson, 2019).

Cryptocurrencies like Ethereum, Bitcoin and Solana enable consumers to bypass traditional retail payment methods and make secure, low-cost financial transactions. These digital currencies use complex cryptographic algorithms to verify and validate transactions, which makes them a fast and efficient way to transfer money and make purchases. By using cryptocurrencies, consumers can avoid the fees and limitations associated with traditional financial systems and enjoy greater control over their financial transactions for two reasons: freedom and secrecy from central organisations like banking institutions (Omane-Adjepong & Alagidede, 2020). One of their key advantages is that cryptocurrencies have rapid transaction speeds and cheap costs. Cryptocurrencies are often transmitted and processed because they are decentralised and rely on advanced cryptographic algorithms to verify and authenticate transactions (Yeong et al., 2022a) faster than traditional cash. Furthermore, because cryptocurrencies do not require the involvement of financial institutions or other intermediaries, the fees associated with utilising them are frequently cheaper than those connected with regular financial transactions. As a result, cryptocurrencies are an appealing choice for people and organisations seeking quick, low-cost financial transfers (Singh & Singh, n.d.).

Academics, corporations, and other stakeholders have expressed interest in cryptocurrency based on decentralised technology. Bitcoin's inventive and disruptive character has aroused curiosity in its possible uses and applications, leading to an explosion of study and discussion on the issue. Many people regard the rise of cryptocurrency as a significant development with the potential to change how we think about money and financial transactions. They are eager to learn more about its potential influence on society and the economy. As a result, the researchers discovered the necessity for cryptocurrency adoption in the Indian digital market. The study of investor's characteristic is important in present and ever-changing scenario (Sharma et. al. 2020). Specifically, after the emergence of ESG concept the study of investor's responsible behavior, their characteristics and its influence in the investment pattern is essential (Vyas et al. 2020). However, several factors influence crypto adoption in India's digital industry. The desire of people to utilize cryptocurrencies determines their success in the digital economy. In other words, consumer acceptance and adoption of cryptocurrencies are critical in determining their success and effect in the digital market. If customers are eager to utilize cryptocurrencies for financial transactions, it is more probable that merchants and other stakeholders will embrace and use them. However, if people are willing to utilize cryptocurrencies, they may need help to gain traction and widespread adoption. Understanding and influencing consumer perceptions regarding bitcoin is therefore critical for anyone interested in promoting its use and success in the digital market (Alaklabi & Kang, 2021). Furthermore, it is determined by what customers anticipate and how they are organized. Before it can function adequately as a trade means, crypto, like any other currency, must efficiently keep its price value (Yeong et al., 2022b). Similarly, facilitating conditions and consumer happiness are the means to boost cryptocurrencies in the digital economy (Abbasi et al., 2021). Transparency in transactions is a critical factor in India's digital economy. It refers to the ability of transactions to be openly and easily traced and verified by all parties involved. In a digital economy, transparency is essential for building trust and confidence among consumers, businesses, and other stakeholders. It helps to ensure that transactions are fair and transparent and that all parties are held accountable for their actions. By promoting transparency in transactions, India's digital economy can foster a more secure and trustworthy environment for financial transactions, which can help to encourage the growth and development of the digital economy (Bhatia & Bedi, 2022). Furthermore, the usage of crypto provides traceability (Kanwalinderjit et al., 2020). It is the critical feature that determines crypto usage and business processes (Abbasi et al., 2021).

The advantage of the selected approach is that it provides instant answers for crypto adoption in India's digital economy. In last couple of years Indian economy suffered the impact of the Covid-19 and now it has come out of the bad effects of it, specifically the manufacturing section (Mehta et. al. 2022) which is the key sector of Indian economy. It also inspired Indian scholars to study the topic. So, this research examines reliability, simplicity of use, social impact, enabling circumstances, and perceived utility in India's digital economy. Second, does Indian customer intent to utilise cryptocurrency affect virtual currency adoption? This research examined Indian consumer bitcoin uptake using theoretical technology acceptance models. The Unified Theory of Acceptance and Use of Technology will be used to study Indian cryptocurrency adoption (UTAUT). This research will examine trustworthiness, usability, social impact, conducive conditions, and perceived usefulness. The

UTAUT model is a commonly used paradigm for predicting and understanding the acceptance and usage of new technologies. It may be utilised in this context to explain cryptocurrency uptake among Indian investors.

Many millennials are interested in investing in cryptocurrency, the digital or virtual money that is decentralised, meaning any government or financial organisation does not control it. Cryptocurrencies are exchanged on internet platforms and may be used to buy products and services; however, they are also frequently purchased and sold as investments. Some millennials may be drawn to cryptocurrencies because of the possibility of significant returns on investment and the technical innovation and decentralisation underlying it (Rey-Ares et al., 2021). On the other hand, investing in cryptocurrencies entails risks such as the danger of losing money owing to price fluctuation, cybersecurity concerns, and regulatory ambiguity (Bonaparte, 2022; Zhao et al., 2018). As a result, Millennials in India, like their counterparts elsewhere, have expressed an interest in several financial products, including cryptocurrencies. The expanding young population in India, increasing acceptance of digital technologies, and the availability of online platforms that make it simpler to purchase and trade cryptocurrencies have all contributed to the country's interest in cryptocurrency.

The studies found that social influence has a significant impact on customers' desire to use mobile banking services. In other words, the behaviour and attitudes of other people, especially friends and family, can influence an individual's decision to use mobile banking services (Hasan et al., 2022; Singh & Singh, n.d.). Therefore, companies that offer mobile banking services should consider the role of social influence in their marketing and outreach efforts, as it can be a powerful tool for encouraging the adoption of their services. Research findings on facilitating conditions, social influence and adoption results in industrialised and developing nations are similar. In other words, the elements influencing technological adoption and acceptance, such as the availability of supporting infrastructure, the influence of people, and the perceived value of the technology, are comparable in industrialised and developing nations (Abbasi et al., 2021). All this shows that a country's degree of development does not necessarily impact technology adoption and acceptability but rather a range of other essential criteria for all countries as was highlighted earlier (Arora et al., 2022). Furthermore, the result of research on the ease of use of cryptocurrency adoption constructs (Muchlis Gazali et al., 2018), is a big step in the future use of cryptocurrencies on a large scale. However, quantitative academic research on the factors driving cryptocurrency adoption in developing nations such as India is still being determined. The present study seeks to close that gap by investigating the factors that influence cryptocurrency adoption in India using the Unified Theory of Acceptance and Use of Technology (UTAUT). The research can help organisations more effectively target their marketing efforts and build their goods and services to match the demands and preferences of Indian customers by giving factual data from the users' perspective.

LITERATURE REVIEW AND BACKGROUND

Cryptocurrencies, such as Bitcoin, introduce a fresh perspective to the global economy by offering a novel take on the monetary system. They are highly liquid, resulting in reduced transaction and verification expenses. (Huhtinen, 2014). The adoption of Cryptocurrency is dependent on its technical importance. However, Cryptocurrency's present status is also unstable, leading to less adoption of these technologies (Michale,2013). Bitcoin's development stage and lack of user-friendly design, which was intended to hasten this development phase, which were deliberate measures to accelerate its development (Evans-Pughe, 2012). Since companies are using cryptocurrency to pay obligations directly or via service providers, the adoption rate is continually rising. Yet, the fluctuation of Bitcoin's exchange rate poses a hurdle to its integrity regarding worldwide acceptability. Cryptocurrencies have certain features, similar to gold and other currencies, but their practical use as a medium of exchange needs to be clarified. The use of virtual money is growing in popularity. Several people now think it's possible to do serious research into Cryptocurrencies such as bitcoin etc., which might have far-reaching implications for the future of money.

The field of information science includes several ideas that attempt to utilise computers to anticipate human characteristics. Initially, Davis (1989) investigated how people feel about cutting-edge technological developments. He discovered two qualities that might predict technology's perceived utilisation, namely, decision-making theory and social cognitive theory. Finally, Venkatesh et al. (2003) examined numerous approaches utilised in recent years to anticipate human-computer interaction. These ideas have been used to determine people's perceived adoption rates to tell companies about their desire to employ new technologies. The Technology Acceptance Model (TAM) provides expected characteristics for comprehending inclinations to embrace digital innovations. TAM has been created and employed in various academic research environments to ascertain the dissemination of technology. Previous studies have utilized varying models or a blend of models to forecast the adoption of new technology. To evaluate cryptocurrency adoption, TAM is used in the current research. Additionally, two critical aspects of adoption have been added, i.e., *Awareness and Perceived Trustworthiness*. In the following section a detailed description of the factors is given.

Perceived Usefulness

The level to which an individual believes that using a particular system or technology would be advantageous and could potentially enhance their overall productivity is considered a crucial indicator of its usefulness. In other words, usefulness measures how beneficial a person believes technology will be in achieving their objectives or completing their duties. According to research, use is significant in determining an individual's inclination to accept and utilise new technology (Ahamad et al., 2022). People are more inclined to explore new technologies and adopt them into their lives or enterprises if they believe they will be beneficial. Conversely, if users perceive technology as ineffective or irrelevant to their needs, they are less inclined to employ it. As a result, increasing a technology's perceived utility may be essential in boosting its acceptance and use(Davis, 1989). The usefulness of technology has a long-term impact on an individual's desire to utilise technological advances in the future (Abdo et al., 2016; Adams et al., 1992; Venkatesh et al., 2003b). If someone feels that utilising a particular technology would benefit them in their job, they are more likely to keep using it. They may even be more driven to seek out and embrace other technologies that will help them even more. This is because they recognise the potential for technology to help them advance in their careers and developments (Shanab & Haider, 2015; Venkatesh & Bala, 2008). According to the study's assumption, perceived utility, enabling circumstances, awareness, perceived ease of use, social impact, and perceived trustworthiness all have a positive association with bitcoin usage intention. The next part goes into data description and analysis.

Perceived Ease of Use

Ease of use measures an individual's view that utilising a specific system or technology would be simple. It represents an individual's opinion of the difficulty or complexity of utilising technology. According to research, perceived ease of use is significant in determining an individual's inclination to accept and utilise new technology. People are more inclined to test technology and adopt it into their lives or enterprises if it is considered simple. People may be less willing to utilise technology if it is difficult or complex (Davis, 1989). It shows a person's self-assurance in their ability to use the system or technology without encountering challenges or difficulties. It has been claimed that growing computer knowledge can boost self-efficacy and lessen computer phobia, allowing for the early adoption of new technology. Self-efficacy is a person's confidence to complete a job or achieve a goal. In contrast, computer anxiety is a fear or discomfort experienced when utilising computers or other digital technology. According to research, persons with high self-efficacy and a low level of computer anxiety are more inclined to explore new technologies and incorporate them into their lives or enterprises. As a result, improving computer knowledge and decreasing computer phobia may be crucial factors in encouraging the early adoption of new technologies. This can be achieved through various means, such as training programs, educational resources, and support from more experienced users (Abdo et al., 2016; Shanab & Haider, 2015; Venkatesh & Bala, 2008). This is a critical component in technology adoption because people are more inclined to embrace and utilise technology if they perceive it as simple. Developers and manufacturers may encourage greater acceptance and usage of technologies by designing them to be simple, which can contribute to economic development.

Social Influence

The efforts which influence a person's beliefs, behaviours or feelings, whether intentional or not, are referred to as "social influence (Delfabbro et al., 2021). Many researchers have studied the topic of social influence and how it influences people's intentions to embrace and accept various forms of digital advancements. The impact of others' conduct and attitudes on an individual's ideas, feelings, and behaviours is social influence. Social influence may play a key role in altering people's attitudes and behaviour toward new technologies adoption. Researchers may better understand how and why individuals embrace new technologies by studying the elements that drive social influence, and they can devise tactics to support or discourage their adoption, e.g., usage of internet banking (Alalwan et al., 2017) or mobile banking (Merhi et al., 2019), digital wallets (Patil et al., 2020) and smartwatches (Beh et al., 2021). When it comes to launching new and innovative goods or services, social influence may be crucial, especially when there is a lack of knowledge accessible about the technology or how it operates. People in these situations may rely on the views and experiences of others to assist them in deciding whether to try a new product or service (Kulviwat et al., 2009). Companies presenting new technologies or services may use social influence to their advantage by establishing a network of advocates or influencers who can promote the product or service and assist in developing trust and credibility among potential users. This may be especially effective when paired with other marketing and outreach initiatives, such as teaching potential consumers about the product's or service's benefits and features (Adapa et al., 2018).

Facilitating Conditions

Facilitating conditions relate to a person's opinion that the essential infrastructure exists so that we can encourage the usage of new technologies (Walton et al., n.d.). To put it another way, facilitating conditions are those variables that make it simpler for people to embrace and use new technologies. These can include technical support, training materials, and other sorts of aid that assist individuals in overcoming any hurdles to adoption. A substantial amount of study in the sector has discovered that facilitating conditions are essential in influencing an individual's desire to embrace new technology. External variables that assist or facilitate adopting and using new technology are referred to as facilitating circumstances. These can include infrastructural availability, the presence of qualified staff, and the presence of enabling rules and regulations (Beh et al., 2021). According to research, significant facilitating factors increase an individual's desire to embrace new technology, but the lack of these variables hinders adoption. Understanding and managing enabling factors is thus a crucial aspect in encouraging the acceptance and usage of new technology (Beza et al., 2018; Venkatesh et al., 2003a). Facilitating conditions are an essential driver of technology adoption. By understanding the role of enabling conditions in technology diffusion, policymakers and other stakeholders can design strategies to promote the acceptance and utilization of technological advances, which can, in turn, contribute to economic development.

Awareness

Tech advancement may considerably influence economic growth, but only if it is widely accepted and employed can its impact be reliably quantified. The process by which technology is embraced and incorporated into society is called its dissemination (Hall & Khan, 2003). Accepting and integrating new technologies into society and the economy is critical in determining their overall influence on economic growth. A new technology's ability to stimulate economic growth will only be allowed if it is universally embraced and employed. Hence, promoting new technologies and maximising their economic impact requires understanding and regulating their adoption and acceptability variables. The spread of technology is frequently aided by a public understanding of its potential advantages. People are more inclined to accept and use new technology if they know how it might benefit their lives or enterprises. Raising public knowledge of new technologies and their potential benefits may be vital in encouraging their acceptance and use (Devanur & Fortnow, 2009; Shareef et al., 2011). This can be achieved through various means, such as marketing and outreach campaigns, media coverage, and educational efforts. By raising awareness of the potential benefits of new technologies, companies and organizations can help to drive their adoption and integration into society. According to the study (Bélanger & Carter, 2008; Krishnan et al., 2017; Krishnaraju et al., 2016), Individuals are not likely to accept and use an innovation if they are uninformed of its existence or its potential benefits; individuals are more likely to embrace and make use of technology if they are well-informed about it and comprehend its potential advantages.

Perceived Trust-Worthiness

According to (Dirsehan & Can, 2020), trust plays an essential factor in the adoption of cryptocurrency. The creation and acceptability of diverse information systems rely heavily on trust. It contributes to developing a favourable attitude toward these systems in society since individuals are more willing to utilise and rely on systems they trust. Many variables can impact trust, including the system's security and privacy, the veracity of the information it offers, and the reputation of the company or people behind it. Therefore, building confidence in information systems is critical for promoting adoption, usage and success. Consumers' faith in blockchain technology is founded on their conviction in complete public transparency, data integrity, and data record of transactions. People trust blockchain technology because it provides for the transparent and secure recording of transactions, protects the accuracy and integrity of data, and necessitates unanimity from all parties engaged in the trade. These principles are fundamental to the operation and security of blockchain technology. They are a significant reason for its rapid acceptance and acknowledgement as a secure and trustworthy platform for financial transactions. The ability to automate service is a factor that impacts cryptocurrencies (Khan & Salah, 2018). So far, that e-commerce should improve the intrinsic and extrinsic factors of service delivery to influence people's positive behaviours (Sharma et al., 2022).

In the subsequent section a detail about the methodology and results are discussed.

RESEARCH METHODOLOGY AND DATA INPUTS

Since the beginning of the 21st century, academics all around the globe have been doing exhaustive study on the topic of how people adopt new technologies (Trivedi et. al. 2021). The research that was carried out used various theories and models to a variety of settings in order to accomplish the goals that were set, and the findings of these investigations varied. This research examined how technology affects financial behaviour and propensity to embrace new currencies. Empirical research was used to study cryptocurrency use and intents. An empirical study methodology was used for the purpose of determining individuals' levels of interest in using cryptocurrency. The purpose of this particular research is to investigate the behavioural tendencies of people specifically millennial with regard to the use of cryptocurrency. In order to accomplish this goal, current research was carried out in India. The research instrument was made by combining the constructs given in a standardized scale by Venkatesh et. al., 2016 (details of each is shown in the following Appendix I) and others on Five-point *Likert*'s scale. We have also added two new constructs to the model i.e., Perceived Trust-worthiness and Awareness. The details of the constructs and items selected for the study is shown in the Appendix I. The questionnaire was sent out to individuals (online) in different Indian cities to understand cryptocurrency adoption attitudes and behaviours. The questionnaire data was analysed to see what variables influence millennial's desire to adopt Cryptocurrency. This research targeted respondents ranging in the age group of 20–40 year. The inclusion of a diverse spectrum of people, from students to working professionals, was intended to promote public involvement in the research. This strategy ensured that the data collected represented a large cross-section of people and that the study's conclusions would be more generalizable. The study also collected more useful perspectives and attitudes from individuals who already know about and have some experience with cryptocurrency. This data helps shape cryptocurrency regulations and activities, supporting digital currency adoption and a more fair and efficient financial system.

The data was collected from the target demographic using a random sampling technique. There were a total of 1250 questionnaires sent out, and 490 replies were collected. However, 126 answers were deemed unreliable due to incomplete or biased responses and were thus excluded from the study in an effort to lower the response error rate. After removing incomplete responses, we used 364 responses as our sample size for this research, for an actual response rate of 30.33%. Harman's single factor score tested for common technique bias to verify the results (CMB). According to the findings, one component accounted for less than half of the total variation (Podsakoff et al., 2012). There was no impact of a single factor or common method bias on our sample. We performed a reliability test, validity check, and EFA using SPSS version 20 to verify the data's reliability and validity. We also used AMOS version 21's Structural Equation Modelling (SEM) to undertake a path analysis and estimate how various factors affect individuals' intents to use cryptocurrency. This helped validate the survey scale and data.

ANALYSIS AND DISCUSSION

Using AMOS v21, the SEM was utilised to establish a link between dependent and independent variables. The research also looked at the individuals' demographics, such as gender, age, and educational level. The findings of a sample of 364 people revealed that 79.95% of the participants were male and 20.5% were female. The plurality of participants, 32.14%, were between the ages of 21 and 30, while 67.86% were between the ages of 31 and 40. These findings suggest that the participants were mostly young, interested in online trading and investing, and were well prepared to comprehend and use digital currencies as a method of exchange. Furthermore, 99.5% of respondents were educated, indicating that they are well-versed in technical breakthroughs and their applications. According to the study, the bulk of the participants were young, male, and highly educated. This suggests that they were more likely to grasp technological developments and the acceptance of digital currency. Furthermore, the results revealed that the majority of participants were between the ages of 21 and 40, and that more than 99.45% of respondents were educated. This emphasises the significance of comprehending the perceptions and behavioural intentions of this young, educated, and technologically aware group regarding the usage of cryptocurrencies as a method of trade. These findings provide valuable insights for businesses and policy-makers looking to promote the use of digital currencies in the future. Before doing the route analysis, the research checked for reliability and validity.

Table 1. Demographic profile of the respondents

		No of Respondents	Percentage in Total Sample
Gender	Male	291	79.95
	Female	73	20.05
		364	100.00
Age	21-30	117	32.14
	31-40	247	67.86
		364	100.00
Education	Graduate	202	55.49
	Postgraduate	108	29.67
	Other Professional education	52	14.29
	Uneducated	2	0.55
		364	100.00

Measurement Model

To identify the total number of variables/factors the exploratory factor analysis (EFA) method was utilised, which confirmed the relationship between variables (Kinnear and Gray, 2010). The components are compacted into a few important and interconnected dimensions, resulting in minimal data loss (Hair et al., 2010). To evaluate if the data was suitable for factor analysis, two tests were run. The KMO & Bartlett's Test of Sphericity is a sample adequacy measure. Their values are KMO (0.858) and Bartlett's values are Approx. Chi-Square 5071.648, df = 465 and sig. 0.000. The values for the determinant (5.49E-007) is also in acceptable limit to conduct the further analysis. The results show that factor analysis is possible with the current data. A preliminary inquiry was conducted to discover eigen values for each element of the data. Hair et al., 1998, advised removing statements with factor loadings below 0.4. In accordance with Kaiser's criterion, there were seven components that had eigen values that were larger than one, and together, these three factors explained 65.642% of the total variance. The results of the data analysis performed using EFA led to the discovery of seven different components. It is important to note that none of the components are subject to cross loading, and their loads all fall within the acceptable range for their respective categories. Table 2 shows the factor loadings derived from the EFA analysis, which may be used to evaluate the survey questions' significance in relation to the relevant variables. Principal component analysis (PCA) utilising the Varimax rotation approach was used to do this, and valid results were obtained for all variables (with values ranging from 0.699 to 0.832) (Rajalahti & Kvalheim, 2011). Evaluating the reliability and validity using the appropriate metrics was done before continuing on to perform additional analysis. Table 2 illustrates that the results of the Cronbach's alpha test reveal that all values are more than 0.7, suggesting that the data is reliable. The fact that all values are greater than 0.7 demonstrates that there is no single factor or common method bias in our sample.. The findings of the composite reliability (CR) analysis varied from 0.745 to 0.812, while the values for the average variance extracted (AVE) were from 0.450 to 0.526. According to the findings presented here, which are summarised in Table 2, there were no problems with the reliability or validity of the data (Fornell & Larcker, 1981; Lam, 2012).

Extraction Method: Principal Component Analysis. Rotation Method: Varimax with Kaiser Normalization.

a. Rotation converged in 6 iterations.

Table 3 displays the square root of the Average Variance Extracted (AVE) values, which reflects each construct's discriminant validity. The results reveal that the square root of AVE values is larger than the correlations between each concept, indicating that there are no discriminant validity difficulties with the survey data (Fornell & Larcker, 1981).

Confirmatory factor analysis (CFA), which was performed using AMOS, was used to analyse the study model in order to determine its consistency and construct validity. The CFA analysis produced the following results: CMIN/df is 1,511, and RMSEA equals 0.038, Both of these fall within the acceptable range. Although the values of GFI= 0.904, NFI= 0.882, CFI= 0.957, and TLI= 0.951 exceed the recommended threshold for a model to be considered a good fit, they still indicate a high level of fitness for the model, TLI= 0.951 has the highest value.

Table 2. EFA results, reliability, and validity of data

Items	Component			
	Loadings	**Cronbach's Alpha**	**CR**	**AVE**
InUCr1	0.786			
InUCr3	0.776			
InUCr4	0.771			
InUCr2	0.763			
InUCr5	0.744	0.86	0.745	0.450
PrEoU3	0.832			
PrEoU2	0.773			
PrEoU4	0.753			
PrEoU5	0.739			
PrEoU1	0.731	0.856	0.782	0.545
PTru3	0.772			
PTru2	0.771			
PTru5	0.768			
PTru1	0.749			
PTru4	0.710	0.844	0.776	0.521
SInf1	0.818			
SInf2	0.810			
SInf3	0.796			
SInf4	0.787	0.847	0.812	0.581
Arns3	0.826			
Arns1	0.775			
Arns4	0.770			
Arns2	0.757	0.838	0.753	0.564
PrUs3	0.803			
PrUs4	0.784			
PrUs2	0.774			
PrUs1	0.735	0.821	0.757	0.549
FCon4	0.811			
FCon1	0.799			
FCon2	0.730			
FCon3	0.699	0.815	0.810	0.526

Table 3. Discriminant validity of all constructs

	PrEoU	FCon	SInf	PrUs	PTru	InUCr	Arns
PrEoU	**0.738**						
FCon	0.387	**0.725**					
SInf	0.206	0.305	**0.762**				
PrUs	0.334	0.309	0.256	**0.741**			
PTru	0.342	0.364	0.229	0.323	**0.722**		
InUCr	0.381	0.43	0.168	0.166	0.416	**0.670**	
Arns	0.276	0.251	0.41	0.41	0.253	0.253	**0.751**

Figure 1. Structural model

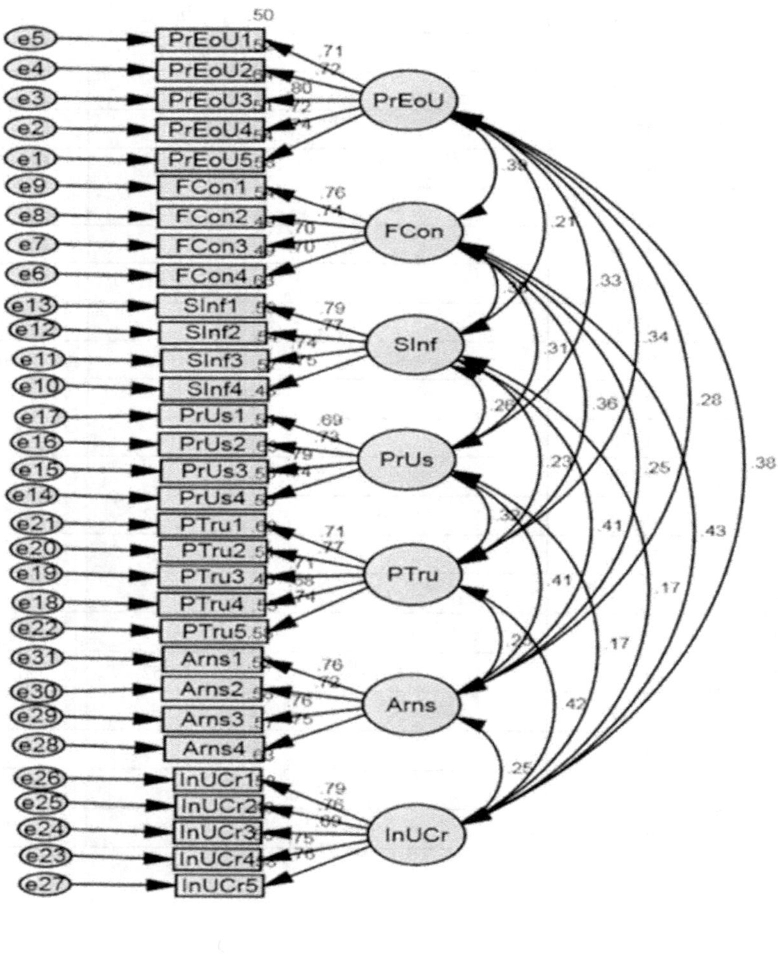

Structural Model

The findings of the measurement model demonstrated that the data is very valid and dependable, which reflected the excellent fitness of the entire model and indicated that it could be utilised for route analysis. The results of the path analysis, which are as follows: CMIN/df = 1.572, RMSEA = 0.040, GFI =0.897, NFI = 0.873, CFI = 0.949, and TLI = 0.945, strongly suggest that the regression model fits the data well and is a good representation of the underlying relationships.

Figure 2. Standardized assessment of the regression weights

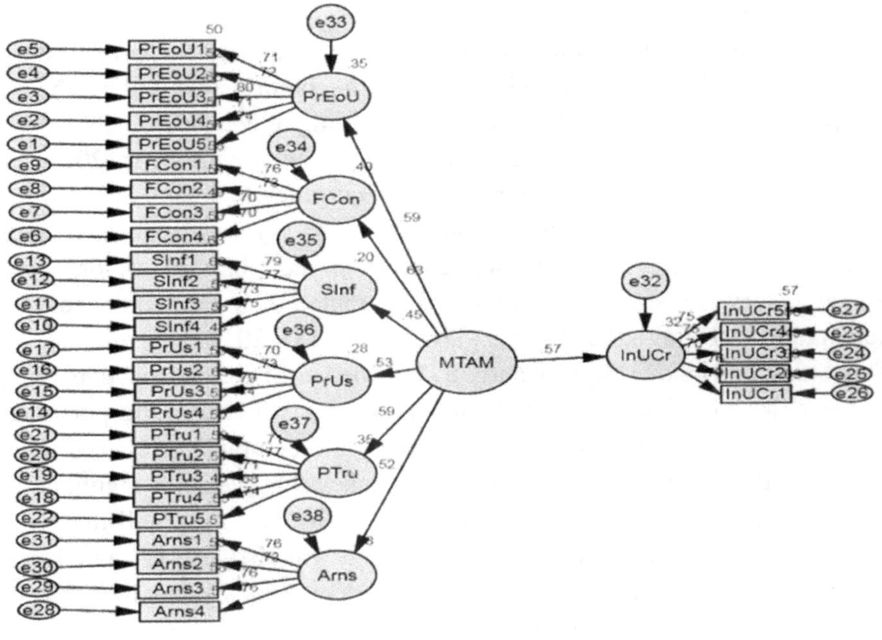

Figure 2 presents a standardized assessment of the regression weights, which was generated using SEM. The values of the path coefficients are significant and positive, suggesting a positive association between the variables that are dependent and those that are independent. Figure 2 also shows the beta coefficients in the analysis. All these values are positive and significant. At 0.01 level of significance. Table 4 shows the value of beta coefficients for all independent variable. The significance of the theoretical model developed for this research may be inferred from the data shown above. All hypotheses of the study are accepted at this stage.

Table 4. Beta values of all variables

	Beta Coefficients		Beta Coefficients
PrEoU	**0.59**	PrUs	0.53
FCon	0.63	PTru	0.59
SInf	0.45	Arns	0.52
MTAM	0.57		

*sig. at 0.01, 0.05

CONCLUSION, RECOMMENDATIONS, AND IMPLICATIONS

Governments throughout the globe are apprehensive of the use of blockchain technology because of the virtual currency's lack of authority and confidentiality, despite its potential advantages. This is the case in countries like India, where the government has yet to legalise Cryptocurrency owing to concerns about its usage in illegal activities like money laundering and tax evasion(Kumar, 2021). The government is hesitant to officially recognise a currency that cannot be managed by institutions (financial). Given the volatility of the cryptocurrency market and blockchain technology's potential applications in the financial sector, a more robust regulatory framework is required to guarantee their safe and accountable implementation ((Desai & Parikh, n.d.; Dyntu & Dykyi, 2019).

This study contributes significantly to knowledge of the perspectives people have about the adoption of a new financial system, which has the potential to result in enhanced interactions between humans and computers. It is essential to acknowledge that crypto is a novel form of currency that seeks for regulation and support from governmental and financial institutions. Not only will this lead to an increase in awareness among individuals, but it will also lead to an increase in trust, which will ultimately result in the acceptance of cryptocurrencies as a way of commerce in the future world's financial system. Regularization and support from governmental and financial institutions cannot be exaggerated in importance because they provide customers with a feeling of safety and integrity, which in turn leads to a wider acceptance of cryptocurrency as a legal medium of transaction. This point cannot be emphasised enough. As a result, the findings of this research shed light on the significant part that governments and other financial institutions play in the effective acceptance and incorporation of cryptocurrencies into the international monetary system.

According to the results of this research, there is a significant and positive connection between each of the characteristics that were investigated and the desire that millennial's having to adopt cryptocurrency. The present concept of technology adoption as a vital component in technological diffusion has also been identified and validated by additional characteristics, such as perceived trustworthiness (b = 0.590) and awareness (b = 0.520). Even if they are not totally aware on the functions and applications of cryptocurrency, our empirical results lead us to believe that millennials are prepared to accept cryptocurrency as a means of exchange if certain conditions are met. When it comes to the government of India, which does not approve the establishment of such a financial system that is not subject to official control, this might weaken confidence, and as a consequence, individuals' desires to adopt cryptocurrency as a currency.

REFERENCES

Abbasi, G. A., Tiew, L. Y., Tang, J., Goh, Y.-N., & Thurasamy, R. (2021). The adoption of cryptocurrency as a disruptive force: Deep learning-based dual stage structural equation modelling and artificial neural network analysis. *PLoS One*, *16*(3), e0247582. doi:10.1371/journal.pone.0247582 PMID:33684120

Abdo, N., Almuraqab, S., & Almuraqab, N. A. S. (2016). *M-Government adoption factors in the UAE: a partial least squares approach M-Government Adoption Factors in the United Arab Emirates: A Partial Least-Squares Approach*. https://www.researchgate.net/publication/315829981

Adams, D. A., Nelson, R. R., & Todd, P. A. (1992). Perceived Usefulness, Ease of Use, and Usage of Information Technology: A Replication. *Management Information Systems Quarterly*, *16*(2), 227. doi:10.2307/249577

Adapa, A., Nah, F. F.-H., Hall, R. H., Siau, K., & Smith, S. N. (2018). Factors Influencing the Adoption of Smart Wearable Devices. *International Journal of Human-Computer Interaction*, *34*(5), 399–409. doi:10.1080/10447318.2017.1357902

Ahamad, S., Gupta, P., Bikash Acharjee, P., Padma Kiran, K., Khan, Z., & Faez Hasan, M. (2022). The role of block chain technology and Internet of Things (IoT) to protect financial transactions in crypto currency market. *Materials Today: Proceedings*, *56*, 2070–2074. doi:10.1016/j.matpr.2021.11.405

Al-Amri, R., Zakaria, N. H., Habbal, A., & Hassan, S. (2019). Cryptocurrency adoption: Current stage, opportunities, and open challenges. *International Journal of Advanced Computer Research*, *9*(44), 293–307. doi:10.19101/IJACR.PID43

Alaklabi, S., & Kang, K. (2021). Perceptions towards Cryptocurrency Adoption: A case of Saudi Arabian Citizens. *Journal of Electronic Banking Systems*, 1–17. doi:10.5171/2021.110411

Alalwan, A. A., Dwivedi, Y. K., & Rana, N. P. (2017). Factors influencing adoption of mobile banking by Jordanian bank customers: Extending UTAUT2 with trust. *International Journal of Information Management*, *37*(3), 99–110. doi:10.1016/j.ijinfomgt.2017.01.002

Arora, M., Sharma, R., & Mehta, K. (2022). Personality Effects on Financial Responses Caused by the Perceived Financial Threat during the COVID-19 Pandemic. *The Journal of Wealth Management*, *25*(3), 72–89. doi:10.3905/jwm.2022.1.183

Beh, P. K., Ganesan, Y., Iranmanesh, M., & Foroughi, B. (2021). Using smartwatches for fitness and health monitoring: The UTAUT2 combined with threat appraisal as moderators. *Behaviour & Information Technology*, *40*(3), 282–299. doi:10.1080/0144929X.2019.1685597

Bélanger, F., & Carter, L. (2008). Trust and risk in e-government adoption. *The Journal of Strategic Information Systems*, *17*(2), 165–176. doi:10.1016/j.jsis.2007.12.002

Beza, E., Reidsma, P., Poortvliet, P. M., Belay, M. M., Bijen, B. S., & Kooistra, L. (2018). Exploring farmers' intentions to adopt mobile Short Message Service (SMS) for citizen science in agriculture. *Computers and Electronics in Agriculture*, *151*, 295–310. doi:10.1016/j.compag.2018.06.015

Bhatia, P., & Bedi, P. (2022). Causal Linkages Among Cryptocurrency and Emerging Market Indices: An Empirical Investigation. *Vision: The Journal of Business Perspective*, *097226292211056*. Advance online publication. doi:10.1177/09722629221105670

Bonaparte, Y. (2022). Time horizon and cryptocurrency ownership: Is crypto not speculative? *Journal of International Financial Markets, Institutions and Money*, *79*, 101609. doi:10.1016/j.intfin.2022.101609

Davis, F. D. (1989). Perceived Usefulness, Perceived Ease of Use, and User Acceptance of Information Technology. *Management Information Systems Quarterly*, *13*(3), 319. doi:10.2307/249008

Delfabbro, P., King, D. L., & Williams, J. (2021). The psychology of cryptocurrency trading: Risk and protective factors. *Journal of Behavioral Addictions*, *10*(2), 201–207. doi:10.1556/2006.2021.00037 PMID:34152998

Desai, K., & Parikh, R. (n.d.). Money laundering and cryptocurrency. *International Research Journal of Commerce Arts and Science*, *10*. http://www.casirj.com

Devanur, N. R., & Fortnow, L. (2009). A computational theory of awareness and decision making. *Proceedings of the 11th Conference on Theoretical Aspects of Rationality and Knowledge - TARK '09*, 99. 10.1145/1562814.1562830

Dirsehan, T., & Can, C. (2020). Examination of trust and sustainability concerns in autonomous vehicle adoption. *Technology in Society*, *63*, 101361. doi:10.1016/j.techsoc.2020.101361

Dyntu, V., & Dykyi, O. (2019). Cryptocurrency in the system of money laundering. *Baltic Journal of Economic Studies*, *4*(5), 75. doi:10.30525/2256-0742/2018-4-5-75-81

Fornell, C., & Larcker, D. F. (1981). Structural Equation Models with Unobservable Variables and Measurement Error: Algebra and Statistics. *JMR, Journal of Marketing Research*, *18*(3), 382–388. doi:10.1177/002224378101800313

Hall, B., & Khan, B. (2003). *Adoption of New Technology*. doi:10.3386/w9730

Hasan, S. Z., Ayub, H., Ellahi, A., & Saleem, M. (2022). A Moderated Mediation Model of Factors Influencing Intention to Adopt Cryptocurrency among University Students. *Human Behavior and Emerging Technologies*, *2022*, 1–14. doi:10.1155/2022/9718920

Kanwalinderjit, & ... , G. (. (2020). Traceability of Cryptocurrency Transactions using Blockchain Analytics. *International Journal of Computing and Digital Systems*, *9*(2), 159–165. doi:10.12785/ijcds/090202

Khan, M. A., & Salah, K. (2018). IoT security: Review, blockchain solutions, and open challenges. *Future Generation Computer Systems*, *82*, 395–411. doi:10.1016/j.future.2017.11.022

Krishnan, S., Teo, T. S. H., & Lymm, J. (2017). Determinants of electronic participation and electronic government maturity: Insights from cross-country data. *International Journal of Information Management*, *37*(4), 297–312. doi:10.1016/j.ijinfomgt.2017.03.002

Krishnaraju, V., Mathew, S. K., & Sugumaran, V. (2016). Web personalization for user acceptance of technology: An empirical investigation of E-government services. *Information Systems Frontiers*, *18*(3), 579–595. doi:10.100710796-015-9550-9

Kulviwat, S., Bruner, G. C. II, & Al-Shuridah, O. (2009). The role of social influence on adoption of high tech innovations: The moderating effect of public/private consumption. *Journal of Business Research*, *62*(7), 706–712. doi:10.1016/j.jbusres.2007.04.014

Kumar, A. (2021). A Study of the Impact of Crypto Currency on the Indian Payment system. *Asian Journal of Management*, 310–316. doi:10.52711/2321-5763.2021.00047

Lam, L. W. (2012). Impact of competitiveness on salespeople's commitment and performance. *Journal of Business Research*, *65*(9), 1328–1334. doi:10.1016/j.jbusres.2011.10.026

Mazambani, L., & Mutambara, E. (2020). Predicting FinTech innovation adoption in South Africa: The case of cryptocurrency. *African Journal of Economic and Management Studies*, *11*(1), 30–50. doi:10.1108/AJEMS-04-2019-0152

Mehta, K., Sharma, R., & Vyas, V. (2022) A quantile regression approach to study the impact of aluminium prices on manufacturing sector of India during COVID era, *Materials Today: Proceedings, 65*(8), 3506-3511. doi:10.1016/j.matpr.2022.06.087

Merhi, M., Hone, K., & Tarhini, A. (2019). A cross-cultural study of the intention to use mobile banking between Lebanese and British consumers: Extending UTAUT2 with security, privacy and trust. *Technology in Society*, *59*, 101151. doi:10.1016/j.techsoc.2019.101151

Muchlis Gazali, H., Hafiz Bin Che Ismail, C. M., & Amboala, T. (2018). Exploring the Intention to Invest in Cryptocurrency: The Case of Bitcoin. *2018 International Conference on Information and Communication Technology for the Muslim World (ICT4M)*, 64–68. 10.1109/ICT4M.2018.00021

Omane-Adjepong, M., & Alagidede, I. P. (2020). High- and low-level chaos in the time and frequency market returns of leading cryptocurrencies and emerging assets. *Chaos, Solitons, and Fractals*, *132*, 109563. doi:10.1016/j.chaos.2019.109563

Patil, P., Tamilmani, K., Rana, N. P., & Raghavan, V. (2020). Understanding consumer adoption of mobile payment in India: Extending Meta-UTAUT model with personal innovativeness, anxiety, trust, and grievance redressal. *International Journal of Information Management*, *54*, 102144. doi:10.1016/j.ijinfomgt.2020.102144

Podsakoff, P. M., MacKenzie, S. B., & Podsakoff, N. P. (2012). Sources of Method Bias in Social Science Research and Recommendations on How to Control It. *Annual Review of Psychology*, *63*(1), 539–569. doi:10.1146/annurev-psych-120710-100452 PMID:21838546

Poongodi, T., Sujatha, R., Sumathi, D., Suresh, P., & Balamurugan, B. (2020). Blockchain in social networking. In *Cryptocurrencies and Blockchain Technology Applications* (pp. 55–76). Wiley. doi:10.1002/9781119621201.ch4

Rajalahti, T., & Kvalheim, O. M. (2011). Multivariate data analysis in pharmaceutics: A tutorial review. *International Journal of Pharmaceutics*, *417*(1–2), 280–290. doi:10.1016/j.ijpharm.2011.02.019 PMID:21335075

Rey-Ares, L., Fernández-López, S., Castro-González, S., & Rodeiro-Pazos, D. (2021). Does self-control constitute a driver of millennials' financial behaviors and attitudes? *Journal of Behavioral and Experimental Economics*, *93*, 101702. doi:10.1016/j.socec.2021.101702

Shanab, E. A., & Haider, S. (2015). Major factors influencing the adoption of m-government in Jordan. *Electronic Government, an International Journal, 11*(4), 223. doi:10.1504/EG.2015.071394

Shareef, M. A., Kumar, V., Kumar, U., & Dwivedi, Y. K. (2011). e-Government Adoption Model (GAM): Differing service maturity levels. *Government Information Quarterly*, *28*(1), 17–35. doi:10.1016/j.giq.2010.05.006

Sharma, M., Antony, R., Sehrawat, R., Cruz, A. C., & Daim, T. U. (2022). Exploring post-adoption behaviors of e-service users: Evidence from the hospitality sector/online travel services. *Technology in Society*, *68*, 101781. doi:10.1016/j.techsoc.2021.101781

Sharma, R., Mehta, K., & Vyas, V. (2020). Responsible Investing: A Study on Non-Economic Goals and Investors' Characteristics. *Applied Finance Letters, 9*(SI), 63-78. doi:10.24135/afl.v9i2.245

Singh, A. K., & Singh, K. V. (n.d.). Cryptocurrency in India-Its effect and future on economy with special reference to bitcoin. *International Journal of Research in Economics and Social Sciences*. http://www.euroasiapub.org

Trivedi, S., Mehta, K., & Sharma, R. (2021). Systematic Literature Review on Application of Blockchain Technology in E-Finance and Financial Services. *Journal of Technology Management & Innovation*, *16*(3), 90–102. doi:10.4067/S0718-27242021000300089

Venkatesh, M., Morris, Davis, & Davis. (2003). User Acceptance of Information Technology: Toward a Unified View. *Management Information Systems Quarterly*, *27*(3), 425. doi:10.2307/30036540

Venkatesh, V., & Bala, H. (2008). Technology Acceptance Model 3 and a Research Agenda on Interventions. *Decision Sciences*, *39*(2), 273–315. doi:10.1111/j.1540-5915.2008.00192.x

Vyas, Mehta, & Sharma. (2020). Investigating socially responsible investing behaviour of Indian investors using structural equation modelling. *Journal of Sustainable Finance & Investment*, 1-23. doi:10.1080/20430795.2020.1790958

Walton, S. M., Thong, J. Y. L., & Xu, X. (n.d.). *Consumer acceptance and use of information technology: Extending the unified theory of acceptance and use of technology*. Academic Press.

Winter, J. S., & Davidson, E. (2019). Big data governance of personal health information and challenges to contextual integrity. *The Information Society*, *35*(1), 36–51. doi:10.1080/01972243.2018.1542648

Yeong, Y.-C., Kalid, K. S., Savita, K. S., Ahmad, M. N., & Zaffar, M. (2022). Sustainable cryptocurrency adoption assessment among IT enthusiasts and cryptocurrency social communities. *Sustainable Energy Technologies and Assessments*, *52*, 102085. doi:10.1016/j.seta.2022.102085

Zhao, N., Cheng, X., & Guo, X. (2018). Impact of information spread and investment behavior on the diffusion of internet investment products. *Physica A*, *512*, 427–436. doi:10.1016/j.physa.2018.08.075

KEY TERMS AND DEFINITIONS

Confirmatory Factor Analysis (CFA): It is a statistical method used to evaluate a measurement model that describes the links between observable variables and latent structures or components.

Cryptocurrency: It is a decentralised, cryptographically secure digital money. Cryptocurrencies leverage blockchain technology for safe, transparent transactions without a central authority.

Exploratory Factor Analysis: EFA (exploratory factor analysis) is a statistical approach for determining the underlying structure of a collection of data. It is a data reduction strategy that aims to find a lesser number of underlying factors that explain the correlations between a greater number of observable variables.

Investor Behaviour: Investor behaviour is the study of people and organisations make investment choices. It entails understanding how investors perceive risks and rewards, assess investment opportunities, arrange their portfolios, and respond to market swings and other external circumstances.

Millennial Investors in India: Millennials are a prominent demographic group in India and are emerging as a new force in the country's financial environment. They were born between 1981 and 1996. As the Indian economy advances and the middle class increases, more millennials get access to financial resources and become interested in investing.

Perceived Trustworthiness: The degree to which someone or something is seen by others as being trustworthy, believable, and sincere is known as perceived trustworthiness. It is a subjective view impacted by a number of variables, including reputation, communication, conduct, and prior experiences.

Unified Theory of Acceptance and Use of Technology: (UTAUT): It is a theoretical framework to understand and predict the adoption and use of new technologies by individuals. In 2005, Venkatesh et al. created the method, and since then, it has had widespread use in the study of information systems.

APPENDIX 1 DETAIL OF CONSTRUCTS USED IN THE STUDY

Figure 3.

Name of construct		Source of items, Abbreviations used
Facilitating Conditions	1. I have the necessary resources to use Cryptocurrencies. 2. I am knowledgeable enough to utilise Cryptocurrencies. 3. Cryptocurrencies work well with the other technology I utilize. 4. When I am having difficulty with Cryptocurrencies, I may seek assistance from others.	Venkatesh et. al., 2012, Beza et al. 2018. (FCon)
Social Influence	1. People that have an impact on my behaviour believe that I should utilise cryptocurrencies. 2 People that matter to me believe that I should utilise cryptocurrencies. 3.When using cryptocurrencies, the crypto digital market comes in handy. 4. In general, bitcoin groups have backed the usage of cryptocurrency.	Venkatesh et. al., 2016 (SInf)
Perceived Usefulness	1. I feel that dealing with cryptocurrency would be simple & straightforward. 2. As an alternative currency, I intend to leverage the valuable Cryptocurrency technology. 3. Using cryptocurrency is preferable to using government funds Due to the privacy of its consumers. 4 Cryptocurrency payment is less expensive than traditional payment options.	Adams, Nelson, & Todd, 1992; F. Davis, 1989; Venkatesh & Davis, 2000 (PrUs)
Perceived Trust-worthiness *(new)*	1. I believe that cryptocurrency would act in my best interest. 2. I expect information about cryptocurrency financial system is sincere. 3. The electronic exchange systems that deals with cryptocurrency should be highly secured from cyber-attacks. 4. To maintain security, I believe cryptocurrency should be endorsed by the government. 5. I believe that cryptocurrency is more reliable and secure currency.	Slade et. al. 2015, Carter et al., 2016; Venkatesh et al., 2011 (Authors self-constructed) (PTru)
Perceived ease of use	1. When I consider the usage of cryptocurrency, I generally feel puzzled. 2. When I consider using cryptocurrency, I am afraid about losing money. 3. I perceived that cryptocurrency is an easy phenomenon to understand or use. 4. I believe cryptocurrency is a simple thing to comprehend and apply. 5. It is easy to remember the functions of cryptocurrency.	Davis et al., 1989; Venkatesh & Davis, 2000 (PrEoU)
Awareness *(new)*	1. I am aware of cryptocurrency. 2. I know cryptocurrency as a mode of exchange or as an alternate currency. 3. I know cryptocurrency is the more attractive type of currency as compared to gold and silver. 4. I am likely to participate educational/training programs regarding the overall features of cryptocurrency.	Shareef et al., 2011, Krishnan, Teo, & Lymm, 2017) (Author self-constructed) (Arns)
Intention to use cryptocurrency	1. I intend to use Bitcoin as an alternative source of currency to buy or sell products in future. 2. I believe using Bitcoin is very helpful to timely fulfil my obligations. 3. I intend to use Bitcoin on a regular basis. 4. I will encourage others to use Bitcoin as a mode of exchange. 5. I prefer to use Bitcoin for the game purposes only.	V. Kumar et al., 2007; Liu et al., 2014; Chen et al., 2016; McKnight, Venkatesh et al., 2016) (InUCr)

Chapter 7
A Bibliometric Analysis of Green Banking:
Present State and Future Directions

Kiran Mehta
Chitkara Business School, Chitkara University, India

Renuka Sharma
https://orcid.org/0000-0002-6514-3411
Chitkara Business School, Chitkara University, India

Samiksha Jalotra
Chitkara Business School, Chitkara University, India

ABSTRACT

The disastrous impacts of catastrophic events, droughts, and severe weather on people throughout the globe forced everyone to think about global warming and its implications and do all they can to fix it. Global warming prevention and sustainability include governments, corporations, and people. The topic of environmentally responsible banking has been widely covered in the media since the turn of the century. As a result, there is an urgent need to understand and categorise the growing body of sustainable banking research. The present study is intended to conduct a bibliometric analysis of green banking literature for the duration of 2001-2022. The findings offer a view on the development of the academic literature relating to sustainable banking all through the course of time as well as throughout academic disciplines and publications.

DOI: 10.4018/978-1-6684-8361-9.ch007

BACKGROUND AND INTRODUCTION

Sustainable development is the process of meeting the needs of the present without compromising the ability of the next generation to do the same. It requires balancing economic expansion with preserving natural resources and societal accountability. Green finance is inextricably linked to sustainable development since it is a vital instrument for improving environmental sustainability. Banks may contribute to foster sustainable economic development and lessen the negative environmental effect of the financial sector by encouraging environmentally sustainable investments and supporting environmentally sustainable enterprises. Green finance and sustainable development are two fundamental ideas that are inextricably linked. By promoting green business practices and backing sustainable economic growth, banks can help make the future safer and more equitable for all people. When a bank practices green banking, it shows that it is a socially responsible organization by improving its internal and external environmental sustainability in its day-to-day operations. Banks that practice sustainability, conservation, or ethics may be referred to by various names (Sharma & Choubey, 2022). In addition, green banking promotes eco-friendly methods of doing business and investing to mitigate the adverse effects of conventional banking on the natural world. It is the promotion of ecologically friendly operations, goods, and services by a financial institution. It entails incorporating environmental factors into the bank's lending, investment, and internal operations and policies. Green banks work to reduce their carbon footprint by utilising renewable energy, reducing waste, and implementing environment conscious operations. Consumers are also urged to adopt ecologically responsible practises such as acquiring environmentally friendly/green technologies, conserving energy, and recycling. Green banking refers to a banking industry that combines new technologies, operational improvements, and shifting customer behaviour. In a market that is becoming more competitive, everyone can benefit from a win-win situation. In addition to being good for the environment, adopting greener banking practises will also lead to improved operational effectiveness, a decreased risk to fraud and manual errors, and cost savings in banking operations. Most of the services that businesses need to take advantage of these opportunities are provided by financial institutions (Biswas, 2011). In 2009, Florida was the first state to adopt green banking. As the largest commercial bank in India, SBI (State Bank of India) has pioneered new approaches to sustainability and "green banking." The Coimbatore wind farm project was officially launched by SBI, the first bank to do so. The term "green banking" is becoming more commonplace. The Indian Banks Association (IBA) defines a "green bank" as an ordinary bank that considers all social, environmental, and ecological concerns, emphasising protecting the planet's ecosystems and its natural resources. It is also commonly referred to as a sustainable bank or ethical bank.

Green banking could help the planet by reducing the carbon footprints of financial institutions and their customers. Online banking is an example of "green banking." Online banking is good for the environment because it reduces paper use, mail delivery, and branch visits. It's important to remember that online banking can potentially boost a bank's productivity and earnings. A paper published by the Reserve Bank of India on November 8, 2010 and titled Policy Environment discusses green banking and green IT initiatives for Indian banks on pages 56 and 57. Indian banks, like many others around the world, are embracing CSR and the importance of protecting natural resources. Technology and services like online banking make it much easier for banks to advocate for sustainable practices (Dipika, 2015). The term "green banking" has only been around for a short time in the banking sector. Sustainable banking is a form of banking that prioritises environmental protection and social responsibility. In the international banking sector, eco-friendly practices are getting serious attention. Some international financial institutions began implementing environmental and social (E&S) risk policies in 1997 in order to control lending practices. Indian financial institutions have only recently begun implementing these features. However, a sizable percentage of them can't wait to start implementing this strategy. The Reserve Bank of India issued a circular (RBI 2007-2008/216) in December 2007 stressing the importance of responsible banking and promoting sustainable development, as well as the need for Indian banks to set up institutional frameworks to accomplish this (Katyal & Nagpal, 2014). DBS Bank India's Green Deposit Program for corporate clients is a newly unveiled, streamlined way for businesses to fund eco-friendly initiatives or projects. Banks are contributing to environmental restoration by encouraging the growth of green industries through "Green Banking," which is beneficial for banks, businesses, and the economy as a whole. DBS Bank is one of the few financial institutions in the world to offer lending and trade credit solutions to environmentally conscious and sustainable green industries, in addition to a new Green Deposit product. Green banking will make it simpler for banks to strengthen their financial standing in the future, in addition to ensuring the greening of sectors (Bhardwaj & Malhotra 2013). In order to thrive, change must permeate all spheres of life. Humanity has made great strides throughout history as economic development has been a global priority. But growth has also brought about negative outcomes like biodiversity loss, climate change, environmental degradation, and so on. Even financial institutions aren't safe from this trend. To create a sustainable and prosperous low-carbon economy, banks can play a pivotal role in driving the necessary economic transformation by creating new opportunities for financing, investment, and portfolio management (Sudhalakshmi & Chinnadorai, 2014). By streamlining customer, business, and internal operational strategies, decisions, and actions, the banking industry can protect the environment and reduce greenhouse gas emissions. Credit risks, startup difficulties, and reputational risks are just some of the dangers that green banks must deal with. The Reserve Bank of India (RBI) and the Government of India (GoI) should spearhead the creation of green policy guidelines and financial incentives to promote the widespread use of green banking practices in India (Bahl, 2012). Even though banks aren't usually thought of as a polluting industry, their current scale of operations has significantly increased their carbon footprint due to factors like their extensive use of energy (for things like lighting, air conditioning, electronic and electrical equipment, IT, etc.), high paper waste, lack of green buildings, and more. Financial institutions must implement carbon footprint-minimising practices and products to ensure long-term viability. Green banking encourages eco-friendly actions while reducing the financial sector's carbon footprint. This can be done in various ways, such as switching to online banking from visiting a physical bank, opening commercial deposits and money market accounts with online banks, and paying bills online instead of by mail (Sudhalakshmi & Chinnadorai, 2014). Green banking isn't just about helping the environment; it will also boost the quality of the bank's assets over time. In order to invest in new energy systems, the International Panel on Climate Change predicts a range of \$1.6–\$3.8 trillion. The European Union needs to spend an extra €180 billion annually on renewable energy and energy efficiency until 2030 to achieve its climate goals. Annual infrastructure spending in Asia should be at least \$1.7 billion US. Therefore, in the coming years, it will be essential for the financial sector to play an active role in sustainable development (Pratap, 2020). Due to the excessive use of non-renewable resources as raw materials by businesses, "green management" has emerged as a necessity in the twenty-first century. Urbanisation and industrialisation have worsened ecological and environmental imbalances around the world by increasing the demand for non-renewable resources. By producing and distributing environmentally friendly goods and services, "green management" creates and implements novel organisational approaches and developments to achieve long-term sustainability, social responsibility, waste reduction, and competitive advantage (Kaur, 2019). The arrival of the twenty-first century and the onset of the globalization age has left us with one significant deficiency: a lack of vegetation. Green banking is the practice of reducing the environmental impact of banking by promoting eco-friendly practices and policies. A sustainable bank is a type of ethical bank. It entails encouraging eco-friendly banking practices by incorporating organizational shifts, technology developments, and shifting customer needs (Prabhu, 2021). Warming of the planet has become a problem on a national and international scale. The primary focus of everyone's efforts to address the global warming crisis should be on green and ecologically friendly projects. The banking business has a positive reputation regarding its impact on pollution and emissions. The banking business in India is one of the largest in the world, and it caters to customers of all income levels. The environmental impact of the expanding economy is significant. Before the start of the twentieth century, banks in India restricted the use of green in their currency. With the advent of ATMs in 2001, the Indian banking sector pioneered the development of a paperless, eco-friendly banking system (Sudarshan Giramkar, 2018).

Online banking, short message service banking, and automated teller machine banking are all examples of "green banking" that eliminate the need for paper transactions. Deforestation may be reduced with the use of paperless finance. Free online bill-paying services. Subsidizes the cost of borrowing money for green projects and goods. The benefits of green financing may be promoted to employers and bank customers. Banks worldwide are "becoming green" by implementing environmentally friendly policies and offering innovative green products. By switching to digital banking, you can save paper and save money. A statement can be sent to a customer's email address electronically. The financial industry may aid in preserving the world by taking eco-friendly measures. Financial institutions may be relied upon. Financial institutions are of the idea that everyone can make a difference in the planet's ecosystem and that even the slightest "GREEN" action taken today will significantly influence bringing about a greener tomorrow. The mission is to provide accessible automated channels at a low cost while raising environmental, national, and social consciousness. By bringing attention to the issue of global warming through "green finance," businesses may help make the world a better place to live. Traditional financial institutions did not engage in "green banking" or seek investment possibilities in green businesses until recently (Aarif & Faizanuddin, 2021).

On the other hand, a bank's day-to-day operations, such as using paper, power, stationery, lighting, air conditioning, and electronic equipment, directly influence the environment. Their rapid expansion has increased their direct impact on the environment, even if their carbon footprint is still relatively small compared to the steel or oil and gas sectors. In addition, banks indirectly influence the environment since they provide long-term funding to businesses that have a detrimental impact on the environment, such as cement, fertilizers, nuclear power, steel, oil and gas, and paper. Implementing greener banking methods is good for the environment, employees' productivity, and customers' wallets since it reduces the likelihood of human mistakes and fraud. Green banking is a priority in our country. Hence, banks should use eco-friendly procedures, from operations to buildings to investments to financing. Green finance may be a valuable tool in the pursuit of sustainable development. In order to reduce its environmental impact, green banking processes transactions digitally and online. Green banking today affects all facets of the business. Green banking has two main components. The first is cutting down on carbon emissions and efficiently using all resources. The second is to promote and support exclusively environmentally beneficial investments. Hence, green banking includes environmentally friendly credit distribution and sustainable resource usage (Soundarya & Soniya, 2020).

Some advanced countries are adopting green banking policies. For instance, the European Investment Bank (EIB) has launched a green bond program to support regional climate action plans throughout Europe. The Bank of England has opened a climate change centre to help financial institutions cope with climate-related risks. JPMorgan Chase, Bank of America, and Goldman Sachs are a few major American financial institutions committed to carbon neutrality or significantly decreased their carbon footprint. Also, the United States Federal Reserve Bank has established a supervisory climate committee to investigate climate risks' impact on the financial sector. In addition, the Japanese Financial Services Agency has established guidelines for incorporating environmental, social, and governance (ESG) considerations into financial institution decision-making. A few examples of developed countries' green banking initiatives are included above.

Green banking and other initiatives to promote sustainability are also gaining traction in the financial sectors of many developing countries. For example, in 2011, the Bangladesh Bank (the country's central bank) enacted a Green Banking Policy to push banks toward more eco-friendly practices. The rule requires banks to allocate at least 5% of their loan portfolios to clean energy and energy efficiency initiatives. Since 2014, the Brazilian Development Bank has funded sustainable energy projects nationwide. Wind and solar power generation expansion projects can apply for grants from the program. As part of its attempts to encourage green finance, the People's Bank of China established guidelines for green bonds in 2015. The Chinese government has committed to reducing carbon emissions and increasing the use of renewable energy. The Reserve Bank of India has implemented regulations to promote "green banking" in India. In 2011, the Reserve Bank of India (RBI) launched a program encouraging financial institutions to invest in clean energy and efficiency initiatives. The Indian government has established goals to enhance the share of renewable energy in the country's total energy output. The Central Bank of Kenya established the Green Bond Program to support activities that improve environmental sustainability. Among the industries that will benefit from this program's money are those involved in renewable energy, energy efficiency, and sustainable agriculture. The countries above are just a small sample of the numerous developing nations making strides toward green finance and a more sustainable financial system.

Research Methodology

To achieve the study's objective, the researchers utilized bibliometric analysis. This technique, first introduced by Pritchard (1969), has become widely popular in aiding quantitative analysis for understanding the literature. Previous research (Ansari and Kant, 2017) has commonly employed this method to highlight crucial aspects such as country, institutions, researchers, publications, and more across various academic topics. Scopus, a database commonly used for bibliometric research (Liu et al., 2012), especially in social sciences (Zupic and Cater, 2015), was the source of our study's 237 peer-reviewed publications, which matched searches for "green banking," "ethical banking," "sustainability," and other relevant phrases related to the term "financial sector/industry." Conference proceedings and non-English language resources were excluded, while our focus was on the business, economics, environment, arts, computing, and social science subjects. The abstracts and full articles of the publications were examined to ensure relevance, reducing the sample size to 125. Our study follows the "institutionalism" research line, concentrating on financial institutions rather than the "welfarist" approach, which focuses more on the customers of financial institutions. Finally, we compared our results with other studies and analysed any discrepancies to arrive at a final sample size of 125 studies spanning 2001-2022.

Information relevant to these publications is retrieved in text format, downloaded, and linked to the VOSviewer for further analysis using the aforementioned parameters (Eck and Waltman, 2017). The VOSviewer is a high-tech tool that may be used to record, visualise, and locate various study maps. More so, maps showing relationships between nations, institutions, publications, writers, and concepts are provided to aid in analysis and interpretation (Castillo-Vergara et al., 2018). In nutshell, following process of the research has been followed in the present study.

1. Defining the field of the study-Green Banking, Sustainability.
2. selection of database-SCOPUS.
3. Criteria for paper selection:
    i. TITLE-ABS-KEY "Green Banking Sustainability"
    ii. Duration is 2001-2022
    iii. Journal articles only
    iv. Language English
4. Analysis of the data collected: Use of VOSviewer for further analysis of the data on the basis of different criteria like keywords, countries, authors, citations, etc.

ANALYSIS AND RESULTS

According to the research on this issue, the popularity of Green Banking, also known as online banking, surged following demonetization. We all know that most people rely on cash transactions in a nation like India. However, once demonetization was enacted, people began using less cash and more internet transactions for their daily necessities, which helped the government of India's green banking project. The newest data from green banking shows that the number of papers has grown between 2016–2017, likely due to the decline in the usage of cash and the rise in the prevalence of digital transactions. Also you can see that after 2016-2017 there is a double digit growth in the documents of green banking in 2018 goes to 14 documents of green banking and we can also see from the above data that after COVID pandemic there is a boost in online transaction and research document i.e. 29 documents which is the highest documents from past more than 20 years study and the least number of documents is 1 which was from year 2001-2007. Since 2009, we've seen a significant increase in articles. Since irresponsible behaviour in the industry was found to be the cause of the crisis, the 2008 financial crisis was a major environmental disaster that stimulated and raised research attention to sustainable banking issues.

Table 1. Yearly publication on green banking

Yearly Publication	No. of Documents
2022	29
2021	29
2020	15
2019	7
2018	14
2017	5
2016	5
2015	2
2014	4
2013	4
2012	2
2011	3
2010	2
2007	1
2005	1
2003	1
2001	1

From Table 2 it can be observed that the top ten countries that are largest contributions to Green Banking research. China is the popular country with 19 publications which basically depicting that China has highest no of publications related to Green Banking topic because China's contribution in fossil fuel emissions before to 2000 is the reason for this. As a result, it started promoting green banking to rebuild its reputation among the European Union. India is second with 13 publication because India started promoting green banking initiative more after demonetization so that people started using less cash and more online transaction which helps them in boosting green banking initiative and Covid is also the reason which also help India to increase in online transaction. Bangladesh is third with 12 publications related to green banking.

Table 2. Countries contribution in green banking

Country Type	No. of Documents as per Country Type
China	19
India	13
Bangladesh	12
Malaysia	11
United States	11
Indonesia	10
United Kingdom	8
Pakistan	6
Germany	5
Italy	5

Sustainability Switzerland, Environment Development And Sustainability, and International Journal Of Green Economics are three of the greatest publications for producing Green Banking content. From the information above, it is clear that Sustainability Switzerland has produced 14 journals on green banking (see Table 3). Although there are many more journals that publish articles on this topic, we are focusing on the top 10 green banking journals in the table above because they publish the most publications on this subject. We can also demonstrate the existence of two journals on green banking in various major publications. There are several more as well, such as the International Journal of Energy Economics and Policy, the lop Conference Series Earth and Environmental Science, and the International Journal of Asian Business and Information Management.

Table 3. Top publications journals of green banking

Source (Top Journal)	No. of Source Titles (Journals)
Sustainability Switzerland	14
Environment Development and Sustainability	4
International Journal of Green Economics	4
Environmental Science and Pollution Research	3
International Journal of Bank Marketing	3
Wit Transactions on Ecology and the Environment	3
Economic Change and Restructuring	2
International Journal of Asian Business and Information Management	2
International Journal of Energy Economics and Policy	2
Iop Conference Series Earth and Environmental Science	2

The subject area covered by green banking research is shown in Table 4. The most popular subject is environmental science, which has 49 articles. This shows that environmental science is a field that supports green banking initiatives and helps the banking industry be more sustainable by facilitating paperless transactions. Second with 45 publications is the field of economics, econometrics, finance, and social science. Researchers in economics have also made contributions to the field of green banking. Third with 38 publications is the subject of business, management, and accounting. The reason they rank among the top three would be that they encourage businesses to adopt online transactions, which save cash and assist firms manage their finances and destroy fewer natural resources. They also promoting different apps that encourage even small vendors to use online transactions rather than cash transactions.

CITATION ANALYSIS ACCORDING TO COUNTRIES

The citation analysis between different nations is displayed in Figure 1. China is the most active country in terms of publications on the subject of green banking, with 19 articles receiving 155 citations. This indicates that China has the strongest cluster of connections with Bangladesh, India, Japan, Malaysia, and many other nations. This is due to China's large pre-2000 contribution to world emissions of fossil fuels. To rebuild its reputation within the European Union, it started to promote green banking. With 13 publications and 79 citations, India ranks in second place and has the second-largest cluster following China. Bangladesh ranks third among the countries with the most citations in the research of green banking, with 12 publications and 104 citations.

Table 4. Top subject covered in green banking

Subject Area	No. of Subject Area
Environmental Science	49
Economics, Econometrics and Finance	45
Social Sciences	45
Business, Management and Accounting	38
Energy	28
Computer Science	21
Engineering	15
Earth and Planetary Sciences	7
Decision Sciences	6
Arts and Humanities	5
Mathematics	4
Agricultural and Biological Sciences	3
Materials Science	2
Chemical Engineering	1
Physics and Astronomy	1

Table 5. Citation analysis according to countries

Country	Documents	Citations
China	19	155
India	13	79
Bangladesh	12	104
Malaysia	11	73
united states	11	117
Indonesia	10	69
United Kingdom	8	36
Pakistan	6	80
Germany	5	10
Italy	5	158
Australia	4	87
France	4	11
Bahrain	3	62
Hungary	3	3
Netherlands	3	25

Figure 1. Citation analysis between different nations is displayed

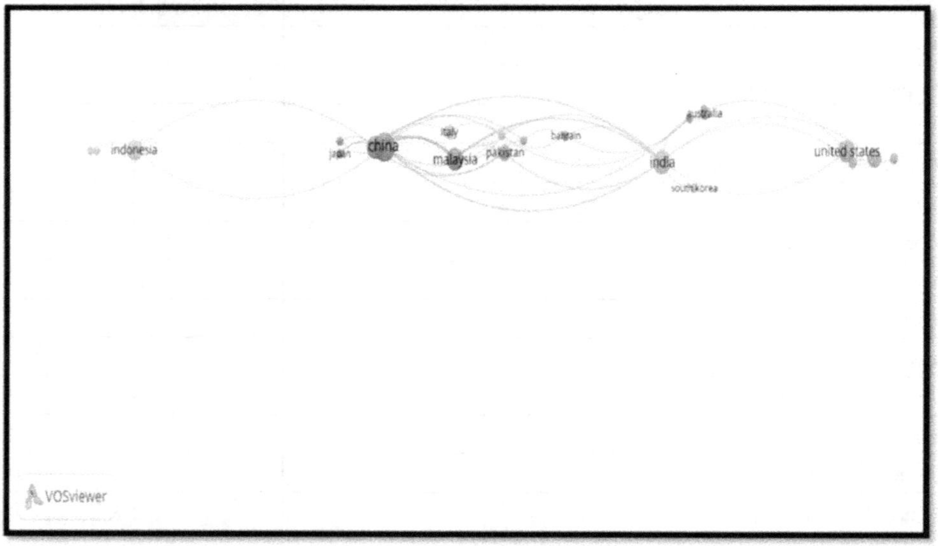

CITATION ANALYSIS BETWEEN VARIOUS AUTHORS

The study of citations between different authors is shown in Figure 2. Fu is the author that has received the most citations in publications on green banking. Fu. q. has coordinated with numerous other authors, authored two articles, and received 58 citations for their work. With 49 citations and 2 publications, Kumar K. and Prakash A. are ranked second, indicating that they have the most citations in research papers. With 43 citations and 2 published publications, Phoumin H., Taghizadeh-hesary F., and Yoshino N. are in third position. These authors have all made significant contributions to the study of green banking.

CO-OCCURRENCE ACCORDING TO KEYWORDS

The final analysis included keywords that were provided by the authors of the publication and those occurred more than twice in the Scopus database. 118 of the 709 keywords actually met the requirements. Sustainability showed up 52 times as the most frequent keyword. Several keywords that have appeared more than twice include sustainable development, green economies, banking, and sustainable banking.

Table 6. Citation analysis between various authors

Author	Documents	Citations
Fu Q.	2	58
Kumar K.	2	49
Prakash A.	2	49
Phoumin H.	2	43
Taghizadeh-Hesary F.	2	43
Yoshino N.	2	43
Julia T.	2	40
Kassim S.	2	40
Nisha N.	5	31
Iqbal M.	3	26

Figure 2. The study of citations between different authors

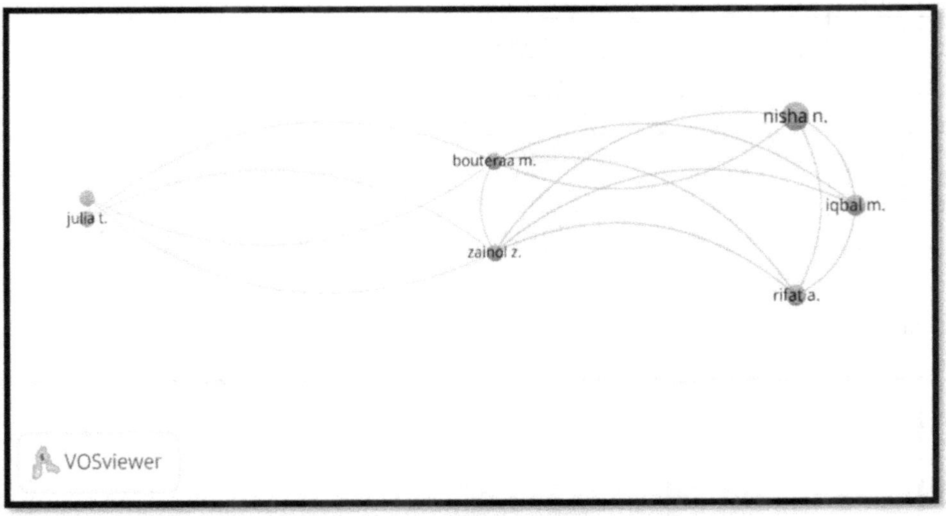

Table 7. Co-occurrence according to keywords

ID	Keyword	Occurrences
626	Sustainability	52
648	Sustainable Development	39
44	Banking	34
319	Green Banking	27
342	Green Finance	17
643	Sustainable Banking	13
29	Bangladesh	11
340	Green Economy	10
128	Corporate Social Responsibility	9
56	Banks	8
247	Environmental Sustainability	7
287	Financial System	7
653	Sustainable Finance	7
96	China	6
266	Finance	6
45	Banking Industry	5
98	Climate Change	5
161	Decision Making	5
280	Financial Market	5
424	Investment	5

Figure 3.

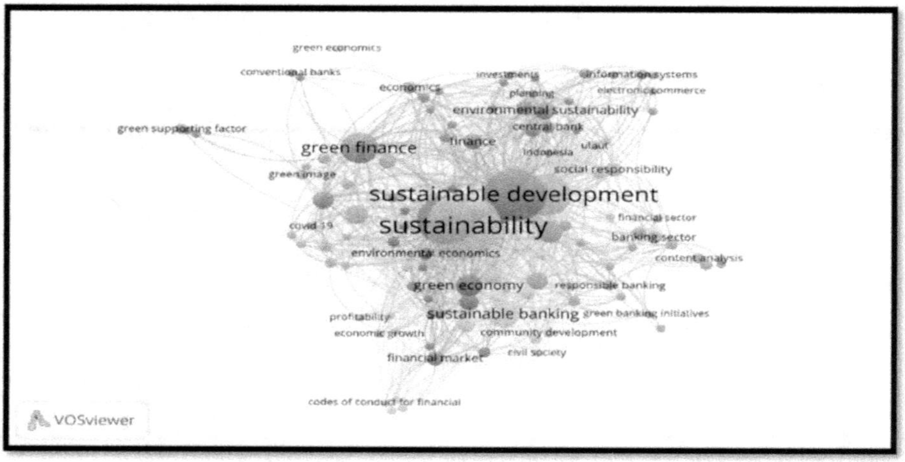

CONCLUSION OF THE STUDY

The concept of "green banking" is relatively new in the financial industry. It is a type of banking that takes into account the effects on society and the environment, and its major goal is to safeguard and preserve the environment. In a market that is becoming more competitive, everyone can benefit from a win-win situation. This study's primary goal is to investigate green banking performance trends and research efforts. The most cited and most recent influential research publications were reviewed in order to undertake numerous analyses using a bibliometric analysis, including citation, co-occurrence of keywords, and discussion. The COVID-19 pandemic and other global shocks have the potential to accelerate the pace of business change towards sustainability. The ongoing crisis has highlighted the interconnectedness of global systems and the urgent need for businesses to adopt more resilient and sustainable practices. In response, there has been a surge in research efforts to better understand the relationship between sustainability and business. The findings of this study indicate that the use of maps and visual trends has been effective in promoting sustainable banking research globally. By providing a visual representation of complex data, maps and trends can help researchers identify patterns and relationships, leading to new insights and discoveries. This, in turn, has contributed to an increase in the number of international publications on sustainable banking studies. As more businesses recognize the importance of sustainability in the wake of global crises, research in this field will continue to grow, further driving the transition towards a more sustainable future. With 19 documents, the China was the nation with the biggest contribution to publications in sustainable banking studies.

In today's society, the term "green banking" is becoming increasingly prevalent. The Indian Banks Association (IBA, 2014) defines a green bank as a financial institution that places equal importance on social, environmental, and ecological factors while prioritizing the preservation of the environment and the Earth's natural resources. The terms "ethical bank" and "sustainable bank" are also commonly used to describe banks that follow environmentally-friendly practices. Green banking initiatives have the potential to benefit both financial institutions and their customers by reducing their carbon footprints. As consumers shift towards more eco-friendly lifestyles, they are increasingly demanding that their banks align with their values by providing sustainable options. Online banking is one example of a green banking effort that has gained popularity in recent years. By offering digital services that eliminate the need for paper-based transactions, online banking reduces paper usage and minimizes the energy consumed by traditional banking operations. As the effects of climate change become more pronounced, the role of green banking in preserving the environment is gaining momentum. Banks and financial institutions have a responsibility to adopt sustainable practices to reduce their negative impact on the environment. The increased adoption of green banking practices not only benefits the environment but also helps build stronger relationships between financial institutions and their customers by demonstrating their commitment to social responsibility.

The Green Banking sector in India is poised for rapid growth due to the government's goal of reducing the country's carbon intensity by 20–25 per cent between 2015 and 2022. The initial cost to remedy the problem of social and environmental norms will be high for Indian institutions. For green banking to be effective in India, the Reserve Bank of India (RBI) and the government must work together to provide green policy guidelines and financial incentives. Banks' chances of survival are inversely proportional to the rate of global warming. Green banking is a business model that Indian banks should immediately embrace if they are serious about practising sustainable banking.

Compared to more conventional banking techniques, online banking has several environmental advantages, such as less paper use, less mail, and fewer travels to branch offices. Internet banking may help boost productivity and earnings for financial institutions. The Reserve Bank of India issued a policy paper on green banking and green IT in India titled Policy Environment on November 8, 2010. Indian banks, like many others throughout the world, are putting greater emphasis on CSR initiatives that benefit society and the environment. Banks in India are more likely to embrace environmentally friendly policies thanks to the widespread use of computers and banking services like online banking. The breadth and depth of the data gained by bibliometric analysis depend heavily on the database used. Scopus, one of the largest and most comprehensive databases, was used extensively in this study to compile information on banking performance research articles published between 2015 and 2022.

Adding other sources, such as book chapters and conference proceedings, might improve the database's comprehensiveness. While the keyword selection technique was considered sufficient for most papers on banking performance, certain studies may have yet to be noticed. Because of this, one may find more relevant articles if one utilizes other or more keywords. The scope of the subsequent bibliometric studies might be widened by including new databases and keywords in the article-gathering process.

In conclusion, "green banking" is a relatively new term in the financial sector that considers the effects of banking activities on society and the natural environment. The study's authors used bibliometric analysis to examine rising worldwide interest in sustainable banking and emerging patterns in green banking performance. Using green banking practices is beneficial for financial institutions and their clients, and the COVID-19 epidemic and other worldwide crises have underscored the necessity for businesses to embrace sustainable methods. The Reserve Bank of India (RBI) and the government of India may help realize India's green banking potential by establishing appropriate regulatory guidelines and offering appropriate financial incentives.

REFERENCES

Ansari, Z., & Kant, R. (2016). A state-of-art literature review reflecting 15 years of focus on sustainable supply chain management. *Journal of Cleaner Production, 142*, 2524–2543. Advance online publication. doi:10.1016/j.jclepro.2016.11.023

Bahl, S. (2012). Green banking-The new strategic imperative. *Asian Journal of Research in Business Economics and Management, 2*(2), 176–185.

Bhardwaj, B. R., & Malhotra, A. (2013). Green banking strategies: Sustainability through corporate entrepreneurship. *Greener Journal of Business and Management Studies, 3*(4), 180–193. doi:10.15580/GJBMS.2013.4.122412343

Biswas, N. (2011). Sustainable green banking approach: The need of the hour. *Business Spectrum, 1*(1), 32–38.

Castillo-Vergara, M., Alvarez-Marin, A., & Placencio-Hidalgo, D. (2018). A bibliometric analysis of creativity in the field of business economics. *Journal of Business Research, 85*, 1–9. doi:10.1016/j.jbusres.2017.12.011

Dipika. (2015). Green Banking in India: A Study of Various Strategies Adopt by Banks for Sustainable Development. *International Journal of Engineering Research & Technology, 3*(10).

Giramkar, S. (2018). Green Banking In India: A Study For Sustainable Development. In *Proceedings of Economics and Finance Conferences*. International Institute of Social and Economic Sciences. 10.20472/EFC.2018.010.010

Katyal, S., & Nagpal, S. (2014). Role of Green Banking in Sustainable Development of India. *International Journal of 360 Management Review, 2*(1), 2320-7132.

Kaur, H. (n.d.). *Study of Green Movement in Indian Corporate Houses For Sustainable Growth*. Academic Press.

Liu, X., Zhan, F. B., Hong, S., Niu, B., & Liu, Y. (2012). A bibliometric study of earthquake research: 1900–2010. *Scientometrics, 92*(3), 747–765. doi:10.100711192-011-0599-z

Prabhu, G. N. (2021). *Green Banking practices–A case study on Indian Green Banking system*. www. ijrpr. com

Pratap, K. (2020). *A study of green banking as an innovative tools in environment sustainability*. Academic Press.

Pritchard, A. (1969). Statistical Bibliography or Bibliometrics? *The Journal of Documentation*, *25*, 348–349.

Sharma, M., & Choubey, A. (2022). Green banking initiatives: A qualitative study on Indian banking sector. *Environment, Development and Sustainability*, *24*(1), 293–319. doi:10.100710668-021-01426-9 PMID:33967597

Sudhalakshmi, K., & Chinnadorai, K. (2014). Green banking practices in Indian banks. *International Journal of Management and Commerce Innovations*, *2*(1), 232–235.

van Eck, N. J., & Waltman, L. (2017). Citation-based clustering of publications using CitNetExplorer and VOSviewer. *Scientometrics*, *111*(2), 1053–1070. doi:10.100711192-017-2300-7 PMID:28490825

Zupic, I., & Cater, T. (2015). Bibliometric Methods in Management and Organization. *Organizational Research Methods*, *18*(3), 429–472. doi:10.1177/1094428114562629

Chapter 8
Prospects of Blockchain Technology in Finance Sustainability

Gurpreet Kaur
Chitkara Business School, Chitkara University, India

Mehak Bansal
Chitkara Business School, Chitkara University, India

Taranpreet Kaur
Chitkara Business School, Chitkara University, India

ABSTRACT

Blockchain technology is a multidisciplinary approach that is growing fast in the economy. The attributes possessed by blockchain are evident in many sectors in the economy such as banking, financial services, innovation, creativity, etc. Blockchain has brought out a revolutionary change in the economy as it provides transparency, cost efficiency, accuracy. Application of blockchain technologies in finance will help in attaining sustainability. The chapter provides comprehensive review of past studies on the role of blockchain technologies in financial services and in enhancing financial performances. The study will provide better insights to the managers of the financial institutions regarding the pros and cons of blockchain technology.

DOI: 10.4018/978-1-6684-8361-9.ch008

INTRODUCTION

A blockchain is a kind of dispersed record innovation that consists of developing arrangements of records that are safely connected together utilizing cryptography. A blockchain was designed by an individual using the name Satoshi Nakamoto in 2008 to act as the public dispersed for bitcoin cryptographic money exchanges (Xu et al., 2019). The implementation of the blockchain in bitcoin made it the first digital currency to address the problem of double spending without the aid of a trusted source of power or central server.

The design of bitcoin has inspired other, transparent to the public, widely used blockchains and applications for digital money. One may think of the blockchain as a type of installation train. The monetary business is perceiving the ground breaking effect of blockchain innovation to create new income, convey process proficiency, further develop end-client experience and diminish risk in business tasks. The acceptance of blockchain into different exchange financing instruments gives an upper hand to banks also, their clients and also improves blockchain transactions in trade finance.

Blockchain with an increased degree of usefulness in exchange finance processes decreases handling time for reports, exchange expenses and expands level of transparency (Bogucharskov et al., 2018). Several financial institutions, ranging from banks and safety net suppliers to review and expert support businesses, are investing in blockchain-based agreements.

Finance is the backbone for the entire economy. Blockchain initially emerged as the technology that underpins virtual currencies like Bitcoin. In view of the fact that trust is established not by powerful delegates like banks and states but rather by network consensus, cryptography, coordinated effort, and clever programming, any remaining types of resources can be moved and kept safely, anonymously, and from one peer to another. (Tapscott & Tapscott, 2017). The present paper provides comprehensive review of past studies on role of blockchain technologies in financial services and in enhancing financial performances. The study will provide better insights to the managers of the financial institutions regarding the pros & cons of blockchain technology.

Review of Literature

Many researchers in the past have studies blockchain as a tool for ensuring finance sustainability. Najjar et al. (2022) examined the role of blockchain technology across multiple supply networks, paper concluded that through the use of blockchain innovation, blockchain can upgrade supplier perceivability by the joining of multi-level stock organizations. Patel et al. (2022) did a bibliometric review on blockchain in banking and finance and concluded that by adopting blockchain based technologies will result into highly interconnected ventures. Kumar et al. (2022) made an attempt to study blockchain as a device towards economic growth and financial development. The paper concluded that the blockchain plays a significant effect in getting the portion and money related nuances of the country and by the adoption of blockchain innovation, people feel more comfortable and secure making exchanges. In a similar study by Kucukaltan et al. (2022) investigation was done on how blockchain emerges as a problematic inventory finance innovation. The paper concluded that blockchain technology neither focused on data security nor on finance as underlined in the composition but it focused on the merits of extending digitalisation in the supply chain.

Casey et al. (2021) concluded that adoption of blockchain technology might change various pieces of the money related organizations area and the greater economy. Park and Li (2021) viewed that blockchain innovation as a instrument for overall development in the economy. Kabanda (2021) studied blockchain development in a Zimbabwean organization security system and inferred that the cybersecurity in Zimbabwe is still below progress and a lot of work needs to be done to ensure that the country is acceptably defended from cybersecurity dangers. Schulz and Feist (2021) investigated role of green climate funds as a creative climate finance and administration arrangement. Kowalski et al. (2021) in a paper recommended that the adoption of blockchain technology, significantly impact the relationship between trading partners and will enhance a trust connection between exchanging partners by working on the security of exchanges and information trades.

Zhang et al. (2020) made an attempt to study the application and the difficulties of blockchain technology. This paper concluded that the blockchain technology is helpful for monetary business to normally and exactly perceive client credit conditions and also rebuild the money related market credit structure.

Ali et al. (2020) perceived blockchain technology as a innovative strategy in the financial area which could help in maintaining financial sustainability in the economy. In a similar study Chen and Bellavitis (2020) investigate that blockchain technology creates a foundation for new business models and can reduce a transaction cost for decentralized business. Wu and Duan (2019) study that blockchain innovation increases the number of monetary organisations and involves the monetary tasks like R3CEV, Hyperledger and Qiwi. This paper also concludes that monetary organisations have begun to apply the blockchain technology to reduce exchange expenses and increase in functional efficiencies. Gurtu and Johny (2019) concluded that the blockchain innovation jumps into supply chain management and will be helpful for researchers in distinguishing the regions where blockchain is the best and can be executed. Zachariadis et al. (2019) made an attempt to study the hurdles of blockchain technology in financial services. Joo et al. (2019) study the usage and responsibility of blockchain advancement in field of finance. Collomb et al. (2019) studied blockchain development as a regulatory advancement, incorporating express standards and goals into the mechanical surface of an ICO. Ozii (2019) concluded that blockchain innovation in finance is a inter mediator in the financial structure by the regulators.

Zagurskiy and Titova (2019) focused on guidelines of blockchain useful application and scattered record improvement in extension of blockchain. The paper concluded that blockchain innovation application can increase high grounds of association and decline a bet by extending reliable information about production. Xu et al. (2019) made an attempt to study the impact of blockchain on finance. The paper concluded that a huge percentage of the population perceives blockchain as a problematic issue wherein on other hand analysts have a favourable opinion on usage of blockchain. Therefore, it can conclude that there is a need to focus on more studies on blockchain & its impact on finance. Polyviou et al. (2019) focuses five unique financial industries that should be definitely different by the use of blockchain innovation and presumed that the blockchain development holds the likelihood to disturb the money related business by changing how different organizations are coordinated in the financial business. Varma (2019) made an attempt to study possibly qualitative elective methods for sorting the finances. The paper concluded that the blockchain is still developing and it is challenging to predict its success simply by use space of cryptographic types of cash. Sheth and Dttani (2019) study the overview of blockchain technology. This paper outlines the functions, kinds and various stages of blockchain technology. Tilooby (2018) made an attempt to study the influence of blockchain on financial transactions. This paper concluded that change in financial trades and present extra open doors for spread out money related foundations too concerning new participants.

Arifin et al. (2018) study that by introducing crowdfunding in monetary consideration arises in monetary innovation. This paper concluded that crowdfunding is a sensible means to progress money related joining, and blockchain development could assist with directing the new worries looked by stage managers. Knezevic (2018) studies the impact of the blockchain innovation on the monetary area and different businesses through digital currency. This paper also concluded that the effect of new advancement on business, over all on financial tasks. Bogucharskov et al. (2018) study the techniques for blockchain application in exchange finance and to recognize key pieces of the additional creating exchanges process. Treleaven et al. (2017) studied how blockchain innovation promises to be tremendously problematic and participating in both public and classified region enlisting applications. Tapscott and Tapscott (2017) study that the blockchain is definitely not an existential risk to the people who embrace the new advancement perspective and disturb from inside.

Yoo (2017) studies how blockchain are used in the financial region. Guyen (2016) investigate that the new development should convey huge advantages to purchasers, current monetary system and society generally.Mori and Taketoshi (2016) study that the layout of new development requires the speculation to involve and apply blockchain development in money related monetary areas. Fanning and Centers (2016) studied on how blockchain works and conclude that blockchain is a scattered data base that keeps a continually creating summary of data records that are cemented against changing.

In reference to the above studies, it can be deduced that that blockchain with its vast potential has the capacity to create finance sustainability. Even after possessing so many advantages it not widely accepted due to lack of trust, awareness. Therefore, there is requirement to explore the blockchain technology and how it can be applied in finance.

Table 1. The table shows the frequency of papers published in different years with name of the journal authors

Year of Publication	Journal Name	Author Name
2022	Journal of sustainable finance and investment	Najjar et.al
2022	Research in international business and finance	Patel et.al
2022	The British journal of Administrative Management	Kumar et.al
2022	International journal of production research	Kucukaltan et.al
2021	Geneva Reports on the world Economy 21	Casey et.al
2021	Zimbabwe Academy of Sciences	Kabanda
2021	earth system governance	Schulz and Marian
2021	Technological forecasting and social change	Kowalski et.al
2021	department of marketing and supply chain management	Park and Li
2020	Systems research and behavioural science	Zhang et.al
2020	International journal of information management	Ali et.al
2020	Journal of business venturing Insights	Chen and Bellavitis
2019	Journal of Physics: conference series	Wu and Duan
2019	International journal of physical distribution and logistics Management	Gurtu and Johny
2019	Information and organization	Zachariadis et. al
2019	Stevens Institute of technology School of Business Research Paper	Chen and Bellavitis
2019	Managerial Finance	Joo et. al
2019	Journal of Corporate accounting and finance	Yu et. al

continues on following page

Table 1. Continued

Year of Publication	Journal Name	Author Name
2019	Cambridge university Press	Collomb et.al
2019	international finance review	Ozii et.al
2019	graduate institute of technology management	Chang et.al
2019	journal of automation and information science	Zagurskkiy and Titova
2019	Financial innovation	Xu et. al
2019	3rd annual decentralized conference	Polyviou et. al
2019	Journal indexing and metrics	Varma
2019	Journal for convergence in technology	Sheth and Dttani
2018	Georgia state university	Al Tilooby
2018	International Journal of Management and applied Research	Arifin et. al
2018	Montenegrin journal of economics	Dusko Knezevic
2018	Journal of reviews on global economics	Bogucharskov et. al
2017	Harvard business Review	Tapscott and Tapscott
2017	Journal of innovation and entrepreneurship	Yoo
2016	International conference on Green Technology and development	Nguyen
2016	Journal of securities operations and custody	Mori and Taketoshi
2016	Journal of corporate accounting and finance	Fanning and Centers

Source: Author's compilation.

Table 2. This table represents the year of publication, name of the journal and title of the paper

Year of Publication	Journal Name	Title of Paper
2022	Journal of sustainable finance and investment	The role of blockchain technology in the integration of sustainability practices across multi-tier supply networks
2022	Research in international business and finance	Blockchain in banking and finance: A bibliometric review
2022	The British journal of Administrative Management	Application of blockchain technology as a support tool in economic & financial development
2022	International journal of production research	Investigating the themes in supply chain finance: The emergence of blockchain as a disruptive technology
2021	Geneva Reports on the world Economy 21	The impact of blockchain technology on finance a catalyst for change

continues on following page

Table 2. Continued

Year of Publication	Journal Name	Title of Paper
2021	Zimbabwe Academy of Sciences	Model structure for blockchain technology and cryptocurrency for the financial services sector in Zimbabwe
2021	earth system governance	Leveraging blockchain technology for innovative climate finance under green climate fund
2021	Technological forecasting and social change	Blockchain technology and trust relationship in trade finance
2021	department of marketing and supply chain management	The effect of blockchain technology on supply chain sustainability performances
2020	Systems research and behavioural science	The challenges and countermeasures of blockchain in finance and economics
2020	International journal of information management	The state of play of blockchain technology in the financial services sector
2020	Journal of business venturing Insights	Blockchain disruption and decentralized finance: The rise of decentralized business models
2019	Journal of Physics: conference series	The application of blockchain technology in financial markets
2019	International journal of physical distribution and logistics Management	Potential of blockchain technology in supply chain management: A literature review
2019	Information and organization	Governance and control in distributed ledgers: Understanding the challenges facing blockchain technology in financial services
2019	Stevens Institute of technology School of Business Research Paper	Decentralized finance: Blockchain technology and the quest for an open financial system
2019	Managerial Finance	Cryptocurrency, a successful application of blockchain technology
2019	Journal of Corporate accounting and finance	Blockchain: The introduction and its application in financial accounting
2019	Cambridge university Press	Blockchain technology and financial regulation: A risk- based approach to the regulation of icos
2019	international finance review	Blockchain finance: Questions regulators ask
2019	graduate institute of technology management	Blockchain enabled trade finance innovation: A potential paradigm shift on using letter of credit
2019	journal of automation and information science	Problems and prospects of blockchain technology usage in supply chains
2019	Financial innovation	A systematic review of blockchain
2019	3rd annual decentralized conference	Blockchain technology: Financial sector application beyond cryptocurrencies
2019	Journal indexing and metrics	Blockchain in finance
2019	Journal for convergence in technology	Overview of blockchain technology

continues on following page

Table 2. Continued

Year of Publication	Journal Name	Title of Paper
2018	Georgia state university	The impact of blockchain technology on financial transactions
2018	International Journal of Management and applied Research	The application of blockchain technology in crowdfunding: Towards financial inclusion via technology
2018	Montenegrin journal of economics	Impact of blockchain technology platform in changing the financial sector and other industries
2018	Journal of reviews on global economics	Adoption of blockchain technology in trade finance process
2017		Blockchain technology in finance
2017	Harvard business Review	How blockchain is changing finance
2017	Journal of innovation and entrepreneurship	Blockchain based financial case analysis and its implications
2016	International conference on Green Technology and development	Blockchain- a financial technology for future sustainable development
2016	Journal of securities operations and custody	Financial technology: Blockchain and securities settlement
2016	Journal of corporate accounting and finance	Blockchain and its coming impact on financial services

Source: Author's compilation.

Table 3. This table shows title of paper with maximum no. of citations

Title of Paper	No. of Citations
Blockchain and its coming impact on financial services	531
Blockchain technology in finance	393
How blockchain is changing finance	383
Blockchain disruption and decentralized finance: The rise of decentralized business models	331
Blockchain- a financial technology for future sustainable development	272
A systematic review of blockchain	255
The state of play of blockchain technology in the financial services sector	167
Governance and control in distributed ledgers: Understanding the challenges facing blockchain technology in financial services	145
Potential of blockchain technology in supply chain management: A literature review	137
The impact of blockchain technology on finance a catalyst for change	133
Blockchain based financial case analysis and its implications	127
Blockchain: The introduction and its application in financial accounting	92

continues on following page

Table 2. Continued

Title of Paper	No. of Citations
Overview of blockchain technology	75
Blockchain in finance	70
Financial technology: Blockchain and securities settlement	69
The challenges and countermeasures of blockchain in finance and economics	68
The application of blockchain technology in crowdfunding: Towards financial inclusion via technology	68
The effect of blockchain technology on supply chain sustainability performances	67
Impact of blockchain technology platform in changing the financial sector and other industries	57
Blockchain enabled trade finance innovation: A potential paradigm shift on using letter of credit	53
Decentralized finance: Blockchain technology and the quest for an open financial system	45

Source: Author's compilation.

CONCLUSION

Blockchain is a crucial piece of technology that enhances economic growth and performance. The purpose of this study is to choose a block chain application method as an aid to financial and economic growth (Kumar et al., 2022).

This paper concludes that the blockchain innovation has been widely applied to monetary market, particularly in monetary note, cross-line installment and resource upheld securitization. Blockchain innovation depends on deviated cryptography, dispersed agreement and smart agreement, the utilization of blockchain innovation is currently at beginning stage. Later on, blockchain innovation can be additionally applied to monetary fields and monetary items. This study investigates the various the benefits and areas of blockchain application in exchange finance, also as additional possibilities for involving innovation around here: expanding online protection, performing exchanges in blockchain, and presenting a discretion debate goal component inside blockchain stage. Blockchain with an elevated degree of usefulness in exchange finance processes lessens handling time for reports, exchange expenses and expands level of straightforwardness. Blockchain which was the fundamental innovation behind bitcoin is presently utilized in monetary area as well as now it has cross industry application. The use of the blockchain technology in monetary bookkeeping has a couple of issues to be settled including confined data taking care of limit, information protection, and administrative difficulties (Chang et al., 2019).

The study has implications on the regulators ad policy makers as the block chain application strategy will act as a guide to monetary and financial development, it is critical piece of innovation that upgrades monetary development and performance.

Implications of the Study

The study is beneficial for the policy makers, decision maker in formulating such framework as will help in maintaining financial sustainability.

REFERENCES

Ali, O., Ally, M., & Dwivedi, Y. (2020). The state of play of blockchain technology in the financial services sector: A systematic literature review. *International Journal of Information Management*, *54*, 102199. doi:10.1016/j.ijinfomgt.2020.102199

Bogucharskov, A. V., Pokamestov, I. E., Adamova, K. R., & Tropina, Z. N. (2018). Adoption of blockchain technology in trade finance process. *Journal of Reviews on Global Economics*, *7*, 510–515. doi:10.6000/1929-7092.2018.07.47

Casey, M., Crane, J., Gensler, G., Johnson, S., & Narula, N. (2018). *The impact of blockchain technology on finance: A catalyst for change*. Academic Press.

Chang, S. E., Luo, H. L., & Chen, Y. (2019). Blockchain-enabled trade finance innovation: A potential paradigm shift on using letter of credit. *Sustainability*, *12*(1), 188. doi:10.3390u12010188

Chen, Y., & Bellavitis, C. (2019). *Decentralized finance: Blockchain technology and the quest for an open financial system*. Stevens Institute of Technology School of Business Research Paper.

Chen, Y., & Bellavitis, C. (2020). Blockchain disruption and decentralized finance: The rise of decentralized business models. *Journal of Business Venturing Insights*, *13*, e00151. doi:10.1016/j.jbvi.2019.e00151

Collomb, A., De Filippi, P., & Klara, S. O. K. (2019). Blockchain technology and financial regulation: A risk-based approach to the regulation of ICOs. *European Journal of Risk Regulation*, *10*(2), 263–314. doi:10.1017/err.2019.41

Fanning, K., & Centers, D. P. (2016). Blockchain and its coming impact on financial services. *Journal of Corporate Accounting & Finance*, *27*(5), 53–57. doi:10.1002/jcaf.22179

Gurtu, A., & Johny, J. (2019). Potential of blockchain technology in supply chain management: A literature review. *International Journal of Physical Distribution & Logistics Management*, *49*(9), 881–900. doi:10.1108/IJPDLM-11-2018-0371

Joo, M. H., Nishikawa, Y., & Dandapani, K. (2019). Cryptocurrency, a successful application of blockchain technology. *Managerial Finance*.

Kabanda, G. (2021). *Model Structure for Block Chain Technology and Cryptocurrency for the financial services sector in Zimbabwe*. Academic Press.

Knezevic, D. (2018). Impact of blockchain technology platform in changing the financial sector and other industries. *Montenegrin Journal of Economics*, *14*(1), 109–120. doi:10.14254/1800-5845/2018.14-1.8

Kowalski, M., Lee, Z. W., & Chan, T. K. (2021). Blockchain technology and trust relationships in trade finance. *Technological Forecasting and Social Change*, *166*, 120641. doi:10.1016/j.techfore.2021.120641

Kucukaltan, B., Kamasak, R., Yalcinkaya, B., & Irani, Z. (2022). Investigating the themes in supply chain finance: The emergence of blockchain as a disruptive technology. *International Journal of Production Research*, 1–20. doi:10.1080/00207543.2022.2118886

Kumar, S., Kumar, B., Nagesh, Y., & Christian, F. (2022). Application of blockchain technology as a support tool in economic & financial development. *Manager-The British Journal of Administrative Management*.

Mori, T. (2016). Financial technology: Blockchain and securities settlement. *Journal of Securities Operations & Custody*, *8*(3), 208–227.

Muneeza, A., Arshad, N. A., & Arifin, A. T. (2018). The application of blockchain technology in crowdfunding: towards financial inclusion via technology. *International Journal of Management and Applied Research, 5*(2), 82-98.

Najjar, M., Alsurakji, I. H., El-Qanni, A., & Nour, A. I. (2022). The role of blockchain technology in the integration of sustainability practices across multi-tier supply networks: Implications and potential complexities. *Journal of Sustainable Finance & Investment*, 1-19.

Nguyen, Q. K. (2016, November). Blockchain-a financial technology for future sustainable development. In *2016 3rd International conference on green technology and sustainable development (GTSD)* (pp. 51-54). IEEE. 10.1109/GTSD.2016.22

Nguyen, Q. K. (2016). Blockchain - A Financial Technology for Future Sustainable Development. *3rd International Conference on Green Technology and Sustainable Development (GTSD)*, 20. 10.1109/GTSD.2016.22

Ozili, P. K. (2019). Blockchain finance: Questions regulators ask. In *Disruptive innovation in business and finance in the digital world*. Emerald Publishing Limited. doi:10.1108/S1569-376720190000020014

Park, A., & Li, H. (2021). The effect of blockchain technology on supply chain sustainability performances. *Sustainability*, *13*(4), 1726. doi:10.3390u13041726

Patel, R., Migliavacca, M., & Oriani, M. (2022). Blockchain in Banking and Finance: Is the best yet to come? A bibliometric review. *Research in International Business and Finance*, *62*, 101718. doi:10.1016/j.ribaf.2022.101718

Polyviou, A., Velanas, P., & Soldatos, J. (2019). Blockchain technology: Financial sector applications beyond cryptocurrencies. *Multidisciplinary Digital Publishing Institute Proceedings*, *28*(1), 7. doi:10.3390/proceedings2019028007

Schulz, K., & Feist, M. (2021). Leveraging blockchain technology for innovative climate finance under the Green Climate Fund. *Earth System Governance*, *7*, 100084. doi:10.1016/j.esg.2020.100084

Sheth, H., & Dattani, J. (2019). Overview of blockchain technology. *Asian Journal For Convergence In Technology*.

Tapscott, A., & Tapscott, D. (2017). How blockchain is changing finance. *Harvard Business Review*, *1*(9), 2–5.

Treleaven, P., Brown, R. G., & Yang, D. (2017). Blockchain technology in finance. *Computer*, *50*(9), 14–17. doi:10.1109/MC.2017.3571047

Trivedi, S., Mehta, K., & Sharma, R. (2021). Systematic literature review on application of blockchain technology in E-finance and financial services. *Journal of Technology Management & Innovation*, *16*(3), 89–102. doi:10.4067/S0718-27242021000300089

Varma, J. R. (2019). Blockchain in finance. *Vikalpa*, *44*(1), 1–11. doi:10.1177/0256090919839897

Wu, B., & Duan, T. (2019, March). The application of blockchain technology in financial markets. *Journal of Physics: Conference Series*, *1176*(4), 042094. doi:10.1088/1742-6596/1176/4/042094

Xu, M., Chen, X., & Kou, G. (2019). A systematic review of blockchain. *Financial Innovation*, *5*(1), 1–14. doi:10.118640854-019-0147-z

Yoo, S. (2017). *Blockchain based financial case analysis and its implications*. Asia Pacific Journal of Innovation and Entrepreneurship. doi:10.1108/APJIE-12-2017-036

Yu, T., Lin, Z., & Tang, Q. (2018). Blockchain: The introduction and its application in financial accounting. *Journal of Corporate Accounting & Finance*, *29*(4), 37–47. doi:10.1002/jcaf.22365

Zachariadis, M., Hileman, G., & Scott, S. V. (2019). Governance and control in distributed ledgers: Understanding the challenges facing blockchain technology in financial services. *Information and Organization*, *29*(2), 105–117. doi:10.1016/j.infoandorg.2019.03.001

Zagurskiy, O. N., & Titova, L. L. (2019). Problems and prospects of blockchain technology usage in supply chains. *Journal of Automation and Information Sciences*, *51*(11), 63–74. doi:10.1615/JAutomatInfScien.v51.i11.60

Zhang, L., Xie, Y., Zheng, Y., Xue, W., Zheng, X., & Xu, X. (2020). The challenges and countermeasures of blockchain in finance and economics. *Systems Research and Behavioral Science*, *37*(4), 691–698. doi:10.1002res.2710

Chapter 9
Sustainability as a Catalyst of Financial Development

Soumya Singhal
Trinity Institute of Professional Studies, Guru Gobind Singh Indraprastha University, India

Khushboo Gulati
Manav Rachna University, India

Isha Chhabra
K.R. Mangalam University, Gurugram, India

ABSTRACT

Sustainable development is a worldwide priority and the main objective of all countries. The sustainability concept focuses on economic, social, and ecological pillars. Every nation tries to bring sustainability to the economy, and financial development plays a major role. The financial sector actively promotes technological advancements in power production to lower emissions, significantly reducing energy pollution. The prior studies have shown mixed results on the interconnection between financial development and carbon dioxide emissions. The results also differ in developed and developing nations. The study shows that seventeen sustainability goals developed by the United Nations to achieve in the year 2030 have been affected due to COVID-19 and the Ukraine War. Hence, it has become imperative for nations to emphasize sustainable development.

DOI: 10.4018/978-1-6684-8361-9.ch009

INTRODUCTION

Sustainable development is a global priority and primary objective for all nations. Sustainable development is an all-encompassing idea composed of economic, social, and ecological sustainability. Yet, environmental degradation caused due to rising production of greenhouse gases (GHGs) with adverse effects on human health and ecological conditions is a global cause of concern (Ulucak et al., 2019) and a significant barrier to achieving sustainable development objectives.

Every nation now strives to meet sustainable development objectives. Therefore, environmental appropriateness has drawn the attention of researchers. The researchers have reported numerous environmental quality drivers, as well as they have recommended sources for constructing a sustainable environment. In addition, globalization, financial development, and energy use have recently received a great deal of attention as important factors of environmental quality.

What Is Sustainability?

The most widely used definition of a company's sustainability is its ability to undergo for numerous years. Helping the world may not be included in a firm's mission statement. Still, a company's success is achieving the maximization of shareholders' value which is further accompanied by a rise in social wealth, which can then be used to help the world. The companies generate profits by providing valuable goods and services for the consumers, which they are willing to pay guarantees not only customers' satisfaction but also other important stakeholders, such as regulators, government, environmentalists, and management taking care of the social environment.

In order to achieve such value, businesses must be well-managed and management should identify whether the financial returns are supporting the business activity or not. Companies should not only focus on profits, but also on the value the organization adds to society. The organization should evaluate the benefits and efficiencies offered to society by focusing on environmental, social, and governance (ESG) and competitive issues. The study focuses upon twin objectives. Firstly, the interconnection between financial development and carbon emissions has been studied. Secondly, the study emphasizes the sustainability goals laid down by the united nation in 2019 to be achieved by 2030.

IMPACT OF FINANCIAL DEVELOPMENT ON THE ENVIRONMENT

Several studies (Tamazian et al., 2009; Islam et al., 2013) have found that businesses should be provided funds from developed countries for investing in green energy and launching sustainable technologies to reduce the degradation of the environment. Contrary to this, researchers also found that industrial development exacerbates the degradation of the environment by providing funds to enterprises at a lower cost for the expansion of their production facilities and also provides consumer finance to individuals for purchasing energy-consumption devices (Dogan & Seker, 2016; Nwani & Omoke, 2020). The increased energy consumption by people dramatically increases Green House Gases (GHG) emissions, accelerating environmental degradation.

Bayar et al. (2020) examined how investment from abroad affected the environment in Europe and reported that FD and energy use hurt the environment quality. On the other side, it is found that financial development will generally initiate research and development, intensify commercial operations, and pull in foreign funds to invest in renewable energy sources for improving environmental sustainability (Frankel & Romer, 1999). Furthermore, by improving the effectiveness of the power sector, a well-established financial market lowers funding rates, streamlines procurement processes, and reduces the spread of oil pollution (Charfeddine, 2017). Yet, financial development will harm the environment's situation through increasing industrial practices, resulting in increased environmental damage (Jensen, 1996) The scholarly evidence (Charfeddine & Kahia, 2019; Salahuddin et al., 2018; Katircioğlu & Taşpinar, 2017) have conflicting opinions on how capital accumulation affects the quality of the environment.

How the Concept of Financial Sustainability Evolved

Our economic models were created during a time of relative abundance of natural resources and relatively low levels of CO_2 emissions. However, economic development has resulted in rising environmental dangers associated with economic policies and activities undertaken for growth and development. So, financial growth and protecting the environment are two of the most important problems the world is facing, and that is why they have become the top priorities globally. Scientists and entrepreneurs worldwide are interested in the topic and are trying to figure out how economic growth affects environmental quality (Fakher, 2019; Uddin et al., 2017). A robust and improved financial sector significantly impacts the efficiency of the financial system and promotes economic development. By eliminating investment barriers and facilitating access to financial resources, consumer and investor confidence is boosted, resulting in more large-ticket purchases and business growth.

In the late 20th century, Lutz & Kakkar (1975) renamed the phenomena of a continuous rise in earth's temperature known as "global warming" to "climate change". Since then, the adverse effects of financial development have started haunting people. Global warming is a severe problem in industrialized and developing nations, and environmental conservation has become a shared objective for all nations (Jahangir Alam et al., 2012). Therefore, sustainable development is a priority or primary objective for every nation. Sustainable development is an all-encompassing concept with three components, including economic, social, and environmental resilience, accompanied by financial development.

Challenges Faced in Financial Development

In theory, academics have a broad agreement about the important part financial integration plays in promoting economic expansion. Financial development promotes capital formation and helps people to learn what they need to know about investment activities and how to use resources efficiently. The financial sector actively promotes technological advancements in power production to lower emissions, which contributes significantly to reducing energy pollution (Jensen, 1996). Research shows that financial progress gauges how easily financial resources are made available to businesses by financial institutions and trade platforms, which can play a significant and beneficial role in halting ecological harm. As a result, financial prosperity lessens environmental deterioration, hence the objective is to narrow this difference.

How Is It Being Supported Globally?

IAS/IFRS, the worldwide accounting standards created by the IASB and supported by EFRAG, have been largely mandated for use in Europe since 2005 by Regulation 1606/02, subject to some restrictions (Biondi et al., 2020).

EFRAG seems to have been tasked with setting standards for corporate sustainability and reporting on sustainability at the European level. But because the IASB's work is bigger and possibly global, Therefore, to get a broader view, IASB work needs to be looked at carefully. The CSRD plan should also apply to privately owned corporations, whereas the IFRS foundation concentrates on publicly traded companies. The implementation of IFRS shows why their current goals differ in terms of what they want to accomplish and who will end up adopting them. (Biondi et al., 2020; Songini et al., 2022; Torre et al., 2020).

Corporate reporting appears to be trending toward emphasizing value more, extending above financial statements, and adding wealth only for shareholders, thanks to the efforts of the IFRS on the worldwide level and EFRAG on the European level.

A new organization designated the "International Sustainability Standards Board" (ISSB) has been proposed by the IFRS Foundation. This group will be in charge of setting accounting standards for sustainability for the upcoming fiscal years. In addition, ISSB will focus its writing on important research in environmental science and pollution.

The IFRS Foundation has explicitly called to focus on the critical macro-decisions that should lead the ISSB's future efforts by establishing international standards and guidelines that will be applied to the sustainability industry. Also, in November 2021, during COP26, the Un International Conference on Changing Climate, the ISSB was established. The IFRS Foundation will essentially undergo a process of strong governance reform by appointing ISSB to establish IFRS sustainability norms, reorganizing its structure to address better the ESG issues that the planet confronts and will experience more of in the future (Barnoussi et al., 2020; Shan et al., 2021).

LITERATURE REVIEW

This section highlights recent literature on financial development, sustainable development, and the impact of carbon emissions on financial development.

Interconnection Between the Economic, Social, and Financial Development in Sustainable Development

Numerous studies have been conducted in the past three decades on the interconnection between any organization's social, environmental, and financial performance. Figure 1. demonstrates the relationship between economic, social, and financial development. This section includes a literature overview of studies conducted on multiple domains to demonstrate the results. Khan et al. (2015) used a dataset to analyze whether the companies with material sustainability investments do better than those without, indicating that investments in these real sustainability issues make the company's shareholders more valuable. Ortas et al. (2013) looked at how well stocks did, based on the Dow Jones Sustainability Asia Pacific Index (DJSI-AP). DJSI-AP is the first investment screening method and is important for making manufacturing cleaner. Using a social and environmental screening procedure doesn't cost businesses more money or hurt how well they do with socially responsible investments (SRI). So, investors can give money to companies that want to be better for the environment by using greener production methods.

Figure 1. Interconnection between social, environmental, and financial performance
Source: Raworth (2017).

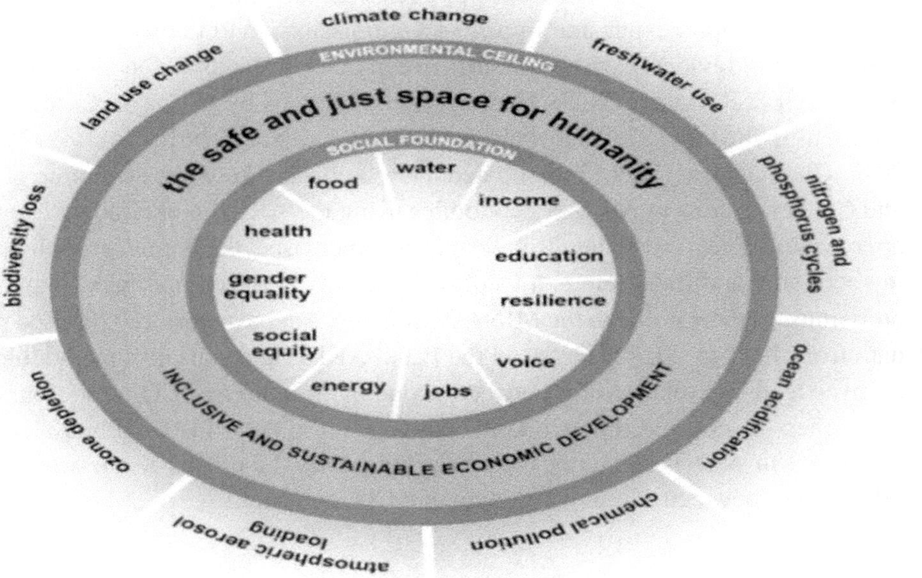

Yet, one of the greatest obstacles to achieving the sustainable development aim is the environmental degradation resulting from the rising production of GHGs. Because of its dangerous impacts on human health and ecological conditions, it has become a significant obstacle to sustainable development and is a matter of great concern (Ulucak et al., 2019). Recent studies have identified a strong relationship between financial development and carbon dioxide emissions (Bekhet et al., 2017; Maji et al., 2017; Shahbaz et al., 2013), but the research findings for developed and developing countries have reached different conclusions. Several studies have demonstrated that financial development reduces CO2 emissions and safeguards the environment (Jalil et al., 2010; King & Levine, 1993; Shahbaz et al., 2013; Zhang, 2011). Contrary to this, numerous researchers have discovered that economic growth exacerbates environmental degradation (Brännlund et al., 2007; Çoban & Topcu, 2013; Tang & Tan, 2014). Further research (Omri et al., 2015; Ozturk & Acaravci, 2013) also suggests no correlation between financial development and CO2 emissions.

Kirikkaleli & Kalmaz (2020) conducted research in Turkey to analyze the relationship between CO_2 emissions and economic growth. The researchers used the ARDL, and wavelet coherence approaches to study this connection. As per the findings, economic expansion impacts CO_2 emissions, and the wavelet coherence approach found evidence of movement between CO_2 emissions and economic growth. Kirikkaleli & Kalmaz's (2020) findings were validated by Adebayo & Odugbesan (2021) utilizing the ARDL and wavelet methods. Utilizing yearly data from 1971 to 2017, Chontanawat (2020) investigated the relationship between economic growth and CO2 emissions in ASEAN economies using the ARDL and Granger causality approaches. The researcher discovered that increased economic growth harms the economy and that there is a feedback causality between real growth and CO_2 emissions. In their study on the MINT economies, Adebayo et al. (2020) used panel data from 1981 to 2018. They used the Panel ARDL and causality methodologies to investigate the relationship between economic growth and CO_2 emissions. The researchers discovered that economic expansion did not substantially affect CO2 emissions in MINT economies. Furthermore, they identified a one-way causal relationship between economic growth and CO_2 emissions.

UNITED NATIONS SUSTAINABLE DEVELOPMENT GOALS

The United Nations produced the 2030 Agenda for Sustainable Development to manage the transition to a more sustainable and inclusive economy (United Nations, 2019). The 17 UN SDGs encourage action in important areas for humankind and the earth from 2015 to 2030. The 17 high-level goals are broken down into 169 targets to make implementation easier

Goal 1: No Poverty: Poverty is the killer of any industry. The whole financial system is based on additional research on financial instruments. The goal of SDG 2019 (Figure 3) is aimed to end poverty by 2030. It can be seen in Figure 3 that 90% of deaths due to disasters happen in low-middle economic countries. So, the world needs to focus on development and reduce poverty. However, per the SDG report 2020 (Figure 4), the last 4 years' progress has been derailed because of COVID-19 and Ukraine War. As a result, there has been an addition of 8 million workers into poverty rather than getting reduced. Not only this, but also the disaster-related death rose by six folds. The working poverty rate has increased for the first time in the last two decades.

Figure 2. No poverty
Source: United Nations (2019).

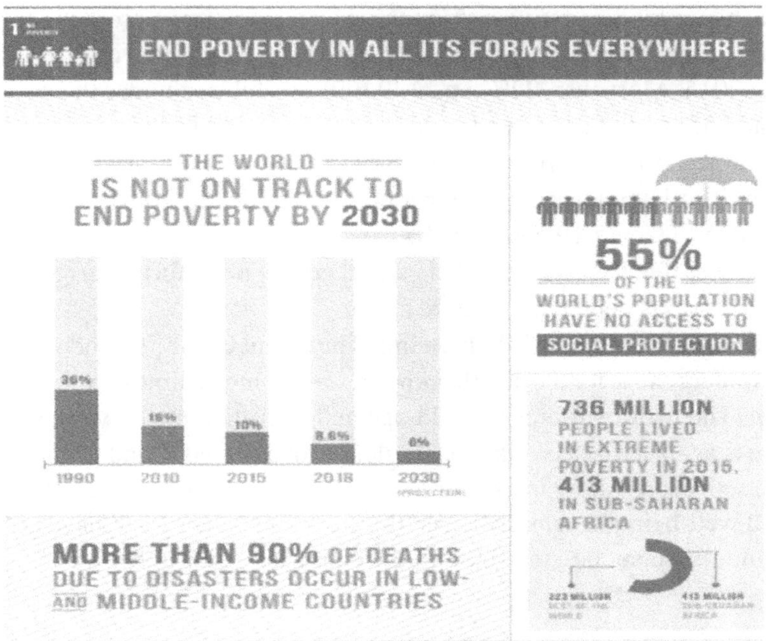

Figure 3. No poverty
Source: United Nations (2022).

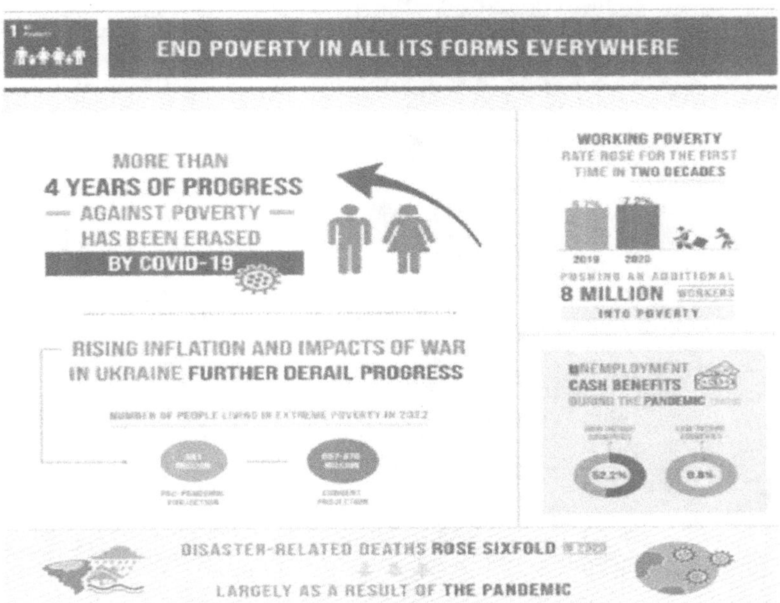

Goal 2: Zero Hunger: The financial growth is limited due to hunger in the economy. That is why the SDG Goal 2019, as presented in Figure 5, aims to end hunger, achieve food security and improved nutrition, and promote sustainable agriculture. Undernourished people increased to 821 million in 2019 from 784 million in 2015. Moreover, 22%, i.e., 149 million children under the age of 5, are stunted, and 5.9% of children under the age of 5, i.e., 40 millings, are overweight. The nations need to end hunger, specifically in South Saharan Africa and Southern Asia, as two third of undernourished people worldwide are from these two regions. However, due to Covid 19, climate change, and growing inequalities, about 1 out of 10 people suffer from hunger. This shortage has been further triggered due to the Ukraine war, as depicted in Figure 5.

Goal 3: Good Health and Well-Being: The recent Covid 19 pandemic emerged as the prominent cause for the poor health and well-being of almost everyone of every age group. The major sufferer was old-age and front-line health workers. Further, the progress against diseases like tuberculosis, malaria, HIV, and tropical diseases has seen a setback resulting in a decline in global life expectancy. Additionally, poor health and well-being have imbalanced the work-life balance and have contributed adversely to the financial growth of all the countries (refer to Figure 7).

Figure 4. Zero hunger
Source: United Nations (2019).

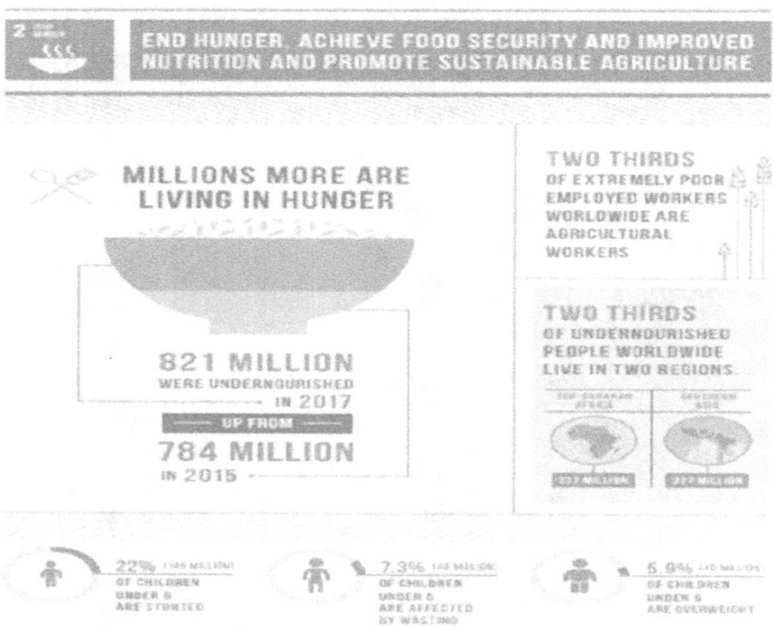

Figure 5. Zero hunger
Source: United Nations (2022).

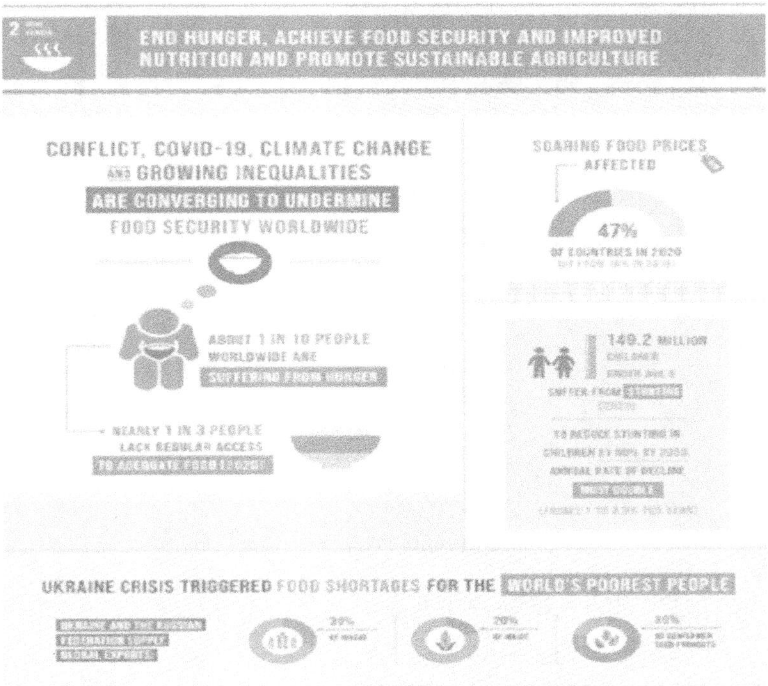

Goal 4: Quality Education: The absence of basic infrastructure of electricity, water, and sanitation in one-fourth of the educational institutions and the unavailability of computers and interest access in around half of the schools worldwide is a serious cause of concern. Moreover, the Russia-Ukraine war and the Covid pandemic have further increased the inequality in education level. It is disheartening to mention that 24 million students will never return to school after the pandemic (refer to Fig 8). Therefore, it is recommended that attempts should be made to develop basic infrastructure so that quality education can be provided to improve the financial health of emerging countries.

Goal 5: Gender Equality: Despite the continuous attempts, still the problem of gender equality will take years to be achieved. The representation of women in managerial positions has not improved much since 2019, as presented in Figure 8. Nearly half of the female population worldwide lacks the basic right to autonomy over their bodies. Moreover, the cases of child marriage have not been abolished until now, and they are expected to increase due to the pandemic. The lower participation of women in the economic system is a serious issue hampering financial growth, as half of the population cannot contribute to the system's financial health.

Figure 6. Good health and well being
Source: United Nations (2022).

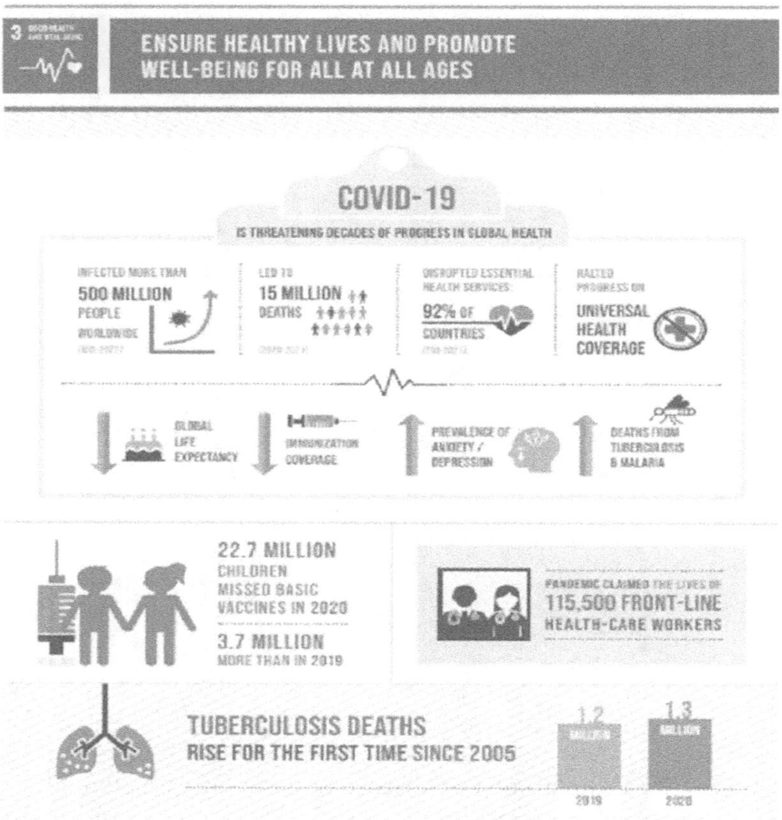

Goal 6: Clean Water and Sanitation: The availability of clean drinking water is essential for human life. But unfortunately, the present scenario depicts that even by 2030, 1.6 billion will not have access to clean drinking water (refer to Figure 10). The progress in providing clean sanitation and hand hygiene facilities is also not being achieved as per the current trends. Therefore, it is suggested to increase the pace of initiatives and activities by almost four-fold to ensure the availability and sustainable management of water and sanitation for all.

Goal 7: Affordable and Clean Energy: The current trend shows that people are moving towards renewable energy sources. In addition, the annual energy-intensity improvement rate is expected to increase to 3.2% from the current 1.9% (refer to Figure 11). On the other side, international financial flows for renewables decreased to $10.9 billion in 2019 from $24.7 billion in 2017, resulting in a decline in the electrification of the developing nations. This slower electrification is halting the financial growth of the countries.

Figure 7. Quality education
Source: United Nations (2022).

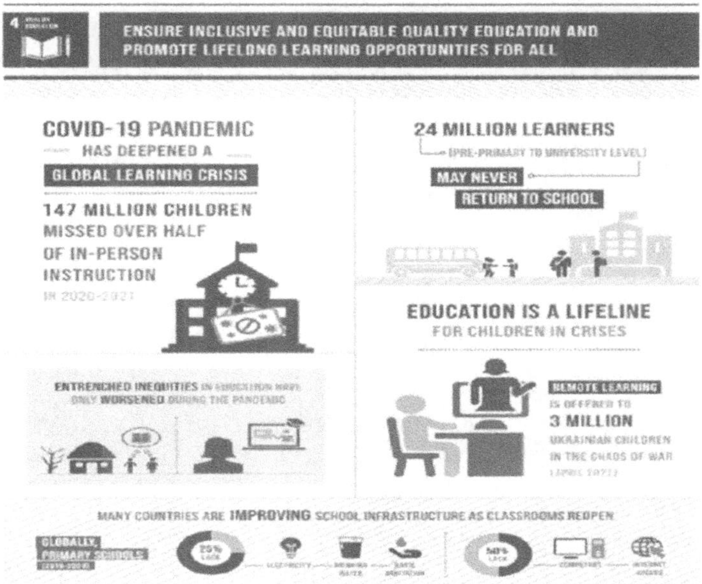

Figure 8. Gender equality
Source: United Nations (2022).

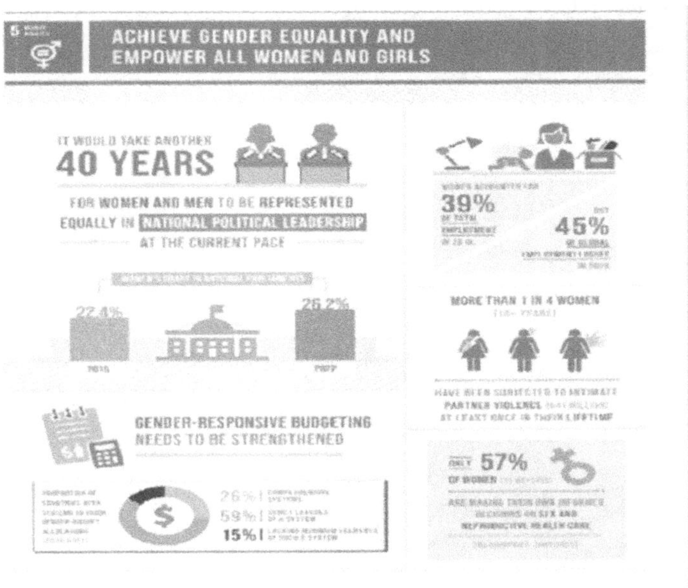

Figure 9. Clean water and sanitation
Source: United Nations (2022).

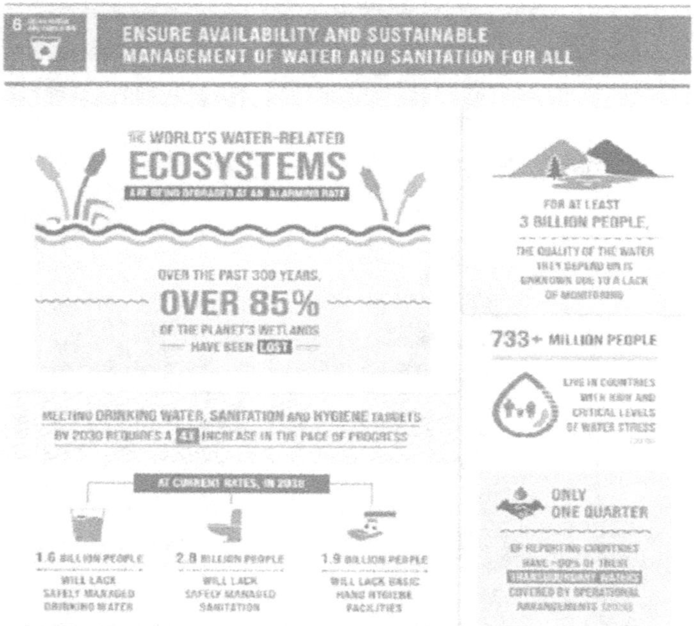

Figure 10. Affordable and clean energy
Source: United Nations (2022).

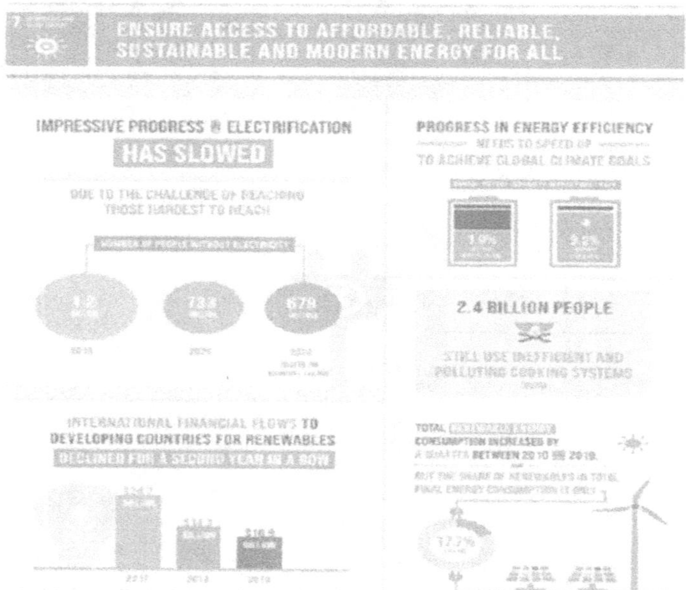

Goal 8: Decent Work and Economic Growth: Covid-19 pandemic and the Ukraine crisis have been the rood blockers for economic growth worldwide. The stoppage of economic activities and recurring lockdowns during the pandemic led to inflation, supply-chain disruptions, policy uncertainties, and global unemployment (refer to Figure 12)—the problems described above caused a setback in global economic recovery resulting in slow financial growth.

Goal 9: Industry, Innovation, and Infrastructure: Passenger airline industry, small-scale industries, and the low-tech industry has suffered have a great setback due to the pandemic situation and are finding it hard to reach their pre covid level production. Also, in Sub-Saharan Africa, mobile network coverage is still very poor, as depicted in Figure 12. Therefore, financial growth is highly dependent on industrial growth and innovation, supported by sound infrastructure.

Figure 11. Decent work and economic growth
Source: United Nations (2022).

Figure 12. Industry, innovation, and infrastructure
Source: United Nations (2022).

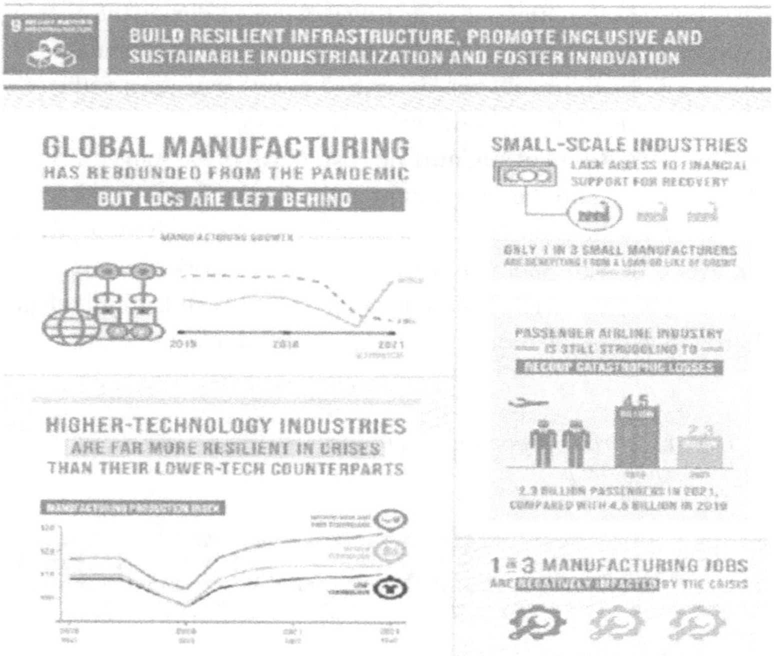

Goal 10: Reduced Inequalities: The Ukraine war has hit the goal of reducing inequality within and among countries. The war forced people to leave their homeland for safe places, resulting in many refugees in other countries (refer to Figure 14). In addition, due to the pandemic, people face discrimination in their countries and other countries due to high competition and slow economic growth.

Goal 11: Sustainable Cities and Communities: Due to large-scale urbanization, the problem of solid waste management has become a cause of concern. Because almost half of this solid waste is left unmanaged, as depicted in Figure 14. Furthermore, industrialization has also contributed to air pollution, and 99% of the world's urban population is forced to breathe polluted air.

Goal 12: Responsible Consumption and Production: There is an immediate need to reduce food wastage at the consumer and distribution level to ensure sustainable consumption and production pattern. Moreover, the e-waste should be safely managed, or else the adverse effects of e-waste and food waste on the environment will continue and worsen the situation for the living beings on this planet (refer to Figure 16).

Figure 13. Reduce inequalities
Source: United Nations (2022).

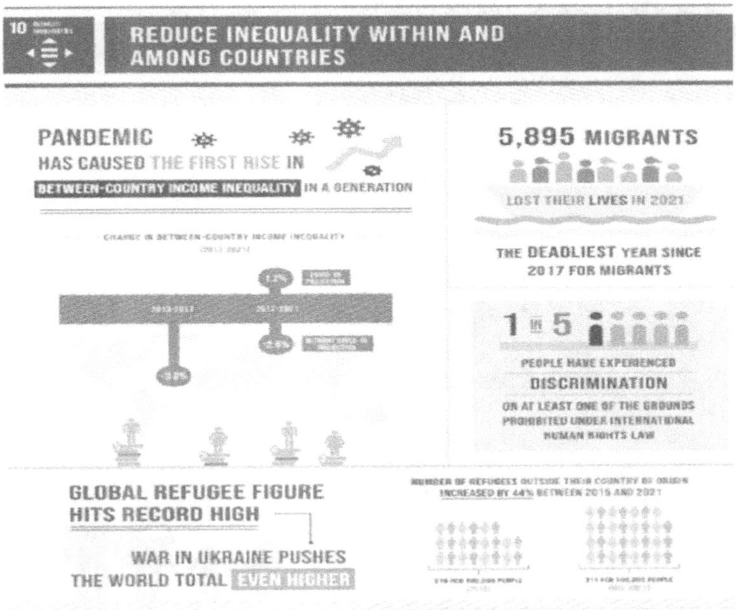

Figure 14. Sustainable cities and communities
Source: United Nations (2022).

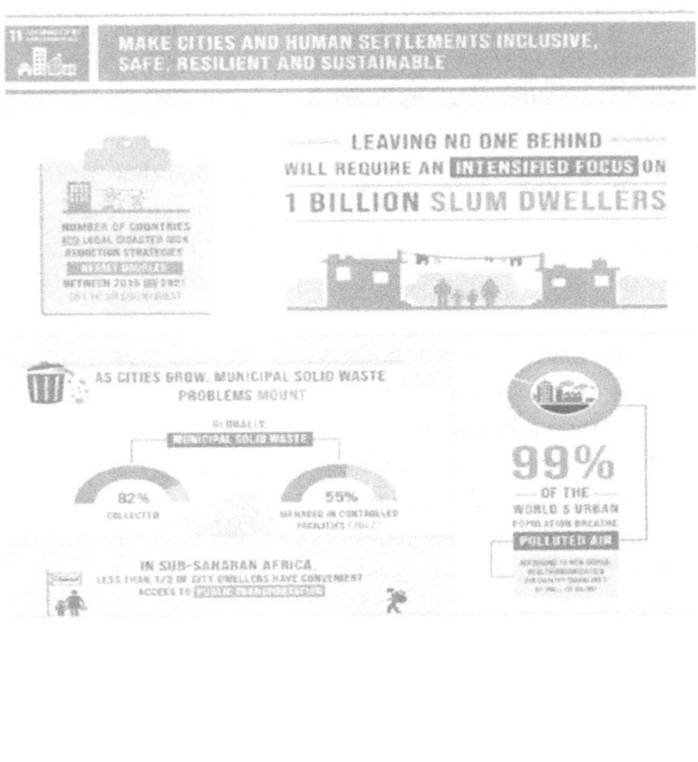

Figure 15. Responsible consumption and production
Source: United Nations (2022).

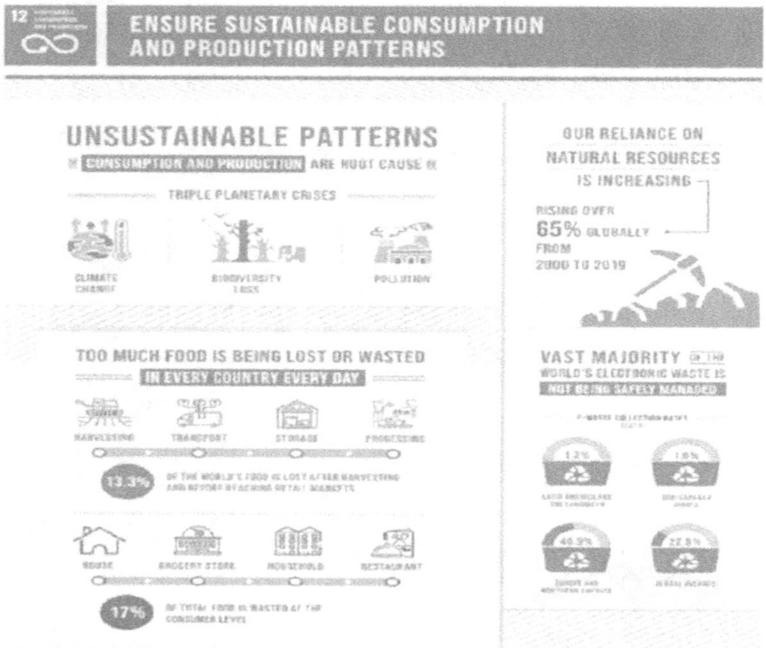

Goal 13: Climate Action: The adverse effects on climate, such as the highest level of CO_2 emissions and ever-rising global temperature, severally affected life on land and sea. The rising sea temperature is harming the coral reefs, and it is also expected that by 21 century, the sea level will rise by 30-60 cm (refer to Figure 17). Similarly, the drought situation is also estimated to displace 700 million people by 2030. Considering the climate situation, it is decided that $100 billion will be committed to climate finance, but even this target is not achieved. Hence, climate change should be urgently looked into. Otherwise, survival on the planet will be very difficult.

Goal 14: Life Below Water: The ocean ecosystem needs to be saved from plastic waste, ocean warming, eutrophication, acidification, and overfishing, as presented in Figure 17. Also, the pandemic has greatly affected fisherman's lives, who need immediate support to continue their work.

Goal 15: Life on Land: There is an immediate need to promote afforestation To protect biodiversity on land(refer to Figure 19). Because deforestation has emerged as the largest culprit for the extinction of wildlife species, it is estimated that 40,000 species will be at risk of extinction in the coming decades.

Figure 16. Climate action
Source: United Nations (2022).

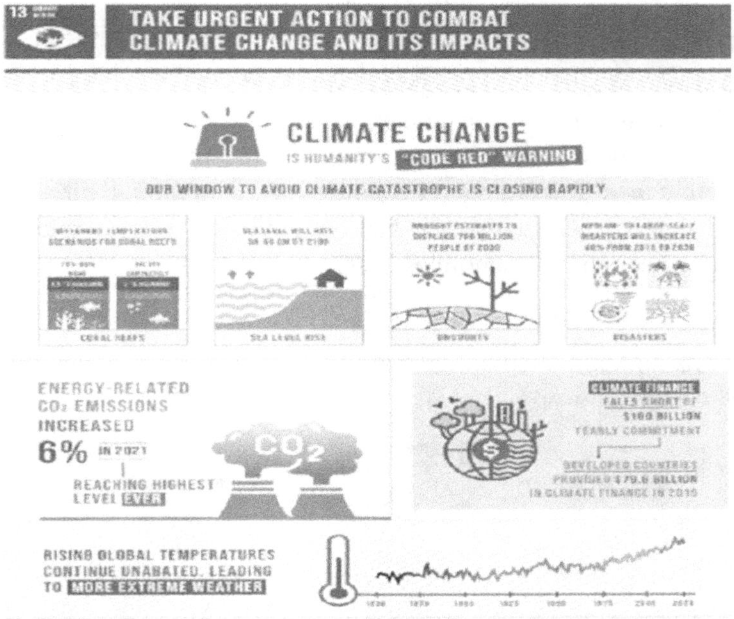

Figure 17. Life below water
Source: United Nations (2022).

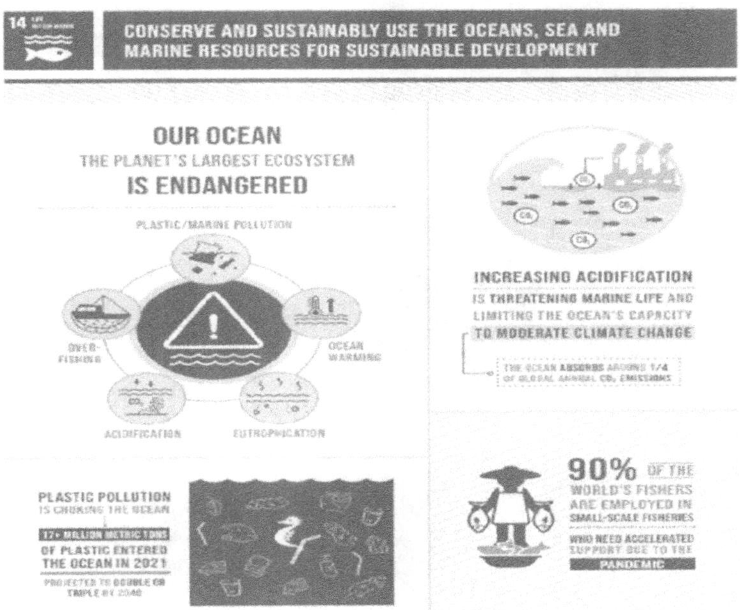

Goal 16: Peace, Justice, and Strong Institutions: For the establishment of peaceful societies, war and conflict situations between countries must be avoided at all costs. Because a record 100 million people had been forcibly displaced worldwide till May 2022, as depicted in Figure 19. Moreover, corruption prevails in almost all economies weakening the judicial system worldwide.

Goal 17: Partnership for the Goals: In times of need, the countries are helping one another to come out of the fiscal crisis and regain financial growth. In this direction, remittance flows to poorer countries, a rise in foreign direct investment, and official development assistance has been playing a great role in uplifting underdeveloped countries' economies (refer to Figure 20).

Figure 18. Life on land
Source: United Nations (2022).

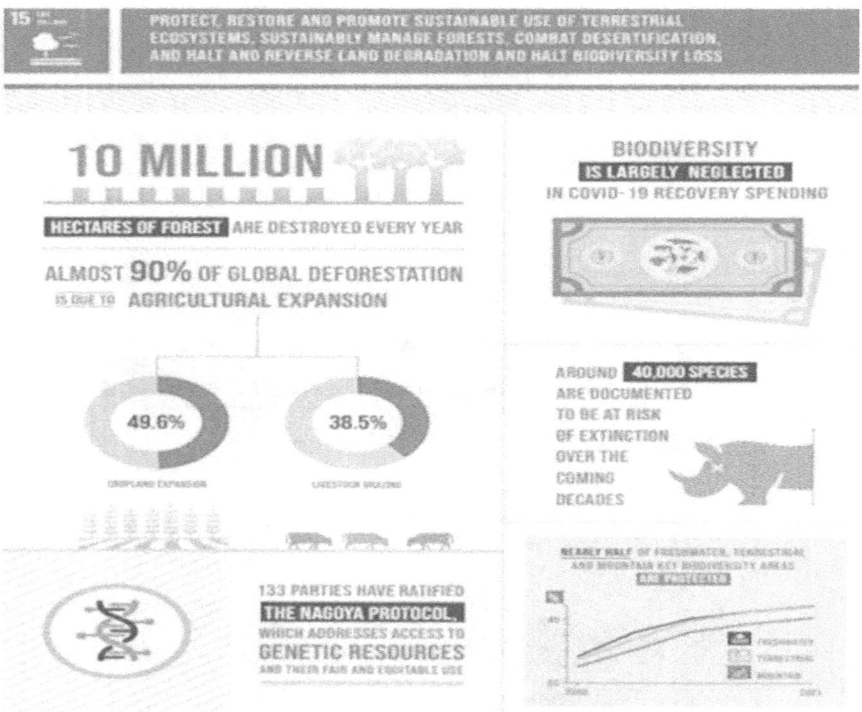

Figure 19. Peace, justice, and strong institutions
Source: United Nations (2022).

Figure 20. Partnership for the goals
Source: United Nations (2022).

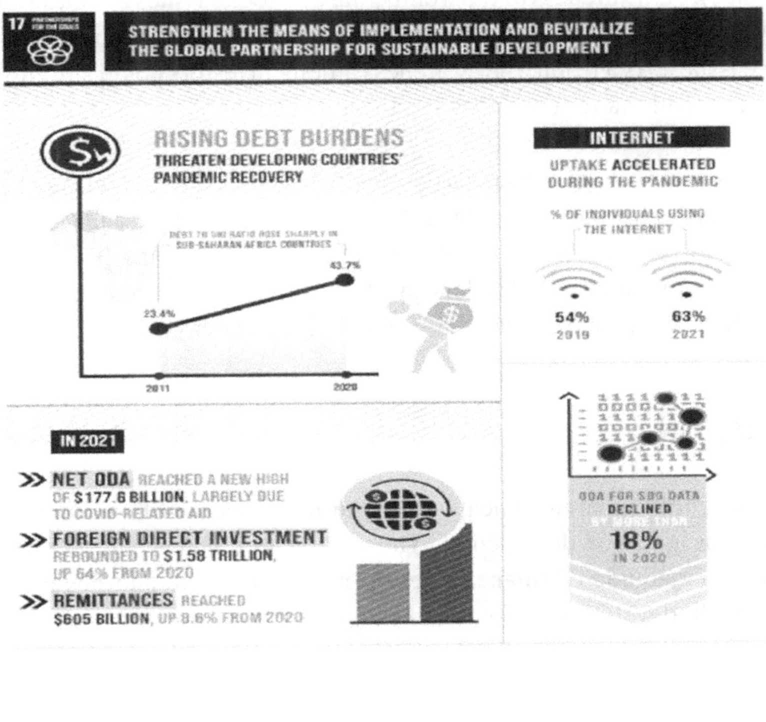

IMPLICATIONS OF THE STUDY

The relationship between financial development and the sustainability environment has significant implications for both the economy and the environment. Here are some potential implications:

1. Financial development can support sustainability efforts: As financial systems become more advanced, they can facilitate investment in sustainable projects, such as renewable energy and environmentally friendly technologies. This financial investment can help to reduce the negative impact of economic activities on the environment.
2. Environmental risks can impact financial stability: Climate change and other environmental risks can significantly impact financial stability, particularly if they lead to widespread damage or disruption. Financial stability can affect the ability of financial institutions to lend and invest and may require new regulatory frameworks to address these risks.
3. Sustainable finance can drive innovation: The development of sustainable finance products and services can drive innovation in the financial sector and other industries. In addition, green products can lead to the development of new technologies and business models that are more environmentally friendly and socially responsible.
4. Social and environmental considerations may become more important for investors: As awareness of environmental and social issues increases, investors may become more interested in investing in companies that positively impact these issues. As a result, the awareness among investors could shift investment patterns, with more funds flowing toward sustainable investments.

The relationship between financial development and the sustainability environment is complex and multifaceted. While financial development can have positive implications for sustainability, some risks and challenges must be addressed. As such, policymakers and stakeholders must work together to promote sustainable finance and ensure economic growth is financially and environmentally sustainable.

CONCLUSION

In conclusion, the research indicates that the influence of FD on environmental quality may be good or detrimental. The aggregate effect would depend on the proportional magnitude of financial development's positive and negative effects. The sustainable development goals indicate that it is important to have financial growth in developing the economy, but the growth should not be harmful to the environment. Companies should not only focus on profit maximization but also consider environmental degradation. This study would be helpful for academicians, management, and scholars to understand the importance of sustainability and how companies can contribute to sustainable development goals framed by the United Nations.

REFERENCES

Adebayo, T. S., Awosusi, A. A., & Adeshola, I. (2020). Determinants of co2 emissions in emerging markets: An empirical evidence from mint economies. *International Journal of Renewable Energy Development*, *9*(3), 411–422. doi:10.14710/ijred.2020.31321

Adebayo, T. S., & Odugbesan, J. A. (2021). Modeling CO2 emissions in South Africa: Empirical evidence from ARDL based bounds and wavelet coherence techniques. *Environmental Science and Pollution Research International*, *28*(8), 9377–9389. doi:10.100711356-020-11442-3 PMID:33145732

Bayar, Y., Maxim, L. D., & Maxim, A. (2020). Financial development and CO2 emissions in post-transition European union countries. *Sustainability (Switzerland)*, *12*(7). Advance online publication. doi:10.3390u12072640

Bekhet, H. A., Matar, A., & Yasmin, T. (2017). CO2 emissions, energy consumption, economic growth, and financial development in GCC countries: Dynamic simultaneous equation models. *Renewable & Sustainable Energy Reviews*, *70*, 117–132. doi:10.1016/j.rser.2016.11.089

Biondi, L., Dumay, J., & Monciardini, D. (2020). Using the International Integrated Reporting Framework to comply with EU Directive 2014/95/EU: Can we afford another reporting façade? *Meditari Accountancy Research*, *28*(5), 889–914. doi:10.1108/MEDAR-01-2020-0695

Brännlund, R., Ghalwash, T., & Nordström, J. (2007). Increased energy efficiency and the rebound effect: Effects on consumption and emissions. *Energy Economics*, *29*(1), 1–17. doi:10.1016/j.eneco.2005.09.003

Charfeddine, L. (2017). The impact of energy consumption and economic development on Ecological Footprint and CO2 emissions: Evidence from a Markov Switching Equilibrium Correction Model. *Energy Economics*, *65*, 355–374. doi:10.1016/j.eneco.2017.05.009

Charfeddine, L., & Kahia, M. (2019). Impact of renewable energy consumption and financial development on CO2 emissions and economic growth in the MENA region: A panel vector autoregressive (PVAR) analysis. *Renewable Energy*, *139*, 198–213. doi:10.1016/j.renene.2019.01.010

Chontanawat, J. (2020). Relationship between energy consumption, CO2 emission and economic growth in ASEAN: Cointegration and causality model. *Energy Reports*, *6*, 660–665. doi:10.1016/j.egyr.2019.09.046

Çoban, S., & Topcu, M. (2013). The nexus between financial development and energy consumption in the EU: A dynamic panel data analysis. *Energy Economics*, *39*, 81–88. doi:10.1016/j.eneco.2013.04.001

Dogan, E., & Seker, F. (2016). The influence of real output, renewable and non-renewable energy, trade and financial development on carbon emissions in the top renewable energy countries. *Renewable & Sustainable Energy Reviews*, *60*, 1074–1085. doi:10.1016/j.rser.2016.02.006

el Barnoussi, A., Howieson, B., & van Beest, F. (2020). Prudential Application of IFRS 9: (Un)Fair Reporting in COVID-19 Crisis for Banks Worldwide?! *Australian Accounting Review*, *30*(3), 178–192. doi:10.1111/auar.12316

Fakher, H.-A. (2019). Investigating the determinant factors of environmental quality (based on ecological carbon footprint index). *Environmental Science and Pollution Research International*, *26*(10), 10276–10291. doi:10.100711356-019-04452-3 PMID:30761494

Frankel, J. A., & Romer, D. (1999). *Does Trade Cause Growth?* Academic Press. doi:10.1016/j.econmod.2012.09.033

Islam, F., Shahbaz, M., Ahmed, A. U., & Alam, M. M. (2013). Financial development and energy consumption nexus in Malaysia: A multivariate time series analysis. *Economic Modelling*, *30*(1), 435–441. doi:10.1016/j.econmod.2012.09.033

Jahangir Alam, M., Ara Begum, I., Buysse, J., & van Huylenbroeck, G. (2012). Energy consumption, carbon emissions and economic growth nexus in Bangladesh: Cointegration and dynamic causality analysis. *Energy Policy*, *45*, 217–225. doi:10.1016/j.enpol.2012.02.022

Jalil, A., Feridun, M., & Ma, Y. (2010). Finance-growth nexus in China revisited: New evidence from principal components and ARDL bounds tests. *International Review of Economics & Finance*, *19*(2), 189–195. doi:10.1016/j.iref.2009.10.005

Jensen, A. L. (1996). *Beverton and Holt life history invariants result from optimal trade-off of reproduction and survival*. Academic Press.

Katircioğlu, S. T., & Taşpinar, N. (2017). Testing the moderating role of financial development in an environmental Kuznets curve: Empirical evidence from Turkey. *Renewable & Sustainable Energy Reviews*, *68*, 572–586. doi:10.1016/j.rser.2016.09.127

Khan, M. N., Serafeim, G., & Yoon, A. (2015). *Corporate Sustainability: First Evidence on Materiality*. Harvard Business School Working Paper. http://nrs.harvard.edu/urn-3:HUL.InstRepos:14369106

King, R. G., & Levine, R. (1993). Finance and Growth: Schumpeter Might Be Right*. *The Quarterly Journal of Economics*, *108*(3), 717–737. doi:10.2307/2118406

Kirikkaleli, D., & Kalmaz, D. B. (2020). Testing the moderating role of urbanization on the environmental Kuznets curve: Empirical evidence from an emerging market. *Environmental Science and Pollution Research International*, *27*(30), 38169–38180. doi:10.100711356-020-09870-2 PMID:32617821

la Torre, M., Sabelfeld, S., Blomkvist, M., & Dumay, J. (2020). Rebuilding trust: Sustainability and non-financial reporting and the European Union regulation. *Meditari Accountancy Research*, *28*(5), 701–725. doi:10.1108/MEDAR-06-2020-0914

Lutz, R. J., & Kakkar, P. (1975). The Psychological Situation As a Determinant of Consumer Behavior. *NA -. Advances in Consumer Research. Association for Consumer Research (U. S.)*, *2*, 439–454.

Maji, I. K., Habibullah, M. S., & Saari, M. Y. (2017). Financial development and sectoral CO2 emissions in Malaysia. *Environmental Science and Pollution Research International*, *24*(8), 7160–7176. doi:10.100711356-016-8326-1 PMID:28097481

Nwani, C., & Omoke, P. C. (2020). Does bank credit to the private sector promote low-carbon development in Brazil? An extended STIRPAT analysis using dynamic ARDL simulations. *Environmental Science and Pollution Research International*, *27*(25), 31408–31426. doi:10.100711356-020-09415-7 PMID:32488699

Omri, A., Daly, S., Rault, C., & Chaibi, A. (2015). Financial development, environmental quality, trade and economic growth: What causes what in MENA countries. *Energy Economics*, *48*, 242–252. doi:10.1016/j.eneco.2015.01.008

Ortas, E., Burritt, R. L., & Moneva, J. M. (2013). Socially Responsible Investment and cleaner production in the Asia Pacific: Does it pay to be good? *Journal of Cleaner Production*, *52*, 272–280. doi:10.1016/j.jclepro.2013.02.024

Ozturk, I., & Acaravci, A. (2013). The long-run and causal analysis of energy, growth, openness and financial development on carbon emissions in Turkey. *Energy Economics*, *36*, 262–267. doi:10.1016/j.eneco.2012.08.025

Raworth, K. (2017). Why it's time for Doughnut Economics. *IPPR Progressive Review, 24*(3), 216–222.

Salahuddin, M., Alam, K., Ozturk, I., & Sohag, K. (2018). The effects of electricity consumption, economic growth, financial development and foreign direct investment on CO2 emissions in Kuwait. *Renewable & Sustainable Energy Reviews*, *81*, 2002–2010. doi:10.1016/j.rser.2017.06.009

Shahbaz, M., Solarin, S. A., Mahmood, H., & Arouri, M. (2013). Does financial development reduce CO2 emissions in Malaysian economy? A time series analysis. *Economic Modelling*, *35*, 145–152. doi:10.1016/j.econmod.2013.06.037

Shan, S., Ahmad, M., Tan, Z., Adebayo, T. S., Man Li, R. Y., & Kirikkaleli, D. (2021). The role of energy prices and non-linear fiscal decentralization in limiting carbon emissions: Tracking environmental sustainability. *Energy*, *234*, 121243. doi:10.1016/j.energy.2021.121243

Songini, L., Pistoni, A., Tettamanzi, P., Fratini, F., & Minutiello, V. (2022). Integrated reporting quality and BoD characteristics: An empirical analysis. *The Journal of Management and Governance*, *26*(2), 579–620. doi:10.100710997-021-09568-8

Tamazian, A., Chousa, J. P., & Vadlamannati, K. C. (2009). Does higher economic and financial development lead to environmental degradation: Evidence from BRIC countries. *Energy Policy*, *37*(1), 246–253. doi:10.1016/j.enpol.2008.08.025

Tang, C. F., & Tan, B. W. (2014). The linkages among energy consumption, economic growth, relative price, foreign direct investment, and financial development in Malaysia. *Quality & Quantity*, *48*(2), 781–797. doi:10.100711135-012-9802-4

Uddin, G. A., Salahuddin, M., Alam, K., & Gow, J. (2017). Ecological footprint and real income: Panel data evidence from the 27 highest emitting countries. *Ecological Indicators*, *77*, 166–175. doi:10.1016/j.ecolind.2017.01.003

Ulucak, R., Yücel, A. G., & Koçak, E. (2019). The Process of Sustainability: From Past to Present. *Environmental Kuznets Curve (EKC)*, 37–53. doi:10.1016/B978-0-12-816797-7.00005-9

United Nations. (2019). *The Sustainable Development Goals Report*. Author.

United Nations. (2022). *The Sustainable Development Goals Report*. Author.

Zhang, Y. J. (2011). The impact of financial development on carbon emissions: An empirical analysis in China. *Energy Policy*, *39*(4), 2197–2203. doi:10.1016/j.enpol.2011.02.026

Chapter 10
Digital Currency and Blockchain Technology in the Financial World

Jyoti Verma
https://orcid.org/0000-0002-7559-4312
Chitkara Business School, Chitkara University, India

Jyotsna Sharma
https://orcid.org/0000-0002-1846-3201
School of Management Studies and Commerce, RIMT University, Mandi Gobindgarh, India

Monica Gupta
Chitkara Business School, Chitkara University, India

ABSTRACT

A distributed ledger, called blockchain, keeps track of every detail about a digital asset. Using this technology, users can utilize the benefits of digital currency. Digital currency has a massive effect on the banking sector. It would be wise to be informed of the technologies that might seriously disrupt the Indian banking sector's operations because it plays a crucial part in the economy and contributes considerably to the nation's gross domestic product. The introduction of this technology in the banking industry significantly reduces fraud resulting from mistakes and identity theft. The specifics of blockchain technology and how it affects the Indian banking industry are discussed in this chapter. It also provides details about various types of digital currency, highlighting their advantages and disadvantages. Much emphasis will be on the importance of blockchain technologies in the future of digital currency. The research's conclusions were strengthened and condensed using SWOT analysis.

DOI: 10.4018/978-1-6684-8361-9.ch010

INTRODUCTION OF BLOCKCHAIN TECHNOLOGY

The concept of Blockchain was first introduced by Satoshi Nakamoto (Nakamoto & Bitcoin, 2008). According to Biais et al. (2019), it is described as a multifunctional and multiusable programmable framework that has been employed to regulate ownership and financial transactions. It is the revolutionary technology that reveals super boom inside a short time interval. Blockchain technology is a based on DLT (Decentralized Distributed Ledger) that keeps track of all a digital asset's transactions (Reiff, 2020). It has drawn a lot of interest from academics, teachers, business professionals, and investors. The exponential growth of digital currency has been extensively demonstrated due to this technology. Due to the fact that this currency has been the main focus of study into financial regulation, security, monetary policy, privacy, and many other topics, this sector is in higher demand (Reid & Harrigan, 2013; Peters & Panayi, 2016). Each coin has two sides. This technology has its own advantages and disadvantages. Immense benefits can be availed by the users on one hand and on the other hand, this technology poses a significant risk to the banking industry as well. The Indian banking industry is being impacted by this technology for the reasons listed below-

- **Reducing Fraudulent Activities:** Blockchain technology provides protection to banks against fraudulent activities. Implementing this technology into the system is considered essential since fraud is growing at a much faster rate. (Andolfatto, 2018).
- **No Intermediary:** Disintermediation is the backbone of blockchain technology, that reduces transaction costs. Due to its being built on a decentralized process, no central authority control is necessary.
- **Add-On Customer Base:** Customers are well equipped with the technology know how and they are developing in a technologically advanced setting. It has huge potential for new innovations in banking industry so as to provide better services to customers. If blockchain technology is used in the financial industry, this may be achievable.
- **International Business Transactions:** In order to make international business transactions easier, more paperwork is required for processing documentation like letter of credit, export documentation, export billing, pre and post shipment financing, factoring, etc. It will become more efficient with the introduction of blockchain technology.
- **Save Transaction Costs:** Blockchain technology provides the ability for rapid, paperless financial transfers. The transaction is free of additional costs. Therefore, this technology may enable banks to cut transaction costs (Grima et al., 2021; Zheng et al., 2017).

Introduction to Digital Currency

Digital currency is regarded as currency that is maintained online and is only available in digital or electronic form. In easy way, we can say that it is cashless currency. Digital Currency consists of central bank digital currency (CBDC), virtual currency, and cryptocurrency. Digital currencies can be centralized or decentralized. For instance, Cryptocurrency is an example of decentralized system and CBDC is an example of centralized system.

Popularity of digital currencies is increasing. This tendency is accelerating due to the increased acceptability of this means of transaction on a global scale. Governments all over the world are attempting to make the most of virtual currencies in different ways, despite the fact that cryptocurrencies attracted a lot of attention owing to its decentralized nature (Verma, 2022). They are able to achieve this by using a Central Bank Digital Currency (CBDC), which the central bank will manage. It issues electronic coins or accounts backed by the government. The acceptance rate of this digital version of currency is in its growing phase. Figure 1 clearly depicts percentage population owing digital currency in 2021 across the world.

Figure 1. Depicts percentage population owing digital currency in 2021 across the world

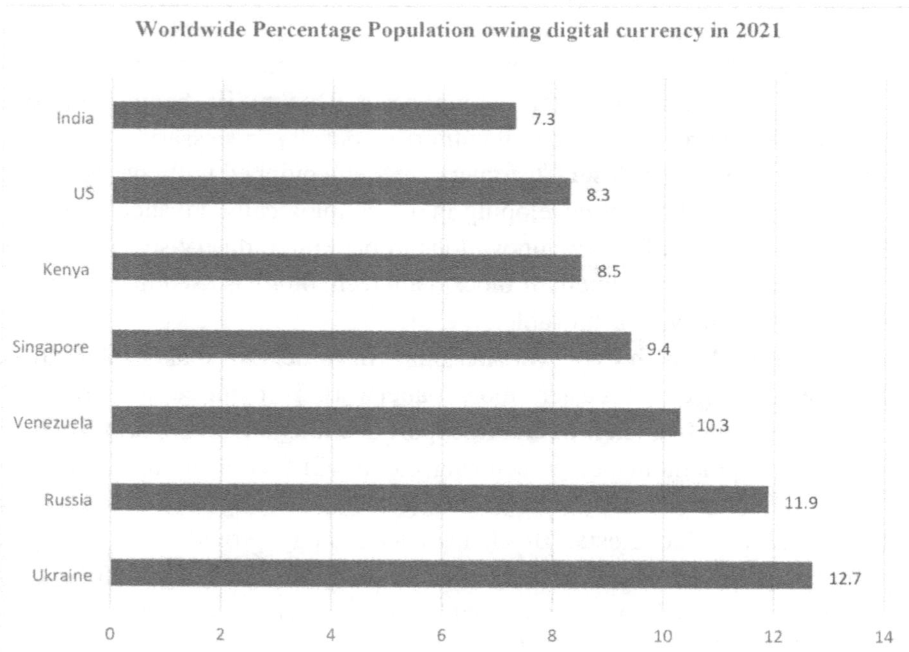

In 2021, according to UN trade and development body (UNCTAD) report, developing countries accounted for the top 15 out of 20 economies in terms of the share of the population that owns digital currency. As per this, with 12.7%, Ukraine dominates the list, followed by Russia at 11.9%, Venezuela at 10.3%, Singapore at 9.4%, Kenya at 8.5%, the US at 8.3%, and India to 7.3%. Here, Ukraine ranked first and India is at the seventh position. Figure 1 shows the large number of people accepting digital version of currency.

Types of Digital Currency

Figure 2. Digital currency

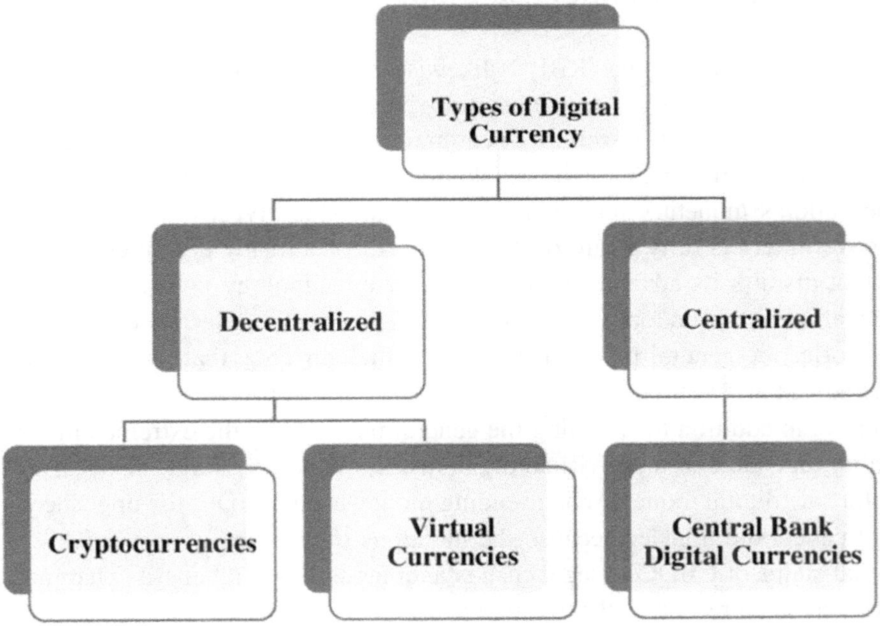

Digital currency is a broader term which consists of various types of currencies which are available in the digital forms. It can be regulated or unregulated but available in electronic forms. Let us discuss these types in detail-

- **Cryptocurrencies:** Cryptocurrencies are one form of digital currency which employ cryptography to secure, verify and control financial transactions in a network. Cryptography is used to control and manage cryptocurrencies.

Bitcoin, Ripple, Dogecoin, Ethereum, etc. are few examples of cryptocurrencies. Since cryptocurrencies are unregulated and only exist in digital form, they are referred to as virtual currencies.

- **Virtual Currencies:** It can be defined as an unregulated digital currency that can be algorithmically managed by a network protocol. These are unregulated digital currencies which is controlled by developers/ founding organization. For instance, it is a gaming network token, and the corporation that developed it also controls and designs its protocols.
- **Central Bank Digital Currencies (CBDCs):** CBDCs are one of the most important type of digital currency because it is regulated and issued by the central bank of a country.

Decentralized vs. Centralized Digital Currency

The Reserve Bank of India (RBI) is likewise concerned about cryptocurrencies' recent surge in popularity. It may cause a rise in crypto assets, which have a high risk of being used to support terrorism or commit other crimes like money laundering. Additionally, it might result in the development of a parallel economy, pose a threat to the nation's monetary policy, and weaken the stability of domestic currency. The government is fully aware of the drawbacks of utilising digital currency, but it cannot dismiss its advantages in terms of the technology involved. Therefore, the government will adopt CBDC in order to protect the interests of the people. It may offer the general public a risk-free virtual currency that would give them all the advantages without the dangers of transacting in private virtual currencies. Therefore, in addition to shielding the general public from the extreme amount of volatility that some of these virtual digital assets encounter, it may also satisfy the need for safe digital money. When sending money using CBDC, the opposite party cannot cancel the transfer because the money is transmitted almost quickly. The potential status of CBDC as legal cash is another significant benefit. That implies that for any legal reasons, all economic participants must accept it. You may use it to pay your taxes, and anyone who loans you money must accept it as payment by law. (Verma & Kaur, 2022).

SWOT Analysis of Digital Currency

For the purpose of generating strategic planning, a company's competitive position is assessed using the SWOT analysis framework. SWOT evaluation evaluates strengths (S), weaknesses (W), opportunities (O), and threats (T).

Strengths

- **Low Transaction Cost:** The cost of transaction becomes much cheaper than physical currencies because there is no middleman involved. Digital currencies enable direct interactions within a network.
- **Easy Transaction:** People from other countries can easily undergo financial transactions at less cost by using digital currency. It will increase revenue of the business who are dealing with digital currency and enables them to serve customers worldwide (Lee et al., 2018; Pereira et al., 2019).
- **Save Time:** The amount of time required for transfers is extremely fast as digital currencies generally exist within the same network and transfers even in the absence of intermediaries.
- **No More Physical Printing of Currency Is Required:** There are lot of requirements for printing physical form of currencies, that consists of printing devices, raw material etc are not required in case of digital currencies. Such currencies are also resistant to physical defects, soiling and theft that might occur with physical form of currency (Verma, 2022).
- **Security:** This technology is based on cryptography and hence makes it most secure form of payment as compared to other physical forms. Crypto security is protected by a hash rate. The higher the hash rate, more power of computing it would require to run over the network (Trivedi et al., 2021). Digital currency transactions are unrectifiable, once done. Digital currency is basically, a warrant by blockchain technology to make them virtually impossible to fake or duplicate (Li et al., 2020).
- **Peer-to-Peer Tokenization Enables New Marketplaces:** Digital currencies are decentralized which means that there are no intermediaries or any third party to control them (Nofer et al., 2017). It is a direct transaction between two or more persons.
- **Convenience to Access:** The biggest strength of digital currency is to provide a hassle-free way to all its users. The acquiring process of a digital currency wallet is quiet easy and fast as compared to opening an account in any financial institution as it does not require ID verification/ documentation/ background details/ credit checks.
- **Traceability:** The transactions are non-traceable in nature. It means no other information is required about users for facilitating a financial transaction on blockchain.
- **Policy Implementation:** In accordance with the existing monetary system, the central bank channels funds into an economy through financial institutions. Bypassing this entire system, CBDCs can let a government send

funds directly to its citizens. Additionally, it makes the processes for creating and distributing the currency that circulates in the system simpler.

Weaknesses

- **Governance:** Since digital currency is not regulated as legal tender in India, neither the individual nor the state is accountable for any transactions made on these platforms. Additionally, the government had denied that private cryptocurrencies would ever be accepted as legal money.
- **Scalability:** Digital currency is receiving exposure in India and around the world. Scalability of the digital currency is the most pressing issue. Everyone is currently prepared to purchase digital coins in large quantities, but the ability of these coins to fluctuate in value is the main issue.
- **Still Experimental:** One of the limitations of digital currency is that it is still in its experimental stage, which implies that occasionally its technology or policy may change. They lack definite norms.
- **Hacking Potential:** Given that they were created digitally, digital currencies may be hacked. Online wallets can be stolen by hackers, or the protocol might be changed to make them unusable.
- **Volatile:** The well-developed decentralized structure of the cryptocurrencies has led to proliferation of weakly funded digital currencies; whose valuations are susceptible to dramatic shifts depending on investor whims.
- **Issues of Accessibility:** The only method to access your digital currency account is with the passwords for your crypto wallet. The digital currency would be permanently gone and impossible to recover in the event that it was misplaced or forgotten.
- **Uncertainty in Regulation:** Due to the lack of sufficient controlling assets in the market for digital currencies, there is a lack of adequate regulation. Anyone can be flawless while purchasing and selling virtual digital assets, but there will always be a danger because regulatory bodies have not accepted cryptocurrencies.
- **Storage Issues:** Digital currencies don't really need physical wallets, but they do have their own storage and processing needs. A few instances are a phone, an Internet connection, and services in relation to their supply. Online wallets with strong security are also required for the storing of digital currency.

Opportunities

- **More Transparency:** It makes the system more transparent. Any attempt to modify a blockchain transaction will require changing every other block in the system, if possible. This renders it impossible to alter system to meet any modifications (Zheng et al., 2018).

- **More Functionality:** In the near future, a single platform might offer a wide range of features or services. This is due to the ease with which any digital currency application may be used to carry out tasks like buying and selling cryptocurrency, earning money, and exchanging it (Monrat et al., 2019).
- **More Opportunities:** Because digital currency is utilized globally, it has a larger consumer base. It has enormous client serviceable marketplaces, generating stronger long-term potential.

Threats

- **Risk-Averse Economic Climate:** Cross-bank settlements have an influence on the economy as they are always evolving. Additionally, the cost of cryptocurrencies is always changing. Your digital currency balance may abruptly increase or decrease.
- **Crypto-Scams:** The likelihood of fraud increases significantly since crypto currencies are still in the early stages of development and because few people are familiar with the systems and protocols required to use them. People are frequently misled into falling for false frauds that use digital currencies.
- **Threat in Smooth Functioning:** Due to specific rules, free moving transactions may be under pressure. The entire globe is concentrating on how to manage this massive enterprise without destroying it.
- **Threat of Regulation:** Tighter regulation is a risk for digital currency. China essentially outlawed mining and holding cryptocurrencies in 2021 for the general public and users. Commercial banks can be superseded by the central bank.

CONCLUSION

When it comes to digital currencies, the entire globe is divided into two radically distinct groups. Some people think that cryptocurrencies are superior than traditional money. On the other side, there are some who oppose it. There could be a disagreement between the regulation of crypto currencies in the near future. Governments would like to control how these digital currencies really operate because numerous cryptocurrencies have been linked to terrorist activities. Additionally, it is predicted that by 2030, cryptocurrencies might account for 25 percent of all national currencies, which would suggest that a significant percentage of the globe will start to accept them as a regular form of payment.

REFERENCES

Andolfatto, D. (2018). Blockchain: What it is, what it does, and why you probably don't need one. *Review - Federal Reserve Bank of St. Louis*, *100*(2), 87–95. doi:10.20955/r.2018.87-95

Biais, B., Bisiere, C., Bouvard, M., & Casamatta, C. (2019). The blockchain folk theorem. *Review of Financial Studies*, *32*(5), 1662–1715. doi:10.1093/rfs/hhy095

Grima, S., Kizilkaya, M., Sood, K., & ErdemDelice, M. (2021). The perceived effectiveness of blockchain for digital operational risk resilience in the European Union insurance market sector. *Journal of Risk and Financial Management*, *14*(8), 363.

Lee, I., & Shin, Y. J. (2018). Fintech: Ecosystem, business models, investment decisions, and challenges. *Business Horizons*, *61*(1), 35–46. doi:10.1016/j.bushor.2017.09.003

Li, X., Jiang, P., Chen, T., Luo, X., & Wen, Q. (2020). A survey on the security of blockchain systems. *Future Generation Computer Systems*, *107*, 841–853. doi:10.1016/j.future.2017.08.020

Monrat, A. A., Schelén, O., & Andersson, K. (2019). A survey of blockchain from the perspectives of applications, challenges, and opportunities. *IEEE Access : Practical Innovations, Open Solutions*, *7*, 117134–117151. doi:10.1109/ACCESS.2019.2936094

Nakamoto, S. (2008). *Bitcoin: A peer-to-peer electronic cash system.* https://bitcoin.org/bitcoin. pdf

Nathan, R. (2020). *Bitcoin explained.* Retrieved From https://www.investopedia.com/terms/b/blockchain.asp

Nofer, M., Gomber, P., Hinz, O., & Schiereck, D. (2017). Blockchain. *Business & Information Systems Engineering*, *59*(3), 183–187. doi:10.100712599-017-0467-3

Pereira, J., Tavalaei, M. M., & Ozalp, H. (2019). Blockchain-based platforms: Decentralized infrastructures and its boundary conditions. *Technological Forecasting and Social Change*, *146*, 94–102. doi:10.1016/j.techfore.2019.04.030

Peters, G. W., & Panayi, E. (2016). Understanding modern banking ledgers through blockchain technologies: Future of transaction processing and smart contracts on the internet of money. In *Banking beyond banks and money* (pp. 239–278). Springer. doi:10.1007/978-3-319-42448-4_13

Reid, F., & Harrigan, M. (2013). An analysis of anonymity in the bitcoin system. In *Security and privacy in social networks* (pp. 197–223). Springer. doi:10.1007/978-1-4614-4139-7_10

Trivedi, S., Mehta, K., & Sharma, R. (2021). Systematic literature review on application of blockchain technology in E-finance and financial services. *Journal of Technology Management & Innovation, 16*(3), 89–102. doi:10.4067/S0718-27242021000300089

Verma, J. (2022a). The Impact of Blockchain Technology and COVID-19 on the Global Banking Industry. *Blockchain Technology in Corporate Governance: Transforming Business and Industries*, 283-301.

Verma, J. (2022b). Factors influencing Driving Demand of Cryptocurrency and its impact on Behavioral Intention: An Indian Perspective. *The Review of Finance and Banking, 14*(1), 35–43. doi:10.24818/rfb.22.14.01.03

Verma, J., & Kaur, J. (2022). Blockchain Technology: How will it impact the Marketing Domain? In Developing Relationships, Personalization, and Data Herald in Marketing 5.0 (pp. 146-160). IGI Global.

Zheng, Z., Xie, S., Dai, H., Chen, X., & Wang, H. (2017). *An overview of blockchain technology: Architecture, consensus, and future trends. In 2017 IEEE international congress on big data (BigData congress)*. IEEE.

Zheng, Z., Xie, S., Dai, H. N., Chen, X., & Wang, H. (2018). Blockchain challenges and opportunities: A survey. *International Journal of Web and Grid Services, 14*(4), 352–375. doi:10.1504/IJWGS.2018.095647

Chapter 11
Application of Blockchain for Sustaining Green Finance

Gurpreet Kaur
Chitkara Business School, Chitkara University, India

Aadheesh
Chitkara Business School, Chitkara University, India

ABSTRACT

Green finance is an important source for raising necessary funds for preserving/ conserving the environment through developments of green projects. It is a loan raised especially for environmentally friendly activities such as biodiversity financing, optimum use of natural resources, etc. Prudent use of green finance attracts the use of digitized technologies which will facilitate prosperous accomplishment of environmental projects. One of the primary and significant digitized technology is blockchain. Further, it ensures effective monitoring of environmental projects, enhances transparency and accountability, and minimizes greenwashing risk. The bank for international settlement (BIS) has stressed blockchain for bringing transparency in usage of green finance thereby improving efficiency. Thus, the present study is an attempt to have insights on the use of blockchain for streamlining green finance. The study proposes the use of digitalized technologies for supporting and promoting green finance.

DOI: 10.4018/978-1-6684-8361-9.ch011

INTRODUCTION

Green finance is any financial activity which ensures a better environmental outcome. It consists of debt mechanisms, array of loans and investments that encourage the development of green projects. It is a new sources of mobilizing and financing existing industries into carbon reduction by establishing new verticals of finance. It will improve liquidity, expanded access to finance, transparency and lower the cost of capital for infrastructure projects.

In the recent years, many research has been done on the green finance. Green finance has been defined by many authors (Wang and Zhi 2016; Zhang et al., 2020; Hafner et al., 2020; Taghizadeh-Hesary and Yoshino (2019) Zhang et al. (2019) has described the present status of green finance and obstacles faced in proper utilisation of green finance. Blockchain technology is widely used in different sectors of the economy. One such application is in financial system (Trivedi & Malik, 2022). Blockchain is a revolutionary tool for ensuring optimum use of green finance by monitoring the climate change, which significantly influences green finance. Blockchain technology is designed in such a way that it is massively resistant to frauds and modifications. It ensure data integrity and reduced the operational costs. Blockchain convert money into digital form wherein transparency increase in use of finance. With the help of block chain, one can easily find out the trading of green bonds & project financed through green finance & its impact on the environment.

"Blockchain is a shared ledger that facilitates the process of recording transactions and track assets, whether it be tangible or intangible". Bitcoin, blockchains first application is known to pollute the environment by emitting vast amount of CO2 in order to make transactions successful with consumption of massive energy. Blockchain can be laid in more efficient ways which won't use more energy.

Blockchain might bring alignment visibility with sustainability goals by enabling everyone to track data on infrastructure projects. He et, al (2020) A blockchain based infrastructure management system could improve transparency in current multi party contract agreements. A blockchain based protocol can support the governance, alignment and monitor infrastructure standards. Debrah et al. (2022) in a study described that in Hong Kong "Leveraging Blockchain Technology and Tokenizing Green Assets is used to Fill the Green Finance Gap". It is a global change as buildings fuel this by accounting for global energy use and carbon emissions further tells us the need for green buildings.

The bank for International Settlement (BIS) has stressed on the blockchain for bringing transparency in usage of green finance thereby improving efficiency.

Sharma et al. (2020) describes that reassessment of infrastructures and services as a need of an hour. New technologies will enable sustaining green finance, thus improving the environment. Naderi et al. (2022) conducted a study in USA to illustrate how emergence of 'Distributed Ledger Technology', such as 'Blockchain' improves current process and systems by being a digital enabler across the infrastructure. Blockchain and Distributed Ledger Technologies can start deeper technological integration and beginning of new business models. Public and private sector will provide guidance on bringing ideas to life through various programme.

Many countries have been achieving green growth while constantly developing their economies. A country must strive towards developing high quality finance and utilise such finance to break economic uncertainty and further promote the economy. Fintech in short can be explained as financial innovation by new technologies. Technology creates products and applications which further impact the working of financial institutions. Green finance promotes the optimization of the economy and maintain its growth.

The green financial system can promote firms to carry green innovation by reducing market transaction costs further leading the customers towards green consumption. Introduction of blockchain helps in promoting rural revitalization, funds will be invested into rural revitalization which will promote rural upliftment by developing rural green financial systems. Blockchain is a facilitator in promoting the green environment by providing necessary green finance.

In this research paper an attempt is made to study the main components of blockchain that are, data privacy, transparency, and process efficiency and automation further helping to deliver a sustainable infrastructure. Further an attempt in made to gets insights as to how blockchain can be helpful in assisting green finance so as to attain sustainable development. The chapter is segregated into different sections. Section 1 consist of introduction, Section 2 describes the insights from past studies. Section 3 present the analysis of Section 2 so as to have better insights. Sections 4 and 5 deal with conclusion and the references.

Review of Literature

Many researchers have studied the relevance of blockchain in facilitating green finance, the details of which are as follows Debrah et al. (2022) in the study looks for incentives for Green finance in Green Buildings and further about AI enabled Green finance software. It concludes the need of blockchain which would help improve green finance to combat climate change.

Zhou et al. (2022) conducted a study China to examines the influence of financial technology on green development and its implementation. It was concluded the mechanism of fintech innovation on green growth will ensure future stability. Naderi et al. (2022) made an attempt to study the Blockchain technology as a innovative climate finance and service provider. It was concluded that Blockchain provides viable solutions to enhance sustainable investments. Some like cryptocurrencies and the other side tech community is motivated to be a part of a sustainable world ensuring transparency.

Hemanand et al. (2022) attempted a study to examine the green finance for ecological advancement in respect of artificial intelligence and minimising carbon impression. Concluding, Green finance resources should be allocated to transportation healthcare needs industrial sectors and financial management. Similar study was done Fahim et al. (2022) in Germany to analyse Green Supply chain management and finance using bitcoin. Ozili (2021) in a study examined the interlink of Digital finance, social finance and green finance. It offers a seamless channel for corporations to fund social projects. Further to conclude it present a framework with concept and suggests a simple interaction between the three terms as they are a topic of highlight in the international development community.

Schulz et al. (2021) did a study in Germany to facilitate transparent and uniformity in transactions by enabling efficient accreditation process and how new technologies like distributed ledger innovation can be used good climate finance. Further it was concluded that Green Climate Fund will leverage emerging Distributed Ledger Techniques and on the other hand digital technologies has huge potential to support the work of the Green Climate Fund

Liu et al. (2021) conducted a study in China to identify the role of green finance in the economic development. Duchene (2020) made an attempt to study the reallocation of capital towards low carbon projects for enhancing energy transition. The paper concluded that by increasing green private investments, the cost of capital will reduce, further promoting green finance. He et al. (2020) attempted to study the upgradation of finance analyse and its role in green finance . It was concluded that Green Finance promotes the making of smart cities and green credit thus ensuring staibility. Sharma et al. (2020) clearly emphasises in creation of an internet of things (IoT) ecosystem and illustrated as to how blockchain technology assisting green finance.. Further it concludes how blockchain technology move towards a sustainable green IoT ecosystem.

Marco et al. (2020) explored tokenization of real assets which would reduce transaction costs thus enhancing transparency and ensure uniformity in green finance. A similar study was done in China to study the development of green finance and it was found that new technologies were explore and less participation rate of financial institutions was done for ensuring sufficient funds for sustaining green environment. Similar studies were done by Puschmann et al. (2020) in Switzerland and Xie et al. (2020) in China. Sachs et al. (2019) in Japan attempted to internalize environmental aspects and lower risk perceptions and increase level of financial flows. It was concluded that green finance is emerging as a priority for public policy as through implementation of block chain many Improvements has been seen in financing options. Cen et al. (2018) described Fintech as a strong driving force for ensuring sustainable economic development, as it supports technological innovation and green finance wants the support of new advanced technologies for gaining popularity.

While analysing the literature review it has been observed that many researchers have explored the usage in blockchain in green finance from 2020 onwards and blockchain is gaining much popularity in recent years

Table 1. The publication years and list of journals wherein the papers are published

Name of the Journal	Year
Building and environment	2022
Ecological economics	2022
Research letters	2022
Computational intelligence and neuroscience	2022
Environmental science and pollution research	2022
Environmental science and pollution research	2022
Earth system governance	2021
Financial internet quarterly	2021
Sustainability	2021
Energy policy	2021
Complexity	2020
Ieee network	2020
The potential for green finance.	2020
International seminar on education innovation and economic management (seiem)	2020
Sustainability	2020
Sustainability	2020
The potential for green finance	2020
Environmental science and pollution research	2020
Energy security and sustainable development.	2019
Adbi working paper series	2019
The rise of green finance in Europe: Opportunities and challenges for issuers, investors and marketplaces	2019
Handbook of green finance	2019
The rise of green finance in Europe: Opportunities and challenges for issuers, investors and marketplaces	2019
Finance research letters	2019
International conference on management, economics, education, arts and humanities	2018
Transforming climate finance and green investment with blockchains	2018

Source: Author's compilation.

Table 2. The papers with maximum number of citations

Title of Paper	Citations	Year
The way to induce private participation in green finance and investment	354	2019
Impact of green finance on economic development and environmental quality: A study based on provincial panel data from China	159	2020
The role of fintech in unlocking green finance	87	2019
The role of fintech in unlocking green finance: Policy insights for developing countries	87	2018
Why is green finance important?	80	2019
Blockchain technology toward green Iot: Opportunities and challenges	73	2020
Handbook of green finance	73	2019
The impact of fintech innovation on green growth in china: Mediating effect of green finance	68	2022
Discovering research trends and opportunities of green finance and energy policy: A data-driven scientometric analysis	57	2021
Green finance gap in green buildings: A scoping review and future research needs	51	2022
Fintech, digitalization and blockchain: Possible applications for green finance	37	2019
Leveraging blockchain technology for innovative climate finance under the green climate fund	35	2021
How green fintech can alleviate the impact of climate change—The case of Switzerland	35	2020
Transforming climate finance and green investment with blockchains	35	2018

Source: Author's compilation

Discussion and Conclusion

Green finance tools in form of green development funds, green insurance, green bonds, new advanced technologies like blockchain, etc. are important sources of funds for ensuring green credit which would further be helpful in ensuring sustainability. Green finance can effectively improve green investments by tokenizing green bonds, bringing transparency and reducing uncertainties, expanding microfinancing which will further facilitate increased financial flows.

Block chain application acts as a catalyst for stimulating green finance. Blockchain technology provides easy methods to improve sustainable investments. Green digital finance is evolving with time as people initiate towards emergence of sustainable growth with green finance. This approach of Financial Technology would create full transparency across complete investments avoiding misappropriation. Further use of blockchain based project bonds to finance infrastructure would generate returns. Such a framework will have better prospects for the developing countries as they can explore more new financial tool for attaining clean & safe environment with help of green finance.

Combination of Blockchain with green finance will be helpful in resolving various global problems. It will assist in saving natural resources by making its optimum utilization (Poberezhna, 2018).

It is suggested that the government can play a key role for developing blockchain so as to create user friendly regulatory framework governing the new technologies so green sustainability can be ensured further international popularity can be gained (Nassiry, 2019). The present paper is an attempt towards describing blockchain as a technology for boosting capital markets or financial institutions which further help in mobilizing sustainable infrastructure investments. This study will further help other researchers to broaden their knowledge about green finance and green chain management. It presents a framework with concept and explains the link between blockchain & green finance.

The papers provide good insights for the policy makers who are interested in exploring new financial technologies like blockchain for green finance and attainment of SDG's. It paves a way for future researchers for developing model showing linkage between the blockchain, green finance and their relation with improving environmental quality thus attaining sustainable development. Further the potential of blockchain should be fully utilized as it will prove to be beneficial tool in the financial system that are decentralized, transparent and innovative (Trivedi et al., 2021).

REFERENCES

Berrou, R., Ciampoli, N., & Marini, V. (2019). Defining green finance: Existing standards and main challenges. *The rise of green finance in Europe: Opportunities and challenges for issuers, investors and marketplaces*, 31-51.

Cen, T., & He, R. (2018, December). Fintech, green finance and sustainable development. In *2018 International Conference on Management, Economics, Education, Arts and Humanities (MEEAH 2018)* (pp. 222-225). Atlantis Press.

Debrah, C., Chan, A. P. C., & Darko, A. (2022). Green finance gap in green buildings: A scoping review and future research needs. *Building and Environment*, *207*, 108443. doi:10.1016/j.buildenv.2021.108443

Dorfleitner, G., & Braun, D. (2019). Fintech, digitalization and blockchain: possible applications for green finance. *The rise of green finance in Europe: opportunities and challenges for issuers, investors and marketplaces*, 207-237.

Fahim, F., & Mahadi, B. (2022). Green supply chain management/green finance: A bibliometric analysis of the last twenty years by using the Scopus database. *Environmental Science and Pollution Research International*, *29*(56), 84714–84740. doi:10.100711356-022-21764-z PMID:35789465

He, Z., Liu, Z., Wu, H., Gu, X., Zhao, Y., & Yue, X. (2020). Research on the impact of green finance and Fintech in smart city. *Complexity*, *2020*, 1–10. doi:10.1155/2020/6673386

Hemanand, D., Mishra, N., Premalatha, G., Mavaluru, D., Vajpayee, A., Kushwaha, S., & Sahile, K. (2022). Applications of intelligent model to analyze the green finance for environmental development in the context of artificial intelligence. *Computational Intelligence and Neuroscience*, *2022*, 1–8. doi:10.1155/2022/2977824 PMID:35845917

Liu, Y., Lei, J., & Zhang, Y. (2021). A study on the sustainable relationship among the green finance, environment regulation and green-total-factor productivity in China. *Sustainability*, *13*(21), 11926. doi:10.3390u132111926

Marke, A. (Ed.). (2018). *Transforming climate finance and green investment with blockchains*. Academic Press.

Meng, F., & Zhang, W. (2022). Digital finance and regional green innovation: Evidence from Chinese cities. *Environmental Science and Pollution Research International*, *29*(59), 89498–89521. doi:10.100711356-022-22072-2 PMID:35854068

Naderi, N., & Tian, Y. (2022). Leveraging Blockchain Technology and Tokenizing Green Assets to Fill the Green Finance Gap. *Energy Research Letters*, *3*, 33907.

Nassiry, D. (2019). The role of fintech in unlocking green finance. In *Handbook of Green Finance* (pp. 315–336). Springer. doi:10.1007/978-981-13-0227-5_27

Ozili, P. K. (2021). Digital finance, green finance and social finance: Is there a link? *Financial Internet Quarterly*, *17*(1), 1–7. doi:10.2478/fiqf-2021-0001

Poberezhna, A. (2018). Addressing water sustainability with blockchain technology and green finance. In *Transforming climate finance and green investment with blockchains* (pp. 189–196). Academic Press. doi:10.1016/B978-0-12-814447-3.00014-8

Puschmann, T., Hoffmann, C. H., & Khmarskyi, V. (2020). How green FinTech can alleviate the impact of climate change—The case of Switzerland. *Sustainability*, *12*(24), 10691. doi:10.3390u122410691

Sachs, J., Woo, W. T., Yoshino, N., & Taghizadeh-Hesary, F. (Eds.). (2019). Handbook of green finance: Energy security and sustainable development. Academic Press.

Sachs, J. D., Woo, W. T., Yoshino, N., & Taghizadeh-Hesary, F. (2019). *Why is green finance important?* Academic Press.

Schletz, M., Nassiry, D., & Lee, M. K. (2020). *Blockchain and tokenized securities: The potential for green finance*. Academic Press.

Schulz, K., & Feist, M. (2021). Leveraging blockchain technology for innovative climate finance under the Green Climate Fund. *Earth System Governance*, *7*, 100084. doi:10.1016/j.esg.2020.100084

Sharma, P. K., Kumar, N., & Park, J. H. (2020). Blockchain technology toward green IoT: Opportunities and challenges. *IEEE Network*, *34*(4), 263–269. doi:10.1109/MNET.001.1900526

Taghizadeh-Hesary, F., & Yoshino, N. (2019). The way to induce private participation in green finance and investment. *Finance Research Letters*, *31*, 98–103. doi:10.1016/j.frl.2019.04.016

Trivedi, S., & Malik, R. (2022). Blockchain Technology as an Emerging Technology in the Insurance Market. In *Big Data: A Game Changer for Insurance Industry* (pp. 81–100). Emerald Publishing Limited. doi:10.1108/978-1-80262-605-620221006

Trivedi, S., Mehta, K., & Sharma, R. (2021). Systematic literature review on application of blockchain technology in E-finance and financial services. *Journal of Technology Management & Innovation*, *16*(3), 89–102. doi:10.4067/S0718-27242021000300089

Wang, M., Li, X., & Wang, S. (2021). Discovering research trends and opportunities of green finance and energy policy: A data-driven scientometric analysis. *Energy Policy*, *154*, 112295. doi:10.1016/j.enpol.2021.112295

Xie, H., Ouyang, Z., & Choi, Y. (2020). Characteristics and influencing factors of green finance development in the Yangtze river delta of China: Analysis based on the spatial durbin model. *Sustainability*, *12*(22), 9753. doi:10.3390u12229753

Yang, X. (2020, May). FinTech in Promoting the Development of Green Finance in China against the Background of Big Data and Artificial Intelligence. In *2020 4th International Seminar on Education Innovation and Economic Management (SEIEM)*. Francis Academic Press.

Zhang, X., Aranguiz, M., Xu, D., Zhang, X., & Xu, X. (2018). Utilizing blockchain for better enforcement of green finance law and regulations. In *Transforming Climate Finance and Green Investment with Blockchains* (pp. 289–301). Academic Press. doi:10.1016/B978-0-12-814447-3.00021-5

Zhongming, Z., Linong, L., Xiaona, Y., & Wei, L. (2018). *The Role of Fintech in Unlocking Green Finance: Policy Insights for Developing Countries*. Academic Press.

Zhou, G., Zhu, J., & Luo, S. (2022). The impact of fintech innovation on green growth in China: Mediating effect of green finance. *Ecological Economics*, *193*, 107308. doi:10.1016/j.ecolecon.2021.107308

Zhou, X., Tang, X., & Zhang, R. (2020). Impact of green finance on economic development and environmental quality: A study based on provincial panel data from China. *Environmental Science and Pollution Research International*, *27*(16), 19915–19932. doi:10.100711356-020-08383-2 PMID:32232752

Chapter 12
Financial Market Innovation, Blockchain, and Sustainability

Manawati Panwar
Department of FMC, Poornima University, India

ABSTRACT

The word 'blockchain' was introduced years ago, but the meaning has changed over time. Initially it was developed only as the tool for bitcoin cryptocurrency transactions. Developed countries like US and China show the positive relationship between blockchain and financial market innovation. In the present era of initialization where people are more concerned about the safety and security of transaction, blockchain is seen as a solution in the financial market sustainability. The Indian government in association with RBI has planned to launch virtual currency for the development of the Indian financial market and economy. This study reveals the relationship between blockchain and financial market innovation in the Indian context and the factors that impact the significance and relationship. The purpose of the study is to estimate the conceptual framework of blockchain in the field of financial market innovation and sustainability. Thus, this study tries to reveal the key factors of blockchain technology that impact the innovation in the field of financial markets.

INTRODUCTION

The centrally trusted party is a necessity for all traditional transactions, which creates numerous issues with transaction cost, efficiency, and security. We must introduce the idea of blockchain technology in order to address these issues and achieve secure, quicker, and more transparent transactions.

DOI: 10.4018/978-1-6684-8361-9.ch012

The Satoshi Nakamoto-created blockchain technology was first used One of the financial uses of blockchain technology is defined as Bitcoin. Distributed ledger technology is what the blockchain is all about (Nakamoto, 2018). Without requiring assistance from a third party, it will handle transactions between people and businesses. Blockchain technology will be a significant source of financial market innovation in the future. it is the backbone technology of financial markets. On the other hand, blockchain is treated as the foundation of Bitcoin (Nakamoto, 2018). It has received widespread attention in a very short span of time. It is a new phenomenon in the financial market that marks its presence in the eyes of the government, media, and enterprises all around the world. Blockchain-based applications are on the rise, covering various fields such as financial services, reputation systems, the Internet of Things (IoT), and so on (Sharma et al., 2022).

Financial services such as digital assets, remittances, and online payments use block chain technology. It will transform financial markets and their operational mode, first by providing more control and clarity of data between users, then by providing a framework for point-to-point connectivity in a very scalable and sustainable way. It enables users to create absolute records of transactions that are accessible to all network participants.

Transparency, data auditability, privacy, value transfer, and process efficiency are the core competencies of block chain technology (Williams & Fernandez, 2019).

This paper's summary is structured as follows. The importance of blockchain technology and in financial notes is comprehensively examined in Section 2. The third portion then examines issues related with blockchain technology and review of literature. The benefits, use, and scope of blockchain technology is then demonstrated in Section 4. The challenges and problems faced by blockchain in India is covered in Section 5. Lastly, Section 6 summarises this study's findings.

BLOCKCHAIN DATABASE

Number of blocks are used to frame a block chain database in which one block is connected with previous block. It is a network of users. Each block records one or more transactions.

The key objective of using block chain database technology is to reduce risk, cost, and time for all of these types of transactions.

Block chain technology provides a number of benefits to participants in the capital market, such as issuers, fund managers, investors, and regulators. The securitization of financial instruments and securities will become both more customised and streamlined through the use of blockchain issuance platforms.

Important Blockchain Features

In conclusion, the following are the main features of blockchain:

- **Decentralization:** Is an important concept. Traditionally, in centralised transaction systems, every transaction must be approved by the central trusted organisation (such as the central bank), which inevitably leads to price and performance bottlenecks at the central servers. In contrast to the centralised mode, blockchain does not require a third party. In a distributed network, data consistency is maintained using consensus techniques (Evans, 2018).
- **Determination:** Sincere miners would not accept faulty transactions because they can be immediately validated. Transactions that have been added to the blockchain are almost impossible to remove or reverse. Invalid transaction-containing blocks could be quickly identified.
- **Anonymity:** With a newly created address, each user can communicate with the blockchain without disclosing their true identity. Keep in mind that, due to an inherent constraint, blockchain cannot ensure absolute privacy preservation.
- **Auditability:** Based on the Unspent Transaction Output (UTXO) architecture, the Bitcoin blockchain retains information regarding user balances. Any transaction must make reference to some previous, unused transactions (Evans, 2018). Those referred to as "unspent transactions" change from being unspent to being spent once the current transaction has been added to the blockchain. So, it would be simple to verify and follow transactions.

Types of Blockchain Technology

Blockchain technology is classified into three types.

- **Public Blockchain:** A decentralised, open-source blockchain technology. Everyone can read transactions, send transactions, and take part in the consensus process. The best example of digital money is Bitcoin.
- **Permissioned Blockchain:** This is a quasi-decentralized system where consensus is managed by a pre-selected group of nodes and participant-only read access is allowed. Letters of credit are the application for trade financing that is most frequently employed.
- **Private Blockchain:** It is entirely centralized, necessitating a "high trust" entity in which one entity is centrally controlled for write permissions while all participants are granted read permissions.

Figure 1. Traditional database vs. blockchain base distributed ledger
Source: Deloitte Report April 2017.

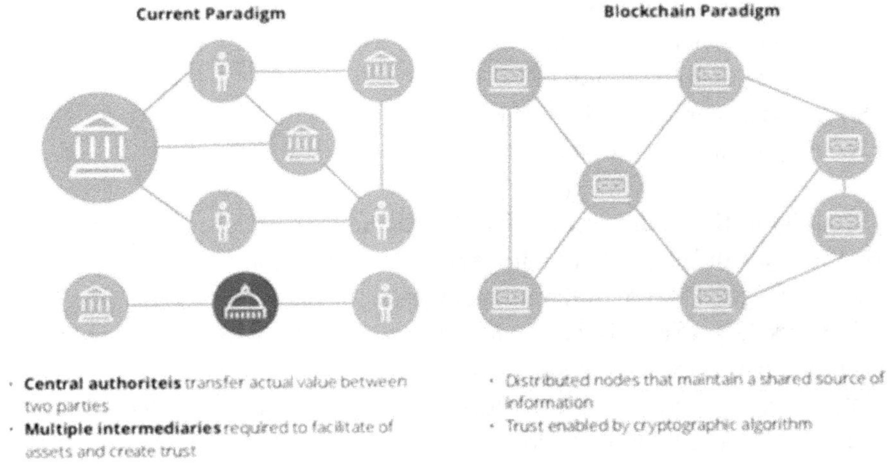

LITERATURE REVIEW

Bitcoin, according to Satoshi Nakamoto (2018), is a chain of digital signatures. Signatures can be used to verify the ownership chain.

Blockchain, as discussed by the author Sri Aruna and Bhaskari (2018) in his paper, is a new technology that is used in applications such as artificial intelligence, human enhancement, and smart contracts, among others..

In his paper, the author Williams and Fernandez (2019) discusses transactional privacy in a decentralised smart contract system.

Issues With Blockchain System Security

The three security concepts of confidentiality, integrity, and availability are what blockchains primarily focus on. Since blockchain is fundamentally a distributed system, it offers availability, and all the chains of transactions between blockchain nodes led to their agreement. The data's integrity is preserved because nodes in the blockchain agreed through a series of transactions. It is possible to protect transaction confidentiality by using the right cryptographic keys (Wu & Duan, 2019).

Blockchain solutions employ a comprehensive strategy that includes protection against unauthorised insiders, compromised nodes, and server failure, as well as entity authentication and authorization via the blockchain, transaction transparency, verification, and infrastructure security.

Blockchain systems should primarily consider the following areas of security:

1. Security on a ledger level.
2. Security on a network level.
3. Security at the transaction level.
4. Surround system-related security.
5. Security for smart contracts.

a. **Security at the Ledger Level:** The blockchain can only be used by authorised members. Valid participants initiate network transactions, and these transactions must be signed by the initiating members.
b. **Network-Level Security:** From the perspective of the network, communication between parts of various nodes must be safe. It must be protected against several internal and external attack vectors within the network. The ledger needs to be able to survive DoS attacks.
c. **Transaction-Level Security:** To ensure that no information is shared with unauthorised parties, PKI principles must be used to encrypt transactions. Identification and authorization of transaction generation must be protected, meaning that only a certain person, "X," may make transactions using that identity.

There is no way for anyone to change or alter the transaction details, and the multi-signature option is accessible for delicate transactions on the blockchain.

d. **Surround System Security Related:** Valid users should only be able to access related system components, like shadow databases. Using authentication and authorization systems will help to achieve this. 420 International Journal of Engineering & Technology In order to protect against malware, worms, and viruses, it also involves document sharing.
e. **Smart Contract Security:** Smart contracts, self-executing contracts, blockchain contracts, and digital contracts all function as agreements because they can be preprogrammed with the ability to self-execute and self-enforce. The network's fundamental guidelines should be adhered to by all contracts placed on the blockchain. These contracts can call for information from a third party that has potentially been altered.

COMPARING THE THREE DIFFERENT TYPES OF BLOCKCHAINS

- **Consensus-Based Decision Making:** Each node could participate in the consensus process on a public blockchain. Also, with a consortium blockchain, only a predetermined group of nodes are in charge of validating blocks. Private chains are wholly under the authority of a single entity, which may also choose the final consensus.
- **Review the Permission:** A private blockchain or a consortium blockchain may or may not make transactions visible to the general public, compared to a public blockchain.
- **Immutability:** It is extremely difficult to alter transactions in a public blockchain because records are maintained on so many different participants. A private blockchain or a consortium blockchain, on the other hand, has a smaller number of members and is therefore more susceptible to manipulation of transaction data.
- **Performance:** Because the public blockchain network has a lot of nodes, it takes a long time for blocks and transactions to spread. As a result, the throughput of transactions is constrained and the latency is significant. Both consortium blockchain and private blockchain may operate more effectively with fewer validators.
- **Centralised:** The three different forms of blockchains have three primary distinctions: public blockchains are decentralised, consortium blockchains are partially centralised, and private blockchains are completely centralised because they are managed by a single entity.
- **The Consensus Procedure:** Everyone in the globe is able to participate in the public blockchain's consensus process. Both consortium blockchain and private blockchain are permissioned, in contrast to public blockchain.

BENEFITS OF BLOCKCHAIN

The advantages of using blockchain vary depending on the circumstance. Blockchain, however, works well most often when there is a large amount of data that is shared across several parties without any type of trust mechanism.

Blockchain technology is the foundation of cryptocurrencies, but it also has numerous other applications and benefits in finance, record keeping, payments, and so on (Ertz & Boily, 2019).

Blockchain technology has the potential to lower infrastructure costs, improve transaction security and data quality, increase efficiency and speed of settlement, and provide transaction transparency (Williams & Fernandez, 2019).

The utility of blockchain technology extends beyond simply keeping a record of financial transaction entries to the automatic implementation of multi-party agreements using digital contracts (Ranjan et al., 2017). Digital contracts auto-execute with a shared database running a blockchain protocol, and all parties validate the outcome instantly without the need for a third-party intermediary.

Figure 2. Chart

Source: https://www2.deloitte.com/content/dam/Deloitte/in/Documents/strategy/in-strategy-innovation-blockchain-technology-india-opportunities-challenges

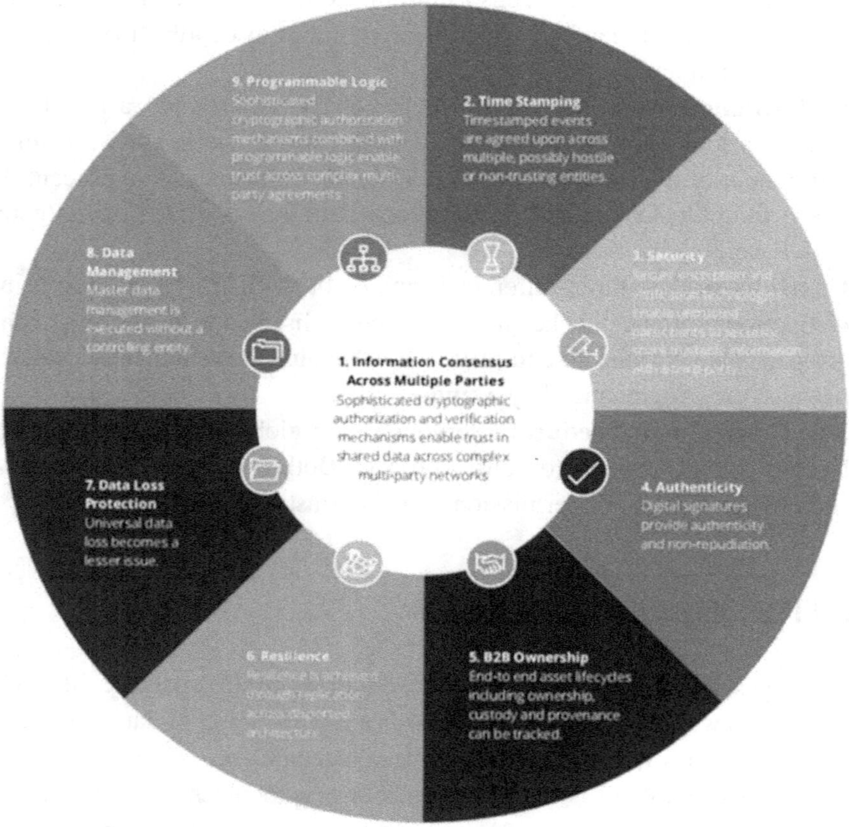

Scope of Blockchain in Financial Markets

Globally, blockchain technology has a bright future. In the world of finance, Blockchain technology has been seen to have an astonishing reach. During demonetization, the financial institutions were unable to cope with the increased workload, which highlighted the issues with having a centralised specialist handle financial operations. The RBI is encouraging banks to promote digitisation as a result. Also, they issued a statement emphasising the potential of Blockchain to combat fraud and the potential for bringing about specific changes to the way financial markets, collateral identification, and payment systems operate.

It is possible to save a large amount of time and money by incorporating Blockchain into financial transactions, including a significant decrease in the amount of time required for processing and validating transactions. The blockchain runs on a distributed database, which facilitates smooth operations, ensures strict security, and protects it from cyberattacks.

Numerous financial organisations have started investing a lot in this specific area after realising the advantages of blockchain technology. Since each address used for transactions is permanently saved on the databases, making all transactions proof and responsible, blockchain can also aid in reducing the flow of black money and dealing with the extensive money cleaning in the economy. The government is looking at blockchain technology as a tool to investigate a number of possibilities that could assist in applying a better control over the national economy.

The interaction between these financial and nonfinancial factors must be carefully considered. Investors are not all the same, and the degree to which they pay attention to ESG factors varies by asset class and the investor's aim. While some investors utilise ESG information only to increase profits and reduce risk, others also do so to support sustainable development. Even though fixed-income assets make up a greater portion of their portfolios and despite new evidence that ESG information also influences the pricing of credit risk for corporate bonds and bank loans, many investors spend far more money on ESG in the area of equity investments. Several investors have also recently focused on the effects of ESG criteria in real estate investments.

Both approaches support the present, contradictory finding that more sustainable development does not always result from more sustainable investments. This paradox can be explained in part by the fact that sustainable investments do not now exist as a category. So, talking about investments that are more sustainable would definitely make more sense. We can currently see just slight gains. A future with more sustainable investments is possible. Ecologically conscientious investors, for instance, make the biggest contribution currently possible to sustainable development in the given circumstances and at the given moment by picking investments in renewable energy companies. Yet, the theoretical claim of really sustainable investments would only be fulfilled if it was possible to make investments in long-lasting and self-supporting ecological and human-social systems.

Figure 3. Agenda for blockchain and financial markets
Source: https://mpra.ub.uni-muenchen.de/99212/2/MPRA_paper_99212

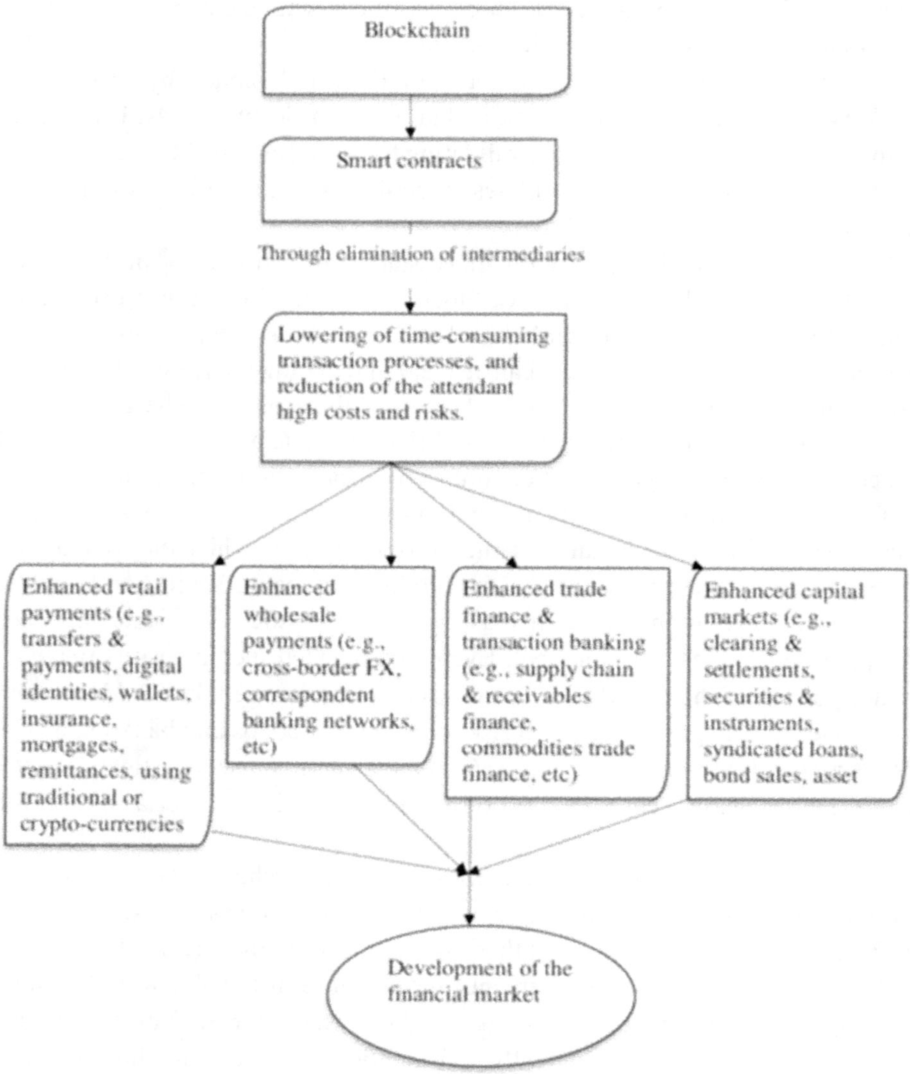

Blockchain Use Cases in the Financial Services Industry

Blockchain is widely explored across industries and multiple use cases are being experimented with financial services players are emerging as the leaders in identifying Blockchain use cases (April, 2017).

Figure 4. Blockchain use cases in financial services industry
Source: Deloitte Report April 2017.

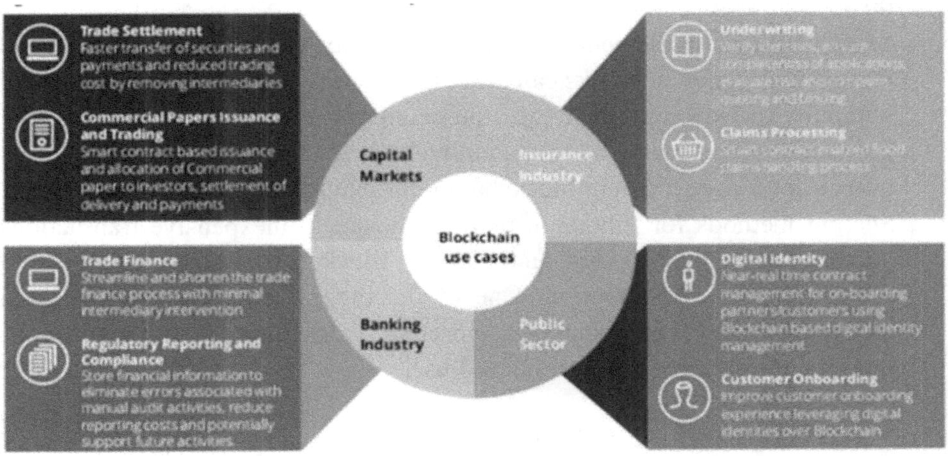

BLOCKCHAIN IN INDIA: CHALLENGES AND PROBLEMS

The major hurdle to Blockchain adoption is being lack of awareness. Users are not aware about its uses and impact (April, 2017) The challenges faced by businesses while performing the proof of concepts (PoC) broadly under the following six major areas:

- **Lack of Adoption:** Blockchains work better and more efficiently when used by a large network of users. For instance, a blockchain ecosystem would require suppliers as well as users to sign up for the network (Buterin, 2015). On the other hand, according to APQC, only 29% of businesses are actively experimenting with or using blockchain. Blockchains will remain inefficient and scalable without widespread usage. There are some signs, nevertheless, that the adoption of blockchain technology may grow. Companies are gradually organising cooperative blockchain working groups to address related issues and offer solutions that can be helpful to everyone without disclosing confidential information.

- **Increased Implementation Costs for Blockchain:** Early financial expenditures are crucial. Investment costs for some businesses could be too high. Even though the majority of existing solutions are free, a sizeable investment is needed for employing skilled software engineers that specialise in blockchain development, licencing costs in the event that a user wants to switch to a paid software version, general management, and more (Zheng et al., 2018). One of the biggest obstacles to the application of blockchain is this.
- **Scalability:** Its implementation faces scalability as its key challenge. Even though transaction networks can process hundreds of transactions per second without experiencing any issues, processing transactions on Bitcoin (3–7 transactions per second) and Ethereum (about 15-20 transactions per second) takes a lot longer, making blockchain unusable for large-scale applications. Scaling methods for Ethereum that permit quick, inexpensive transactions include Lightning Network and Plasma. Blockchain technology needs to accelerate for wide adoption. One of the biggest issues with blockchain technology, and consequently, enterprise blockchain technology, is its inability to support a large number of users.

Due to the increasing demand for enterprise blockchain and related apps, businesses that can expand their enterprise blockchain platforms successfully will prosper.

- **Challenges With Security and Privacy:** What are some of the most crucial inquiries you should think about? What about all the privacy and security worries? While cryptocurrencies offer pseudonymity, many possible blockchain applications require smart transactions and contracts to be undeniably connected to real persons, presenting serious privacy and data security concerns.

Today, many companies must abide by legal requirements. When it comes to sensitive information, their clients entrust them. This information won't be completely private, though, if it's all recorded on a public ledger. Blockchain technology can be used in this case, either privately or in consortiums. Your private information would still be protected, and you would only have access to what is necessary.

Security is yet another crucial component. Yet, there are very few situations where this is possible with efficient protocols. While being more secure than traditional computer systems, blockchain-based applications, systems, and organisations are nevertheless susceptible to hacking.

- **Regulations:** The absence of regulation will be the next place where you can run into trouble. It is possible for scams and market manipulation to cause a worldwide economic catastrophe. As a result, Bitcoin has received a lot of unfavourable press on a global scale.
- **Contraband Behaviour:** Blockchain technology is still in its infancy, and the lack of strict regulations has encouraged the growth of shady ventures and other bad actors looking to take advantage of unsophisticated investors. In addition, there have been some well-publicized thefts from cryptocurrency exchanges, notably the infamous bitcoin robbery from Mt. Gox in 2014, which almost brought down the entire sector.
- **Usage of Energy:** Another issue is that Proof of Work, the most popular consensus algorithm, consumes a lot of energy. This limits access to PoW networks for common users, promotes the creation of massive mining pools, prevents decentralisation by pressuring users to join large mining pools, and creates environmental issues.
- **Low Availability of Workers:** The nonfungible token (NFT) and DeFi businesses have experienced a sharp increase in nonfungible tokens and projects over the last year, which has caused problems in the labour market. Recent data shows that as startups and established companies search for top talent, the demand for blockchain talent has surged by more than 300%.

The shortage of experienced engineers in the blockchain sector has gotten worse as a result of intense competition among businesses that provide extremely competitive salary packages to recruit and retain their staff. As a result, several companies in the cryptocurrency industry pay employees in particular job categories more than $1 million annually. In order to fill the blockchain talent vacuum, businesses are hiring coders. One of the implementation issues with blockchain technology is getting closer to being resolved every day.

- **Interoperability:** Interoperability is one of the most crucial problems that needs to be solved because it's one of the main reasons why businesses haven't fully adopted blockchain technology. Since they are unable to transmit and receive data from other blockchain-based systems, most blockchains are kept in isolation and do not interact with other peer networks.
- **Inconsistency With Standards:** At this time, what standards does blockchain follow? No global standard exists despite the abundance of networks. As a result of the lack of a global standard, interoperability issues, cost increases, and complicated procedures exist. It discourages new developers and investors from entering the market because there is no specific version of blockchain technology.

- **Adaptation to Existing Systems:** Another issue is how to integrate blockchain technology with an existing system. If a business chooses to use blockchain, they must typically entirely replace their outdated system or create a plan to successfully connect the two technologies.

Another problem is that businesses without blockchain developers lack access to the skill pool needed to take part in this process. Reliance on an external source may make this issue worse. Yet, to implement the majority of market solutions, the business must commit a substantial amount of time and money.

CONCLUSION

we are now entering a phase where Blockchain may do the same by ushering in a new paradigm comprising 'Internet of Trust' and 'Internet of Value'. The financial services industry may be one of the firsts to be impacted by wider adoption of Blockchain and its associated Distributed Ledger Technologies. Trade Finance, Cross-border Payments, Bill Discounting, Supply chain financing, Loyalty and Digital Identity areas are major field where number of usage of blockchain have tested by Indian Players. Blockchains enable trustworthy, auditable peer-to-peer interactions and strong, distributed peer-to-peer systems. Government should establish uniform legislation for this technology as business prepares to use blockchain technologies.

Blockchain's primary technology is its consensus process. Focus on developing algorithms based on the Blockchain technology's consensus mechanisms for various scenarios in future work. Integration challenges, Lack of awareness & Identification of right platform is another hindrance to blockchain technology. To overcome this challenge, organizations need to take serious steps such as cross-functional teams, conducted focused group discussions with the IT team of the partner firm.

The four main qualities of blockchain—decentralization, persistency, anonymity, and auditability—have demonstrated their potential to revolutionise traditional industries. We provide a thorough introduction of blockchain in this essay. We begin by providing a general review of blockchain technologies, including its architecture and salient features. The common blockchain consensus algorithms are then covered. We looked at and contrasted these protocols in various ways.

In addition, we outlined a number of difficulties and issues that might obstruct blockchain development and outlined some current solutions. Furthermore suggested are some potential directions for the future. Blockchain-based applications are becoming more prevalent these days, and we intend to investigate them in-depth in the future.

This study looked at how blockchain technology affected financial markets. The findings have demonstrated that blockchain technology and the financial market have a good and important link. Blockchain technology is still in its early stages, but it is gaining traction in financial markets. However, it is clear from this study that technology has the potential to empower investors. Because the technology is still in its early stages, a better understanding of how the potentials can be realised in financial markets is needed. More research is needed to determine how blockchain technology can be applied to the real-world financial challenges that people face, particularly in different political and cultural contexts.

REFERENCES

Buterin, V. (2015). *On public and private blockchains*. Available: https://blog.ethereum.org/2015/08/07/on-public-and-private-blockchains/

Dib, O., Brousmiche, K. L., Durand, A., Thea, E., & Hamida, E. B. (2018). Consortium blockchains: Overview, applications and challenges. *International Journal On Advances in Telecommunications*, *11*(1&2), 51–64.

Ertz, M., & Boily, É. (2019). The rise of the digital economy: Thoughts on blockchain technology and cryptocurrencies for the collaborative economy. *International Journal of Innovation Studies*, *3*(4), 84–93. doi:10.1016/j.ijis.2019.12.002

Evans, O. (2018). https://mpra.ub.uni-muenchen.de/99212/2/MPRA_paper_99212.pdf

Garay, J., Kiayias, A., & Leonardos, N. (2015). The Bitcoin Backbone Protocol: Analysis and Applications. Springer Berlin Heidelberg.

Janssen, M., Weerakkody, V., Ismagilova, E., Sivarajah, U., & Irani, Z. (2020). A framework for analysing blockchain technology adoption: Integrating institutional, market and technical factors. *International Journal of Information Management*, *50*, 302–309. doi:10.1016/j.ijinfomgt.2019.08.012

Kosba, A., Miller, A., Shi, E., Wen, Z., & Papamanthou, C. (2016). Hawk: The blockchain model of cryptography and privacy-preserving smartcontracts. *IEEE Symposium on Security and Privacy*, 839-858. 10.1109/SP.2016.55

Nakamoto, S. (n.d.). *Bitcoin: A Peer-to-Peer Electronic Cash System*. https://www.researchgate.net/publication/336242531_The_Impact_of_Blockchain_Technology_on_Financial_Technology_FinTech

NRI. (2015). *Survey on blockchain technologies and related services.* Tech. Rep. Available: http://www.meti.go.jp/english/press/ 2016/pdf/0531 01f.pdf

Rajasekaran, A. S., Azees, M., & Al-Turjman, F. (2022). A comprehensive survey on blockchain technology. *Sustainable Energy Technologies and Assessments, 52*, 102039. doi:10.1016/j.seta.2022.102039

Ranjan, R., McParthland, J.W., & Lewis, R. (2017). Blockchain and Financial Market Innovation. *Economic Perspectives, 41*(7).

Sarmah, S.S. (2018). *Understanding blockchain technology*. https://www.researchgate.net/publication/336130918_Understanding_Blockchain_Technology

Schuetz, S., & Venkatesh, V. (2020). Blockchain, adoption, and financial inclusion in India: Research opportunities. *International Journal of Information Management, 52*, 101936. doi:10.1016/j.ijinfomgt.2019.04.009

Sharma, P., Jindal, R., & Borah, M. D. (2022). A Review of Blockchain-Based Applications and Challenges. *Wireless Personal Communications, 123*(2), 1201–1243. doi:10.100711277-021-09176-7

Sri Aruna, P. S. G., & Bhaskari, D. L. (2018). A study on blockchain technology. *IACSIT International Journal of Engineering and Technology.*

Swan, M. (2015). Blockchain thinking: The brain as a DAC (decentralized autonomous organization). *Texas Bitcoin Conference*, 27-29.

Tschorsch, F., & Scheuermann, B. (2016). *Bitcoin and Beyond: A Technical Survey on Decentralized Digital Currencies.* ieeexplore.ieee.org/document/7423672

Wang, He, & Ji. (2017). *Designated-Verifier Proof of Assets for Bitcoin Exchange Using Elliptic Curve Cryptography*. Academic Press.

White Paper on Applications of Blockchain technology to Banking and Financial sector in India. (2017). IDRBT.

WilliamsH.FernandezJ. (2019). www.ibm.com/blogs/blockchain/2019/04/how-transparency-through-blockchain-helps-the-cybersecurity-community/

Wu, B., & Duan, T. (2019, March). The application of blockchain technology in financial markets. *Journal of Physics: Conference Series, 1176*(4), 042094. doi:10.1088/1742-6596/1176/4/042094

Zhang, A., Zhong, R. Y., Farooque, M., Kang, K., & Venkatesh, V. G. (2020). Blockchain-based life cycle assessment: An implementation framework and system architecture. *Resources, Conservation and Recycling*, *152*, 104512. doi:10.1016/j.resconrec.2019.104512

Zheng, Z., Xie, S., Dai, H.-N., Chen, X., & Wang, H. (2018). Blockchain challenges and opportunities: A survey. *International Journal of Web and Grid Services*, *14*(4), 352–375. doi:10.1504/IJWGS.2018.095647

Chapter 13
Importance of Blockchain Technology in Green Innovation

Tushti Prasant Bakrania
Atmiya University, India

Chirag Vipulbhai Erda
Atmiya University, India

ABSTRACT

Large-scale and small-scale industries as well as entrepreneurs are struggling to find various ways to reduce pollution and move towards a more ecofriendly environment. One of the most forthcoming technologies is blockchain, which has entered the market but is not yet that prominent amongst people. Food suppliers in many countries have started using this technology, and various other companies have also taken interest in using this system to reduce their paperwork and to become faster and more reliable in their work. Blockchain technology is not a popular term for small entrepreneurs or small business, so to justify the above problem, this chapter gives brief idea about how blockchain can be helpful for sustainable growth with green innovation. It sheds light on the importance of blockchain technology in various innovations, which are ecofriendly. The study will add in the broader idea about green innovation and its link with blockchain technology.

DOI: 10.4018/978-1-6684-8361-9.ch013

INTRODUCTION

Marketing is one major factor which allows the companies to derive the value a customer or consumer perceives from the received service or product. (Larivière et al., 2013). Customer centric marketing is critical part for firms those who wish to sustain in B2C competitive environment. (Sheth et al., 2000). The methods which companies select to communicate to consumers may vary from company to company. But nevertheless the main objective should be related to consumers involvement and interest which has to be same. The rapid increase in the latest products and changing in taste and preference have often given a tuff competition to smaller firms by larger companies. The major problem which was faced by smaller firms was not having latest technology due to huge investments. But still many start ups and smaller firms are investing into technology to grab market and sustain their position.

Companies today are developing various forms of technology and exploiting various channels of media and advertising methods to position their brands and capture more market through their services and products. Digital marketing is leading the market in current situation through various new channels across social media which is more innovative, cost effective and more influential with customers (Melewar et al., 2017). The growth of the Internet with various latest technology, has made considerable impact on traditional marketing mix.

For example, advanced technologies often termed as big data analytics have allowed firms to aggregate large and complex data sets and use sophisticated analytics to gain additional consumer insights (Stone and Woodcock, 2014). Likewise, retailers and online businesses are increasingly investing in social media as part of their marketing communications practices and attempts to outperform their competitors (Vend, 2018). In this regard, DeMers (2016) forecasted that the trend toward cyber shopping is likely to intensify with an increased future consumer propensity to engage in online shopping experiences. As a consequence, more people in the United States prefer to do their shopping online than to purchase from brick and mortar stores (Marketo, 2017). Modern technologies put consumers at the forefront of security, privacy, trust, and transparency challenges. Prabhaker (2000) argues that each time individuals engage in an online transaction, they leave behind a digital trail of detailed information about their identity, their buying preferences, spending habits, credit card details, and other personally identifiable information (PII) (i.e., data that can be used to identify a particular person). From a privacy perspective, this situation has worsened over the years as data collection practices have become more versatile and ubiquitous. Online businesses regularly fail to meet regulatory requirements, and privacy leaks are frequent and have a lasting impact on consumers' trust (Ingram et al., 2018; Martin, 2018; Bodoni, 2019).

In various business and there models it is becoming really a complicated part to understand and investigate which technology is best for green market which is an upcoming market in near future. Due to huge environmental issues being faced globally companies and starts up are taking initiatives in green projects and even government is promoting to this. The technologies which are recently developed like AI – Artificial Intelligence, Cloud Computing, Internet of things, Robotics and block chains. These technologies plays a very crucial role in business development specially block chain. Block chain has helped many firms in managing - information, tampering of records, and supply chain management. The above were major problems faced by companies and block chain was common solution to prevent all these problems.

Block chain technology is a ledger (transaction records) which allows for information to be apprehend and shared in a known network. This network is being used by the registered members of the same company. Through this network they can maintain there own records and keep the information which is needed by them. This technology is useful to organizations where the same information has to be passed to various departments simultaneously. This technology becomes the strong source of single information through out the company. The best part of block chain is that once data is added it cannot be changed or modified so record tampering can be reduced or it will be negligible. There are mainly three basic features it has. The first one is BCT allows direct one to one transaction sharing in same organization. The second one is BCT is fully transparent and very much secure data storage. The third one is it allows for logic and agreements to be executed automatically

LITERATURE REVIEW

In Supply chain management (SCM) integration green supply chain is one of the latest emerging management model which has better efficiency, environmental impact and constant touch with manufacturers, suppliers as well as consumers. (Chen et al., 2012). According to Mathivathanan in 2018 defined Green SCM as a set of practices which has various activities starting from generation of ideas, evolving through design of eco friendly products, purchasing, logistics, manufacturing as well as waste management. Current situation has brought the whole world together to improve the environmental conditions which has become worst. The consumers as well as manufacturers are understanding the importance of nature and environment and they demand more of eco friendly products.

The GSCM concept comprises of implementation of many procedures, processes and different policies that includes minimizing the negative impacts which arises from different activities which includes supply chain. It ensures mergers with partners for the same. The best SC of today's state of the art information, technological as well as environmental friendly communication systems such as global positioning system scanners, personal data assistant and various tagging methods like RFID and barcodes are used at pace. (Jonsson et al., 2013). These technologies are more of environment friendly with different single point database systems. But however they have a drawback in terms of information sharing as these systems are totally based on different database systems. These all technologies are based on centralized database system. It can be easily exposed to failure point as if one fails the whole system fails at a stretch. Mubarak and Petraite (2020) said that block chain technology has pro environment features along with other technological states which provides a unified decentralised database system where firms can share all information as well as data within their control with system settings. This is the most advanced technology amongst all. Due to this reason majority of the companies specifically financial firms prefer it due to its reliability, more efficiency, better speed, organized structure and so on. Currently there is a separate system which is based on technology which is cryptocurrency, i.e., bitcoin. This information is not limited to finance only but it includes products information, information related to project, talent flow, processes information amongst others. Businesses need to undertake and forecast variations in their customers demand to provide them more efficiently. In such a situation, transparency, and extended collaboration with suppliers as well as customers are crucial for meeting the demand fluctuation (Pirvulescu & Enevoldsen, 2019b).

Santomier (2008) believes that in new economy brands are not going for solely one campaign after another instead of that they are capitalizing on various forms of consumer engagement and dialogue to expand their market coverage and enforce more synergistic to increase marketing communication strategy. Currently firms are building a portfolio of technologies and exploiting various media channels and publicity methods to position their brands as well as sell their products, ideas as well as services (McAllister & Turow, 2002).

Attributes of Blockchain and Its Importance in Green Innovation

Block chain as the name itself says it describes the way the technology function: say it stores information on various blocks which are then linked together and constitute a chain of data which is verified. According to Tillemann et al. (2019) has describes three basic steps on how Block chain works as explained in Figure 1. These steps are as given below:

Figure 1. Steps on how blockchain works
Source: Author compilation.

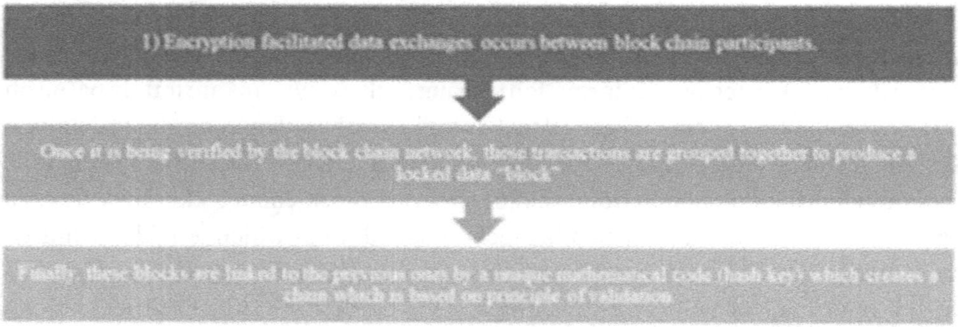

Layers of block chain which are describes as below:

1. The storing and securing of permanent, auditable, and unchangeable digital records which provides data security.
2. The exchange of digital assets in real time, which will provide better transparency.
3. The execution of smart contracts which contributes to efficiency.

Figure 2. Attributes of blockchain
Source: Author compilation.

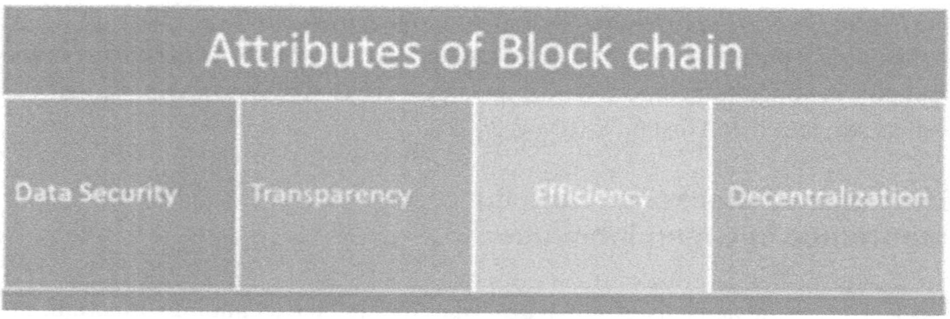

Attributes of blockchain as mentioned in Figure 2 are explained below:

1. **Data Security:** Highest secure way for storing various data is Block chain. It is secure as each and every transaction is verified in case a new block in added (Crosby et al., 2016). This mechanism is termed as 'peer-to-peer' which makes it difficult for violators to modify the data (Wang et al., 2021). Additionally,

any information cannot be deleted once it is approved by each and every node (Yli-Huumo et al., 2016). All these attributes of blockchain makes it secure.

2. **Transparency:** The transparency of blockchain is increased by its visibility publicly and access only to authorized entities (Mukkamala et al., 2018). Thus, every peer is able to view the data but cannot edit it (Kim and Shin, 2019). Additionally, the authenticity is ensured by digital signature (Galen et al., 2019). Thus, blockchain is both secure and transparent.
3. **Efficiency:** Blockchain is efficient as the data is shared instantly and digitally which has created various opportunities like smart contracts, a free and secure agreement (Szabo, 1997). Blockchain is efficient as the chances of error are less and transaction cost is low (Mukkamala et al., 2018; Tillemann et al., 2019). Thus, the attributes of blockchain that it is quick, secure, transparent and low cost makes it efficient for data storage and sharing.
4. **Decentralization:** The structure of blockchain is decentralized which makes all members to collectively make an environment of peer-to-peer network (Trivedi et al., 2021). Thus, another attribute of blockchain is that it is decentralized which makes it robust to external disruptions.

Importance of Blockchain in Green Innovation

Due to their reduced environmental impact compared to fossil fuels, renewable energy sources have recently been a major factor in the adoption of blockchain technology. Renewable energy sources include the sun, wind, rain, and geothermal heat. All of these can be used to produce electricity. The utilisation of these resources results in the production of clean, renewable energy. Now that renewable energy technology have advanced, people can produce their own electricity without having to rely on pricy fossil fuels. The smart grid can help us in this situation by enabling us to utilise all of the cost-free and plentiful green energy sources in our immediate vicinity. An updated electrical system called the "smart grid" uses information technology and analogue or digital communications.

Smart grids must also overcome the challenges of security, interoperability, and data transfer. Renewable energy sources are erratic and unpredictable, thus the existing network must incorporate sophisticated technology. In order to encourage the use of renewable resources and create a better environment, a blockchain-based smart-grid is employed. The forking attack that was recently introduced is applied invertedly to the blockchain in the suggested paradigm. Stakeholders are represented in the energy grid concept by a central authority and dispersed peers. This technology has the potential to enhance moral smart grid systems and create a greener planet.

The application of green certificates in an industrial operating system may be achieved using blockchain technology. The possibility of peer-to-peer energy exchanges using a microgrid design and blockchain was investigated. It is believed that a blockchain-based system could be used to accurately assess and monitor the environmental impact of energy-related assets. It is possible to go greener as a result of blockchain's potential to improve the energy supply chain. Blockchain technology has enabled energy-sharing economy applications, leading to various authors advocating new market models and the democratization of energy supplies. Blockchains, when combined with smart contracts, promise transparent, tamper-proof, and secure platforms capable of delivering creative, environmentally responsible business solutions.

CONCLUSION

Blockchain technology has the potential to enhance the management of financial markets, e-government, smart cities, and energy systems, leading to a greener IoT ecosystem and green innovation. Finally, there is blockchain technology, which ensures that transactions are secure, open, unchangeable, and guarded against fraud. IoT research and development technology is being quickly incorporated into blockchain technology, which can get around problems and bottlenecks. The use of blockchain technology is rising. Because of this, the study's emphasis was on the potential contribution of blockchain technology to the creation of an Internet of Things ecosystem that is more environmentally friendly as well as on important issues that blockchain technology can address.

The results of this study indicate that societal perception, sustainability attitude, and sustainability orientation all have a significant impact on the development of green endeavours and mindsets. The results of this study on green innovation could help the Peruvian government create a programme for mindfulness or an educational system that places more emphasis on sustainability and green innovation. These initiatives could aid Peru in achieving its objective of establishing a green economy because they have the potential to generate more environmentally friendly businesses. The green economy focuses on encouraging green innovation and a green attitude among small- and medium-sized business owners in order to guarantee that economic gains fully adhere to the green agenda. This is a must-have condition.

REFERENCES

Ageron, B., Gunasekaran, A., & Spalanzani, A. (2012). Sustainable supply management: An empirical study. *International Journal of Production Economics*, *140*(1), 168–182. doi:10.1016/j.ijpe.2011.04.007

Ahlstrand, A. (2018). *The Potential of Blockchain Technology in Solving Green Supply Chain Management Challenges*. Academic Press.

Ahmed, M., Mubarik, M. S., & Shahbaz, M. (2021). Factors affecting the outcome of corporate sustainability policy: A review paper. *Environmental Science and Pollution Research International, 28*(9), 10335–10356. doi:10.100711356-020-12143-7 PMID:33403636

Al-Ghdabi, R. R., Almomani, R. Z. Q., & Banyhamdan, K. M. (2019). Impact of the green supply chain management practices on corporate image of chemical industries in Jordan. *International Journal of Scientific and Technology Research, 8*(12), 2546–2554.

Alauthaman, M., Aslam, N., Zhang, L., Alasem, R., & Hossain, M. A. (2018). A P2P botnet detection scheme based on decision tree and adaptive multilayer neural networks. *Neural Computing & Applications, 29*(11), 991–1004. doi:10.100700521-016-2564-5 PMID:29769759

Allaway, A. W., Gooner, R. M., Berkowitz, D., & Davis, L. (2006). Deriving and exploring behavior segments within a retail loyalty card program. *European Journal of Marketing, 40*(11/12), 1317–1339. doi:10.1108/03090560610702830

Alvarenga, I. D., Rebello, G. A., & Duarte, O. C. M. (2018). Securing configuration management and migration of virtual network functions using blockchain. *NOMS 2018-2018 IEEEIFIP Network Operations and Management Symposium*, 1–9. 10.1109/NOMS.2018.8406249

Archa, A. B., & Achuthan, K. (2018). Trace and track: enhanced pharma supply chain infrastructure to prevent fraud. *Lecture Notes of the Institute for Computer Sciences, Social-Informatics and Telecommunications Engineering, LNICST, 218*(1), 189-195. . doi:10.1007/978-3-319-73423-1_17

Aslam, U., Manzoor, S., & Babar, M. I. (2019). Systematic literature review of blockchain in requisites of big data and its applications. *Journal of Software Engineering and Intelligent Systems*. Available at: www.jseis.org

Bag, S., Viktorovich, D. A., Sahu, A. K., & Sahu, A. K. (2021). Barriers to adoption of blockchain technology in green supply chain management. *Journal of Global Operations and Strategic Sourcing, 14*(1), 104–133. doi:10.1108/JGOSS-06-2020-0027

Baldimtsi, F., Kiayias, A., & Samari, K. (2017). Watermarking public- key cryptographic functionalities and implementations. In P. Q. Nguyen & J. Zhou (Eds.), *Information Security Lecture Notes in Computer Science* (pp. 173–191). Springer International Publishing. doi:10.1007/978-3-319-69659-1_10

Beales, H. (2010). The value of behavioral targeting. *Netw. Advert. Initiat.*, *1*, 1–23. Available online at: https://www.networkadvertising.org/pdfs/Beales_NAI_Study.pdf

Berman, S. J., & McClellan, B. E. (2002). Ten strategies for survival in the attention economy. *Strategy and Leadership*, *30*(3), 28–33. doi:10.1108/10878570210697513

Blattberg, R. C., & Deighton, J. (1996). Manage marketing by the customer equity test. *Harvard Business Review*, *74*, 136–144. PMID:10158473

Bodoni, S. (2019). *Mastercard Alerts Privacy Watchdogs After Loyalty Program Leak*. Available online at: https://www.bloomberg.com/news/articles/2019 08-23/ mastercard-tells-belgian-german-privacy-watchdogs-of-breach

Bond Brand Loyalty. (2016). *The 2016 Bond Loyalty Report*. Available online at: https://cdn2.hubspot.net/hubfs/352767/Resources/2016_Bond_Loyalty_ Report_ Executive_Summary_CAN_Launch_Edition.pdf

Bu, X., Dang, W. V. T., Wang, J., & Liu, Q. (2020). Environmental orientation, green supply chain management, and firm performance: Empirical evidence from Chinese small and medium-sized enterprises. *International Journal of Environmental Research and Public Health*, *17*(4), 1199. Advance online publication. doi:10.3390/ ijerph17041199 PMID:32069931

Castorani, V., Landi, D., & Germani, M. (2016). Determination of the optimal configuration of energy recovery ventilator through virtual prototyping and DoE techniques. *Procedia CIRP*, *50*, 52–57. doi:10.1016/j.procir.2016.05.019

Chan, R. Y. K., He, H., Chan, H. K., & Wang, W. Y. C. (2012). Environmental orientation and corporate performance: The mediation mechanism of green supply chain management and moderating effect of competitive intensity. *Industrial Marketing Management*, *41*(4), 621–630. doi:10.1016/j.indmarman.2012.04.009

Chen, C. C., Shih, H. S., Shyur, H. J., & Wu, K. S. (2012). A business strategy selection of green supply chain management via an analytic network process. *Computers & Mathematics with Applications (Oxford, England)*, *64*(8), 2544–2557. doi:10.1016/j.camwa.2012.06.013

Chichoni, J., & Webb, S. (2018). The digital global supply chain: The growing case for blockchain technology expansion within global supply chain. *Marriott Student Review*, *2*(2), 1–84.

Chin, T. A., Tat, H. H., & Sulaiman, Z. (2015). Green supply chain management, environmental collaboration and sustainability performance. *Procedia CIRP*, *26*, 695–699. doi:10.1016/j.procir.2014.07.035

Crosby, M., Pattanayak, P., Verma, S., & Kalyanaraman, V. (2016). BlockChain technology: beyond bitcoin: applied innovation review. *Applied Innovation Review*, *2*, 5–20.

De Giovanni, P., & Cariola, A. (2020). Process innovation through industry 4.0 technologies, lean practices and green supply chains. *Research in Transportation Economics*, *4*, 100869. doi:10.1016/j.retrec.2020.100869

Dhull, S., & Narwal, M. S. (2016). Drivers and barriers in green supply chain management adaptation: A state-of-art review. *Uncertain Supply Chain Management*, *4*(1), 61–76. doi:10.5267/j.uscm.2015.7.003

Li, G., Li, L., Choi, T. M., & Sethi, S. P. (2020). Green supply chain management in Chinese firms: Innovative measures and the moderating role of quick response technology. *Journal of Operations Management*, *66*(7-8), 958–988. doi:10.1002/joom.1061

Liu, B., & De Giovanni, P. (2019). Green process innovation through Industry 4.0 technologies and supply chain coordination. *Annals of Operations Research*, 1–36. doi:10.100710479-019-03498-3

Mahmood, T., & Mubarik, M. S. (2020). Balancing innovation and exploitation in the fourth industrial revolution: Role of intellectual capital and technology absorptive capacity. *Technological Forecasting and Social Change*, *160*, 120248. doi:10.1016/j.techfore.2020.120248 PMID:32839626

Malaysia Productivity Corporation. (2019). *Productivity Report 2018-2019*. Available at: http://www. mpc.gov.my/wp-content/uploads/2019/09/Productivity-Report-18_19-latest-as-at-250919-1.pdf

Mathivathanan, D., Kannan, D., & Haq, A. N. (2018). Sustainable supply chain management practices in Indian automotive industry: A multi-stakeholder view. *Resources, Conservation and Recycling*, *128*, 284–305. doi:10.1016/j.resconrec.2017.01.003

Menguc, B., & Ozanne, L. K. (2005). Challenges of the "green imperative": A natural resource-based approach to the environmental orientation-business performance relationship. *Journal of Business Research, 58*(4), 430–438. doi:10.1016/j.jbusres.2003.09.002

Milani, F., Garcıa-Ban~uelos, L., & Dumas, M. (2016). Blockchain and business process improvement. *BPTrends, 4*. Available at: www.bptrends.com

Mubarak, M. F., & Petraite, M. (2020). Industry 4.0 technologies, digital trust and technological orientation: What matters in open innovation? *Technological Forecasting and Social Change, 161*, 120332. doi:10.1016/j.techfore.2020.120332

Mubarak, M. F., Shaikh, F. A., Mubarik, M., Samo, K. A., & Mastoi, S. (2019). The impact of digital transformation on business performance. *Engineering, Technology and Applied Science Research, 9*(6), 5056–5061. doi:10.48084/etasr.3201

Mubarik, M., Zuraidah, R., & Rasi, B. R. M. (2019b). Triad of big data supply chain analytics, supply chain integration and supply chain performance: Evidences from oil and gas sector. *Humanities and Social Sciences Letters, 7*(4), 209–224. doi:10.18488/journal.73.2019.74.209.224

Mubarik, M., Zuraidah binti Raja Mohd Rasi, R., & Faraz Mubarak, M. (2020). Fostering supply chain integration through blockchain technology: A study of Malaysian manufacturing sector. *International Journal of Management and Sustainability, 9*(3), 135–147. doi:10.18488/journal.11.2020.93.135.147

Mubarik, M. S., Bontis, N., Mubarik, M., & Mahmood, T. (2021b). Intellectual capital and supply chain resilience. *Journal of Intellectual Capital*. Advance online publication. doi:10.1108/JIC-06-2020-0206

Mubarik, M. S., Kazmi, S. H. A., & Zaman, S. I. (2021a). Application of gray DEMATEL-ANP in green- strategic sourcing. *Technology in Society, 64*, 101524. doi:10.1016/j.techsoc.2020.101524

Mubarik, M. S., Naghavi, N., & Mubarak, M. F. (2019a). Impact of supplier relational capital on supply chain performance in Pakistani textile industry. *Asian Economic and Financial Review, 9*(3), 318–328. doi:10.18488/journal.aefr.2019.93.318.328

Mubarik, M. S., Naghavi, N., Mubarik, M., Kusi-Sarpong, S., Khan, S. A., Zaman, S. I., & Kazmi, S. H. A. (2021c). Resilience and cleaner production in industry 4.0: Role of supply chain mapping and visibility. *Journal of Cleaner Production, 292*, 126058. doi:10.1016/j.jclepro.2021.126058

Nakamoto, S. (2008). *Bitcoin: What's in the Whitepaper?* Academic Press.

Nascimento, D. L. M., Alencastro, V., Quelhas, O. L. G., Caiado, R. G. G., Garza-Reyes, J. A., Lona, L. R., & Tortorella, G. (2019). Exploring Industry 4.0 technologies to enable circular economy practices in a manufacturing context: A business model proposal. *Journal of Manufacturing Technology Management*, *30*(3), 607–627. doi:10.1108/JMTM-03-2018-0071

Olah, J., Aburumman, N., Popp, J., Khan, M. A., Haddad, H., & Kitukutha, N. (2020). Impact of industry 4.0 on environmental sustainability. *Sustainability (Switzerland)*, *12*(11), 1–21. doi:10.3390u12114674

Trivedi, S. (2023). Blockchain Framework for Insurance industry. *International Journal of Innovation and Technology Management.*

Trivedi, S., & Malik, R. (2022). Blockchain Technology as an Emerging Technology in the Insurance Market. In *Big Data: A Game Changer for Insurance Industry* (pp. 81–100). Emerald Publishing Limited. doi:10.1108/978-1-80262-605-620221006

Trivedi, S., Mehta, K., & Sharma, R. (2021). Systematic literature review on application of blockchain technology in E-finance and financial services. *Journal of Technology Management & Innovation*, *16*(3), 89–102. doi:10.4067/S0718-27242021000300089

Chapter 14
Blockchain Technology Use to Streamline Climate Investment

Surabhi Sugathan
Metas Adventist College, India

ABSTRACT

The main objective of this chapter is to contour the climate investing by implementing blockchain technology, which will lead to transparency within the network. Climate investing aids the companies that are involved in reducing carbon emissions, subsidising the usage of fossil fuels and manufacturing alternate options. This investment will be directly propositional to the "green revolution," which the Indian government is making efforts towards. Blockchain technology will help towards this investment by creating a transparent and secured network that is impossible to hack. The database management will be designed using the latest programming techniques, which may also include artificial intelligence. Climate finance includes the financial resources which has been used to support the sustainability and climate change.

INTRODUCTION

It is necessary to take a closer look at the design, capabilities, and governance implications of these emerging technologies in order to provide an answer to the question of how blockchain and DLTs might be used for creative climate funding under the GCF. The distinction between the technical terminology "blockchain" and "DLT" has been stressed, despite the fact that there are significant overlaps between technological clusters.

DOI: 10.4018/978-1-6684-8361-9.ch014

Bitcoin has brought together many community groups and has gradually evolved into a technical foundation for transforming productive relationships and building a trusting society. Blockchain is a distributed and distributed technology with trackable and consistent data that can establish trust relationships in participating nodes in a network environment without a trust center. Smart contract technologies in the next generation of blockchain, such as Ether and Hyperledger Fabric, extend blockchain from a distributed database for storing critical data to a decentralized, distributed computing platform. Blockchain technically solves the security issues of access control methods that use centralized authorized decisionmaking entities. Access control of blockchain-based can reduce the dependence of access control on a single trusted entity and improve the reliability of access control and data security. Meanwhile, Devices of IoT can use blockchain as the underlying network architecture to form the IoT, thus strengthening the IoT's ability to resist external cyber-attacks.

This article provided an overview of the use of blockchain technology in related fields and the challenges IoT faces in terms of security and privacy. This article provided an overview of the use of blockchain technology in related fields and the challenges IoT faces in terms of security and privacy. This article fully introduces the use of blockchain technology in related fields and the challenges IoT faces in terms of security and privacy.

This chapter has the following parts. Introduce the origins of blockchain technology, technology principles and blockchain industry development and applications; reveals the basic concepts of IoT technology and summarizes the security and privacy issues as well as the major security threats IoT faces in the first phase. The second section briefly introduced the concept of climate investment. The third section discussed combination of blockchain and climate investment, focusing on a detailed discussion of the existing challenges and issues facing. The fourth section discussed the whole article and summarizes the risks and challenges faced by Blockchain application in climate investment in terms of the security and privacy. The fifth section summarizes future research applications and guide.

LITERATURE REVIEW

Blockchain

The Overview of Blockchain

Blockchain Definitions

A blockchain is essentially a continually increasing distributed database maintained by numerous participants (Sipthorpe et al., 2022). The Distributed Shared Ledger (DSL) blockchain maintains a growing and ordered chain of data through smart contracts that allow any number of nodes participating in the system to put together a time system of all nodes through cryptographic algorithms that can Encryption algorithms calculate and record all information exchanged in the system to a data block and generate a data block thumbprint that can be used to chain the following data (Hwa, 2016).

Blocks and verify it (Sivarethinamohan & Sujatha, 2021). The core of the system also lies in the development from information connectivity to value connectivity by establishing trust between the two parties of a transaction through a distributed network, a time-series tamperproof cryptographic ledger and a decentralized consensus mechanism, and by programming and manipulating data with smart contracts consisting of automation scripts (Bird et al., 2019).

The Technical Characteristics of Blockchain

Blockchain is an integrated innovation of many existing technologies and is mainly used to achieve multi-party trust and university cooperation. In general, mature blockchain systems have four characteristics: transparency, tamper-proof traceability, privacy security, and high reliability of the system (Bosco et al., 2018).

Transparency

In a decentralized system, all nodes in the network are peer-topeer and they send and receive information in the network equally (Trivedi et al., 2021). Therefore, each node in the system has full observation of all actions in the network and maintains a local ledger of these actions in each node and the whole system is transparent to each node.

Tamper-Proof Traceability

Tamper-proof means that once a transaction is verified across the network and added to the blockchain, it is difficult to modify or delete it (Sipthorpe et al., 2022).

Traceability signifies that every exchange on the blockchain is fully tracked. We can track all historical transactions associated with a certain state on the blockchain (Trivedi & Malik, 2022).

Privacy Security

As any node in the blockchain system contains the complete blockchain authentication logic, no node needs to depend on any other node to accomplish the verification process of transactions in the blockchain (Schletz et al., 2020). The de-trust features make it unnecessary for nodes to reveal their identities to each other, as no node needs to judge the validity of a transaction based on the identity of other nodes, which provides the basis for the blockchain system to protect user privacy (Trivedi, 2023).

Blockchain and IoT Convergence

IoT devices are connected to networks, generating large amounts of data and integrating powerful data analytics capabilities that are expected to change the way people produce and live (Trivedi et al., 2021). However, while providing development opportunities, there are still many problems in scalability, compatibility, and security in the IoT industry at this stage, which seriously limit the space for the integration and development of IoT with various industry sectors and hinder the realization of its potential value. Blockchain, as an emerging technology fused with IoT, can be an effective solution to the problems of trust, data management, security, and privacy problems in the IoT growth (Yan et al., 2022).

Climate Investment

Climate finance, in general, refers to the flows of financial resources utilised to support a wide range of climate-related initiatives. Sustainability and change - These might encourage both mitigation and adaptation efforts (Bender et al., 2019). Actions that lessen the effects of the existing dangers and inevitable consequences of climate change are the main focus of adaptation initiatives. The goal of adaptation initiatives is to increase how resilient natural and human systems are to such changes. On the other side, mitigation aims to reduce and lessen the effects of climate change, primarily through lowering or regulating greenhouse gas emissions.

Climate finance include climate-specific funding mechanisms and mitigation and adaptation strategies to encourage and facilitate the shift to low-carbon, climate-resilient growth and development through human resource development, research and development, and economic development. In a more general sense, the term is used to describe all financial flows related to initiatives for climate change mitigation and adaptation from both public and private actors. The term has been used in a narrow sense to refer to transfers of public resources from developed to developing countries in light of their obligations to provide "new and additional financial resources" under the UN Climate Convention. The topic of the climate change discussion has recently focused on the foreign cash flows intended to finance climate projects (Bird et al., 2019). The sheer amount of resources and the variety of financing options have made it extremely difficult to manage and ensure the effectiveness of the funding.

A wide range of procedures and financial instruments are required to run this massive stream of climate resources, with the goal of funding the measures to combat climate change (Forstater, 2012). The National Climate Funds are a key component of the Mechanisms. National funds are often how nations pool, combine, and manage all the resources coming from domestic sources as well as foreign grants, loans, etc.

Given that the Climate Investment Funds (CIF), which is now operational, represents the new international climate finance architecture, and that the Climate Investment Funds (CIF) was initially designed as an interim solution, it is important to evaluate the CIF's position in relation to other sources of concessional financing and in light of the changing financial needs of developing nations.

Several channels of climate finance exist. It comes from a range of public and/or private sources, is channelled through a range of multilateral, bilateral, and national public or private channels, and is invested in a variety of ways — at commercial or concessional terms — to address the needs and circumstances unique to an activity and its recipient.

The people who receive money vary as well, ranging from fully public organisations like local or national governments to purely private individuals like small-scale landowners or business owners.

In order to promote climate-relevant investment, this chapter examines the role of public actors, notably various concessional climate finance sources (Parmentola et al., 2022).

Concessional financing for climate-related investments in poor countries is channelled through MDBs by the CIF, the GEF, and other bilateral and multilateral donor trust funds and developing nations (Fankhauser & Lavric, 2003). In addition to these outside resources, several MDBs use their own concessional resources (commonly referred to as "soft ending windows") to offer grants and loans at zero or low interest rates to specific member countries (Hainaut & Cochran, 2018). These internal resources, whose main goals are to reduce poverty and achieve economic and social development objectives, include the Asian Development Fund (ADF) of the Asian Development Bank, the African Development Fund of the African Development Bank, the Multilateral Investment Fund and Fund for Special Operations (FSO) of the International Development Bank, and the International Development Association of the World Bank (IDA).

Since they offer financing (or other instruments) under more lenient or "softer" terms than the MDBs may through their regular capital resources, all of these concessional sources are significant. With their particular focus on climate-related goals, the external sources of concessional money that are channelled via the MDBs have played a particularly significant role in supporting the MDBs' climate agenda.

Blockchain Contribution for Climate Investment

The principal framework model (public-permissionless) portrays a framework where the exchange or information history is freely noticeable and each hub in the organization has consent to check and add exchanges to the blockchain (Calandra et al., 2022). One prominent example is bitcoin. In the second system model, the data or transaction history is also publicly visible (public-permitted), but nodes in the network need special permission to verify and add transactions (Bosco et al., 2018). Even privileged parties can be appointed by the network maintainer (Javaid et al., 2022). An illustration of such a model is Ripple, a financial transaction, currency exchange, and remittance system designed for banks and payment networks. Ripple's (XRP) distributed consensus ledger replaces the traditional blockchain (Dorfleitner & Braun, 2019). The third model, known as private-permissionless, is a network in which anyone can verify or add transactions, but only a select group of nodes that have been approved beforehand can view the relevant data or transaction history (Kim & Kim, 2017). The LTO Network, a platform for running trustless workflows geared toward governments and multinational corporations, is one illustration. LTO utilizes a cross breed blockchain with a confidential layer for information sharing and cycle mechanization, and a public layer which goes about as a permanent computerized legal official (Howson, 2020). A private consortium ledger is one way to describe the fourth system model, which is called private-permitted (Lee & Kim, 2016). Viewing the history of data or transactions, as well as verifying and adding data or transactions, can only be done by pre-approved nodes (Dorfleitner, Muck, & Scheckenbach, 2021). Innovative supply chain management systems, banking consortia, and Hyperledger Fabric, a private permissioned blockchain supported by IBM, are examples of use cases.

These four distinct system models make it abundantly clear that initial design choices, in addition to general technological capabilities and the actors involved in DLT implementation or regulation, will be crucial to the successful application of DLTs for climate finance (Lohmann, 2009). Because they may result in path dependencies or lock-ins with specific governance implications, the initial design choices that are made are crucial if the GCF is to be used to investigate specific DLT application areas (Dorfleitner, Muck, & Scheckenbach, 2021). In contrast to permissioned systems like consortium blockchains, which restrict interactions to pre-approved members (nodes), permissionless systems allow participants to collaborate with any other party on a case-by-case basis (Schinckus, 2020). Design choices also have an impact on whether the DLT network is based on proprietary and commercial principles or openness, cooperation, and transparency (Guo & Liang, 2016). Because it is necessary to ensure that the advantages of data-driven innovation are balanced with concerns about privacy, ethics, sustainability, and fundamental human rights, this particular design decision is also closely linked to issues of legal regulation (Qin et al., 2023).

We believe it is necessary to define blockchain as a particular kind of DLT because the technical terms "blockchain" and "DLT" are frequently used interchangeably (Zhang et al., 2023). The underlying DLT system is then divided into at least four distinct models: (1) public-permissionless ledgers; (2) public-permissioned ledgers; (3) private-permissioned ledgers; and (4) private-permissioned ledgers.

It is essential to be aware that the design of DLT systems is inherently political. Due to the numerous effects that digital products have on people's behavior, attitudes, and needs, DLT design decisions have a significant impact on users' lives (Trivedi & Malik, 2022). In other words, by defining specific rules for users interacting through the network, DLT system design encourages particular forms of social interaction and human behavior. Because of this political aspect, discussions about DLT design are clearly positioned within broader discussions about the governance of and through emerging technologies (Trivedi et al., 2021). The fact that distributed ledger technologies (DLTs) are neither a one-size-fits-all nor stand-alone solution to major political issues in climate finance is one of the most important insights that can be gleaned from ongoing debates regarding the governance of emerging technologies (Puri et al., 2020). Instead, DLTs ought to be viewed as adaptable tools that can be applied to solve clearly defined operational and interorganizational issues in their current state of development.

DISCUSSION AND RECOMMENDATIONS

Underdeveloped capital markets typically impede domestic resource mobilization for infrastructure investment, despite the fact that the majority of developing and emerging economies face an urgent need to scale up sustainable finance for low-carbon and climate-resilient infrastructure investment. Domestic savers in many developing and emerging economies also face a lack of "safe" assets in the local currency, forcing them to export capital to advanced economies' financial centers. We talk about how fintech can complement traditional capital markets and get money for long-term infrastructure investments. By combining timestamp, public and private key mechanisms, and smart contract technologies, we propose blockchain-based project bonds to raise funding through a digital crowdfunding platform. These bonds can also record and verify the use of proceeds, sustainability impact, and revenue streams of projects. Not only would this strategy enable issuers like municipalities to raise funds for sustainable infrastructure investment, but it would also give investors of all sizes the chance to purchase assets in local currencies. It would also make project management easier once the project is running, like billing and metering, and it would make the investment's entire life cycle transparent, which would help prevent money from being misused.

CONCLUSION AND FUTURE WORK

According to the forecast of related organizations, the amount of global IoT devices are going to reach tens of billions by 2023. As the number of devices in the IoT rises dramatically, the demand for services continues to increase, the cost of data center infrastructure construction and maintenance investment rises significantly, and the security risks and performance bottlenecks of related IoT business platforms are increasing day by day. Designing new IoT service models has become a strategic focus for enterprise and organizational innovation, and combining blockchain technologies to build a "decentralized" IoT structure has become one of the key models.

REFERENCES

Bender, J., Bridges, T. A., & Shah, K. (2019). Reinventing climate investing: Building equity portfolios for climate risk mitigation and adaptation. *Journal of Sustainable Finance & Investment*, *9*(3), 191–213. doi:10.1080/20430795.2019.1579512

Bird, N., Cao, Y., & Quevedo, A. (2019). *Transformational change in the climate investment funds*. See www. odi. org/sites/odi.org.uk/files/resource-documents/12587. pdf

Bosco, F., Croce, V., & Raveduto, G. (2018). Blockchain Technology for Financial Services Facilitation in RES Investments. *Proceedings of the 2018 IEEE 4th International Forum on Research and Technology for Society and Industry (RTSI)*, 1–5. 10.1109/RTSI.2018.8548505

Calandra, D., Secinaro, S., Massaro, M., Dal Mas, F., & Bagnoli, C. (2022). The link between sustainable business models and Blockchain: A multiple case study approach. *Business Strategy and the Environment*, bse.3195. doi:10.1002/bse.3195

Dorfleitner, G., & Braun, D. (2019). Fintech, digitalization and blockchain: possible applications for green finance. *The rise of green finance in Europe: opportunities and challenges for issuers, investors and marketplaces*, 207-237.

Dorfleitner, G., Muck, F., & Scheckenbach, I. (2021). Blockchain applications for climate protection: A global empirical investigation. *Renewable & Sustainable Energy Reviews*, *149*, 111378. doi:10.1016/j.rser.2021.111378

Fankhauser, S., & Lavric, L. (2003). The investment climate for climate investment: Joint Implementation in transition countries. *Climate Policy*, *3*(4), 417–434. doi:10.1016/S1469-3062(03)00050-0

Guo, Y., & Liang, C. (2016). Blockchain application and outlook in the banking industry. *Financ. Innovat*, *2*(1), 24. doi:10.118640854-016-0034-9

Hainaut, H., & Cochran, I. (2018). The Landscape of domestic climate investment and finance flows: Methodological lessons from five years of application in France. *Inter Economics*, *155*, 69–83. doi:10.1016/j.inteco.2018.06.002

Howson, P. (2020). Climate crises and Crypto-Colonialism: Conjuring value on the Blockchain frontiers of the global South. *Frontiers in Blockchain*, *3*, 22. doi:10.3389/fbloc.2020.00022

Hwa, C. S. (2016). Legal issues for the introduction of distributed ledger based on Blockchain technology focused on the financial industry. Korea Financial Law Association, 13(2), 107-138.

Javaid, M., Haleem, A., Singh, R. P., Suman, R., & Khan, S. (2022). A review of Blockchain Technology applications for financial services. *BenchCouncil Transactions on Benchmarks, Standards and Evaluations*, 100073.

Kim, Y.J., & Kim, D. (2017). A Study on a strategic planning and trend of Blockchain standardization. *The Journal of the Institute of Internet Broadcasting and Communication*.

Lee, S.-H., & Kim, K. (2016). Device Authentication in Smart Grid System Using Blockchain. KAIST.

Lohmann, L. (2009). Climate as investment. *Development and Change*, *40*(6), 1063–1083. doi:10.1111/j.1467-7660.2009.01612.x

Parmentola, A., Petrillo, A., Tutore, I., & De Felice, F. (2022). Is blockchain able to enhance environmental sustainability? A systematic review and research agenda from the perspective of Sustainable Development Goals (SDGs). *Business Strategy and the Environment*, *31*(1), 194–217. doi:10.1002/bse.2882

Puri, J., Rastogi, A., Prowse, M., & Asfaw, S. (2020). Good will hunting: Challenges of theory-based impact evaluations for climate investments in a multilateral setting. *World Development*, *127*, 104784. doi:10.1016/j.worlddev.2019.104784

Qin, M., Zhang, X., Li, Y., & Badarcea, R. M. (2023). Blockchain market and green finance: The enablers of carbon neutrality in China. *Energy Economics*, *118*, 106501. doi:10.1016/j.eneco.2022.106501

Schinckus, C. (2020). The good, the bad and the ugly: An overview of the sustainability of blockchain technology. *Energy Research & Social Science*, *69*, 101614. doi:10.1016/j.erss.2020.101614

Schletz, M., Nassiry, D., & Lee, M. K. (2020). *Blockchain and tokenized securities: The potential for green finance*. Academic Press.

Sipthorpe, A., Brink, S., Van Leeuwen, T., & Staffell, I. (2022). Blockchain solutions for carbon markets are nearing maturity. *One Earth*, *5*(7), 779–791. doi:10.1016/j.oneear.2022.06.004

Sivarethinamohan, R., & Sujatha, S. (2021). Unraveling the potential of artificial intelligence-driven blockchain technology in environment management. In *Advances in Mechanical Engineering: Select Proceedings of CAMSE 2020* (pp. 693-700). Springer Singapore. 10.1007/978-981-16-0942-8_66

Trivedi, S. (2023). Blockchain Framework for Insurance industry. *International Journal of Innovation and Technology Management*.

Trivedi, S., & Malik, R. (2022). Blockchain Technology as an Emerging Technology in the Insurance Market. In *Big Data: A Game Changer for Insurance Industry* (pp. 81–100). Emerald Publishing Limited. doi:10.1108/978-1-80262-605-620221006

Trivedi, S., Mehta, K., & Sharma, R. (2021). Systematic literature review on application of blockchain technology in E-finance and financial services. *Journal of Technology Management & Innovation*, *16*(3), 89–102. doi:10.4067/S0718-27242021000300089

Yan, L., Mirza, N., & Umar, M. (2022). The cryptocurrency uncertainties and investment transitions: Evidence from high and low carbon energy funds in China. *Technological Forecasting and Social Change*, *175*, 121326. doi:10.1016/j.techfore.2021.121326

Zhang, D., Chen, X. H., Lau, C. K. M., & Xu, B. (2023). Implications of cryptocurrency energy usage on climate change. *Technological Forecasting and Social Change*, *187*, 122219. doi:10.1016/j.techfore.2022.122219

Compilation of References

Abbasi, G. A., Tiew, L. Y., Tang, J., Goh, Y.-N., & Thurasamy, R. (2021). The adoption of cryptocurrency as a disruptive force: Deep learning-based dual stage structural equation modelling and artificial neural network analysis. *PLoS One*, *16*(3), e0247582. doi:10.1371/journal.pone.0247582 PMID:33684120

Abdo, N., Almuraqab, S., & Almuraqab, N. A. S. (2016). *M-Government adoption factors in the UAE: a partial least squares approach M-Government Adoption Factors in the United Arab Emirates: A Partial Least-Squares Approach*. https://www.researchgate.net/publication/315829981

Abramova, S., & Böhme, R. (2016). *Perceived benefit and risk as multidimensional determinants of bitcoin use: A quantitative exploratory study*. Academic Press.

Adams, D. A., Nelson, R. R., & Todd, P. A. (1992). Perceived Usefulness, Ease of Use, and Usage of Information Technology: A Replication. *Management Information Systems Quarterly*, *16*(2), 227. doi:10.2307/249577

Adams, R., Kewell, B., & Parry, G. (2018). Blockchain for good? Digital ledger technology and sustainable development goals. In *Handbook of sustainability and social science research* (pp. 127–140). Springer. doi:10.1007/978-3-319-67122-2_7

Adapa, A., Nah, F. F.-H., Hall, R. H., Siau, K., & Smith, S. N. (2018). Factors Influencing the Adoption of Smart Wearable Devices. *International Journal of Human-Computer Interaction*, *34*(5), 399–409. doi:10.1080/10447318.2017.1357902

Adebayo, T. S., Awosusi, A. A., & Adeshola, I. (2020). Determinants of co2 emissions in emerging markets: An empirical evidence from mint economies. *International Journal of Renewable Energy Development*, *9*(3), 411–422. doi:10.14710/ijred.2020.31321

Adebayo, T. S., & Odugbesan, J. A. (2021). Modeling CO2 emissions in South Africa: Empirical evidence from ARDL based bounds and wavelet coherence techniques. *Environmental Science and Pollution Research International*, *28*(8), 9377–9389. doi:10.100711356-020-11442-3 PMID:33145732

AfDB. (2018). *African Development Bank, Nordic Development Fund, Global Environment Facility and Calvert Impact Capital partner in US $55-million investment into Off-Grid Energy Access Fund.* Retrieved December 10, 2022, from https://www.afdb.org/ar/news-and-events/african-development-bank-nordic-development-fund-global-environment-facility-and-calvert-impact-capital-partner-in-us-55-million-investment-into-off-grid-energy-access-fund-17743

Ageron, B., Gunasekaran, A., & Spalanzani, A. (2012). Sustainable supply management: An empirical study. *International Journal of Production Economics, 140*(1), 168–182. doi:10.1016/j.ijpe.2011.04.007

Aggarwal, S., Chaudhary, R., Aujla, G. S., Kumar, N., Choo, K. K. R., & Zomaya, A. Y. (2019). Blockchain for smart communities: Applications, challenges and opportunities. *Journal of Network and Computer Applications, 144*, 13–48. doi:10.1016/j.jnca.2019.06.018

Ahamad, S., Gupta, P., Bikash Acharjee, P., Padma Kiran, K., Khan, Z., & Faez Hasan, M. (2022). The role of block chain technology and Internet of Things (IoT) to protect financial transactions in crypto currency market. *Materials Today: Proceedings, 56*, 2070–2074. doi:10.1016/j.matpr.2021.11.405

Ahlstrand, A. (2018). *The Potential of Blockchain Technology in Solving Green Supply Chain Management Challenges.* Academic Press.

Ahmed, M., Mubarik, M. S., & Shahbaz, M. (2021). Factors affecting the outcome of corporate sustainability policy: A review paper. *Environmental Science and Pollution Research International, 28*(9), 10335–10356. doi:10.100711356-020-12143-7 PMID:33403636

Akesson, U., Wingqvist, G. Ö., Ek, G., & César, E. (2016). *Environmental and climate change policy brief Zimbabwe.* Gothernburg: Sida's Helpdesk for Environment and Climate Change. Retrieved December 1, 2022, from https://sidaenvironmenthelpdesk.se/digitalAssets/1725/1725303_zimbabwe_environment-cc_policybrief-2016-04-13.pdf

Akomea-Frimpong, I., Adeabah, D., Ofosu, D., & Tenakwah, E. J. (2021). A review of studies on green finance of banks research gap and future directions. *Journal of Sustainable Finance and Investment, 12*(4), 1241–1264. doi:10.1080/20430795.2020.1870202

Alaklabi, S., & Kang, K. (2021). Perceptions towards Cryptocurrency Adoption: A case of Saudi Arabian Citizens. *Journal of Electronic Banking Systems*, 1–17. doi:10.5171/2021.110411

Alalwan, A. A., Dwivedi, Y. K., & Rana, N. P. (2017). Factors influencing adoption of mobile banking by Jordanian bank customers: Extending UTAUT2 with trust. *International Journal of Information Management, 37*(3), 99–110. doi:10.1016/j.ijinfomgt.2017.01.002

Al-Amri, R., Zakaria, N. H., Habbal, A., & Hassan, S. (2019). Cryptocurrency adoption: Current stage, opportunities, and open challenges. *International Journal of Advanced Computer Research, 9*(44), 293–307. doi:10.19101/IJACR.PID43

Alauthaman, M., Aslam, N., Zhang, L., Alasem, R., & Hossain, M. A. (2018). A P2P botnet detection scheme based on decision tree and adaptive multilayer neural networks. *Neural Computing & Applications*, *29*(11), 991–1004. doi:10.100700521-016-2564-5 PMID:29769759

Al-Ghdabi, R. R., Almomani, R. Z. Q., & Banyhamdan, K. M. (2019). Impact of the green supply chain management practices on corporate image of chemical industries in Jordan. *International Journal of Scientific and Technology Research*, *8*(12), 2546–2554.

Al-Hashedi, K. G., & Magalingam, P. (2021). Financial fraud detection applying data mining techniques: A comprehensive review from 2009 to 2019. *Computer Science Review*, *40*, 100402. doi:10.1016/j.cosrev.2021.100402

Ali, O., Ally, M., & Dwivedi, Y. (2020). The state of play of blockchain technology in the financial services sector: A systematic literature review. *International Journal of Information Management*, *54*, 102199. doi:10.1016/j.ijinfomgt.2020.102199

Allaway, A. W., Gooner, R. M., Berkowitz, D., & Davis, L. (2006). Deriving and exploring behavior segments within a retail loyalty card program. *European Journal of Marketing*, *40*(11/12), 1317–1339. doi:10.1108/03090560610702830

Almakhour, M., Sliman, L., Samhat, A., & Mellouk, A. (2020). *Verification of smart contracts: A survey* (Vol. 67). Pervasive and Mobile Computing.

Al-SheryaniK.NobaneeH. (2020). *Green Finance: A Mini-Review*. Available at SSRN 3538696.

Alvarenga, I. D., Rebello, G. A., & Duarte, O. C. M. (2018). Securing configuration management and migration of virtual network functions using blockchain. *NOMS 2018-2018 IEEEIFIP Network Operations and Management Symposium*, 1–9. 10.1109/NOMS.2018.8406249

Andolfatto, D. (2018). Blockchain: What it is, what it does, and why you probably don't need one. *Review - Federal Reserve Bank of St. Louis*, *100*(2), 87–95. doi:10.20955/r.2018.87-95

Ansari, Z., & Kant, R. (2016). A state-of-art literature review reflecting 15 years of focus on sustainable supply chain management. *Journal of Cleaner Production*, *142*, 2524–2543. Advance online publication. doi:10.1016/j.jclepro.2016.11.023

Anshari, M., Almunawar, M. N., & Masri, M. (2020). An overview of financial technologies in Indonesia. *The Financial Technology and Disruptive Innovation in ASEAN,* 216-224.

Ante, L. (2020). Smart contracts on the blockchain–a bibliometric analysis and review. *Telematics and Informatics*, 101519.

Archa, A. B., & Achuthan, K. (2018). Trace and track: enhanced pharma supply chain infrastructure to prevent fraud. *Lecture Notes of the Institute for Computer Sciences, Social-Informatics and Telecommunications Engineering, LNICST, 218*(1), 189-195.. doi:10.1007/978-3-319-73423-1_17

Arksey, H., & O'Malley, L. (2005). Scoping studies: Towards a methodological framework. *International Journal of Social Research Methodology*, *8*(1), 19–32. doi:10.1080/1364557032000119616

Aromataris, E., Fernandez, R., Godfrey, C. M., Holly, C., Khalil, H., & Tungpunkom, P. (2015). Summarizing systematic reviews: Methodological development, conduct and reporting of an umbrella review approach. *JBI Evidence Implementation*, *13*(3), 132–140. PMID:26360830

Arora, M., Sharma, R., & Mehta, K. (2022). Personality Effects on Financial Responses Caused by the Perceived Financial Threat during the COVID-19 Pandemic. *The Journal of Wealth Management*, *25*(3), 72–89. doi:10.3905/jwm.2022.1.183

Arslan, S. S., Jurdak, R., Jelitto, J., & Krishnamachari, B. (2020). *Advancements in distributed ledger technology for Internet of Things*. Academic Press.

Arslanian, H., & Fischer, F. (2019). Blockchain as an enabling technology. In *The Future of Finance* (pp. 113–121). Palgrave Macmillan. doi:10.1007/978-3-030-14533-0_10

Asadollahfardi, G., Panahandeh, A., Khalvati, A. A., & Sekhavati, A. (2017). Life cycle assessment of construction phase of monorail project in Qom, Iran. *Pollution*, *3*(1), 81–99.

Aslam, U., Manzoor, S., & Babar, M. I. (2019). Systematic literature review of blockchain in requisites of big data and its applications. *Journal of Software Engineering and Intelligent Systems*. Available at: www.jseis.org

Avgouleas, E., & Kiayias, A. (2019). The promise of blockchain technology for global securities and derivatives markets: The new financial ecosystem and the 'holy grail' of systemic risk containment. *European Business Organization Law Review*, *20*(1), 81–110. doi:10.100740804-019-00133-3

Babel, K., Daian, P., Kelkar, M., & Juels, A. (2021). *Clockwork finance: Automated analysis of economic security in smart contracts*. arXiv preprint arXiv:2109.04347

Bag, S., Viktorovich, D. A., Sahu, A. K., & Sahu, A. K. (2021). Barriers to adoption of blockchain technology in green supply chain management. *Journal of Global Operations and Strategic Sourcing*, *14*(1), 104–133. doi:10.1108/JGOSS-06-2020-0027

Bahl, S. (2012). Green banking-The new strategic imperative. *Asian Journal of Research in Business Economics and Management*, *2*(2), 176–185.

Bai, J., Chen, Z., Yan, X., & Zhang, Y. (2022). Research on the impact of green finance on carbon emissions: Evidence from China. *Economic Research-Ekonomska Istraživanja*, *35*(1), 6965–6984. doi:10.1080/1331677X.2022.2054455

Baldimtsi, F., Kiayias, A., & Samari, K. (2017). Watermarking public- key cryptographic functionalities and implementations. In P. Q. Nguyen & J. Zhou (Eds.), *Information Security Lecture Notes in Computer Science* (pp. 173–191). Springer International Publishing. doi:10.1007/978-3-319-69659-1_10

Batrancea, I., Batrancea, L., Maran Rathnaswamy, M., Tulai, H., Fatacean, G., & Rus, M. I. (2020). Greening the financial system in USA, Canada and Brazil: A panel data analysis. *Mathematics*, *8*(12), 2217. doi:10.3390/math8122217

Baudoin, M. A., Vogel, C., Nortje, K., & Naik, M. (2017). Living with drought in South Africa: Lessons learnt from the recent El Niño drought period. *International Journal of Disaster Risk Reduction, 23*, 128–137. doi:10.1016/j.ijdrr.2017.05.005

Bayar, Y., Maxim, L. D., & Maxim, A. (2020). Financial development and CO2 emissions in post-transition European union countries. *Sustainability (Switzerland), 12*(7). Advance online publication. doi:10.3390u12072640

Beales, H. (2010). The value of behavioral targeting. *Netw. Advert. Initiat., 1*, 1–23. Available online at: https://www.networkadvertising.org/pdfs/Beales_ NAI_Study.pdf

Beck, R., Avital, M., Rossi, M., & Thatcher, J. B. (2017). *Blockchain technology in business and information systems research.* Academic Press.

Beck, R., Avital, M., Rossi, M., & Thatcher, J. B. (2017). Blockchain technology in business and information systems research. *Business & Information Systems Engineering, 59*(6), 381–384. doi:10.100712599-017-0505-1

Beh, P. K., Ganesan, Y., Iranmanesh, M., & Foroughi, B. (2021). Using smartwatches for fitness and health monitoring: The UTAUT2 combined with threat appraisal as moderators. *Behaviour & Information Technology, 40*(3), 282–299. doi:10.1080/0144929X.2019.1685597

Bekhet, H. A., Matar, A., & Yasmin, T. (2017). CO2 emissions, energy consumption, economic growth, and financial development in GCC countries: Dynamic simultaneous equation models. *Renewable & Sustainable Energy Reviews, 70*, 117–132. doi:10.1016/j.rser.2016.11.089

Bélanger, F., & Carter, L. (2008). Trust and risk in e-government adoption. *The Journal of Strategic Information Systems, 17*(2), 165–176. doi:10.1016/j.jsis.2007.12.002

Bender, J., Bridges, T. A., & Shah, K. (2019). Reinventing climate investing: Building equity portfolios for climate risk mitigation and adaptation. *Journal of Sustainable Finance & Investment, 9*(3), 191–213. doi:10.1080/20430795.2019.1579512

Berman, S. J., & McClellan, B. E. (2002). Ten strategies for survival in the attention economy. *Strategy and Leadership, 30*(3), 28–33. doi:10.1108/10878570210697513

Bernstein, D. J., & Lange, T. (2016). *SafeCurves: Choosing safe curves for elliptic-curve cryptography.* https://safecurves.cr.yp.to/

Berrou, R., Ciampoli, N., & Marini, V. (2019). Defining green finance: Existing standards and main challenges. *The rise of green finance in Europe: Opportunities and challenges for issuers, investors and marketplaces*, 31-51.

Beza, E., Reidsma, P., Poortvliet, P. M., Belay, M. M., Bijen, B. S., & Kooistra, L. (2018). Exploring farmers' intentions to adopt mobile Short Message Service (SMS) for citizen science in agriculture. *Computers and Electronics in Agriculture, 151*, 295–310. doi:10.1016/j.compag.2018.06.015

Bhardwaj, B. R., & Malhotra, A. (2013). Green banking strategies: Sustainability through corporate entrepreneurship. *Greener Journal of Business and Management Studies*, *3*(4), 180–193. doi:10.15580/GJBMS.2013.4.122412343

Bhatia, P., & Bedi, P. (2022). Causal Linkages Among Cryptocurrency and Emerging Market Indices: An Empirical Investigation. *Vision: The Journal of Business Perspective, 097226292211056.* Advance online publication. doi:10.1177/09722629221105670

Bhattacharjee, A., & Jahanshahi, A. A. (2021). Artificial landscape strategy: A business growth recovery plan in the post pandemic world. *Academia Letters*. Advance online publication. doi:10.20935/AL2311

Biais, B., Bisiere, C., Bouvard, M., & Casamatta, C. (2019). The blockchain folk theorem. *Review of Financial Studies*, *32*(5), 1662–1715. doi:10.1093/rfs/hhy095

Biondi, L., Dumay, J., & Monciardini, D. (2020). Using the International Integrated Reporting Framework to comply with EU Directive 2014/95/EU: Can we afford another reporting façade? *Meditari Accountancy Research*, *28*(5), 889–914. doi:10.1108/MEDAR-01-2020-0695

Bird, N., Cao, Y., & Quevedo, A. (2019). *Transformational change in the climate investment funds.* See www. odi. org/sites/odi.org.uk/files/resource-documents/12587.pdf

Biswas, N. (2011). Sustainable green banking approach: The need of the hour. *Business Spectrum*, *1*(1), 32–38.

Blattberg, R. C., & Deighton, J. (1996). Manage marketing by the customer equity test. *Harvard Business Review*, *74*, 136–144. PMID:10158473

Blau, J. (2017). *The Paris Agreement: climate change, solidarity, and human rights*. Springer. doi:10.1007/978-3-319-53541-8

Bodoni, S. (2019). *Mastercard Alerts Privacy Watchdogs After Loyalty Program Leak.* Available online at: https://www.bloomberg.com/news/articles/201908-23/mastercard-tells-belgian-german-privacy-watchdogs-of-breach

Bogucharskov, A. V., Pokamestov, I. E., Adamova, K. R., & Tropina, Z. N. (2018). Adoption of blockchain technology in trade finance process. *Journal of Reviews on Global Economics*, *7*, 510–515. doi:10.6000/1929-7092.2018.07.47

Bonaparte, Y. (2022). Time horizon and cryptocurrency ownership: Is crypto not speculative? *Journal of International Financial Markets, Institutions and Money*, *79*, 101609. doi:10.1016/j.intfin.2022.101609

Bond Brand Loyalty. (2016). *The 2016 Bond Loyalty Report.* Available online at: https://cdn2.hubspot.net/hubfs/352767/Resources/2016_Bond_Loyalty_Report_Executive_Summary_CAN_Launch_Edition.pdf

Bosco, F., Croce, V., & Raveduto, G. (2018). Blockchain Technology for Financial Services Facilitation in RES Investments. *Proceedings of the 2018 IEEE 4th International Forum on Research and Technology for Society and Industry (RTSI)*, 1–5. 10.1109/RTSI.2018.8548505

Bowman, M., & Minas, S. (2019). Resilience through interlinkage: The green climate fund and climate finance governance. *Climate Policy*, *19*(3), 342–353. doi:10.1080/14693062.2018.1513358

Brandão, A., São Mamede, H., & Gonçalves, R. (2018, March). Systematic review of the literature, research on blockchain technology as support to the trust model proposed applied to smart places. In *World conference on information systems and technologies* (pp. 1163-1174). Springer. 10.1007/978-3-319-77703-0_113

Brännlund, R., Ghalwash, T., & Nordström, J. (2007). Increased energy efficiency and the rebound effect: Effects on consumption and emissions. *Energy Economics*, *29*(1), 1–17. doi:10.1016/j.eneco.2005.09.003

Brophy, R. (2019). Blockchain and insurance: a review for operations and regulation. *Journal of Financial Regulation and Compliance, 28*(2), 215-234.

Brown. (2016). *SECG SEC 1: Elliptic Curve Cryptography (Version 2.0)*. https://www.secg.org/sec1-v2.pdf

Buchner, B., Clark, A., Falconer, A., Macquarie, R., Meattle, C., & Wetherbee, C. (2019). *Global landscape of climate finance 2019*. http://119.78.100.173/C666/handle/2XK7JSWQ/242591

Burtraw, D., Palmer, K., Bharvirkar, R., & Paul, A. (2002). The effect on asset values of the allocation of carbon dioxide emission allowances. *The Electricity Journal*, *5*(5), 51–62. doi:10.1016/S1040-6190(02)00316-0

Buterin, V. (2015). *On public and private blockchains*. Available: https://blog.ethereum.org/2015/08/07/on-public-and-private-blockchains/

Bu, X., Dang, W. V. T., Wang, J., & Liu, Q. (2020). Environmental orientation, green supply chain management, and firm performance: Empirical evidence from Chinese small and medium-sized enterprises. *International Journal of Environmental Research and Public Health*, *17*(4), 1199. Advance online publication. doi:10.3390/ijerph17041199 PMID:32069931

Calandra, D., Secinaro, S., Massaro, M., Dal Mas, F., & Bagnoli, C. (2022). The link between sustainable business models and Blockchain: A multiple case study approach. *Business Strategy and the Environment*, bse.3195. doi:10.1002/bse.3195

Casey, M., Crane, J., Gensler, G., Johnson, S., & Narula, N. (2018). *The impact of blockchain technology on finance: A catalyst for change*. Academic Press.

Casino, F., Dasaklis, T. K., & Patsakis, C. (2019). A systematic literature review of blockchain-based applications: Current status, classification and open issues. *Telematics and Informatics*, *36*, 55–81. doi:10.1016/j.tele.2018.11.006

Castillo-Vergara, M., Alvarez-Marin, A., & Placencio-Hidalgo, D. (2018). A bibliometric analysis of creativity in the field of business economics. *Journal of Business Research*, *85*, 1–9. doi:10.1016/j.jbusres.2017.12.011

Castorani, V., Landi, D., & Germani, M. (2016). Determination of the optimal configuration of energy recovery ventilator through virtual prototyping and DoE techniques. *Procedia CIRP*, *50*, 52–57. doi:10.1016/j.procir.2016.05.019

Cen, T., & He, R. (2018, December). Fintech, green finance and sustainable development. In *2018 International Conference on Management, Economics, Education, Arts and Humanities (MEEAH 2018)* (pp. 222-225). Atlantis Press.

Chan, A.P.C., Darko, A., Ameyaw, E.E., & Owusu-Manu, D.G. (2016). Barriers affecting the adoption of green building technologies. *Journal of Management in Engineering*, *33*(3). doi: ME.1943-5479.0000507. doi:10.1061/(ASCE)

Chang, S. E., Luo, H. L., & Chen, Y. (2019). Blockchain-enabled trade finance innovation: A potential paradigm shift on using letter of credit. *Sustainability*, *12*(1), 188. doi:10.3390u12010188

Chang, V., Baudier, P., Zhang, H., Xu, Q., Zhang, J., & Arami, M. (2020). How Blockchain can impact financial services–The overview, challenges and recommendations from expert interviewees. *Technological Forecasting and Social Change*, *158*, 120166. doi:10.1016/j.techfore.2020.120166 PMID:32834134

Chan, R. Y. K., He, H., Chan, H. K., & Wang, W. Y. C. (2012). Environmental orientation and corporate performance: The mediation mechanism of green supply chain management and moderating effect of competitive intensity. *Industrial Marketing Management*, *41*(4), 621–630. doi:10.1016/j.indmarman.2012.04.009

Charfeddine, L. (2017). The impact of energy consumption and economic development on Ecological Footprint and CO2 emissions: Evidence from a Markov Switching Equilibrium Correction Model. *Energy Economics*, *65*, 355–374. doi:10.1016/j.eneco.2017.05.009

Charfeddine, L., & Kahia, M. (2019). Impact of renewable energy consumption and financial development on CO2 emissions and economic growth in the MENA region: A panel vector autoregressive (PVAR) analysis. *Renewable Energy*, *139*, 198–213. doi:10.1016/j.renene.2019.01.010

Chen, Y., & Bellavitis, C. (2019). *Decentralized finance: Blockchain technology and the quest for an open financial system*. Stevens Institute of Technology School of Business Research Paper.

Chen, C. C., Shih, H. S., Shyur, H. J., & Wu, K. S. (2012). A business strategy selection of green supply chain management via an analytic network process. *Computers & Mathematics with Applications (Oxford, England)*, *64*(8), 2544–2557. doi:10.1016/j.camwa.2012.06.013

Chen, C. L., Deng, Y. Y., Tsaur, W. J., Li, C. T., Lee, C. C., & Wu, C. M. (2021). A traceable online insurance claims system based on blockchain and smart contract technology. *Sustainability*, *13*(16), 9386. doi:10.3390u13169386

Chen, Y., & Bellavitis, C. (2020). Blockchain disruption and decentralized finance: The rise of decentralized business models. *Journal of Business Venturing Insights*, *13*, e00151. doi:10.1016/j.jbvi.2019.e00151

Chichoni, J., & Webb, S. (2018). The digital global supply chain: The growing case for blockchain technology expansion within global supply chain. *Marriott Student Review*, *2*(2), 1–84.

Chien, F., Ngo, Q. T., Hsu, C. C., Chau, K. Y., & Iram, R. (2021). Assessing the mechanism of barriers towards green finance and public spending in small and medium enterprises from developed countries. *Environmental Science and Pollution Research International*, *28*(43), 60495–60510. doi:10.100711356-021-14907-1 PMID:34156623

Chin, T. A., Tat, H. H., & Sulaiman, Z. (2015). Green supply chain management, environmental collaboration and sustainability performance. *Procedia CIRP*, *26*, 695–699. doi:10.1016/j.procir.2014.07.035

Chirisa, I., Gumbo, T., Gundu-Jakarasi, V. N., Zhakata, W., Karakadzai, T., Dipura, R., & Moyo, T. (2021). Interrogating climate adaptation financing in Zimbabwe: Proposed direction. *Sustainability*, *13*(12), 6517. doi:10.3390u13126517

ChohanU. W. (2022). Web 3.0: The future architecture of the internet? doi:10.2139/ssrn.4037693

Chontanawat, J. (2020). Relationship between energy consumption, CO2 emission and economic growth in ASEAN: Cointegration and causality model. *Energy Reports*, *6*, 660–665. doi:10.1016/j.egyr.2019.09.046

Çoban, S., & Topcu, M. (2013). The nexus between financial development and energy consumption in the EU: A dynamic panel data analysis. *Energy Economics*, *39*, 81–88. doi:10.1016/j.eneco.2013.04.001

Cobbinah, P. B., Erdiaw-Kwasie, M. O., & Amoateng, P. (2015). Rethinking sustainable development within the framework of poverty and urbanisation in developing countries. *Environmental Development*, *13*, 18–32. doi:10.1016/j.envdev.2014.11.001

Collomb, A., De Filippi, P., & Klara, S. O. K. (2019). Blockchain technology and financial regulation: A risk-based approach to the regulation of ICOs. *European Journal of Risk Regulation*, *10*(2), 263–314. doi:10.1017/err.2019.41

Colquhoun, H. L., Levac, D., O'Brien, K. K., Straus, S., Tricco, A. C., Perrier, L., & Moher, D. (2014). Scoping reviews: Time for clarity in definition, methods, and reporting. *Journal of Clinical Epidemiology*, *67*(12), 1291–1294. doi:10.1016/j.jclinepi.2014.03.013 PMID:25034198

Crosby, M., Pattanayak, P., Verma, S., & Kalyanaraman, V. (2016). BlockChain technology: beyond bitcoin: applied innovation review. *Applied Innovation Review*, *2*, 5–20.

Cucari, N., Lagasio, V., Lia, G., & Torriero, C. (2021). The impact of blockchain in banking processes: The Interbank Spunta case study. *Technology Analysis and Strategic Management*, 1–13.

Cucari, N., Wankowicz, E., & De Falco, S. E. (2019). Rural tourism and Albergo Diffuso: A case study for sustainable land-use planning. *Land Use Policy*, *82*, 105–119. doi:10.1016/j.landusepol.2018.11.050

Cui, H., Wang, R., & Wang, H. (2020). An evolutionary analysis of green finance sustainability based on multi-agent game. *Journal of Cleaner Production*, *269*, 121799. doi:10.1016/j.jclepro.2020.121799

Darko, A., & Chan, A. P. C. (2017). Review of barriers to green building adoption. *Sustainable Development*, *25*(3), 167–179. doi:10.1002d.1651

Daudt, H. M., van Mossel, C., & Scott, S. J. (2013). Enhancing the scoping study methodology: A large, inter-professional team's experience with Arksey and O'Malley's framework. *BMC Medical Research Methodology*, *13*(1), 1–9. doi:10.1186/1471-2288-13-48 PMID:23522333

Davis, F. D. (1989). Perceived Usefulness, Perceived Ease of Use, and User Acceptance of Information Technology. *Management Information Systems Quarterly*, *13*(3), 319. doi:10.2307/249008

Davis, K., Drey, N., & Gould, D. (2009). What are scoping studies? A review of the nursing literature. *International Journal of Nursing Studies*, *46*(10), 1386–1400. doi:10.1016/j.ijnurstu.2009.02.010 PMID:19328488

De Giovanni, P., & Cariola, A. (2020). Process innovation through industry 4.0 technologies, lean practices and green supply chains. *Research in Transportation Economics*, *4*, 100869. doi:10.1016/j.retrec.2020.100869

Debrah, C., Chan, A. P. C., & Darko, A. (2022). Green finance gap in green buildings: A scoping review and future research needs. *Building and Environment*, *207*, 108443. doi:10.1016/j.buildenv.2021.108443

Delfabbro, P., King, D. L., & Williams, J. (2021). The psychology of cryptocurrency trading: Risk and protective factors. *Journal of Behavioral Addictions*, *10*(2), 201–207. doi:10.1556/2006.2021.00037 PMID:34152998

Desai, K., & Parikh, R. (n.d.). Money laundering and cryptocurrency. *International Research Journal of Commerce Arts and Science*, *10*. http://www.casirj.com

Desalegn, G., & Tangl, A. (2022). Enhancing green finance for inclusive green growth: A systematic approach. *Sustainability*, *14*(12), 7416. doi:10.3390u14127416

Devanur, N. R., & Fortnow, L. (2009). A computational theory of awareness and decision making. *Proceedings of the 11th Conference on Theoretical Aspects of Rationality and Knowledge - TARK '09*, 99. 10.1145/1562814.1562830

Dhull, S., & Narwal, M. S. (2016). Drivers and barriers in green supply chain management adaptation: A state-of-art review. *Uncertain Supply Chain Management*, *4*(1), 61–76. doi:10.5267/j.uscm.2015.7.003

Di Vaio, A., Palladino, R., Hassan, R., & Escobar, O. (2020). Artificial intelligence and business models in the sustainable development goals perspective: A systematic literature review. *Journal of Business Research, 121*, 283–314. doi:10.1016/j.jbusres.2020.08.019

Dib, O., Brousmiche, K. L., Durand, A., Thea, E., & Hamida, E. B. (2018). Consortium blockchains: Overview, applications and challenges. *International Journal On Advances in Telecommunications, 11*(1&2), 51–64.

Dikau, S., & Volz, U. (2021). Central bank mandates, sustainability objectives and the promotion of green finance. *Ecological Economics, 184*, 107022. doi:10.1016/j.ecolecon.2021.107022

Dipika. (2015). Green Banking in India: A Study of Various Strategies Adopt by Banks for Sustainable Development. *International Journal of Engineering Research & Technology, 3*(10).

Dirsehan, T., & Can, C. (2020). Examination of trust and sustainability concerns in autonomous vehicle adoption. *Technology in Society, 63*, 101361. doi:10.1016/j.techsoc.2020.101361

Dogan, E., & Seker, F. (2016). The influence of real output, renewable and non-renewable energy, trade and financial development on carbon emissions in the top renewable energy countries. *Renewable & Sustainable Energy Reviews, 60*, 1074–1085. doi:10.1016/j.rser.2016.02.006

Dorfleitner, G., & Braun, D. (2019). Fintech, digitalization and blockchain: possible applications for green finance. *The rise of green finance in Europe: opportunities and challenges for issuers, investors and marketplaces*, 207-237.

Dorfleitner, G., Muck, F., & Scheckenbach, I. (2021). Blockchain applications for climate protection: A global empirical investigation. *Renewable & Sustainable Energy Reviews, 149*, 111378. doi:10.1016/j.rser.2021.111378

Drummer, D., & Neumann, D. (2020). Is code law? Current legal and technical adoption issues and remedies for blockchain-enabled smart contracts. *Journal of Information Technology, 35*(4), 337–360. doi:10.1177/0268396220924669

Dwaikat, L. N., & Ali, K. N. (2018). Green buildings life cycle cost analysis and life cycle budget development: Practical applications. *Journal of Building Engineering, 18*, 303–311. doi:10.1016/j.jobe.2018.03.015

Dyntu, V., & Dykyi, O. (2019). Cryptocurrency in the system of money laundering. *Baltic Journal of Economic Studies, 4*(5), 75. doi:10.30525/2256-0742/2018-4-5-75-81

Dzingirai, M., & Ndava, R. (2022). Global institutional role to promote achievement of the sustainable development goals in Zimbabwe. In N. Baporikar (Ed.), *Handbook of Research on Global Institutional Roles for Inclusive Development* (pp. 99–117). IGI Global. doi:10.4018/978-1-6684-2448-3.ch006

Dziwok, E., & Jager, J. (2021). A classification of different approaches to green finance and green monetary policy. *Sustainability, 13*(21), 11902. doi:10.3390u132111902

Ebekozien, A., Aigbavboa, C., & Samsurijan, M. S. (2022). An appraisal of blockchain technology relevance in the 21st century Nigerian construction industry: perspective from the built environment professionals. *Journal of Global Operations and Strategic Sourcing*. doi:10.1108/JGOSS-01-2022-0005

Efanov, D., & Roschin, P. (2018). The all-pervasiveness of the blockchain technology. *Procedia Computer Science*, *123*, 116–121. doi:10.1016/j.procs.2018.01.019

el Barnoussi, A., Howieson, B., & van Beest, F. (2020). Prudential Application of IFRS 9: (Un) Fair Reporting in COVID-19 Crisis for Banks Worldwide?! *Australian Accounting Review*, *30*(3), 178–192. doi:10.1111/auar.12316

Eling, M., & Lehmann, M. (2018). The impact of digitalization on the insurance value chain and the insurability of risks. *The Geneva Papers on Risk and Insurance. Issues and Practice*, *43*(3), 359–396. doi:10.105741288-017-0073-0

Ertz, M., & Boily, É. (2019). The rise of the digital economy: Thoughts on blockchain technology and cryptocurrencies for the collaborative economy. *International Journal of Innovation Studies*, *3*(4), 84–93. doi:10.1016/j.ijis.2019.12.002

Evans, O. (2018). https://mpra.ub.uni-muenchen.de/99212/2/MPRA_paper_99212.pdf

Fadaeddini, A., Majidi, B., & Eshghi, M. (2020). Secure decentralized peer-to-peer training of deep neural networks based on distributed ledger technology. *The Journal of Supercomputing*, *76*(12), 10354–10368. doi:10.100711227-020-03251-9

Fahim, F., & Mahadi, B. (2022). Green supply chain management/green finance: A bibliometric analysis of the last twenty years by using the Scopus database. *Environmental Science and Pollution Research International*, *29*(56), 84714–84740. doi:10.100711356-022-21764-z PMID:35789465

Fakher, H.-A. (2019). Investigating the determinant factors of environmental quality (based on ecological carbon footprint index). *Environmental Science and Pollution Research International*, *26*(10), 10276–10291. doi:10.100711356-019-04452-3 PMID:30761494

Fankhauser, S., & Lavric, L. (2003). The investment climate for climate investment: Joint Implementation in transition countries. *Climate Policy*, *3*(4), 417–434. doi:10.1016/S1469-3062(03)00050-0

Fanning, K., & Centers, D. P. (2016). Blockchain and its coming impact on financial services. *Journal of Corporate Accounting & Finance*, *27*(5), 53–57. doi:10.1002/jcaf.22179

Fonseca, L. M., Domingnes, J. P., & Dima, A. M. (2020). Mapping the SDGs relationships. *Sustainability*, *12*(8), 3359. doi:10.3390u12083359

Fonta, W. M., Ayuk, E. T., & van Huysen, T. (2018). Africa and the Green Climate Fund: Current challenges and future opportunities. *Climate Policy*, *18*(9), 1210–1225. doi:10.1080/14693062.2018.1459447

Fornell, C., & Larcker, D. F. (1981). Structural Equation Models with Unobservable Variables and Measurement Error: Algebra and Statistics. *JMR, Journal of Marketing Research*, *18*(3), 382–388. doi:10.1177/002224378101800313

Frankel, J. A., & Romer, D. (1999). *Does Trade Cause Growth?* Academic Press. doi:10.1016/j.econmod.2012.09.033

French, A., Shim, J. P., Risius, M., Larsen, K. R., & Jain, H. (2021). The 4th Industrial Revolution powered by the integration of AI, blockchain, and 5G. *Communications of the Association for Information Systems*, *49*(1), 6. doi:10.17705/1CAIS.04910

Frizzo-Barker, J., Chow-White, P. A., Adams, P. R., Mentanko, J., Ha, D., & Green, S. (2020). Blockchain as a disruptive technology for business: A systematic review. *International Journal of Information Management*, *51*, 102029. doi:10.1016/j.ijinfomgt.2019.10.014

Fusco, A., Dicuonzo, G., Dell'Atti, V., & Tatullo, M. (2020). Blockchain in healthcare: Insights on COVID-19. *International Journal of Environmental Research and Public Health*, *17*(19), 7167. doi:10.3390/ijerph17197167 PMID:33007951

Galiautdinov, R. (2020). Brain machine interface: The accurate interpretation of neurotransmitters' signals targeting the muscles. *International Journal of Applied Research in Bioinformatics*, *10*(1), 26–36. Advance online publication. doi:10.4018/IJARB.2020010102

Galiautdinov, R., & Mkrttchian, V. (2019a). Math model of neuron and nervous system research, based on AI constructor creating virtual neural circuits: Theoretical and Methodological Aspects. In V. Mkrttchian, E. Aleshina, & L. Gamidullaeva (Eds.), *Avatar-Based Control, Estimation, Communications, and Development of Neuron Multi-Functional Technology Platforms* (pp. 320–344). IGI Global. doi:10.4018/978-1-7998-1581-5.ch015

Galiautdinov, R., & Mkrttchian, V. (2019b). Brain machine interface – for Avatar Control & Estimation in Educational purposes Based on Neural AI plugs: Theoretical and Methodological Aspects. In V. Mkrttchian, E. Aleshina, & L. Gamidullaeva (Eds.), *Avatar-Based Control, Estimation, Communications, and Development of Neuron Multi-Functional Technology Platforms* (pp. 345–360). IGI Global. doi:10.4018/978-1-7998-1581-5.ch016

Gallagher, K. P., & Irwin, A. (2015). China's economic statecraft in Latin America: Evidence from China's policy banks. *Pacific Affairs*, *88*(1), 99–121. doi:10.5509/201588199

Garay, J., Kiayias, A., & Leonardos, N. (2015). The Bitcoin Backbone Protocol: Analysis and Applications. Springer Berlin Heidelberg.

Gatteschi, V., Lamberti, F., Demartini, C., Pranteda, C., & Santamaría, V. (2018). Blockchain and smart contracts for insurance: Is the technology mature enough?. *Future Internet, 10*(2), 20.

Geddes, A., Schmid, N., Schmidt, T. S., & Steffen, B. (2020). The politics of climate finance: Consensus and partisanship in designing green state investment banks in the United Kingdom and Australia. *Energy Research & Social Science*, *69*, 101583. doi:10.1016/j.erss.2020.101583

Giglio, S., Kelly, B., & Stroebel, J. (2021). Climate finance. *Annual Review of Financial Economics*, *13*(1), 15–36. doi:10.1146/annurev-financial-102620-103311

Giramkar, S. (2018). Green Banking In India: A Study For Sustainable Development. In *Proceedings of Economics and Finance Conferences.* International Institute of Social and Economic Sciences. 10.20472/EFC.2018.010.010

Gleim, M. R., & Stevens, J. L. (2021). Blockchain: A game changer for marketers? *Marketing Letters*, *32*(1), 123–128. doi:10.100711002-021-09557-9

Government of Zimbabwe. (2021). *Zimbabwe Revised Nationally Determined Contribution.* Retrived November 25, 2022, from https://unfccc.int/sites/default/files/NDC/2022-06/Zimbabwe%20Revised%20Nationally%20Determined%20Contribution%202021%20Final.pdf

Graaf, T. J. de. (2019). *From old to new: From internet to smart contracts and from people to smart contracts.* Academic Press.

Grant, M. J., & Booth, A. (2009). A typology of reviews: An analysis of 14 review types and associated methodologies. *Health Information and Libraries Journal*, *26*(2), 91–108. doi:10.1111/j.1471-1842.2009.00848.x PMID:19490148

Grima, S., Kizilkaya, M., Sood, K., & ErdemDelice, M. (2021). The perceived effectiveness of blockchain for digital operational risk resilience in the European Union insurance market sector. *Journal of Risk and Financial Management*, *14*(8), 363.

Grima, S., Spiteri, J., & Romānova, I. (2020). A STEEP framework analysis of the key factors impacting the use of blockchain technology in the insurance industry. *The Geneva Papers on Risk and Insurance. Issues and Practice*, *45*(3), 398–425. doi:10.105741288-020-00162-x

Guo, Y., & Liang, C. (2016). Blockchain application and outlook in the banking industry. *Financ. Innovat*, *2*(1), 24. doi:10.118640854-016-0034-9

Gurtu, A., & Johny, J. (2019). Potential of blockchain technology in supply chain management: A literature review. *International Journal of Physical Distribution & Logistics Management*, *49*(9), 881–900. doi:10.1108/IJPDLM-11-2018-0371

Hainaut, H., & Cochran, I. (2018). The Landscape of domestic climate investment and finance flows: Methodological lessons from five years of application in France. *Inter Economics*, *155*, 69–83. doi:10.1016/j.inteco.2018.06.002

Hak, T., Janoušková, S., & Moldan, B. (2016). Sustainable Development Goals: A need for relevant indicators. *Ecological Indicators*, *60*, 565–573. doi:10.1016/j.ecolind.2015.08.003

Hall, B., & Khan, B. (2003). *Adoption of New Technology*. doi:10.3386/w9730

Hasan, S. Z., Ayub, H., Ellahi, A., & Saleem, M. (2022). A Moderated Mediation Model of Factors Influencing Intention to Adopt Cryptocurrency among University Students. *Human Behavior and Emerging Technologies*, *2022*, 1–14. doi:10.1155/2022/9718920

Hasnaoui, J. A., Rizvi, S. K. A., Reddy, K., Mirza, N., & Naqvi, B. (2021). Human capital efficiency, performance, market, and volatility timing of Asian equity funds during COVID-19 outbreak. *Journal of Asset Management*, *22*(5), 360–375. doi:10.105741260-021-00228-y

Hassani, H., Huang, X., & Silva, E. (2018). Banking with blockchain-ed big data. *Journal of Management Analytics*, *5*(4), 256–275. doi:10.1080/23270012.2018.1528900

Hemanand, D., Mishra, N., Premalatha, G., Mavaluru, D., Vajpayee, A., Kushwaha, S., & Sahile, K. (2022). Applications of intelligent model to analyze the green finance for environmental development in the context of artificial intelligence. *Computational Intelligence and Neuroscience*, *2022*, 1–8. doi:10.1155/2022/2977824 PMID:35845917

Heuvel, S. (2014). The demand for short-term, safe assets and financial stability: Some evidence and implications for central bank policies. *Introduction to web3*. Available: https://ethereum.org/en/web3

Hewa, T., Ylianttila, M., & Liyanage, M. (2020). Survey on blockchain based smart contracts: Applications, opportunities and challenges. *Journal of Network and Computer Applications*, 102857.

He, Z., Liu, Z., Wu, H., Gu, X., Zhao, Y., & Yue, X. (2020). Research on the impact of green finance and Fintech in smart city. *Complexity*, *2020*, 1–10. doi:10.1155/2020/6673386

Hodson, C. J. (2019). *Cyber risk management: Prioritize threats, identify vulnerabilities and apply controls*. Kogan Page Publishers.

Hoegh-Guldberg, O., Jacob, D., Bindi, M., Brown, S., Camilloni, I., Diedhiou, A., . . . Zougmoré, R. B. (2018). Impacts of 1.5 C global warming on natural and human systems. Global warming of 1.5 C. An IPCC Special Report.

Howson, P. (2020). Climate crises and Crypto-Colonialism: Conjuring value on the Blockchain frontiers of the global South. *Frontiers in Blockchain*, *3*, 22. doi:10.3389/fbloc.2020.00022

Huang, Y., Duan, K., & Urquhart, A. (2023). Time-varying dependence between Bitcoin and green financial assets: A comparison between pre-and post-COVID-19 periods. *Journal of International Financial Markets, Institutions and Money*, *82*, 101687. doi:10.1016/j.intfin.2022.101687

Huang, Z., Liao, G., & Li, Z. (2019). Loaning scale and government subsidy for promoting green innovation. *Technological Forecasting and Social Change*, *144*, 148–156. doi:10.1016/j.techfore.2019.04.023

Hunjra, A. I., Hassan, M. K., Zaied, Y. B., & Managi, S. (2023). Nexus between green finance, environmental degradation, and sustainable development: Evidence from developing countries. *Resources Policy*, *81*, 103371. doi:10.1016/j.resourpol.2023.103371

Hwa, C. S. (2016). Legal issues for the introduction of distributed ledger based on Blockchain technology focused on the financial industry. Korea Financial Law Association, 13(2), 107-138.

International Trade Administration. (2022). *Zimbabwe - Country Commercial Guide*. Retrieved December 5, 2022, from https://www.trade.gov/country-commercial-guides/zimbabwe-investment-climate-statement

Jahangir Alam, M., Ara Begum, I., Buysse, J., & van Huylenbroeck, G. (2012). Energy consumption, carbon emissions and economic growth nexus in Bangladesh: Cointegration and dynamic causality analysis. *Energy Policy*, *45*, 217–225. doi:10.1016/j.enpol.2012.02.022

Jahanshahi, A. A., Bhattacharjee, A., & Maghsoudi, T. (2021). Internal capabilities as the source of achieving competitive advantage in small-sized businesses. *International Journal of Business Innovation and Research*, *26*(2), 141–162. doi:10.1504/IJBIR.2021.118446

Jalil, A., Feridun, M., & Ma, Y. (2010). Finance-growth nexus in China revisited: New evidence from principal components and ARDL bounds tests. *International Review of Economics & Finance*, *19*(2), 189–195. doi:10.1016/j.iref.2009.10.005

Janssen, M., Weerakkody, V., Ismagilova, E., Sivarajah, U., & Irani, Z. (2020). A framework for analysing blockchain technology adoption: Integrating institutional, market and technical factors. *International Journal of Information Management*, *50*, 302–309. doi:10.1016/j.ijinfomgt.2019.08.012

Javaid, M., Haleem, A., Singh, R. P., Suman, R., & Khan, S. (2022). A review of Blockchain Technology applications for financial services. *BenchCouncil Transactions on Benchmarks, Standards and Evaluations*, 100073.

Jensen, A. L. (1996). *Beverton and Holt life history invariants result from optimal trade-off of reproduction and survival*. Academic Press.

Jiakui, C., Abbas, J., Najam, H., Liu, J., & Abbas, J. (2023). Green technological innovation, green finance, and financial development and their role in green total factor productivity: Empirical insights from China. *Journal of Cleaner Production*, *382*, 135131. doi:10.1016/j.jclepro.2022.135131

Jia, Q. (2023). The impact of green finance on the level of decarbonization of the economies: An analysis of the United States', China's, and Russia's current agenda. *Business Strategy and the Environment*, *32*(1), 110–119. doi:10.1002/bse.3120

Joanna Briggs Institute. (2011). The Joanna Briggs Institute best practice information sheet: Music as an intervention in hospitals. *Nursing & Health Sciences*, *13*(1), 99–102. doi:10.1111/j.1442-2018.2011.00583.x PMID:21426462

Jones, M. L. (2004). Application of systematic review methods to qualitative research: Practical issues. *Journal of Advanced Nursing*, *48*(3), 271–278. doi:10.1111/j.1365-2648.2004.03196.x PMID:15488041

Joo, M. H., Nishikawa, Y., & Dandapani, K. (2019). Cryptocurrency, a successful application of blockchain technology. *Managerial Finance*.

Kabanda, G. (2021). *Model Structure for Block Chain Technology and Cryptocurrency for the financial services sector in Zimbabwe*. Academic Press.

Kanwalinderjit, & ... , G. (. (2020). Traceability of Cryptocurrency Transactions using Blockchain Analytics. *International Journal of Computing and Digital Systems*, *9*(2), 159–165. doi:10.12785/ijcds/090202

Kar, A. K., & Navin, L. (2021). Diffusion of blockchain in insurance industry: An analysis through the review of academic and trade literature. *Telematics and Informatics*, *58*, 101532. doi:10.1016/j.tele.2020.101532

Katircioğlu, S. T., & Taşpinar, N. (2017). Testing the moderating role of financial development in an environmental Kuznets curve: Empirical evidence from Turkey. *Renewable & Sustainable Energy Reviews*, *68*, 572–586. doi:10.1016/j.rser.2016.09.127

Katyal, S., & Nagpal, S. (2014). Role of Green Banking in Sustainable Development of India. *International Journal of 360 Management Review*, *2*(1), 2320-7132.

Kaur, H. (n.d.). *Study of Green Movement in Indian Corporate Houses For Sustainable Growth*. Academic Press.

Kewell, B., Adams, R., & Parry, G. (2017). Blockchain for good? *Strategic Change*, *26*(5), 429–437. doi:10.1002/jsc.2143

Khan, M. N., Serafeim, G., & Yoon, A. (2015). *Corporate Sustainability: First Evidence on Materiality*. Harvard Business School Working Paper. http://nrs.harvard.edu/urn-3:HUL.InstRepos:14369106

Khan, M. A., & Salah, K. (2018). IoT security: Review, blockchain solutions, and open challenges. *Future Generation Computer Systems*, *82*, 395–411. doi:10.1016/j.future.2017.11.022

Khan, R., Kumar, P., Jayakody, D. N. K., & Liyanage, M. (2019). A survey on security and privacy of 5G technologies: Potential solutions, recent advancements, and future directions. *IEEE Communications Surveys and Tutorials*, *22*(1), 196–248. doi:10.1109/COMST.2019.2933899

Khatoon, A. (2020). A blockchain-based smart contract system for healthcare management. *Electronics (Basel)*, *9*(1), 94. doi:10.3390/electronics9010094

Kim, Y.J., & Kim, D. (2017). A Study on a strategic planning and trend of Blockchain standardization. *The Journal of the Institute of Internet Broadcasting and Communication*.

King, R. G., & Levine, R. (1993). Finance and Growth: Schumpeter Might Be Right*. *The Quarterly Journal of Economics*, *108*(3), 717–737. doi:10.2307/2118406

Kirikkaleli, D., & Kalmaz, D. B. (2020). Testing the moderating role of urbanization on the environmental Kuznets curve: Empirical evidence from an emerging market. *Environmental Science and Pollution Research International*, *27*(30), 38169–38180. doi:10.100711356-020-09870-2 PMID:32617821

Klarin, A. (2020). The decade-long cryptocurrencies and the blockchain rollercoaster: Mapping the intellectual structure and charting future directions. *Research in International Business and Finance*, *51*, 101067. doi:10.1016/j.ribaf.2019.101067

Knezevic, D. (2018). Impact of blockchain technology platform in changing the financial sector and other industries. *Montenegrin Journal of Economics*, *14*(1), 109–120. doi:10.14254/1800-5845/2018.14-1.8

Kołodziej, M. (2021). Development Factors of Blockchain Technology Within Banking Sector. In *Contemporary Trends and Challenges in Finance* (pp. 125–138). Springer. doi:10.1007/978-3-030-73667-5_8

Kongmanee, J., Kijsanayothin, P., & Hewett, R. (2019). Securing smart contractsin blockchain. In *2019 34th IEEE/ACM International Conference on Automated Software Engineering Workshop (ASEW)*. IEEE.

Kosba, A., Miller, A., Shi, E., Wen, Z., & Papamanthou, C. (2016). Hawk: The blockchain model of cryptography and privacy-preserving smartcontracts. *IEEE Symposium on Security and Privacy*, 839-858. 10.1109/SP.2016.55

Kouwenberg, R., & Zheng, C. (2023). A Review of the Global Climate Finance Literature. *Sustainability*, *15*(2), 1255. doi:10.3390u15021255

Kowalski, M., Lee, Z. W., & Chan, T. K. (2021). Blockchain technology and trust relationships in trade finance. *Technological Forecasting and Social Change*, *166*, 120641. doi:10.1016/j.techfore.2021.120641

Krezmien, M. P., Camacho, K. A., & Travers, J. C. (2017). Using methodological reviews and meta-analyses to identify current best practices in school-based counseling. In *International handbook for policy research on school-based counseling* (pp. 105–120). Springer. doi:10.1007/978-3-319-58179-8_8

Krishnan, S., Teo, T. S. H., & Lymm, J. (2017). Determinants of electronic participation and electronic government maturity: Insights from cross-country data. *International Journal of Information Management*, *37*(4), 297–312. doi:10.1016/j.ijinfomgt.2017.03.002

Krishnaraju, V., Mathew, S. K., & Sugumaran, V. (2016). Web personalization for user acceptance of technology: An empirical investigation of E-government services. *Information Systems Frontiers*, *18*(3), 579–595. doi:10.100710796-015-9550-9

Kucukaltan, B., Kamasak, R., Yalcinkaya, B., & Irani, Z. (2022). Investigating the themes in supply chain finance: The emergence of blockchain as a disruptive technology. *International Journal of Production Research*, 1–20. doi:10.1080/00207543.2022.2118886

Kulviwat, S., Bruner, G. C. II, & Al-Shuridah, O. (2009). The role of social influence on adoption of high tech innovations: The moderating effect of public/private consumption. *Journal of Business Research*, *62*(7), 706–712. doi:10.1016/j.jbusres.2007.04.014

Kumar, A. (2021). A Study of the Impact of Crypto Currency on the Indian Payment system. *Asian Journal of Management*, 310–316. doi:10.52711/2321-5763.2021.00047

Kumar, S., Kumar, B., Nagesh, Y., & Christian, F. (2022). Application of blockchain technology as a support tool in economic & financial development. *Manager-The British Journal of Administrative Management.*

Kurebwa, J. (2021). Implications of illicit financial flows on Zimbabwe's development. *International Journal of World Policy and Development Studies*, *7*(2), 27–34. doi:10.32861/ijwpds.72.27.34

la Torre, M., Sabelfeld, S., Blomkvist, M., & Dumay, J. (2020). Rebuilding trust: Sustainability and non-financial reporting and the European Union regulation. *Meditari Accountancy Research*, *28*(5), 701–725. doi:10.1108/MEDAR-06-2020-0914

Lam, L. W. (2012). Impact of competitiveness on salespeople's commitment and performance. *Journal of Business Research*, *65*(9), 1328–1334. doi:10.1016/j.jbusres.2011.10.026

Le Gear, A. (2020). A Blockchain Supported Solution for Compliant Digital Security Offerings. In *Blockchain and Distributed Ledger Technology Use Cases* (pp. 113–131). Springer. doi:10.1007/978-3-030-44337-5_6

Le Page, D., Tyler-Davie, G., & Hamilton, G. (2019). Climate change must be a central pillar of SA's economic growth. *Business Day*, *6*, 1–2.

Leal Filho, W., Wall, T., Mucova, S. A. R., Nagy, G. J., Balogun, A. L., Luetz, J. M., ... Gandhi, O. (2022). Deploying artificial intelligence for climate change adaptation. *Technological Forecasting and Social Change*, *180*, 121662. doi:10.1016/j.techfore.2022.121662

Lee, S.-H., & Kim, K. (2016). Device Authentication in Smart Grid System Using Blockchain. KAIST.

Lee, I., & Shin, Y. J. (2018). Fintech: Ecosystem, business models, investment decisions, and challenges. *Business Horizons*, *61*(1), 35–46. doi:10.1016/j.bushor.2017.09.003

Lele, A. (2019). Blockchain. In *Disruptive Technologies for the Militaries and Security* (pp. 197–202). Springer. doi:10.1007/978-981-13-3384-2_12

Lemieux, V. L. (2016). Trusting records: Is Blockchain technology the answer? *Records Management Journal*, *26*(2), 110–139. doi:10.1108/RMJ-12-2015-0042

Leong, Y. Y., & Chen, Y. C. (2020). Cyber risk cost and management in IoT devices-linked health insurance. *The Geneva Papers on Risk and Insurance. Issues and Practice*, *45*(4), 737–759. doi:10.105741288-020-00169-4

Levac, D., Colquhoun, H., & O'Brien, K. K. (2010). Scoping studies: Advancing the methodology. *Implementation Science; IS*, *5*(1), 1–9. doi:10.1186/1748-5908-5-69 PMID:20854677

Liang, C., Wei, Y., & Zhang, Y. (2020). Is implied volatility more informative for forecasting realized volatility: An international perspective. *Journal of Forecasting*, *39*(8), 1253–1276. doi:10.1002/for.2686

Li, G., Li, L., Choi, T. M., & Sethi, S. P. (2020). Green supply chain management in Chinese firms: Innovative measures and the moderating role of quick response technology. *Journal of Operations Management*, *66*(7-8), 958–988. doi:10.1002/joom.1061

Lipton, A. (2018). Blockchains and distributed ledgers in retrospective and perspective. *The Journal of Risk Finance*, *19*(1), 4–25. doi:10.1108/JRF-02-2017-0035

Liu, B., & De Giovanni, P. (2019). Green process innovation through Industry 4.0 technologies and supply chain coordination. *Annals of Operations Research*, 1–36. doi:10.100710479-019-03498-3

Liu, S., & Wang, Y. (2023). Green innovation effect of pilot zones for green finance reform: Evidence of quasi natural experiment. *Technological Forecasting and Social Change*, *186*, 122079. doi:10.1016/j.techfore.2022.122079

Liu, X., Farahani, B., & Firouzi, F. (2020). Distributed ledger technology. In *Intelligent Internet of Things* (pp. 393–431). Springer. doi:10.1007/978-3-030-30367-9_8

Liu, X., Zhan, F. B., Hong, S., Niu, B., & Liu, Y. (2012). A bibliometric study of earthquake research: 1900–2010. *Scientometrics*, *92*(3), 747–765. doi:10.100711192-011-0599-z

Liu, Y., Lei, J., & Zhang, Y. (2021). A study on the sustainable relationship among the green finance, environment regulation and green-total-factor productivity in China. *Sustainability*, *13*(21), 11926. doi:10.3390u132111926

Li, W., Andreina, S., Bohli, J.-M., & Karame, G. (2017). Securing Proof-of-Stake Blockchain Protocols. In J. Garcia-Alfaro, G. Navarro-Arribas, H. Hartenstein, & J. Herrera-Joancomartí (Eds.), *Data Privacy Management, Cryptocurrencies and Blockchain Technology* (pp. 297–315). Springer International Publishing., doi:10.1007/978-3-319-67816-0_17

Li, X., Jiang, P., Chen, T., Luo, X., & Wen, Q. (2020). A survey on the security of blockchain systems. *Future Generation Computer Systems*, *107*, 841–853. doi:10.1016/j.future.2017.08.020

Lohmann, L. (2009). Climate as investment. *Development and Change*, *40*(6), 1063–1083. doi:10.1111/j.1467-7660.2009.01612.x

Loureiro, S. M. C., Guerreiro, J., & Tussyadiah, I. (2021). Artificial intelligence in business: State of the art and future research agenda. *Journal of Business Research*, *129*, 911–926. doi:10.1016/j.jbusres.2020.11.001

Lutz, R. J., & Kakkar, P. (1975). The Psychological Situation As a Determinant of Consumer Behavior. *NA -. Advances in Consumer Research. Association for Consumer Research (U. S.)*, *2*, 439–454.

Lu, Y. (2019). The blockchain: State-of-the-art and research challenges. *Journal of Industrial Information Integration*, *15*, 80–90. doi:10.1016/j.jii.2019.04.002

Mahmood, T., & Mubarik, M. S. (2020). Balancing innovation and exploitation in the fourth industrial revolution: Role of intellectual capital and technology absorptive capacity. *Technological Forecasting and Social Change*, *160*, 120248. doi:10.1016/j.techfore.2020.120248 PMID:32839626

Maji, I. K., Habibullah, M. S., & Saari, M. Y. (2017). Financial development and sectoral CO2 emissions in Malaysia. *Environmental Science and Pollution Research International*, *24*(8), 7160–7176. doi:10.100711356-016-8326-1 PMID:28097481

Malaysia Productivity Corporation. (2019). *Productivity Report 2018-2019*. Available at: http://www. mpc.gov.my/wp-content/uploads/2019/09/Productivity-Report-18_19-latest-as-at-250919-1.pdf

Mao, H., & Motohashi, K. (2016). A Comparative Study on Tenant Firms in Beijing Tsinghua University Science Park and Shenzhen Research Institute of Tsinghua University. *Asian Journal of Innovation and Policy*, *5*(3), 225–250. doi:10.7545/ajip.2016.5.3.225

Marke, A. (Ed.). (2018). *Transforming climate finance and green investment with blockchains*. Academic Press.

Mathivathanan, D., Kannan, D., & Haq, A. N. (2018). Sustainable supply chain management practices in Indian automotive industry: A multi-stakeholder view. *Resources, Conservation and Recycling*, *128*, 284–305. doi:10.1016/j.resconrec.2017.01.003

Matzutt, R., Hiller, J., Henze, M., Ziegeldorf, J. H., Müllmann, D., Hohlfeld, O., & Wehrle, K. (2018, February). A quantitative analysis of the impact of arbitrary blockchain content on bitcoin. In *International Conference on Financial Cryptography and Data Security* (pp. 420-438). Springer. 10.1007/978-3-662-58387-6_23

Maull, R., Godsiff, P., Mulligan, C., Brown, A., & Kewell, B. (2017). Distributed ledger technology: Applications and implications. *Strategic Change*, *26*(5), 481–489. doi:10.1002/jsc.2148

Mazambani, L., & Mutambara, E. (2020). Predicting FinTech innovation adoption in South Africa: The case of cryptocurrency. *African Journal of Economic and Management Studies*, *11*(1), 30–50. doi:10.1108/AJEMS-04-2019-0152

Mazzucato, M., Kattel, R., & Ryan-Collins, J. (2020). Challenge-driven innovation policy: Towards a new policy toolkit. *Journal of Industry, Competition and Trade*, *20*(2), 421–437. doi:10.100710842-019-00329-w

Mehta, K., Sharma, R., & Vyas, V. (2022) A quantile regression approach to study the impact of aluminium prices on manufacturing sector of India during COVID era, *Materials Today: Proceedings, 65*(8), 3506-3511. doi:10.1016/j.matpr.2022.06.087

Meng, F., & Zhang, W. (2022). Digital finance and regional green innovation: Evidence from Chinese cities. *Environmental Science and Pollution Research International*, *29*(59), 89498–89521. doi:10.100711356-022-22072-2 PMID:35854068

Menguc, B., & Ozanne, L. K. (2005). Challenges of the "green imperative": A natural resource-based approach to the environmental orientation-business performance relationship. *Journal of Business Research*, *58*(4), 430–438. doi:10.1016/j.jbusres.2003.09.002

Merediz-Solà, I., & Bariviera, A. F. (2019). A bibliometric analysis of bitcoin scientific production. *Research in International Business and Finance*, *50*, 294–305. doi:10.1016/j.ribaf.2019.06.008

Merhi, M., Hone, K., & Tarhini, A. (2019). A cross-cultural study of the intention to use mobile banking between Lebanese and British consumers: Extending UTAUT2 with security, privacy and trust. *Technology in Society*, *59*, 101151. doi:10.1016/j.techsoc.2019.101151

Milani, F., Garcıa-Ban~uelos, L., & Dumas, M. (2016). Blockchain and business process improvement. *BPTrends, 4*. Available at: www.bptrends.com

Min, H. (2019). Blockchain technology for enhancing supply chain resilience. *Business Horizons*, *62*(1), 35–45. doi:10.1016/j.bushor.2018.08.012

Mkrttchian, V., Gamidullaeva, L., & Galiautdinov, R. (2019). Design of Nano-scale Electrodes and Development of Avatar-Based Control System for Energy-Efficient Power Engineering: Application of an Internet of Things and People (IOTAP) Research Center. *International Journal of Applied Nanotechnology Research*, *4*(1), 41–48. Advance online publication. doi:10.4018/IJANR.2019010104

Mohanta, B. K., Jena, D., Panda, S. S., & Sobhanayak, S. (2019). Blockchain technology: A survey on applications and security privacy challenges. *Internet of Things*, *8*, 100107. doi:10.1016/j.iot.2019.100107

Mohanta, B. K., Jena, D., Satapathy, U., & Patnaik, S. (2020). Survey on IoT security: Challenges and solution using machine learning, artificial intelligence and blockchain technology. *Internet of Things*, *11*, 100227. doi:10.1016/j.iot.2020.100227

Monrat, A. A., Schelén, O., & Andersson, K. (2019). A survey of blockchain from the perspectives of applications, challenges, and opportunities. *IEEE Access : Practical Innovations, Open Solutions*, *7*, 117134–117151. doi:10.1109/ACCESS.2019.2936094

Mori, T. (2016). Financial technology: Blockchain and securities settlement. *Journal of Securities Operations & Custody*, *8*(3), 208–227.

Moyano, J. P., & Ross, O. (2017). KYC optimization using distributed ledger technology. *Business & Information Systems Engineering*, *59*(6), 411–423. doi:10.100712599-017-0504-2

Mubarak, M. F., & Petraite, M. (2020). Industry 4.0 technologies, digital trust and technological orientation: What matters in open innovation? *Technological Forecasting and Social Change*, *161*, 120332. doi:10.1016/j.techfore.2020.120332

Mubarak, M. F., Shaikh, F. A., Mubarik, M., Samo, K. A., & Mastoi, S. (2019). The impact of digital transformation on business performance. *Engineering, Technology and Applied Science Research*, *9*(6), 5056–5061. doi:10.48084/etasr.3201

Mubarik, M. S., Bontis, N., Mubarik, M., & Mahmood, T. (2021b). Intellectual capital and supply chain resilience. *Journal of Intellectual Capital*. Advance online publication. doi:10.1108/JIC-06-2020-0206

Mubarik, M. S., Kazmi, S. H. A., & Zaman, S. I. (2021a). Application of gray DEMATEL-ANP in green- strategic sourcing. *Technology in Society*, *64*, 101524. doi:10.1016/j.techsoc.2020.101524

Mubarik, M. S., Naghavi, N., & Mubarak, M. F. (2019a). Impact of supplier relational capital on supply chain performance in Pakistani textile industry. *Asian Economic and Financial Review*, *9*(3), 318–328. doi:10.18488/journal.aefr.2019.93.318.328

Mubarik, M. S., Naghavi, N., Mubarik, M., Kusi-Sarpong, S., Khan, S. A., Zaman, S. I., & Kazmi, S. H. A. (2021c). Resilience and cleaner production in industry 4.0: Role of supply chain mapping and visibility. *Journal of Cleaner Production*, *292*, 126058. doi:10.1016/j.jclepro.2021.126058

Mubarik, M., Zuraidah binti Raja Mohd Rasi, R., & Faraz Mubarak, M. (2020). Fostering supply chain integration through blockchain technology: A study of Malaysian manufacturing sector. *International Journal of Management and Sustainability*, *9*(3), 135–147. doi:10.18488/journal.11.2020.93.135.147

Mubarik, M., Zuraidah, R., & Rasi, B. R. M. (2019b). Triad of big data supply chain analytics, supply chain integration and supply chain performance: Evidences from oil and gas sector. *Humanities and Social Sciences Letters*, *7*(4), 209–224. doi:10.18488/journal.73.2019.74.209.224

Muchlis Gazali, H., Hafiz Bin Che Ismail, C. M., & Amboala, T. (2018). Exploring the Intention to Invest in Cryptocurrency: The Case of Bitcoin. *2018 International Conference on Information and Communication Technology for the Muslim World (ICT4M)*, 64–68. 10.1109/ICT4M.2018.00021

Muneeza, A., Arshad, N. A., & Arifin, A. T. (2018). The application of blockchain technology in crowdfunding: towards financial inclusion via technology. *International Journal of Management and Applied Research, 5*(2), 82-98.

Munn, Z., Aromataris, E., Tufanaru, C., Stern, C., Porritt, K., Farrow, J., ... Jordan, Z. (2019). The development of software to support multiple systematic review types: The Joanna Briggs Institute System for the Unified Management, Assessment and Review of Information (JBI SUMARI). *JBI Evidence Implementation*, *17*(1), 36–43. PMID:30239357

Naderi, N., & Tian, Y. (2022). Leveraging Blockchain Technology and Tokenizing Green Assets to Fill the Green Finance Gap. *Energy Research Letters, 3*, 33907.

Najjar, M., Alsurakji, I. H., El-Qanni, A., & Nour, A. I. (2022). The role of blockchain technology in the integration of sustainability practices across multi-tier supply networks: Implications and potential complexities. *Journal of Sustainable Finance & Investment*, 1-19.

Nakamoto, S. (2008). *Bitcoin: A peer-to-peer electronic cash system.* https://bitcoin. org/bitcoin. pdf

Nakamoto, S. (2008). *Bitcoin: What's in the Whitepaper?* Academic Press.

Nakamoto, S. (n.d.). *Bitcoin: A Peer-to-Peer Electronic Cash System*. https://www.researchgate.net/publication/336242531_The_Impact_of_Blockchain_Technology_on_Financial_Technology_FinTech

Nakhuva, B., & Champaneria, T. (2015). Study of various internet of things platforms. *International Journal of Computer Science & Engineering Survey*, *6*(6), 61–74. doi:10.5121/ijcses.2015.6605

Narayan, R., & Tidström, A. (2020). Tokenizing coopetition in a blockchain for a transition to circular economy. *Journal of Cleaner Production*, *263*, 121437. doi:10.1016/j.jclepro.2020.121437

Nascimento, D. L. M., Alencastro, V., Quelhas, O. L. G., Caiado, R. G. G., Garza-Reyes, J. A., Lona, L. R., & Tortorella, G. (2019). Exploring Industry 4.0 technologies to enable circular economy practices in a manufacturing context: A business model proposal. *Journal of Manufacturing Technology Management*, *30*(3), 607–627. doi:10.1108/JMTM-03-2018-0071

Nassiry, D. (2019). The role of fintech in unlocking green finance. In *Handbook of Green Finance* (pp. 315–336). Springer. doi:10.1007/978-981-13-0227-5_27

Nathan, R. (2020). *Bitcoin explained.* Retrieved From https://www.investopedia.com/terms/b/blockchain.asp

Ndlovu, R. (2022). *CBZ to invest two percent of income in green projects*. Retrieved December 10, 2022, from https://vicfallslive.co.zw/cbz-to-invest-two-percent-of-income-in-green-projects/

Nguyen, Q. K. (2016, November). Blockchain-a financial technology for future sustainable development. In *2016 3rd International conference on green technology and sustainable development (GTSD)* (pp. 51-54). IEEE. 10.1109/GTSD.2016.22

Nguyen, C. T., Hoang, D. T., Nguyen, D. N., Niyato, D., Nguyen, H. T., & Dutkiewicz, E. (2019). Proof-of-Stake Consensus Mechanisms for Future Blockchain Networks: Fundamentals, Applications and Opportunities. *IEEE Access : Practical Innovations, Open Solutions*, *7*, 85727–85745. doi:10.1109/ACCESS.2019.2925010

Ngwenya, N. (2019). *South Africa's green bonds show there are massive opportunities for growth.* Retrieved December 12, 2022, from https://www.businesslive.co.za/bd/opinion/2019-06-20-sas-green-bonds-show-there-are-massive-opportunities-for-growth/

Niranjanamurthy, M., Nithya, B. N., & Jagannatha, S. (2019). Analysis of Blockchain technology: Pros, cons and SWOT. *Cluster Computing*, *22*(6), 14743–14757. doi:10.100710586-018-2387-5

Nishimura, M. (2017). Business Model for a Low-Carbon Economy. *Journal of International Management*, *1*, 112–122.

Niyazbekova, S., Jazykbayeva, B., Mottaeva, A., Beloussova, E., Suleimenova, B., & Zueva, A. (2021). The Growth of "Green" finance at the global level in the context of sustainable economic development. In E3S Web of Conferences (Vol. 244, p. 10058). EDP Sciences. doi:10.1051/e3sconf/202124410058

Nofer, M., Gomber, P., Hinz, O., & Schiereck, D. (2017). Blockchain. *Business & Information Systems Engineering*, *59*(3), 183–187. doi:10.100712599-017-0467-3

NRI. (2015). *Survey on blockchain technologies and related services.* Tech. Rep. Available: http://www.meti.go.jp/english/press/ 2016/pdf/0531 01f.pdf

Nwani, C., & Omoke, P. C. (2020). Does bank credit to the private sector promote low-carbon development in Brazil? An extended STIRPAT analysis using dynamic ARDL simulations. *Environmental Science and Pollution Research International*, *27*(25), 31408–31426. doi:10.100711356-020-09415-7 PMID:32488699

Nyarugwe, R. T. (2020). *An analysis of the Zimbabwean money laundering and proceeds of crime amendment act of 2018.* Retrieved December 2, 2022, from https://etd.uwc.ac.za/handle/11394/8057

Nyemba, W. R., & Mbohwa, C. (2018). Challenges and opportunities in adopting and implementing sustainability plans in engineering, mining and processing companies in Zimbabwe. *Procedia Manufacturing*, *21*, 181–188. doi:10.1016/j.promfg.2018.02.109

Olah, J., Aburumman, N., Popp, J., Khan, M. A., Haddad, H., & Kitukutha, N. (2020). Impact of industry 4.0 on environmental sustainability. *Sustainability (Switzerland)*, *12*(11), 1–21. doi:10.3390u12114674

Ølnes, S., Ubacht, J., & Janssen, M. (2017). *Blockchain in government: Benefits and implications of distributed ledger technology for information sharing*. Academic Press.

Olubunmi, O. A., Xia, P. B., & Skitmore, M. (2016). Green building incentives: A review. *Renewable & Sustainable Energy Reviews*, *59*, 1611–1621. doi:10.1016/j.rser.2016.01.028

Omane-Adjepong, M., & Alagidede, I. P. (2020). High- and low-level chaos in the time and frequency market returns of leading cryptocurrencies and emerging assets. *Chaos, Solitons, and Fractals*, *132*, 109563. doi:10.1016/j.chaos.2019.109563

Omri, A., Daly, S., Rault, C., & Chaibi, A. (2015). Financial development, environmental quality, trade and economic growth: What causes what in MENA countries. *Energy Economics*, *48*, 242–252. doi:10.1016/j.eneco.2015.01.008

Ortas, E., Burritt, R. L., & Moneva, J. M. (2013). Socially Responsible Investment and cleaner production in the Asia Pacific: Does it pay to be good? *Journal of Cleaner Production*, *52*, 272–280. doi:10.1016/j.jclepro.2013.02.024

Ozbayoglu, A. M., Gudelek, M. U., & Sezer, O. B. (2020). Deep learning for financial applications: A survey. *Applied Soft Computing*, *93*, 106384. doi:10.1016/j.asoc.2020.106384

Ozili, P. K. (2022). Green finance research around the world: A review of literature. *International Journal of Green Economics*. Retrieved October 30, 2022, from https://papers.ssrn.com/sol3/papers.cfm?abstract_id=4066900

Ozili, P. K. (2019). Blockchain finance: Questions regulators ask. In *Disruptive innovation in business and finance in the digital world.* Emerald Publishing Limited. doi:10.1108/S1569-376720190000020014

Ozili, P. K. (2021). Digital finance, green finance and social finance: Is there a link? *Financial Internet Quarterly, 17*(1), 1–7. doi:10.2478/fiqf-2021-0001

Ozturk, I., & Acaravci, A. (2013). The long-run and causal analysis of energy, growth, openness and financial development on carbon emissions in Turkey. *Energy Economics, 36*, 262–267. doi:10.1016/j.eneco.2012.08.025

Page, D. (2008). Systematic literature searching and the bibliographic database haystack. *Electronic Journal of Business Research Methods, 6*(2), 199–208.

Park, A., & Li, H. (2021). The effect of blockchain technology on supply chain sustainability performances. *Sustainability, 13*(4), 1726. doi:10.3390u13041726

Parkhill, A. J., Nixon, M., & McEwan, T. E. (2022). A critical analysis of stalking theory and implications for research and practice. *Behavioral Sciences & the Law, 40*(5), 562–583. doi:10.1002/bsl.2598 PMID:36134723

Parmentola, A., Petrillo, A., Tutore, I., & De Felice, F. (2022). Is blockchain able to enhance environmental sustainability? A systematic review and research agenda from the perspective of Sustainable Development Goals (SDGs). *Business Strategy and the Environment, 31*(1), 194–217. doi:10.1002/bse.2882

Patel, R., Migliavacca, M., & Oriani, M. (2022). Blockchain in Banking and Finance: Is the best yet to come? A bibliometric review. *Research in International Business and Finance, 62*, 101718. doi:10.1016/j.ribaf.2022.101718

Patil, P., Tamilmani, K., Rana, N. P., & Raghavan, V. (2020). Understanding consumer adoption of mobile payment in India: Extending Meta-UTAUT model with personal innovativeness, anxiety, trust, and grievance redressal. *International Journal of Information Management, 54*, 102144. doi:10.1016/j.ijinfomgt.2020.102144

Pedersen, A. B., Risius, M., & Beck, R. (2019). A ten-step decision path to determine when to use blockchain technologies. *MIS Quarterly Executive, 18*(2), 99–115. doi:10.17705/2msqe.00010

Peng, H., Feng, T., & Zhou, C. (2018). International experiences in the development of green finance. *American Journal of Industrial and Business Management, 8*(02), 385–392. doi:10.4236/ajibm.2018.82024

Pereira, J., Tavalaei, M. M., & Ozalp, H. (2019). Blockchain-based platforms: Decentralized infrastructures and its boundary conditions. *Technological Forecasting and Social Change, 146*, 94–102. doi:10.1016/j.techfore.2019.04.030

Pestovska, Z. (2021). Changes in the financial services market under the influence of AI. *Artificial Intelligence as a Basis for the Development of the Digital Economy*, 85.

Peters, G. W., & Panayi, E. (2016). Understanding modern banking ledgers through blockchain technologies: Future of transaction processing and smart contracts on the internet of money. In *Banking beyond banks and money* (pp. 239–278). Springer. doi:10.1007/978-3-319-42448-4_13

Peters, M. D., Godfrey, C. M., Khalil, H., McInerney, P., Parker, D., & Soares, C. B. (2015). Guidance for conducting systematic scoping reviews. *JBI Evidence Implementation*, *13*(3), 141–146. PMID:26134548

Poberezhna, A. (2018). Addressing water sustainability with blockchain technology and green finance. In *Transforming climate finance and green investment with blockchains* (pp. 189–196). Academic Press. doi:10.1016/B978-0-12-814447-3.00014-8

Podsakoff, P. M., MacKenzie, S. B., & Podsakoff, N. P. (2012). Sources of Method Bias in Social Science Research and Recommendations on How to Control It. *Annual Review of Psychology*, *63*(1), 539–569. doi:10.1146/annurev-psych-120710-100452 PMID:21838546

Polyviou, A., Velanas, P., & Soldatos, J. (2019). Blockchain technology: Financial sector applications beyond cryptocurrencies. *Multidisciplinary Digital Publishing Institute Proceedings*, *28*(1), 7. doi:10.3390/proceedings2019028007

Poongodi, T., Sujatha, R., Sumathi, D., Suresh, P., & Balamurugan, B. (2020). Blockchain in social networking. In *Cryptocurrencies and Blockchain Technology Applications* (pp. 55–76). Wiley. doi:10.1002/9781119621201.ch4

Prabhu, G. N. (2021). *Green Banking practices–A case study on Indian Green Banking system*. www. ijrpr. com

Pranto, T. H., Noman, A. A., Mahmud, A., & Haque, A. B. (2021). Blockchain and smart contract for IoT enabled smart agriculture. *PeerJ. Computer Science*, *7*, e407. doi:10.7717/peerj-cs.407 PMID:33834098

Pratap, K. (2020). *A study of green banking as an innovative tools in environment sustainability*. Academic Press.

Pritchard, A. (1969). Statistical Bibliography or Bibliometrics? *The Journal of Documentation*, *25*, 348–349.

Puri, J., Rastogi, A., Prowse, M., & Asfaw, S. (2020). Good will hunting: Challenges of theory-based impact evaluations for climate investments in a multilateral setting. *World Development*, *127*, 104784. doi:10.1016/j.worlddev.2019.104784

Puschmann, T., Hoffmann, C. H., & Khmarskyi, V. (2020). How green FinTech can alleviate the impact of climate change—The case of Switzerland. *Sustainability*, *12*(24), 10691. doi:10.3390u122410691

Qerimi, Q., & Sergi, B. S. (2022). The case for global regulation of carbon capture and storage and artificial intelligence for climate change. *International Journal of Greenhouse Gas Control*, *120*, 103757. doi:10.1016/j.ijggc.2022.103757

Qin, M., Zhang, X., Li, Y., & Badarcea, R. M. (2023). Blockchain market and green finance: The enablers of carbon neutrality in China. *Energy Economics, 118*, 106501. doi:10.1016/j.eneco.2022.106501

Quatrini, S. (2021). Challenges and opportunities to scale up sustainable finance after the COVID-19 crisis: Lessons and promising innovations from science and practice. *Ecosystem Services*, *48*, 101240. doi:10.1016/j.ecoser.2020.101240 PMID:36568712

Radanović, I., & Likić, R. (2018). Opportunities for use of blockchain technology in medicine. *Applied Health Economics and Health Policy*, *16*(5), 583–590. doi:10.100740258-018-0412-8 PMID:30022440

Rajalahti, T., & Kvalheim, O. M. (2011). Multivariate data analysis in pharmaceutics: A tutorial review. *International Journal of Pharmaceutics*, *417*(1–2), 280–290. doi:10.1016/j.ijpharm.2011.02.019 PMID:21335075

Rajasekaran, A. S., Azees, M., & Al-Turjman, F. (2022). A comprehensive survey on blockchain technology. *Sustainable Energy Technologies and Assessments*, *52*, 102039. doi:10.1016/j.seta.2022.102039

Ranjan, R., McParthland, J.W., & Lewis, R. (2017). Blockchain and Financial Market Innovation. *Economic Perspectives*, *41*(7).

Rashideh, W. (2020). Blockchain technology framework: Current and future perspectives for the tourism industry. *Tourism Management*, *80*, 104125. doi:10.1016/j.tourman.2020.104125

Raworth, K. (2017). Why it's time for Doughnut Economics. *IPPR Progressive Review, 24*(3), 216–222.

Reedy, P. (2020). Interpol review of digital evidence 2016-2019. *Forensic Science International: Synergy*.

Reid, F., & Harrigan, M. (2013). An analysis of anonymity in the bitcoin system. In *Security and privacy in social networks* (pp. 197–223). Springer. doi:10.1007/978-1-4614-4139-7_10

Rey-Ares, L., Fernández-López, S., Castro-González, S., & Rodeiro-Pazos, D. (2021). Does self-control constitute a driver of millennials' financial behaviors and attitudes? *Journal of Behavioral and Experimental Economics*, *93*, 101702. doi:10.1016/j.socec.2021.101702

Rouhani & Deters. (2019). Security, performance, and applications of smart contracts: A systematic survey. *IEEE Access, 7*(50), 759–779.

Sachs, J. D., Woo, W. T., Yoshino, N., & Taghizadeh-Hesary, F. (2019). *Why is green finance important?* Academic Press.

Sachs, J., Woo, W. T., Yoshino, N., & Taghizadeh-Hesary, F. (2019). Importance of green finance for achieving sustainable development goals and energy security. Handbook of green finance: Energy security and sustainable development, 3-12.

Sachs, J., Woo, W. T., Yoshino, N., & Taghizadeh-Hesary, F. (Eds.). (2019). Handbook of green finance: Energy security and sustainable development. Academic Press.

Salahuddin, M., Alam, K., Ozturk, I., & Sohag, K. (2018). The effects of electricity consumption, economic growth, financial development and foreign direct investment on CO2 emissions in Kuwait. *Renewable & Sustainable Energy Reviews*, *81*, 2002–2010. doi:10.1016/j.rser.2017.06.009

Saleh, F. (2021). Blockchain without Waste: Proof-of-Stake. *The Review of Financial Studies*, *34*(3), 1156–1190. doi:10.1093/rfs/hhaa075

Sanka, A. I., Irfan, M., Huang, I., & Cheung, R. C. (2021). A survey of breakthrough in blockchain technology: Adoptions, applications, challenges and future research. *Computer Communications*, *169*, 179–201. doi:10.1016/j.comcom.2020.12.028

Sarmah, S.S. (2018). *Understanding blockchain technology*. https://www.researchgate.net/publication/336130918_Understanding_Blockchain_Technology

Saxena, S., Bhushan, B., & Ahad, M. A. (2021). Blockchain based solutions to secure IoT: Background, integration trends and a way forward. *Journal of Network and Computer Applications*, *181*, 103050. doi:10.1016/j.jnca.2021.103050

Schinckus, C. (2020). The good, the bad and the ugly: An overview of the sustainability of blockchain technology. *Energy Research & Social Science*, *69*, 101614. doi:10.1016/j.erss.2020.101614

Schletz, M., Nassiry, D., & Lee, M. K. (2020). *Blockchain and tokenized securities: The potential for green finance*. Academic Press.

Schuetz, S., & Venkatesh, V. (2020). Blockchain, adoption, and financial inclusion in India: Research opportunities. *International Journal of Information Management*, *52*, 101936. doi:10.1016/j.ijinfomgt.2019.04.009

Schulz, K., & Feist, M. (2021). Leveraging blockchain technology for innovative climate finance under the Green Climate Fund. *Earth System Governance*, *7*, 100084. doi:10.1016/j.esg.2020.100084

Shahbaz, M., Solarin, S. A., Mahmood, H., & Arouri, M. (2013). Does financial development reduce CO2 emissions in Malaysian economy? A time series analysis. *Economic Modelling*, *35*, 145–152. doi:10.1016/j.econmod.2013.06.037

Shanab, E. A., & Haider, S. (2015). Major factors influencing the adoption of m-government in Jordan. *Electronic Government, an International Journal*, *11*(4), 223. doi:10.1504/EG.2015.071394

Shan, S., Ahmad, M., Tan, Z., Adebayo, T. S., Man Li, R. Y., & Kirikkaleli, D. (2021). The role of energy prices and non-linear fiscal decentralization in limiting carbon emissions: Tracking environmental sustainability. *Energy*, *234*, 121243. doi:10.1016/j.energy.2021.121243

Shareef, M. A., Kumar, V., Kumar, U., & Dwivedi, Y. K. (2011). e-Government Adoption Model (GAM): Differing service maturity levels. *Government Information Quarterly*, *28*(1), 17–35. doi:10.1016/j.giq.2010.05.006

Sharma, R., Mehta, K., & Vyas, V. (2020). Responsible Investing: A Study on Non-Economic Goals and Investors' Characteristics. *Applied Finance Letters, 9*(SI), 63-78. doi:10.24135/afl.v9i2.245

Sharma, M., Antony, R., Sehrawat, R., Cruz, A. C., & Daim, T. U. (2022). Exploring post-adoption behaviors of e-service users: Evidence from the hospitality sector /online travel services. *Technology in Society*, *68*, 101781. doi:10.1016/j.techsoc.2021.101781

Sharma, M., & Choubey, A. (2022). Green banking initiatives: A qualitative study on Indian banking sector. *Environment, Development and Sustainability*, *24*(1), 293–319. doi:10.100710668-021-01426-9 PMID:33967597

Sharma, P. K., Kumar, N., & Park, J. H. (2020). Blockchain technology toward green IoT: Opportunities and challenges. *IEEE Network*, *34*(4), 263–269. doi:10.1109/MNET.001.1900526

Sharma, P., Jindal, R., & Borah, M. D. (2022). A Review of Blockchain-Based Applications and Challenges. *Wireless Personal Communications*, *123*(2), 1201–1243. doi:10.100711277-021-09176-7

Shermin, V. (2017). Disrupting governance with blockchains and smart contracts. *Strategic Change*, *26*(5), 499–509. doi:10.1002/jsc.2150

Sheth, H., & Dattani, J. (2019). Overview of blockchain technology. *Asian Journal For Convergence In Technology*.

Shipalana, P. (2020). *Green finance mechanisms in developing countries: Emerging practice*. Retrieved November 2, 2022, from https://cer.org.za/wp-content/uploads/2021/07/Shipalana-Policy-Briefing-.pdf

Singh, A. K., & Singh, K. V. (n.d.). Cryptocurrency in India-Its effect and future on economy with special reference to bitcoin. *International Journal of Research in Economics and Social Sciences*. http://www.euroasiapub.org

Sipthorpe, A., Brink, S., Van Leeuwen, T., & Staffell, I. (2022). Blockchain solutions for carbon markets are nearing maturity. *One Earth*, *5*(7), 779–791. doi:10.1016/j.oneear.2022.06.004

Sivarethinamohan, R., & Sujatha, S. (2021). Unraveling the potential of artificial intelligence-driven blockchain technology in environment management. In *Advances in Mechanical Engineering: Select Proceedings of CAMSE 2020* (pp. 693-700). Springer Singapore. 10.1007/978-981-16-0942-8_66

Slany, A., Cherel-Robson, M., & Picard, L. (2020). *Economic development in Africa Report 2020 tackling illicit financial flows for sustainable development in Africa*. Retrieved December 5, 2022, from https://unctad.org/system/files/official-document/aldcafrica2020_en.pdf

Songini, L., Pistoni, A., Tettamanzi, P., Fratini, F., & Minutiello, V. (2022). Integrated reporting quality and BoD characteristics: An empirical analysis. *The Journal of Management and Governance*, *26*(2), 579–620. doi:10.100710997-021-09568-8

Sorgente, A., & Lanz, M. (2017). Emerging adults' financial well-being: A scoping review. *Adolescent Research Review*, *2*(4), 255–292. doi:10.100740894-016-0052-x

Sreehari, P., Nandakishore, M., Krishna, G., Jacob, J., & Shibu, V. (2017). Smartwill converting the legal testament into a smart contract. In *2017 Interna-tional Conference on Networks & Advances in Computational Technolo-gies (NetACT)*. IEEE.

Sri Aruna, P. S. G., & Bhaskari, D. L. (2018). A study on blockchain technology. *IACSIT International Journal of Engineering and Technology*.

Stratopoulos, T. C., Wang, V. X., & Ye, J. (2020). Blockchain technology adoption. *Accounting Horizons, 36*(1), 197-220.

Sudhalakshmi, K., & Chinnadorai, K. (2014). Green banking practices in Indian banks. *International Journal of Management and Commerce Innovations*, *2*(1), 232–235.

Sultana, T., Almogren, A., Akbar, M., Zuair, M., Ullah, I., & Javaid, N. (2020). Data sharing system integrating access control mechanism using blockchain-based smart contracts for IoT devices. *Applied Sciences (Basel, Switzerland)*, *10*(2), 488. doi:10.3390/app10020488

Sunyaev, A. (2020). Distributed ledger technology. In *Internet Computing* (pp. 265–299). Springer. doi:10.1007/978-3-030-34957-8_9

Suryono, R. R., Budi, I., & Purwandari, B. (2020). Challenges and trends of financial technology (Fintech): A systematic literature review. *Information (Basel)*, *11*(12), 590. doi:10.3390/info11120590

Swan, M. (2015). Blockchain thinking: The brain as a DAC (decentralized autonomous organization). *Texas Bitcoin Conference*, 27-29.

Taghizadeh-Hesary, F., & Yoshino, N. (2019). The way to induce private participation in green finance and investment. *Finance Research Letters*, *31*, 98–103. doi:10.1016/j.frl.2019.04.016

Tamazian, A., Chousa, J. P., & Vadlamannati, K. C. (2009). Does higher economic and financial development lead to environmental degradation: Evidence from BRIC countries. *Energy Policy*, *37*(1), 246–253. doi:10.1016/j.enpol.2008.08.025

Tang, C. F., & Tan, B. W. (2014). The linkages among energy consumption, economic growth, relative price, foreign direct investment, and financial development in Malaysia. *Quality & Quantity*, *48*(2), 781–797. doi:10.100711135-012-9802-4

Tan, J., Su, X., & Wang, R. (2023). The impact of natural resource dependence and green finance on green economic growth in the context of COP26. *Resources Policy*, *81*, 103351. doi:10.1016/j.resourpol.2023.103351

Tapscott, A., & Tapscott, D. (2017). How blockchain is changing finance. *Harvard Business Review*, *1*(9), 2–5.

Tasca, P., & Tessone, C. J. (2019). A Taxonomy of Blockchain Technologies: Principles of Identification and Classification. *Ledger, 4*. doi:10.5195/ledger.2019.140

Taylor, P. J., Dargahi, T., Dehghantanha, A., Parizi, R. M., & Choo, K. K. R. (2020). A systematic literature review of blockchain cyber security. *Digital Communications and Networks*, *6*(2), 147–156. doi:10.1016/j.dcan.2019.01.005

Tian, Y., Lu, Z., Adriaens, P., Minchin, R. E., Caithness, A., & Woo, J. (2020). Finance infrastructure through blockchain-based tokenization. *Frontiers of Engineering Management*, *7*(4), 485–499. doi:10.100742524-020-0140-2

Tollefson, J. (2018). IPCC says limiting global warming to 1.5 C will require drastic action. *Nature*, *562*(7726), 172–173. doi:10.1038/d41586-018-06876-2 PMID:30301994

Tong, D., Zhang, Q., Davis, S. J., Liu, F., Zheng, B., Geng, G., Xue, T., Li, M., Hong, C., Lu, Z., Streets, D. G., Guan, D., & He, K. (2018). Targeted emission reductions from global super-polluting power plant units. *Nature Sustainability*, *1*(1), 59–68. doi:10.103841893-017-0003-y

Treleaven, P., Brown, R. G., & Yang, D. (2017). Blockchain technology in finance. *Computer*, *50*(9), 14–17. doi:10.1109/MC.2017.3571047

Tricco, A. C., Langlois, E., Straus, S. E., & World Health Organization. (2017). *Rapid reviews to strengthen health policy and systems: a practical guide*. World Health Organization.

Trivedi, S. (2023). Blockchain Framework for Insurance industry. *International Journal of Innovation and Technology Management.*

Trivedi, S., & Malik, R. (2022). Blockchain Technology as an Emerging Technology in the Insurance Market. In *Big Data: A Game Changer for Insurance Industry* (pp. 81–100). Emerald Publishing Limited. doi:10.1108/978-1-80262-605-620221006

Trivedi, S., Mehta, K., & Sharma, R. (2021). Systematic Literature Review on Application of Blockchain Technology in E-Finance and Financial Services. *Journal of Technology Management & Innovation*, *16*(3), 90–102. doi:10.4067/S0718-27242021000300089

Tschorsch, F., & Scheuermann, B. (2016). *Bitcoin and Beyond: A Technical Survey on Decentralized Digital Currencies*. ieeexplore.ieee.org/document/7423672

Uddin, G. A., Salahuddin, M., Alam, K., & Gow, J. (2017). Ecological footprint and real income: Panel data evidence from the 27 highest emitting countries. *Ecological Indicators*, *77*, 166–175. doi:10.1016/j.ecolind.2017.01.003

Ukpong, M. S., & Acha, I. A. (2019). A Critique of Micro-Insurance Models for Microfinance Banks to Boost SMEs in Nigeria. *Noble International Journal of Economics and Financial Research, 4*(1), 1-9.

Ulucak, R., Yücel, A. G., & Koçak, E. (2019). The Process of Sustainability: From Past to Present. *Environmental Kuznets Curve (EKC)*, 37–53. doi:10.1016/B978-0-12-816797-7.00005-9

United Nations. (2019). *The Sustainable Development Goals Report*. Author.

United Nations. (2022). *The Sustainable Development Goals Report*. Author.

van Eck, N. J., & Waltman, L. (2017). Citation-based clustering of publications using CitNetExplorer and VOSviewer. *Scientometrics*, *111*(2), 1053–1070. doi:10.100711192-017-2300-7 PMID:28490825

Varma, J. R. (2019). Blockchain in finance. *Vikalpa*, *44*(1), 1–11. doi:10.1177/0256090919839897

Venegas, P. (2020, July). Trustable Risk Scoring for Non-bank Gateways in Blockchain and DLT Financial Networks. In *International Conference on Complex Systems* (pp. 165-178). Springer.

Venkatesh, M., Morris, Davis, & Davis. (2003). User Acceptance of Information Technology: Toward a Unified View. *Management Information Systems Quarterly*, *27*(3), 425. doi:10.2307/30036540

Venkatesh, V., & Bala, H. (2008). Technology Acceptance Model 3 and a Research Agenda on Interventions. *Decision Sciences*, *39*(2), 273–315. doi:10.1111/j.1540-5915.2008.00192.x

Verma, J. (2022a). The Impact of Blockchain Technology and COVID-19 on the Global Banking Industry. *Blockchain Technology in Corporate Governance: Transforming Business and Industries*, 283-301.

Verma, J., & Kaur, J. (2022). Blockchain Technology: How will it impact the Marketing Domain? In Developing Relationships, Personalization, and Data Herald in Marketing 5.0 (pp. 146-160). IGI Global.

Verma, J. (2022b). Factors influencing Driving Demand of Cryptocurrency and its impact on Behavioral Intention: An Indian Perspective. *The Review of Finance and Banking*, *14*(1), 35–43. doi:10.24818/rfb.22.14.01.03

Vial, G. (2019). Understanding digital transformation: A review and a research agenda. *The Journal of Strategic Information Systems*, *28*(2), 118–144. doi:10.1016/j.jsis.2019.01.003

Vranken, H. (2017). Sustainability of bitcoin and blockchains. *Current Opinion in Environmental Sustainability*, *28*, 1–9. doi:10.1016/j.cosust.2017.04.011

Vyas, Mehta, & Sharma. (2020). Investigating socially responsible investing behaviour of Indian investors using structural equation modelling. *Journal of Sustainable Finance & Investment*, 1-23. doi:10.1080/20430795.2020.1790958

Walton, S. M., Thong, J. Y. L., & Xu, X. (n.d.). *Consumer acceptance and use of information technology: Extending the unified theory of acceptance and use of technology*. Academic Press.

Wang, He, & Ji. (2017). *Designated-Verifier Proof of Assets for Bitcoin Exchange Using Elliptic Curve Cryptography*. Academic Press.

Wang, M., Li, X., & Wang, S. (2021). Discovering research trends and opportunities of green finance and energy policy: A data-driven scientometric analysis. *Energy Policy*, *154*, 112295. doi:10.1016/j.enpol.2021.112295

Weber, G., & Cabras, I. (2017). The transition of Germany's energy production, green economy, low-carbon economy, socio-environmental conflicts, and equitable society. *Journal of Cleaner Production*, *167*, 1222–1231. doi:10.1016/j.jclepro.2017.07.223

White Paper on Applications of Blockchain technology to Banking and Financial sector in India. (2017). IDRBT.

Whittemore, R., Chao, A., Jang, M., Minges, K. E., & Park, C. (2014). Methods for knowledge synthesis: An overview. *Heart & Lung*, *43*(5), 453–461. doi:10.1016/j.hrtlng.2014.05.014 PMID:25012634

WilliamsH.FernandezJ. (2019). www.ibm.com/blogs/blockchain/2019/04/how-transparency-through-blockchain-helps-the-cybersecurity-community/

Winter, J. S., & Davidson, E. (2019). Big data governance of personal health information and challenges to contextual integrity. *The Information Society*, *35*(1), 36–51. doi:10.1080/01972243.2018.1542648

Wu, B., & Duan, T. (2019, March). The application of blockchain technology in financial markets. *Journal of Physics: Conference Series*, *1176*(4), 042094. doi:10.1088/1742-6596/1176/4/042094

Wu, X., Sadiq, M., Chien, F., Ngo, Q. T., Nguyen, A. T., & Trinh, T.-T. (2021). Testing role of green financing on climate change mitigation: Evidences from G7 and E7 countries. *Environmental Science and Pollution Research International*, *28*(47), 66736–66750. doi:10.100711356-021-15023-w PMID:34235703

Wu, X., Zhu, X., Wu, G. Q., & Ding, W. (2013). Data mining with big data. *IEEE Transactions on Knowledge and Data Engineering*, *26*(1), 97–107.

Xie, H., Ouyang, Z., & Choi, Y. (2020). Characteristics and influencing factors of green finance development in the Yangtze river delta of China: Analysis based on the spatial durbin model. *Sustainability*, *12*(22), 9753. doi:10.3390u12229753

Xu, M., Chen, X., & Kou, G. (2019). A systematic review of blockchain. *Financial Innovation*, *5*(1), 1–14. doi:10.118640854-019-0147-z

Yang, X. (2020, May). FinTech in Promoting the Development of Green Finance in China against the Background of Big Data and Artificial Intelligence. In *2020 4th International Seminar on Education Innovation and Economic Management (SEIEM)*. Francis Academic Press.

Yan, L., Mirza, N., & Umar, M. (2022). The cryptocurrency uncertainties and investment transitions: Evidence from high and low carbon energy funds in China. *Technological Forecasting and Social Change*, *175*, 121326. doi:10.1016/j.techfore.2021.121326

Yeong, Y.-C., Kalid, K. S., Savita, K. S., Ahmad, M. N., & Zaffar, M. (2022). Sustainable cryptocurrency adoption assessment among IT enthusiasts and cryptocurrency social communities. *Sustainable Energy Technologies and Assessments*, *52*, 102085. doi:10.1016/j.seta.2022.102085

Yong, W. (2019). Report on the Development of Qianhai, Shenzhen. In *Annual Report on the Development of China's Special Economic Zones (2018)* (pp. 41–57). Springer. doi:10.1007/978-981-13-9837-7_4

Yoo, S. (2017). *Blockchain basedfinancial case analysis and its implications*. Asia Pacific Journal of Innovation and Entrepreneurship. doi:10.1108/APJIE-12-2017-036

Yuan, F., & Gallagher, K. P. (2015). *Greening development finance in the Americas.* Global Economic Governance Initiative, Boston University. Retrieved November 28, 2022, from https://www.bu.edu/pardeeschool/files/2014/12/Greening.Development.Final_.pdf

Yu, T., Lin, Z., & Tang, Q. (2018). Blockchain: The introduction and its application in financial accounting. *Journal of Corporate Accounting & Finance*, *29*(4), 37–47. doi:10.1002/jcaf.22365

Zachariadis, M., Hileman, G., & Scott, S. V. (2019). Governance and control in distributed ledgers: Understanding the challenges facing blockchain technology in financial services. *Information and Organization*, *29*(2), 105–117. doi:10.1016/j.infoandorg.2019.03.001

Zagurskiy, O. N., & Titova, L. L. (2019). Problems and prospects of blockchain technology usage in supply chains. *Journal of Automation and Information Sciences*, *51*(11), 63–74. doi:10.1615/JAutomatInfScien.v51.i11.60

Zeb, S., Shah, I. A., Rashid, A., & Raza, H. (2021). Impact of corporate social responsibility and corporate governance on firm performance. *Journal of Business and Economics*, *13*(1), 18–34.

Zhang, R., & Chan, W. K. (2020). Evaluation of Energy Consumption in Block-Chains with Proof of Work and Proof of Stake. *Journal of Physics: Conference Series, 1584*(1), 012023. doi:10.1088/1742-6596/1584/1/012023

Zhang, Y., Ma, S., Li, J., Li, K., Nepal, S., & Gu, D. (2020). Smartshield: Automatic smart contract protection made easy. In *2020 IEEE 27thInternational Conference on Software Analysis, Evolution and Reengi-neering (SANER)*. IEEE.

Zhang, A., Zhong, R. Y., Farooque, M., Kang, K., & Venkatesh, V. G. (2020). Blockchain-based life cycle assessment: An implementation framework and system architecture. *Resources, Conservation and Recycling*, *152*, 104512. doi:10.1016/j.resconrec.2019.104512

Zhang, D., Chen, X. H., Lau, C. K. M., & Xu, B. (2023). Implications of cryptocurrency energy usage on climate change. *Technological Forecasting and Social Change*, *187*, 122219. doi:10.1016/j.techfore.2022.122219

Zhang, L., Xie, Y., Zheng, Y., Xue, W., Zheng, X., & Xu, X. (2020). The challenges and countermeasures of blockchain in finance and economics. *Systems Research and Behavioral Science*, *37*(4), 691–698. doi:10.1002res.2710

Zhang, X., Aranguiz, M., Xu, D., Zhang, X., & Xu, X. (2018). Utilizing blockchain for better enforcement of green finance law and regulations. In *Transforming Climate Finance and Green Investment with Blockchains* (pp. 289–301). Academic Press. doi:10.1016/B978-0-12-814447-3.00021-5

Zhang, Y. J. (2011). The impact of financial development on carbon emissions: An empirical analysis in China. *Energy Policy*, *39*(4), 2197–2203. doi:10.1016/j.enpol.2011.02.026

Zhao, N., Cheng, X., & Guo, X. (2018). Impact of information spread and investment behavior on the diffusion of internet investment products. *Physica A*, *512*, 427–436. doi:10.1016/j.physa.2018.08.075

Zheng, Z., Xie, S., Dai, H. N., Chen, X., & Wang, H. (2018). Blockchain challenges and opportunities: A survey. *International Journal of Web and Grid Services*, *14*(4), 352–375. doi:10.1504/IJWGS.2018.095647

Zheng, Z., Xie, S., Dai, H., Chen, X., & Wang, H. (2017). *An overview of blockchain technology: Architecture, consensus, and future trends. In 2017 IEEE international congress on big data (BigData congress)*. IEEE.

Zhongming, Z., Linong, L., Xiaona, Y., & Wei, L. (2018). *The Role of Fintech in Unlocking Green Finance: Policy Insights for Developing Countries*. Academic Press.

Zhou, G., Zhu, J., & Luo, S. (2022). The impact of fintech innovation on green growth in China: Mediating effect of green finance. *Ecological Economics*, *193*, 107308. doi:10.1016/j.ecolecon.2021.107308

Zhou, X., Tang, X., & Zhang, R. (2020). Impact of green finance on economic development and environmental quality: A study based on provincial panel data from China. *Environmental Science and Pollution Research International*, *27*(16), 19915–19932. doi:10.100711356-020-08383-2 PMID:32232752

Zimbabwe Financial Inclusion Report C. E. N. F. R. I. (2016). *Making Access Possible*. Retrieved November 27, 2022, from https://cenfri.org/wp-content/uploads/2016/01/MAP-Zimbabwe_Synthesis-report_Cenfri-FinMark-Trust-UNCDF_October-2016.pdf

Zimbabwe Integrated Solid Waste Management Plan. (2011). *Zimbabwe Integrated Solid Waste Management Plan statistics for the year 2011, (IES, 2014)*. Retrieved December 6, 2022, from https://www.yumpu.com/en/document/view/62915014/zimbabwe-integrated-solid-waste-management-plan

Zupic, I., & Cater, T. (2015). Bibliometric Methods in Management and Organization. *Organizational Research Methods*, *18*(3), 429–472. doi:10.1177/1094428114562629

Zvirevo, W. (2019). *Green Financing in Zimbabwe: Case of the Infrastructure Development Bank of Zimbabwe*. Elephant Hills Hotel.

About the Contributors

Sonal Trivedi has more than 10 years of experience in academics. She has authored two national books and published 5 Scopus indexed papers. She has chaired 5 conferences and file 6 Patents. She has attended and presented papers in various international and national conference. She is also reviewer of various Scopus indexed journals.

Rashmi Aggarwal is working as Professor and Assistant Dean (Under-Graduation) at Chitkara Business School, Chitkara University, Punjab, India. She is an astute professional with over 22 years of experience teaching MCA, BCA, BBA, B.Com, Computer Science, Electrical Engg., Mass Communication & Hospitality. She has undertaken a Consultancy Project on Cost Accounting and received excellence Award for Most Collaborating Employee. She has contributed in various books, journals, FDPs and workshops.

Gurmeet Singh has more than 25 years of teaching experience in higher-educational multicultural settings. He received Best Research Collaborator award for 2014 from School of Management and Public Administration. He is awarded Certificate of recognition for high quality ranked publications in 2016, 2015, 2014, 2013 (for 2014,2013 and 2012 publications) by The University of The South Pacific for publishing in high quality journals. He is recipient of Amity Academic Excellence Award for 2016 for excellent academic background and contribution in the field of education and research. He is recipient of 2008, "Japanese award for outstanding research on development"

* * *

Ankita is a student of BA economics of Chitkara University, Punjab India.

Tushti P. Bakrania is a Research Scholar at Atmiya University Rajkot, Gujarat. Working in Metas Adventist College Surat. Gujarat as an Assistant Professor, In Department of Management and Commerce. Have teaching experience of 6 years. Have published 7 different category of papers in the field of management and one chapter for book.

Vikram Bansal is Faculty of Atal Bihari Vajpayee School of Management and Entrepreneurship, Jawaharlal Nehru University, New Delhi, India. He previously worked at Shri Vishwakarma Skill University in Gurugram, India, and Lincoln University College in Malaysia. He has over 15 years of experience in teaching and research. He has presented and published over 25 research papers in prestigious national and international journals. His areas of research interest include marketing management, entrepreneurship development, and tourism management. In the areas of business and product development, he has continued to serve as a consultant/mentor to leading organizations and startups. He has also represented on the editorial boards of several international and national journals. Dr. Bansal has traveled to many countries on academic visits, including Thailand, Malaysia, and Singapore.

Amitab Bhattacharjee has been working as a bifoliate manner, Associate Researcher & Lecturer and also continuing affiliated research projects internationally. His major research concentrations are entrepreneurship, financial sustainability, SQM and green strategic management. He is the author of several articles in Sustainability Journal, Journal of Public Affairs, International Journal of Organizational Analysis and International Journal of Business Innovation and Research. In Japan, he has experience as a project coordinator in several international research projects. Accordingly, now acting as a service professional along with being an independent researcher in Japan.

Isha Chhabra is currently working as Assistant Professor with K.R Mangalam University, Gurugram (Haryana). She is also pursuing her PH.D in the field of financial performance of public sector enterprises. She has publication in Scopus indexed journals. She also received best paper award in an international conference organized by Delhi University. She graduated from Delhi University with distinction. Her areas of interest are financial accounting, financial management.

Mufaro Dzingirai is a full-time lecturer in the Department of Business Management, Midlands State University, and a PhD candidate in Business Management at Midlands State University. He is also currently a Senior Fellow at the Nexus Think Tank (Zarawi Trust). Notably, he is a Monitoring and Evaluation Specialist (Internship) at Midlands AIDS Services Organization. Interestingly, he received the Best

Paper Presentation Award from the University of Johannesburg (UJ) in 2022. He attended the UNCTAD YSI Summer School 2022 on Globalization and Development Strategies, jointly organized by the United Nations Conference on Trade and Development (UNCTAD) and the Institute of New Economic Thinking's Young Scholars Initiative (YSI) held from August 1-5, 2022. He earned his Master of Commerce in Strategic Management and Corporate Governance degree from Midlands State University in 2016. He was hired as a teacher by the Ministry of Education from 2014 to 2016. In 2013, he received the MSU Book Prize as the best graduating student. He completed his Bachelor of Commerce in Business Management Honours Degree in 2013. Given his deep interest in community development, he manage to complete his Bachelor of Social Science in Monitoring and Evaluation in 2021. His research interests include Higher Education, Strategy, Management, Finance, Entrepreneurship, and Development. He publishes in high-impact journals accredited by Scopus and also reviewed many scientific papers in databases like Emerald Insight. More interestingly, he has been hired as a research consultant by both private and public organizations. Lastly, he supervises postgraduate students and has linkages with various universities (national and international) as an external examiner or moderator.

Chirag V. Erda is Assistant Professor in Department of Management, Faculty of Business & Commerce Atmiya University, Rajkot (Gujarat) India.

Rinat Galiautdinov is a Principal Software Developer and Software Architect having the expertise in Information Technology and Computer Science. Mr. Galiautdinov is also an expert in Banking/Financial industry as well as in Neurobiological sphere. Mr. Rinat Galiautdinov works on the number of highly important researches (including such the spheres as: Drones, Financial Systems and Private Money, Brain interface and neuro-biology) as an independent researcher and projects holder and developer.

Khushboo Gulati is working as an Assistant Professor with Manav Rachna University. She completed her Ph.D. from Amity Business School, Amity University, Noida. Her research interests include corporate governance and management accounting. She has published research papers in Scopus Indexed papers and presented papers in international Conferences.

Neha Kamboj is working as an Assistant Professor in the School of Management and Commerce, K.R. Mangalam University, Gurugram. She has chaired 2 conferences and filed 6 Patents. She is also reviewer of various Scopus indexed journals. Since 2013 she has taught many courses to under graduate (UG) and post graduate

(PG) students of business administration programme at reputed management. She is teaching various Finance subjects like Financial Management, Corporate Accounting, Accounting for Business, Financial Reporting & Analysis, Multinational Financial Management, Capital Market, Elements of Banking and Indian Financial System & Financial Markets, to BBA, B.Com, MBA students. She has participated in various national and international workshops, seminars, conferences, Faculty Development Programs to keep herself updated and well equipped with latest innovations and changes in the field of Finance and Banking.

Gurpreet Kaur is Assistant professor (Finance and accounting) in Chitkara Business School, Chitkara University, Punjab. She has more than 12 years' experience in teaching & is awarded for her academic performance Her areas of specialization includes accounting and finance related subjects (taxation, operation research, cost accounting, management accounting, financial management). Her area of interest in research is financial risk. She has published/presented research papers in journals/ conferences (national & international).

Herbert Masukume is a lecturer in the Faculty of Business Sciences at Midlands State University. He holds a MSc in Strategic Management from Great Zimbabwe University and a BSc in Human Resources Management from Midlands State University (Zimbabwe). His interests are in increasing Industrial Relations with a focus on improving workplace relations for the maintenance of industrial harmony.

Kiran Mehta (Ph.D.) is an educator, trainer, consultant, and researcher. She has almost twenty years of experience. She has published several research articles in a variety of international publications, including Emerald, Taylor & Francis, and Sage. She is the author of "Financial Services," a textbook published by CENGAGE. She has created study materials for a number of Indian institutes. Her areas of interest include climate finance, sustainable business, portfolio management, stock market efficiency, technology and education, entrepreneurship, and venture capital.

Manawati Panwar has both experience in corporates (HDFC Bank, India) and in academics. Her specialization is in Finance. She has more than 10 years experience in academics.

Ritik Rana is a student of MBA in finance and banking at Chitkara Business School, Chitkara University, Rajpura. Hailing from Himachal Pradesh and currently residing in Chandigarh, he completed his undergraduate degree in BSc Non-Medical from DAV College, Chandigarh. Ritik is passionate about finance and personal finance, and has chosen to pursue his MBA in finance and banking in order to further his knowledge and expertise in this field. He is particularly interested in learning about financial planning, investment strategies, and wealth management, and enjoys reading about these topics in his free time.

Jyotsna Sharma is working as Assistant Professor at RIMT University. She is Post graduate in Business Management and holds a doctorate in the area of Banking. She also holds a post-graduate diploma in International Business and is qualified UGC-NET. She has work experience of over fourteen years and actively involved in teaching for more than ten years in diverse areas of Business Management, Finance, and Marketing. She has authored a book Titled "Career Planning and Management". She has published various research papers in various journals, seminars/conferences of national and international repute. Also, she has contributed research papers that have been included as chapters in different books with ISBN numbers. She has participated in several Faculty Development Programmes (FDPs).

Renuka Sharma is a Professor (Finance) at Chitkara Business School at Chitkara University in Punjab. She has over 18 years of teaching and research experience (more than ten years post-doctoral and eight years before to obtaining her PhD). She has authored numerous research papers, a few of which have been published in international/national journals (Taylor&Francis, Emerald, Sage, Inderscience, etc.) and the rest have been presented at international/national conferences (IIM Bangalore, Shillong, Calcutta, Indore, and Kozhikode, among others), with numerous papers selected for Best Paper Awards. She also serves as a reviewer for numerous prestigious journals published by Emerald, Elsevier, and Inderscience, among others. Currently, she is guiding two PhD scholars and has successfully defended five others. She has been a consultant for several start-ups and MSMEs. She is the author of two textbooks for Cengage Pub. and Vikas Pub. Additionally, she has developed study materials for a variety of business-related courses for prominent Indian universities and institutions She has served as a resource person for several MDPs and FDPs related to research and finance. She is an entrepreneur too.

Soumya Singhal is a recognized person who started her academic career as a Research Associate at IIM Indore. She has a knack for finance, which her Ph.D. has complemented in Intellectual Capital and her post-graduation and graduation with M.Com & B.Com(H), respectively, from the University of Delhi. She has worked as an audit associate at KPMG Global and have industry experience. She is also UGC-NET qualified. She has always inspired students to enrich themselves through various portals like Swayam Prabha, intellectual classrooms, and research projects. She has taught subjects such as Income Tax, Financial Management, Business Research, and Accounting.

Surabhi Sugathan has more than 5 years of experience in academics. Her area of research is investor behavior.

Jyoti Verma is a faculty at Chitkara Business School, Chitkara University, Punjab, India. With more than 19 research papers to her credit published in various journals and conferences at the national & international levels, Dr. Verma has developed her core expertise in the area of service quality, blockchain, and behavioral finance. She has authored 1 book titled 'Accelerating the Development of Quality of IT-Enabled Banking Services' by international publishers and published many book chapters in edited books at the international level. She has published many patents and has prepared and delivered many E-Content programs on Research Methodology (MHRD Projects).

Kudakwashe Zvitambo was born 1972. He is a Senior Lecturer at Midlands State University, Zimbabwe. Dr Zvitambo holds a PhD in Management Sciences specializing in Corporate Governance. He obtained his doctorate degree at Durban University of Technology, South Africa. Dr Zvitambo has research interests in Corporate Governance, Humanistic Philosophy, Finance and Business Ethics.

Index

www.ingramcontent.com/pod-product-compliance
Lightning Source LLC
LaVergne TN
LVHW081339300926
849161LV00008B/2018